ULTIMATE SUCCESS

THE MENTAL MAGIC TO CREATING WEALTH

A TarcherPerigee Book

ULTIMATE SUCCESS

FEATURING

Think and Grow Rich, As a Man Thinketh,
and *The Power of Your Subconscious Mind*

Napoleon Hill, James Allen,
and Joseph Murphy

tarcherperigee

An imprint of Penguin Random House LLC
375 Hudson Street
New York, New York 10014

Think and Grow Rich was originally published 1937. *As a Man Thinketh* was originally published 1903.
The Power of Your Subconscious Mind was originally published 1963. Anthologized as *Ultimate Success* by TarcherPerigee in 2018.

This volume reproduces these works largely as they appeared in their original editions. Except for adjustments that bring the text in line with contemporary typology standards, the publisher has mostly retained the original spelling, usage, and style of the author. As these works were written in early eras, they occasionally feature an antiquated reference or word choice. For purposes of historical accuracy, the publisher has largely left these intact.

LIBRARY OF CONGRESS CATALOGING-IN-PUBLICATION DATA

Names: Hill, Napoleon, 1883-1970. Think and grow rich. | Allen, James,
1864-1912. As a man thinketh. | Murphy, Joseph, 1898-1981. Power of your subconscious mind.
Title: Ultimate success, featuring, Think and grow rich, As a man thinketh, and
The power of your subconscious mind : the mental magic to creating wealth / Napoleon Hill, James Allen, and Joseph Murphy.
Description: New York : TarcherPerigee, 2018. Identifiers: LCCN 2017049827 (print) | LCCN 2017053703 (ebook) |
ISBN 9780525504399 | ISBN 9780143132417 (pbk.)
Subjects: LCSH: New Thought. | Success. | Success in business. | Mental discipline.
Classification: LCC BF639 (ebook) | LCC BF639 .U58 2018 (print) | DDC 650.1—dc23
LC record available at https://lccn.loc.gov/2017049827

Printed in the United States of America

1 3 5 7 9 10 8 6 4 2

Book design by Katy Riegel

CONTENTS

THINK AND GROW RICH

By Napoleon Hill

1937

CONTENTS

PUBLISHER'S PREFACE

This book conveys the experience of more than five hundred men of great wealth, who began at scratch, with nothing to give in return for riches except thoughts, ideas, and organized plans.

Here you have the entire philosophy of money-making, just as it was organized from the actual achievements of the most successful men known to the American people during the past fifty years. It describes what to do, also, how to do it!

It presents complete instructions on how to sell your personal services.

It provides you with a perfect system of self-analysis that will readily disclose what has been standing between you and "the big money" in the past.

It describes the famous Andrew Carnegie formula of personal achievement by which he accumulated hundreds of millions of dollars for himself and made no fewer than a score of millionaires of men to whom he taught his secret.

Perhaps you do not need all that is to be found in the book—no one of the five hundred men from whose experiences it was written did—but you may need one idea, plan, or suggestion to start you toward your goal. Somewhere in the book you will find this needed stimulus.

The book was inspired by Andrew Carnegie, after he had made his millions and retired.

It was written by the man to whom Carnegie disclosed the astounding secret of his riches—the same man to whom the five hundred wealthy men revealed the source of their riches.

In this volume will be found the thirteen principles of money-making essential to every person who accumulates sufficient money to guarantee financial independence. It is estimated that the research which went into the preparation, before the book was written, or could be written—research covering more than twenty-five years of continuous effort—could not be duplicated at a cost of less than $100,000.00.

Moreover, the knowledge contained in the book never can be duplicated, at any cost, for the reason that more than half of the five hundred men who supplied the information it brings have passed on.

Riches cannot always be measured in money!

Money and material things are essential for freedom of body and mind, but there are some who will feel that the greatest of all riches can be evaluated only in terms of lasting friendships, harmonious family relationships, sympathy and understanding between business associates, and introspective harmony which brings one peace of mind measurable only in spiritual values!

All who read, understand, and apply this philosophy will be better prepared to attract and enjoy these higher estates which always have been and always will be denied to all except *those who are ready for them.*

Be prepared, therefore, when you expose yourself to the influence of this philosophy, to experience a changed life which may help you not only to negotiate your way through life with harmony and understanding, but also to prepare you for the accumulation of material riches in abundance.

THE PUBLISHER

AUTHOR'S PREFACE

In every chapter of this book, mention has been made of the money-making secret which has made fortunes for more than five hundred exceedingly wealthy men whom I have carefully analyzed over a long period of years.

The secret was brought to my attention by Andrew Carnegie, more than a quarter of a century ago. The canny, lovable old Scotsman carelessly tossed it into my mind, when I was but a boy. Then he sat back in his chair, with a merry twinkle in his eyes, and watched carefully to see if I had brains enough to understand the full significance of what he had said to me.

When he saw that I had grasped the idea, he asked if I would be willing to spend twenty years or more, preparing myself to take it to the world, to men and women who, without the secret, might go through life as failures. I said I would, and with Mr. Carnegie's cooperation, I have kept my promise.

This book contains the secret, after having been put to a practical test by thousands of people, in almost every walk of life. It was Mr. Carnegie's idea that the magic formula, which gave him a stupendous fortune, ought to be placed within reach of people who do not have time to investigate how men make money, and it was his hope that I might test and demonstrate the soundness of the formula through the experience of men and women in every calling. He believed the formula should be taught in all public schools and colleges, and expressed the opinion that if it were properly taught it would so revolutionize the entire educational system that the time spent in school could be reduced to less than half.

His experience with Charles M. Schwab, and other young men of Mr. Schwab's type, convinced Mr. Carnegie that much of that which is taught in the schools is of no value whatsoever in connection with the business of earning a living or accumulating riches. He had arrived at this decision, because he had taken into his business one young man after another, many of them with but little schooling, and by coaching them in the use of this formula, developed in them rare leadership. Moreover, *his coaching made fortunes for every one of them who followed his instructions.*

In the chapter on Faith, you will read the astounding story of the organization of the giant United States Steel Corporation, as it was conceived and carried out by one of the young men through whom Mr. Carnegie proved that his formula will work *for all who are ready for it.* This single application of the secret, by that young man—Charles M. Schwab—made him a huge fortune in both money and opportunity. Roughly speaking, this particular application of the formula was worth *six hundred million dollars.*

These facts—and they are facts well known to almost everyone who knew Mr. Carnegie—give you a fair idea of what the reading of this book may bring to you, provided you *know what it is that you want.*

Even before it had undergone twenty years of practical testing, the secret was passed on to more than one hundred thousand men and women who have used it for their personal benefit, as Mr. Carnegie planned that they should. Some have made fortunes with it. Others have used it successfully in creating harmony in their homes. A clergyman used it so effectively that it brought him an income of upwards of $75,000.00 a year.

Arthur Nash, a Cincinnati tailor, used his near-bankrupt business as a "guinea pig" on which to test the formula. The business came to life and made a fortune for its owners. It is still thriving, although Mr. Nash has gone. The experiment was so unique that newspapers and magazines gave it more than a million dollars' worth of laudatory publicity.

The secret was passed on to Stuart Austin Wier, of Dallas, Texas. He was ready for it—so ready that he gave up his profession and studied law. Did he succeed? That story is told too.

I gave the secret to Jennings Randolph, the day he graduated from college, and he has used it so successfully that he is now serving his third term as a Member of Congress, with an excellent opportunity to keep on using it until it carries him to the White House.

While serving as Advertising Manager of the LaSalle Extension University, when it was little more than a name, I had the privilege of seeing J. G. Chapline, President of the University, use the formula so effectively that he has since made the LaSalle one of the great extension schools of the country.

The secret to which I refer has been mentioned no fewer than a hundred times, throughout this book. It has not been directly named, for it seems to work more successfully when it is merely uncovered and left in sight, where those who are ready, and searching for it, may pick it up. That is why Mr. Carnegie tossed it to me so quietly, without giving me its specific name.

If you are ready to put it to use, you will recognize this secret at least once in every chapter. I wish I might feel privileged to tell you how you will know if you are ready, but that would deprive you of much of the benefit you will receive when you make the discovery in your own way.

While this book was being written, my own son, who was then finishing the last year of his college work, picked up the manuscript of chapter two, read it, and discovered the secret for himself. He used the information so effectively that he went directly into a responsible position at a beginning salary greater than the average man ever earns. His story has been briefly described in chapter two. When you read it, perhaps you will dismiss any feeling you may have had, at the beginning of the book, that it promised too much. And, too, if you have ever been discouraged, if you have had difficulties to surmount which took the very soul out of you, if you have tried and failed, if you were ever handicapped by illness or physical affliction, this story of my son's discovery and use of the Carnegie formula may prove to be the oasis in the Desert of Lost Hope, for which you have been searching.

This secret was extensively used by President Woodrow Wilson, during the world war. It was passed on to every soldier who fought in the war, carefully wrapped in the training received before going to the front. President Wilson told me it was a strong factor in raising the funds needed for the war.

More than twenty years ago, Hon. Manuel L. Quezon (then Resident Commissioner of the Philippine Islands), was inspired by the secret to gain freedom for his people. He has gained freedom for the Philippines, and is the first President of the free state.

A peculiar thing about this secret is that those who once acquire it and use it find themselves literally swept on to success, with but little effort, and they never again submit to failure! If you doubt this, study the names of those who have used it, wherever they have been mentioned, check their records for yourself, and be convinced.

There is no such thing as something for nothing!

The secret to which I refer cannot be had without a price, although the price is far less than its value. It cannot be had at any price by those who are not intentionally searching for it. It cannot be given away, it cannot be purchased for money, for the reason that it comes in two parts. One part is already in possession of those who are ready for it.

The secret serves equally well, all who are ready for it. Education has nothing to do with it. Long before I was born, the secret had found its way into the possession of Thomas

A. Edison, and he used it so intelligently that he became the world's leading inventor, although he had but three months of schooling.

The secret was passed on to a business associate of Mr. Edison. He used it so effectively that, although he was then making only $12,000 a year, he accumulated a great fortune, and retired from active business while still a young man. You will find his story at the beginning of the first chapter. It should convince you that riches are not beyond your reach, that you can still be what you wish to be, that money, fame, recognition and happiness can be had by all who are ready and determined to have these blessings.

How do I know these things? You should have the answer before you finish this book. You may find it in the very first chapter, or on the last page.

While I was performing the twenty-year task of research, which I had undertaken at Mr. Carnegie's request, I analyzed hundreds of well-known men, many of whom admitted that they had accumulated their vast fortunes through the aid of the Carnegie secret; among these men were:—

Henry Ford
William Wrigley Jr.
John Wanamaker
James J. Hill
George S. Parker
E. M. Statler
Henry L. Doherty
Cyrus H. K. Curtis
George Eastman
Dr. Frank Gunsaulus
King Gillette

Theodore Roosevelt
John W. Davis
Elbert Hubbard
Wilbur Wright
William Jennings Bryan
Dr. David Starr Jordan
J. Odgen Armour
Charles M. Schwab
Harris F. Williams
Daniel Willard
Ralph A. Weeks

Judge Daniel T. Wright
Thomas A. Edison
F. W. Woolworth
Edward A. Filene
Arthur Brisbane
Wm. Howard Taft
Edward W. Bok
Elbert H. Gary
John H. Patterson
Stuart Austin Wier
George M. Alexander
Hon. Jennings Randolph
Clarence Darrow
John D. Rockefeller
Frank A. Vanderlip
Col. Robert A. Dollar
Edwin C. Barnes
Woodrow Wilson
Luther Burbank
Frank A. Munsey
Dr. Alexander Graham Bell
Julius Rosenwald
Dr. Frank Crane
J. G. Chapline
Arthur Nash

These names represent but a small fraction of the hundreds of well-known Americans whose achievements, financially and otherwise, prove that those who understand and apply the Carnegie secret reach high stations in life. I have never known anyone who was inspired to use the secret, who did not achieve noteworthy success in his chosen calling. I have never known any person to distinguish himself, or to accumulate riches of any consequence, without possession of the secret. From these two facts I draw the conclusion that the secret is more important, as a part of the knowledge essential for self-determination, than any which one receives through what is popularly known as "education."

What is education, anyway? This has been answered in full detail.

As far as schooling is concerned, many of these men had very little. John Wanamaker once told me that what little schooling he had, he acquired in very much the same manner as a modern locomotive takes on water, by "scooping it up as it runs." Henry Ford never reached high school, let alone college. I am not attempting to minimize the value of schooling, but I am trying to express my earnest belief that those who master and apply the secret will reach high stations, accumulate riches, and bargain with life on their own terms, even if their schooling has been meager.

Somewhere, as you read, the secret to which I refer will jump from the page and stand boldly before you, if you are ready for it! When it appears, you will recognize it. Whether you receive the sign in the first or the last chapter, stop for a moment when it presents itself, and turn down a glass, for that occasion will mark the most important turning-point of your life.

We pass now, to chapter one, and to the story of my very dear friend, who has generously acknowledged having seen the mystic sign, and whose business achievements are evidence enough that he turned down a glass. As you read his story, and the others, remember that they deal with the important problems of life, such as all men experience. The problems arising from one's endeavor to earn a living, to find hope, courage, contentment and peace of mind; to accumulate riches and to enjoy freedom of body and spirit.

Remember, too, as you go through the book, that it deals with facts and not with fiction, its purpose being to convey a great universal truth through which all who are ready may learn, not only *what* to do, but also *how* to do it! and receive, as well, the needed stimulus to make a start.

As a final word of preparation, before you begin the first chapter, may I offer one brief suggestion which may provide a clue by which the Carnegie secret may be recognized? It is this—*all achievement, all earned riches, have their beginning in an idea!* If you are ready for the secret, you already possess one half of it; therefore, you will readily recognize the other half the moment it reaches your mind.

THE AUTHOR

CHAPTER 1

INTRODUCTION

THE MAN WHO "THOUGHT" HIS WAY INTO PARTNERSHIP WITH THOMAS A. EDISON

Truly, "thoughts are things," and powerful things at that, when they are mixed with definiteness of purpose, persistence, and a burning desire for their translation into riches, or other material objects.

A little more than thirty years ago, Edwin C. Barnes discovered how true it is that men really do think and grow rich. His discovery did not come about at one sitting. It came little by little, beginning with a burning desire to become a business associate of the great Edison.

One of the chief characteristics of Barnes' desire was that it was *definite.* He wanted to work *with* Edison, not *for* him. Observe, carefully, the description of how he went about translating his desire into reality, and you will have a better understanding of the thirteen principles which lead to riches.

When this desire, or impulse of thought, first flashed into his mind he was in no position to act upon it. Two difficulties stood in his way. He did not know Mr. Edison, and he did not have enough money to pay his railroad fare to Orange, New Jersey.

These difficulties were sufficient to have discouraged the majority of men from making any attempt to carry out the desire. But his was no ordinary desire! He was so determined to find a way to carry out his desire that he finally decided to travel by "blind baggage," rather than be defeated. (To the uninitiated, this means that he went to East Orange on a freight train.)

He presented himself at Mr. Edison's laboratory, and announced he had come to go into business with the inventor. In speaking of the first meeting between Barnes and Edison, years later, Mr. Edison said, "He stood there before me, looking like an ordinary tramp, *but there was something in the expression of his face which conveyed the impression that he was determined to get what he had come after.* I had learned, from years of experience with men, that when a man really desires a thing so deeply that he is willing to stake his entire future on a single turn of the wheel in order to get it, he is sure to win. I gave him the opportunity he asked for, *because I saw he had made up his mind to stand by until he succeeded.* Subsequent events proved that no mistake was made."

Just what young Barnes said to Mr. Edison on that occasion was far less important than *that which he thought*. Edison, himself, said so! It could not have been the young man's appearance which got him his start in the Edison office, for that was definitely against him. It was what he thought that counted.

If the significance of this statement could be conveyed to every person who reads it, there would be no need for the remainder of this book.

Barnes did not get his partnership with Edison on his first interview. He did get a chance to work in the Edison offices, at a very nominal wage, doing work that was unimportant to Edison, but most important to Barnes, because it gave him an opportunity to display his "merchandise" where his intended "partner" could see it.

Months went by. Apparently nothing happened to bring the coveted goal which Barnes had set up in his mind as his definite major purpose. But something important was happening in Barnes' mind. He was constantly intensifying his desire to become the business associate of Edison.

Psychologists have correctly said that "when one is truly ready for a thing, it puts in its appearance." Barnes was ready for a business association with Edison; moreover, he was determined to remain ready until he got that which he was seeking.

He did not say to himself, "Ah well, what's the use? I guess I'll change my mind and try for a salesman's job." But, he did say, "I came here to go into business with Edison, and I'll accomplish this end if it takes the remainder of my life." *He meant it!* What a different story men would have to tell if only they would adopt a definite purpose, and stand by that purpose until it had time to become an all-consuming obsession!

Maybe young Barnes did not know it at the time, but his bulldog determination, his persistence in standing back of a single desire, was destined to mow down all opposition, and bring him the opportunity he was seeking.

When the opportunity came, it appeared in a different form, and from a different direction than Barnes had expected. That is one of the tricks of opportunity. It has a sly habit of slipping in by the back door, and often it comes disguised in the form of misfortune, or temporary defeat. Perhaps this is why so many fail to recognize opportunity.

Mr. Edison had just perfected a new office device, known at that time as the Edison Dictating Machine (now the Ediphone). His salesmen were not enthusiastic over the machine. They did not believe it could be sold without great effort. Barnes saw his opportunity. It had crawled in quietly, hidden in a queer-looking machine which interested no one but Barnes and the inventor.

Barnes knew he could sell the Edison Dictating Machine. He suggested this to Edison, and promptly got his chance. He did sell the machine. In fact, he sold it so successfully that Edison gave him a contract to distribute and market it all over the nation. Out of that business association grew the slogan "Made by Edison and installed by Barnes."

The business alliance has been in operation for more than thirty years. Out of it Barnes has made himself rich in money, but he has done something infinitely greater: he has proved that one really may "Think and Grow Rich."

How much actual cash that original desire of Barnes' has been worth to him, I have no way of knowing. Perhaps it has brought him two or three million dollars, but the amount, whatever it is, becomes insignificant when compared with the greater asset he acquired in the form of definite knowledge that *an intangible impulse of thought can be transmuted into its physical counterpart* by the application of known principles.

Barnes literally *thought* himself into a partnership with the great Edison! He thought himself into a fortune. He had nothing to start with, except the capacity to know what he wanted, and the determination to stand by that desire until he realized it.

He had no money to begin with. He had but little education. He had no influence. But he did have initiative, faith, and the will to win. With these intangible forces he *made himself* number one man with the greatest inventor who ever lived.

Now, let us look at a different situation, and study a man who had plenty of tangible evidence of riches, but lost it, *because he stopped* three feet short of the goal he was seeking.

THREE FEET FROM GOLD

One of the most common causes of failure is the habit of quitting when one is overtaken by *temporary defeat.* Every person is guilty of this mistake at one time or another.

An uncle of R. U. Darby was caught by the "gold fever" in the gold-rush days, and went west to dig and grow rich. He had never heard that *more gold has been mined from the brains of men than has ever been taken from the earth.* He staked a claim and went to work with pick and shovel. The going was hard, but his lust for gold was definite.

After weeks of labor, he was rewarded by the discovery of the shining ore. He needed machinery to bring the ore to the surface. Quietly, he covered up the mine, retraced his footsteps to his home in Williamsburg, Maryland, told his relatives and a few neighbors of the "strike." They got together money for the needed machinery, and had it shipped. The uncle and Darby went back to work the mine.

The first car of ore was mined, and shipped to a smelter. The returns proved they had one of the richest mines in Colorado! A few more cars of that ore would clear the debts. Then would come the big killing in profits.

Down went the drills! Up went the hopes of Darby and Uncle! Then something happened! The vein of gold ore disappeared! They had come to the end of the rainbow, and the pot of gold was no longer there! They drilled on, desperately trying to pick up the vein again—all to no avail.

Finally, they decided to quit.

They sold the machinery to a "junk" man for a few hundred dollars, and took the train back home. Some "junk" men are dumb, but not this one! He called in a mining engineer to look at the mine and do a little calculating. The engineer advised that the project had failed, because the owners were not familiar with "fault lines." His calculations showed that the vein would be found just three feet from where the Darbys had stopped drilling! That is exactly where it was found!

The "junk" man took millions of dollars in ore from the mine, because he knew enough to seek expert counsel before giving up.

Most of the money which went into the machinery was procured through the efforts of R. U. Darby, who was then a very young man. The money came from his relatives and neighbors, because of their faith in him. He paid back every dollar of it, although he was years in doing so.

Long afterward, Mr. Darby recouped his loss many times over, *when he made the discovery* that desire can be transmuted into gold. The discovery came after he went into the business of selling life insurance.

Remembering that he lost a huge fortune, because he stopped three feet from gold, Darby profited by the experience in his chosen work, by the simple method of saying to himself, "I stopped three feet from gold, but I will never stop *because men say 'no'* when I ask them to buy insurance."

Darby is one of a small group of fewer than fifty men who sell more than a million dollars in life insurance annually. He owes his "stickability" to the lesson he learned from his "quitability" in the gold mining business.

Before success comes in any man's life, he is sure to meet with much temporary defeat, and, perhaps, some failure. When defeat overtakes a man, the easiest and most logical thing to do is to quit. That is exactly what the majority of men do.

More than five hundred of the most successful men this country has ever known told the author their greatest success came just one step *beyond* the point at which defeat had overtaken them. Failure is a trickster with a keen sense of irony and cunning. It takes great delight in tripping one when success is almost within reach.

A FIFTY CENT LESSON IN PERSISTENCE

Shortly after Mr. Darby received his degree from the "University of Hard Knocks," and had decided to profit by his experience in the gold mining business, he had the good fortune to be present on an occasion that proved to him that "No" does not necessarily mean no.

One afternoon he was helping his uncle grind wheat in an old-fashioned mill. The uncle operated a large farm on which a number of colored sharecrop farmers lived. Quietly, the door was opened, and a small colored child, the daughter of a tenant, walked in and took her place near the door.

The uncle looked up, saw the child, and barked at her roughly, "What do you want?"

Meekly, the child replied, "My mama says send her fifty cents."

"I'll not do it," the uncle retorted. "Now you run on home."

"Yes sir," the child replied. *But she did not move.*

The uncle went ahead with his work, so busily engaged that he did not pay enough attention to the child to observe that she did not leave. When he looked up and saw her still standing there, he yelled at her, "I told you to go on home! Now go, or I'll take a switch to you."

The little girl said, "Yes sir," *but she did not budge an inch.*

The uncle dropped a sack of grain he was about to pour into the mill hopper, picked up a barrel stave, and started toward the child with an expression on his face that indicated trouble.

Darby held his breath. He was certain he was about to witness a murder. He knew his uncle had a fierce temper. He knew that colored children were not supposed to defy white people in that part of the country.

When the uncle reached the spot where the child was standing, she quickly stepped forward one step, looked up into his eyes, and screamed at the top of her shrill voice, *"My mama's gotta have that fifty cents!"*

The uncle stopped, looked at her for a minute, then slowly laid the barrel stave on the floor, put his hand in his pocket, took out half a dollar, and gave it to her.

The child took the money and slowly backed toward the door, never taking her eyes off the man *whom she had just conquered.* After she had gone, the uncle sat down on a box and looked out the window into space for more than ten minutes. He was pondering, with awe, over the whipping he had just taken.

Mr. Darby, too, was doing some thinking. That was the first time in all his experience that he had seen a colored child deliberately *master* an adult white person. How did she do it? What happened to his uncle that caused him to lose his fierceness and become as docile as a lamb? What strange power did this child use that made her master over her superior? These and other similar questions flashed into Darby's mind, but he did not find the answer until years later, when he told me the story.

Strangely, the story of this unusual experience was told to the author in the old mill, on the very spot where the uncle took his whipping. Strangely, too, I had devoted nearly a quarter of a century to the study of the power which enabled an ignorant, illiterate colored child to conquer an intelligent man.

As we stood there in that musty old mill, Mr. Darby repeated the story of the unusual conquest, and finished by asking, "What can you make of it? What strange power did that child use, that so completely whipped my uncle?"

The answer to his question will be found in the principles described in this book. The answer is full and complete. It contains details and instructions sufficient to enable anyone to understand, and apply the same force which the little child accidentally stumbled upon.

Keep your mind alert, and you will observe exactly what strange power came to the rescue of the child; you will catch a glimpse of this power in the next chapter. Somewhere in the book you will find an idea that will quicken your receptive powers, and place at your command, for your own benefit, this same irresistible power. The awareness of this power may come to you in the first chapter, or it may flash into your mind in some subsequent chapter. It may come in the form of a single idea. Or, it may come in the nature of a plan, or a purpose. Again, it may cause you to go back into your past experiences of failure or defeat, and bring to the surface some lesson by which you can regain all that you lost through defeat.

After I had described to Mr. Darby the power unwittingly used by the little colored child, he quickly retraced his thirty years of experience as a life insurance salesman, and frankly acknowledged that his success in that field was due, in no small degree, to the lesson he had learned from the child.

Mr. Darby pointed out: "Every time a prospect tried to bow me out, without buying, I saw that child standing there in the old mill, her big eyes glaring in defiance, and I said to myself, 'I've gotta make this sale.' The better portion of all sales I have made were made after people had said 'no.'"

He recalled, too, his mistake in having stopped only three feet from gold. "But," he said, "that experience was a blessing in disguise. It taught me *to keep on keeping on,* no matter how hard the going may be, a lesson I needed to learn before I could succeed in anything."

This story of Mr. Darby and his uncle, the colored child and the gold mine, doubtless will be read by hundreds of men who make their living by selling life insurance, and to all of these, the author wishes to offer the suggestion that Darby owes to these two experiences his ability to sell more than a million dollars of life insurance every year.

Life is strange, and often imponderable! Both the successes and the failures have their roots in simple experiences. Mr. Darby's experiences were common-place and simple enough, yet they held the answer to his destiny in life, therefore they were as important (to him) as life itself. He profited by these two dramatic experiences, because *he analyzed them,* and found the lesson they taught. But what of the man who has neither the time nor the inclination to study failure in search of knowledge that may lead to success? Where, and how, is he to learn the art of converting defeat into stepping stones to opportunity?

In answer to these questions, this book was written.

The answer called for a description of thirteen principles, but remember, as you read, the answer *you* may be seeking, to the questions which have caused you to ponder over the strangeness of life, may be found *in your own mind,* through some idea, plan, or purpose which may spring into your mind as you read.

One sound idea is all that one needs to achieve success. The principles described in this book contain the best, and the most practical of all that is known, concerning ways and means of creating useful ideas.

Before we go any further in our approach to the description of these principles, we believe you are entitled to receive this important suggestion. . . . When riches begin to come, they come so quickly, in such great abundance, that one wonders where they have been hiding during all those lean years. This is an astounding statement, and all the more so when we take into consideration the popular belief that riches come only to those who work hard and long.

When you begin to think and grow rich, you will observe that riches begin with a state of mind, with definiteness of purpose, with little or no hard work. You, and every other person, ought to be interested in knowing how to acquire that state of mind which will attract riches. I spent twenty-five years in research, analyzing more than 25,000 people, because I, too, wanted to know "how wealthy men become that way."

Without that research, this book could not have been written.

Here take notice of a very significant truth, viz: The business depression started in 1929, and continued on to an all-time record of destruction, until sometime after President Roosevelt entered office. Then the depression began to fade into nothingness. Just as an electrician in a theatre raises the lights so gradually that darkness is transmuted into light before you realize it, so did the spell of fear in the minds of the people gradually fade away and become faith.

Observe very closely: As soon as you master the principles of this philosophy, and begin to follow the instructions for applying those principles, your financial status will begin to improve, and everything you touch will begin to transmute itself into an asset for your benefit. Impossible? Not at all!

One of the main weaknesses of mankind is the average man's familiarity with the word "impossible." He knows all the rules which will not work. He knows all the things which cannot be done. This book was written for those who seek the rules which have made others successful, and are willing to *stake everything* on those rules.

A great many years ago I purchased a fine dictionary. The first thing I did with it was to turn to the word "impossible," and neatly clip it out of the book. That would not be an unwise thing for you to do.

Success comes to those who become success conscious.

Failure comes to those who indifferently allow themselves to become failure conscious.

The object of this book is to help all who seek it, to learn the art of changing their minds from failure consciousness to success consciousness.

Another weakness found in altogether too many people is the habit of measuring everything, and everyone, by *their own* impressions and beliefs. Some who will read this will believe that no one can think and grow rich. They cannot think in terms of riches, because their thought habits have been steeped in poverty, want, misery, failure, and defeat.

These unfortunate people remind me of a prominent Chinese man, who came to America to be educated in American ways. He attended the University of Chicago. One day President Harper met this young man on the campus, stopped to chat with him for a few minutes, and asked what had impressed him as being the most noticeable characteristic of the American people.

"Why," the man exclaimed, "the queer slant of your eyes. Your eyes are off slant!"

What do we say about the Chinese?

We refuse to believe that which we do not understand. We foolishly believe that our own limitations are the proper measure of limitations. Sure, the other fellow's eyes are "off slant," because they are not the same as our own.

Millions of people look at the achievements of Henry Ford, after he has arrived, and envy him, because of his good fortune, or luck, or genius, or whatever it is that they credit for Ford's fortune. Perhaps one person in every hundred thousand knows the secret of Ford's success, and those who do know are too modest, or too reluctant, to speak of it, *because of its simplicity.* A single transaction will illustrate the "secret" perfectly.

A few years back, Ford decided to produce his now famous V-8 motor. He chose to build an engine with the entire eight cylinders cast in one block, and instructed his engineers to produce a design for the engine. The design was placed on paper, but the engineers agreed, to a man, that it was simply *impossible* to cast an eight cylinder gas engine block in one piece.

Ford said, "Produce it anyway."

"But," they replied, "it's impossible!"

"Go ahead," Ford commanded, "and stay on the job until you succeed no matter how much time is required."

The engineers went ahead. There was nothing else for them to do, if they were to remain on the Ford staff. Six months went by, nothing happened. Another six months passed, and still nothing happened. The engineers tried every conceivable plan to carry out the orders, but the thing seemed out of the question: *"Impossible!"*

At the end of the year Ford checked with his engineers, and again they informed him they had found no way to carry out his orders.

"Go right ahead," said Ford, "I want it, and I'll have it."

They went ahead, and then, as if by a stroke of magic, the secret was discovered.

The Ford determination had won once more!

This story may not be described with minute accuracy, but the sum and substance of it is correct. Deduce from it, you who wish to think and grow rich, the secret of the Ford millions, if you can. You'll not have to look very far.

Henry Ford is a success, because he understands, and *applies* the principles of success.

One of these is desire: knowing what one wants. Remember this Ford story as you read, and pick out the lines in which the secret of his stupendous achievement have been described. If you can do this, if you can lay your finger on the particular group of principles which made Henry Ford rich, you can equal his achievements in almost any calling for which you are suited.

YOU ARE "THE MASTER OF YOUR FATE, THE CAPTAIN OF YOUR SOUL," BECAUSE . . .

When Henley wrote the prophetic lines "I am the Master of my Fate, I am the Captain of my Soul," he should have informed us that we are the Masters of our Fate, the Captains of our Souls, *because* we have the power to control our thoughts.

He should have told us that the ether in which this little earth floats, in which we move and have our being, is a form of energy moving at an inconceivably high rate of vibration, and that the ether is filled with a form of universal power which adapts itself to the nature of the thoughts we hold in our minds; and influences us, in natural ways, to transmute our thoughts into their physical equivalent.

If the poet had told us of this great truth, we would know why it is that we are the Masters of our Fate, the Captains of our Souls. He should have told us, with great emphasis, that this power makes no attempt to discriminate between destructive thoughts and constructive thoughts, that it will urge us to translate into physical reality thoughts of poverty just as quickly as it will influence us to act upon thoughts of riches.

He should have told us, too, that our brains become magnetized with the dominating thoughts which we hold in our minds, and, by means with which no man is familiar, these "magnets" attract to us the forces, the people, the circumstances of life which harmonize with the nature of our *dominating* thoughts.

He should have told us that before we can accumulate riches in great abundance, we must magnetize our minds with intense desire for riches, that we must become "money conscious" until the desire for money drives us to create definite plans for acquiring it.

But, being a poet, and not a philosopher, Henley contented himself by stating a great truth in poetic form, leaving those who followed him to interpret the philosophical meaning of his lines.

Little by little, the truth has unfolded itself, until it now appears certain that the principles described in this book hold the secret of mastery over our economic fate.

We are now ready to examine the first of these principles. Maintain a spirit of open-mindedness, and remember as you read, they are the invention of no one man. The principles were gathered from the life experiences of more than five hundred men who actually accumulated riches in huge amounts; men who began in poverty, with but little education, without influence. The principles worked for these men. You can put them to work for your own enduring benefit.

You will find it easy, not hard, to do.

Before you read the next chapter, I want you to know that it conveys factual information which might easily change your entire financial destiny, as it has so definitely brought changes of stupendous proportions to two people described.

I want you to know, also, that the relationship between these two men and myself is such that I could have taken no liberties with the facts, even if I had wished to do so. One of them has been my closest personal friend for almost twenty-five years, the other is my own son. The unusual success of these two men, success which they generously accredit to the principle described in the next chapter, more than justifies this personal reference as a means of emphasizing the far-flung power of this principle.

Almost fifteen years ago, I delivered the Commencement Address at Salem College, Salem, West Virginia. I emphasized the principle described in the next chapter, with so much intensity that one of the members of the graduating class definitely appropriated it, and made it a part of his own philosophy. The young man is now a Member of Congress, and an important factor in the present administration. Just before this book went to the publisher, he wrote me a letter in which he so clearly stated his opinion of the principle outlined in the next chapter that I have chosen to publish his letter as an introduction to that chapter.

It gives you an idea of the rewards to come.

My dear Napoleon:

My service as a Member of Congress having given me an insight into the problems of men and women, I am writing to offer a suggestion which may become helpful to thousands of worthy people.

With apologies, I must state that the suggestion, if acted upon, will mean several years of labor and responsibility for you, but I am enheartened to make the suggestion, because I know your great love for rendering useful service.

In 1922, you delivered the Commencement Address at Salem College, when I was a member of the graduating class. In that address, you planted in my mind an idea which has been responsible for the opportunity I now have to serve the people of my State, and will be responsible, in a very large measure, for whatever success I may have in the future.

The suggestion I have in mind is that you put into a book the sum and substance of the address you delivered at Salem College, and in that way give the people of America an opportunity to profit by your many years of experience and association with the men who, by their greatness, have made America the richest nation on earth.

I recall, as though it were yesterday, the marvelous description you gave of the method by which Henry Ford, with but little schooling, without a dollar, with no influential friends, rose to great heights. I made up my mind then, even before you had finished your speech, that I would make a place for myself, no matter how many difficulties I had to surmount.

Thousands of young people will finish their schooling this year, and within the next few years. Every one of them will be seeking just such a message of practical encouragement as the one I received from you. They will want to know where to turn, what to do, to get started in life. You can tell them, because you have helped to solve the problems of so many, many people.

If there is any possible way that you can afford to render so great a service, may I offer the suggestion that you include with every book one of your Personal Analysis Charts, in order that the purchaser of the book may have the benefit of a complete self-inventory, indicating, as you indicated to me years ago, exactly what is standing in the way of success.

Such a service as this, providing the readers of your book with a complete, unbiased picture of their faults and their virtues, would mean to them the difference between success and failure. The service would be priceless.

Millions of people are now facing the problem of staging a come-back, because of the depression, and I speak from personal experience when I say, I know these earnest people would welcome the opportunity to tell you their problems, and to receive your suggestions for the solution.

You know the problems of those who face the necessity of beginning all over again. There are thousands of people in America today who would like to know how they can convert ideas into money, people who must start at scratch, without finances, and recoup their losses. If anyone can help them, you can.

If you publish the book, I would like to own the first copy that comes from the press, personally autographed by you.

With best wishes, believe me,
Cordially yours,
Jennings Randolph

CHAPTER 2

DESIRE

THE STARTING POINT OF ALL ACHIEVEMENT

The First Step Toward Riches

When Edwin C. Barnes climbed down from the freight train in Orange, New Jersey, more than thirty years ago, he may have resembled a tramp, but his thoughts were those of a king!

As he made his way from the railroad tracks to Thomas A. Edison's office, his mind was at work. He saw himself *standing in Edison's presence.* He heard himself asking Mr. Edison for an opportunity to carry out the one consuming obsession of his life, a burning desire to become the business associate of the great inventor.

Barnes' desire was not a *hope!* It was not a *wish!* It was a keen, pulsating desire, which transcended everything else. It was definite.

The desire was not new when he approached Edison. It had been Barnes' *dominating desire* for a long time. In the beginning, when the desire first appeared in his mind, it may have been, probably was, only a wish, but it was no mere wish when he appeared before Edison with it.

A few years later, Edwin C. Barnes again stood before Edison, in the same office where he first met the inventor. This time his desire had been translated into reality. *He was in business with Edison.* The dominating dream of his life had become a reality. Today, people who know Barnes envy him, because of the "break" life yielded him. They see him in the days of his triumph, without taking the trouble to investigate the *cause* of his success.

Barnes succeeded because he chose a definite goal, placed all his energy, all his will power, all his effort, everything back of that goal. He did not become the partner of Edison the day he arrived. He was content to start in the most menial work, as long as it provided an opportunity to take even one step toward his cherished goal.

Five years passed before the chance he had been seeking made its appearance. During all those years not one ray of hope, not one promise of attainment of his desire had been held out to him. To everyone, except himself, he appeared only another cog in the Edison business wheel, but in his own mind, he was the partner of Edison every minute of the time, from the very day that he first went to work there.

It is a remarkable illustration of the power of a definite desire. Barnes won his goal, because he wanted to be a business associate of Mr. Edison, more than he wanted anything else. He created a plan by which to attain that purpose. But he burned all bridges behind him. He stood by his desire until it became the dominating obsession of his life—and—finally, a fact.

When he went to Orange, he did not say to himself, "I will try to induce Edison to give me a job of some sort." He said, "I will see Edison, and put him on notice that I have come to go into business with him."

He did not say, "I will work there for a few months, and if I get no encouragement, I will quit and get a job somewhere else." He did say, "I will start anywhere. I will do anything Edison tells me to do, but *before I am through,* I will be his associate."

He did not say, "I will keep my eyes open for another opportunity, in case I fail to get what I want in the Edison organization." He said, "There is but one thing in this world that I am determined to have, and that is a business association with Thomas A. Edison. I will burn all bridges behind me, and stake my entire future on my ability to get what I want."

He left himself no possible way of retreat. He had to win or perish!

That is all there is to the Barnes story of success!

A long while ago, a great warrior faced a situation which made it necessary for him to make a decision which insured his success on the battlefield. He was about to send his armies against a powerful foe, whose men outnumbered his own. He loaded his soldiers into boats, sailed to the enemy's country, unloaded soldiers and equipment, then gave the order to burn the ships that had carried them. Addressing his men before the first battle, he said, "You see the boats going up in smoke. That means that we cannot leave these shores alive unless we win! We now have no choice—*we win—or we perish!*" They won.

Every person who wins in any undertaking must be willing to burn his ships and cut all sources of retreat. Only by so doing can one be sure of maintaining that state of mind known as a burning desire to win, essential to success.

The morning after the great Chicago fire, a group of merchants stood on State Street, looking at the smoking remains of what had been their stores. They went into a conference to decide if they would try to rebuild, or leave Chicago and start over in a more promising section of the country. They reached a decision—all except one—to leave Chicago.

The merchant who decided to stay and rebuild pointed a finger at the remains of his store, and said, "Gentlemen, on that very spot I will build the world's greatest store, no matter how many times it may burn down."

That was more than fifty years ago. The store was built. It stands there today, a towering monument to the power of that state of mind known as a burning desire. The easy thing for Marshall Field to have done, would have been exactly what his fellow merchants did. When the going was hard, and the future looked dismal, they pulled up and went where the going seemed easier.

Mark well this difference between Marshall Field and the other merchants, because it is the same difference which distinguishes Edwin C. Barnes from thousands of other young men who have worked in the Edison organization. It is the same difference which distinguishes practically all who succeed from those who fail.

Every human being who reaches the age of understanding of the purpose of money wishes for it. *Wishing* will not bring riches. But *desiring* riches with a state of mind that becomes an obsession, then planning definite ways and means to acquire riches, and backing those plans with persistence which *does not recognize failure,* will bring riches.

The method by which desire for riches can be transmuted into its financial equivalent consists of six definite, practical steps, viz:

FIRST. Fix in your mind the exact amount of money you desire. It is not sufficient merely to say, "I want plenty of money." Be definite as to the amount. (There is a psychological reason for definiteness which will be described in a subsequent chapter.)

SECOND. Determine exactly what you intend to give in return for the money you desire. (There is no such reality as "something for nothing.")

THIRD. Establish a definite date when you intend to *possess* the money you desire.

FOURTH. Create a definite plan for carrying out your desire, and begin *at once,* whether you are ready or not, to put this plan into *action.*

FIFTH. Write out a clear, concise statement of the amount of money you intend to acquire, name the time limit for its acquisition, state what you intend to give in return for the money, and describe clearly the plan through which you intend to accumulate it.

SIXTH. Read your written statement aloud, twice daily, once just before retiring at night, and once after arising in the morning. As you read—see and feel and believe yourself already in possession of the money.

It is important that you follow the instructions described in these six steps. It is especially important that you observe and follow the instructions in the sixth paragraph. You may complain that it is impossible for you to "see yourself in possession of money" before you actually have it. Here is where a burning desire will come to your aid. If you truly desire money so keenly that your desire is an obsession, you will have no difficulty in convincing yourself that you will acquire it. The object is to want money, and to become so determined to have it that you convince yourself you will have it.

Only those who become "money conscious" ever accumulate great riches. "Money consciousness" means that the mind has become so thoroughly saturated with the desire for money, that one can see one's self already in possession of it.

To the uninitiated, who has not been schooled in the working principles of the human mind, these instructions may appear impractical. It may be helpful, to all who fail to recognize the soundness of the six steps, to know that the information they convey was received from Andrew Carnegie, who began as an ordinary laborer in the steel mills, but managed, despite his humble beginning, to make these principles yield him a fortune of considerably more than one hundred million dollars.

It may be of further help to know that the six steps here recommended were carefully scrutinized by the late Thomas A. Edison, who placed his stamp of approval upon them as being not only the steps essential for the accumulation of money, but necessary for the attainment of *any definite goal.*

The steps call for no "hard labor." They call for no sacrifice. They do not require one to become ridiculous, or credulous. To apply them calls for no great amount of education.

But the successful application of these six steps does call for sufficient *imagination* to enable one to see, and to understand, that accumulation of money cannot be left to chance, good fortune, and luck. One must realize that all who have accumulated great fortunes first did a certain amount of dreaming, hoping, wishing, desiring, and planning *before* they acquired money.

You may as well know, right here, that you can never have riches in great quantities, unless you can work yourself into a white heat of desire for money, and actually believe you will possess it.

You may as well know, also, that every great leader, from the dawn of civilization down to the present, was a dreamer. Christianity is the greatest potential power in the world today, because its founder was an intense dreamer who had the vision and the imagination to see realities in their mental and spiritual form before they had been transmuted into physical form.

If you do not see great riches in your imagination, you will never see them in your bank balance.

Never in the history of America has there been so great an opportunity for practical dreamers as now exists. The six-year economic collapse has reduced all men, substantially, to the same level. A new race is about to be run. The stakes represent huge fortunes which will be accumulated within the next ten years. The rules of the race have changed, because we now live in a changed world that definitely favors the masses, those who had but little or no opportunity to win under the conditions existing during the depression, when fear paralyzed growth and development.

We who are in this race for riches should be encouraged to know that this changed world in which we live is demanding new ideas, new ways of doing things, new leaders, new inventions, new methods of teaching, new methods of marketing, new books, new literature, new features for the radio, new ideas for moving pictures. Back of all this demand for new and better things, there is one quality which one must possess to win, and that is definiteness of purpose, the knowledge of what one wants, and a burning desire to possess it.

The business depression marked the death of one age, and the birth of another. This changed world requires practical dreamers who can *and will* put their dreams into action. The practical dreamers have always been and always will be the pattern-makers of civilization.

We who desire to accumulate riches should remember the real leaders of the world always have been men who harnessed, and put into practical use, the intangible, unseen forces of unborn opportunity, and have converted those forces (or impulses of thought), into skyscrapers, cities, factories, airplanes, automobiles, and every form of convenience that makes life more pleasant.

Tolerance and an open mind are practical necessities of the dreamer of today. Those who are afraid of new ideas are doomed before they start. Never has there been a time more favorable to pioneers than the present. True, there is no wild and woolly west to be conquered, as in the days of the Covered Wagon; but there is a vast business, financial, and industrial world to be remolded and redirected along new and better lines.

In planning to acquire your share of the riches, let no one influence you to scorn the dreamer. To win the big stakes in this changed world, you must catch the spirit of the great pioneers of the past, whose dreams have given to civilization all that it has of value, the spirit which serves as the life-blood of our own country—your opportunity, and mine, to develop and market our talents.

Let us not forget, Columbus dreamed of an Unknown world, staked his life on the existence of such a world, and discovered it!

Copernicus, the great astronomer, dreamed of a multiplicity of worlds, and revealed them! No one denounced him as "impractical" *after* he had triumphed. Instead, the world worshipped at his shrine, thus proving once more that "success requires no apologies, failure permits no alibis."

If the thing you wish to do is right, and *you believe in it,* go ahead and do it! Put your dream across, and never mind what "they" say if you meet with temporary defeat, for "they," perhaps, do not know that every failure brings with it the seed of an equivalent success.

Henry Ford, poor and uneducated, dreamed of a horseless carriage, went to work with what tools he possessed, without waiting for opportunity to favor him, and now evidence of his dream belts the entire earth. He has put more wheels into operation than any man who ever lived, because he was not afraid to back his dreams.

Thomas Edison dreamed of a lamp that could be operated by electricity, began where he stood to put his dream into action, and despite more than *ten thousand failures,* he stood by that dream until he made it a physical reality. Practical dreamers do not quit!

Whelan dreamed of a chain of cigar stores, transformed his dream into action, and now the United Cigar Stores occupy the best corners in America.

Lincoln dreamed of freedom for the black slaves, put his dream into action, and barely missed living to see a united North and South translate his dream into reality.

The Wright brothers dreamed of a machine that would fly through the air. Now one may see evidence all over the world that they dreamed soundly.

Marconi dreamed of a system for harnessing the intangible forces of the ether. Evidence that he did not dream in vain may be found in every wireless and radio in the world. Moreover, Marconi's dream brought the humblest cabin, and the most stately manor house side by side. It made the people of every nation on earth back-door neighbors. It gave the President of the United States a medium by which he may talk to all the people of America at one time, and on short notice. It may interest you to know that

Marconi's "friends" had him taken into custody, and examined in a psychopathic hospital, when he announced he had discovered a principle through which he could send messages through the air, without the aid of wires, or other direct physical means of communication. The dreamers of today fare better.

The world has become accustomed to new discoveries. Nay, it has shown a willingness to reward the dreamer who gives the world a new idea.

"The greatest achievement was, at first, and for a time, but a dream."

"The oak sleeps in the acorn. The bird waits in the egg, and in the highest vision of the soul, a waking angel stirs. Dreams are the seedlings of reality."

Awake, arise, and assert yourself, you dreamers of the world. Your star is now in the ascendency. The world depression brought the opportunity you have been waiting for. It taught people humility, tolerance, and openmindedness.

The world is filled with an abundance of opportunity which the dreamers of the past never knew.

A burning desire to be and to do is the starting point from which the dreamer must take off. Dreams are not born of indifference, laziness, or lack of ambition.

The world no longer scoffs at the dreamer, nor calls him impractical. If you think it does, take a trip to Tennessee, and witness what a dreamer President has done in the way of harnessing and using the great water power of America. A score of years ago, such a dream would have seemed like madness.

You have been disappointed, you have undergone defeat during the depression, you have felt the great heart within you crushed until it bled. Take courage, for these experiences have tempered the spiritual metal of which you are made—they are assets of incomparable value.

Remember, too, that all who succeed in life get off to a bad start, and pass through many heartbreaking struggles before they "arrive." The turning point in the lives of those who succeed usually comes at the moment of some crisis, through which they are introduced to their "other selves."

John Bunyan wrote the *Pilgrim's Progress,* which is among the finest of all English literature, after he had been confined in prison and sorely punished, because of his views on the subject of religion.

O. Henry discovered the genius which slept within his brain after he had met with great misfortune, and was confined in a prison cell, in Columbus, Ohio. Being forced, through misfortune, to become acquainted with his "other self," and to use his imagination, he discovered himself to be a great author instead of a miserable criminal and outcast. Strange and varied are the ways of life, and stranger still are the ways of Infinite Intelligence, through which men are sometimes forced to undergo all sorts of punishment before discovering their own brains, and their own capacity to create useful ideas through imagination.

Edison, the world's greatest inventor and scientist, was a "tramp" telegraph operator; he failed innumerable times before he was driven, finally, to the discovery of the genius which slept within his brain.

Charles Dickens began by pasting labels on blacking pots. The tragedy of his first love penetrated the depths of his soul, and converted him into one of the world's truly great authors. That tragedy produced, first, *David Copperfield,* then a succession of other works that made this a richer and better world for all who read his books. Disappointment over love affairs generally has the effect of driving men to drink, and women to ruin; and this, because most people never learn the art of transmuting their strongest emotions into dreams of a constructive nature.

Helen Keller became deaf, dumb, and blind shortly after birth. Despite her greatest misfortune, she has written her name indelibly in the pages of the history of the great. Her entire life has served as evidence that *no one ever is defeated until defeat has been accepted as a reality.*

Robert Burns was an illiterate country lad; he was cursed by poverty, and grew up to be a drunkard in the bargain. The world was made better for his having lived, because he clothed beautiful thoughts in poetry, and thereby plucked a thorn and planted a rose in its place.

Booker T. Washington was born in slavery, handicapped by race and color. Because he was tolerant, had an open mind at all times, on all subjects, and was a dreamer, he left his impress for good on an entire race.

Beethoven was deaf, Milton was blind, but their names will last as long as time endures, because they dreamed and translated their dreams into organized thought.

Before passing to the next chapter, kindle anew in your mind the fire of hope, faith, courage, and tolerance. If you have these states of mind, and a working knowledge of the principles described, all else that you need will come to you, when you are ready for it. Let Emerson state the thought in these words: "Every proverb, every book, every byword that belongs to thee for aid and comfort shall surely come home through open or winding passages. Every friend whom not thy fantastic will, but the great and tender soul in thee craveth, shall lock thee in his embrace."

There is a difference between wishing for a thing and being ready to receive it. No one is *ready* for a thing until he *believes* he can acquire it. The state of mind must be belief, not mere hope or wish. Open-mindedness is essential for belief. Closed minds do not inspire faith, courage, and belief.

Remember, no more effort is required to aim high in life, to demand abundance and prosperity, than is required to accept misery and poverty. A great poet has correctly stated this universal truth through these lines:

I bargained with Life for a penny,
And Life would pay no more,
However I begged at evening
When I counted my scanty store.

For Life is a just employer,
He gives you what you ask,
But once you have set the wages,
Why, you must bear the task.

I worked for a menial's hire,
Only to learn, dismayed,
That any wage I had asked of Life,
Life would have willingly paid.

DESIRE OUTWITS MOTHER NATURE

As a fitting climax to this chapter, I wish to introduce one of the most unusual persons I have ever known. I first saw him twenty-four years ago, a few minutes after he was born. He came into the world without any physical sign of ears, and the doctor admitted, when pressed for an opinion, that the child might be deaf, and mute for life.

I challenged the doctor's opinion. I had the right to do so; I was the child's father. I, too, reached a decision, and rendered an opinion, but I expressed the opinion silently, in the secrecy of my own heart. I decided that my son would hear and speak. Nature could send me a child without ears, but Nature *could not induce me to accept* the reality of the affliction.

In my own mind I knew that my son would hear and speak. How? I was sure there must be a way, and I knew I would find it. I thought of the words of the immortal Emerson: "The whole course of things goes to teach us faith. We need only obey. There is guidance for each of us, and by lowly listening, we shall hear *the right word*."

The right word? Desire! More than anything else, I desired that my son should not be a deaf mute. From that desire I never receded, not for a second.

Many years previously, I had written, "Our only limitations are those we set up in our own minds." For the first time, I wondered if that statement were true. Lying on the bed in front of me was a newly born child, without the natural equipment of hearing. Even though he might hear and speak, he was obviously disfigured for life. Surely, this was a limitation which that child had not set up in his own mind.

What could I do about it? Somehow I would find a way to transplant into that child's mind my own burning desire for ways and means of conveying sound to his brain without the aid of ears.

As soon as the child was old enough to cooperate, I would fill his mind so completely with a burning desire to hear, that Nature would, by methods of her own, translate it into physical reality.

All this thinking took place in my own mind, but I spoke of it to no one. Every day I renewed the pledge I had made to myself, not to accept a deaf mute for a son.

As he grew older, and began to take notice of things around him, we observed that he had a slight degree of hearing. When he reached the age when children usually begin talking, he made no attempt to speak, but we could tell by his actions that he could hear certain sounds slightly. That was all I wanted to know! I was convinced that if he could hear, even slightly, he might develop still greater hearing capacity. Then something happened which gave me hope. It came from an entirely unexpected source.

We bought a victrola. When the child heard the music for the first time, he went into ecstasies, and promptly appropriated the machine. He soon showed a preference for certain records, among them, "It's a Long Way to Tipperary." On one occasion, he played that piece over and over, for almost two hours, standing in front of the victrola, *with his teeth clamped on the edge of the case.* The significance of this self-formed habit of his did not become clear to us until years afterward, for we had never heard of the principle of "bone conduction" of sound at that time.

Shortly after he appropriated the victrola, I discovered that he could hear me quite clearly when I spoke with my lips touching his mastoid bone, or at the base of the brain. These discoveries placed in my possession the necessary media by which I began to translate into reality my *Burning Desire* to help my son develop hearing and speech. By that time he was making stabs at speaking certain words. The outlook was far from encouraging, but desire backed by faith knows no such word as impossible.

Having determined that he could hear the sound of my voice plainly, I began, immediately, to transfer to his mind the desire to hear and speak. I soon discovered that the child enjoyed bedtime stories, so I went to work, creating stories designed to develop in him self-reliance, imagination, and a *keen desire to hear and to be normal.*

There was one story in particular which I emphasized by giving it some new and dramatic coloring each time it was told. It was designed to plant in his mind the thought that his affliction was not a liability, but an asset of great value. Despite the fact that all the philosophy I had examined clearly indicated that every adversity brings with it the seed of an equivalent advantage, I must confess that I had not the slightest idea *how* this affliction could ever become an asset. However, I continued my practice of wrapping that philosophy in bedtime stories, hoping the time would come when he would find some plan by which his handicap could be made to serve some useful purpose.

Reason told me plainly that there was no adequate compensation for the lack of ears and natural hearing equipment. Desire backed by faith pushed reason aside, and inspired me to carry on.

As I analyze the experience in retrospect, I can see now that my *son's faith in me* had much to do with the astounding results. He did not question anything I told him. I sold him the idea that he had a distinct *advantage* over his older brother, and that this advantage would reflect itself in many ways. For example, the teachers in school would observe that he had no ears, and, because of this, they would show him special attention and treat him with extraordinary kindness. They always did. His mother saw to that, by visiting the teachers and arranging with them to give the child the extra attention necessary. I sold him the idea, too, that when he became old enough to sell newspapers (his older brother had already become a newspaper merchant), he would have a big advantage over his brother, for the reason that people would pay him extra money for his wares, because they could see that he was a bright, industrious boy, despite the fact he had no ears.

We could notice that, gradually, the child's hearing was improving. Moreover, he had not the slightest tendency to be self-conscious because of his affliction. When he was about seven, he showed the first evidence that our method of servicing his mind was bearing fruit. For several months he begged for the privilege of selling newspapers, but his mother would not give her consent. She was afraid that his deafness made it unsafe for him to go on the street alone.

Finally, he took matters in his own hands. One afternoon, when he was left at home with the servants, he climbed through the kitchen window, shinnied to the ground, and set out on his own. He borrowed six cents in capital from the neighborhood shoemaker, invested it in papers, sold out, reinvested, and kept repeating until late in the evening. After balancing his accounts, and paying back the six cents he had borrowed from his banker, he had a net profit of forty-two cents. When we got home that night, we found him in bed asleep, with the money tightly clenched in his hand.

His mother opened his hand, removed the coins, and cried. Of all things! Crying over her son's first victory seemed so inappropriate. My reaction was the reverse. I laughed heartily, for I knew that my endeavor to plant in the child's mind an attitude of faith in himself had been successful.

His mother saw, in his first business venture, a little deaf boy who had gone out in the streets and risked his life to earn money. I saw a brave, ambitious, self-reliant little business man whose stock in himself had been increased a hundred percent, because he had gone into business on his own initiative, and had won. The transaction pleased me, because I knew that he had given evidence of a trait of resourcefulness that would go with him all through life. Later events proved this to be true. When his older brother wanted something, he would lie down on the floor, kick his feet in the air, cry for it—and get it. When the "little deaf boy" wanted something, he would plan a way to earn the money, then buy it for himself. He still follows that plan!

Truly, my own son has taught me that handicaps can be converted into stepping stones on which one may climb toward some worthy goal, unless they are accepted as obstacles, and used as alibis.

The little deaf boy went through the grades, high school, and college without being able to hear his teachers, excepting when they shouted loudly, at close range. He did not go to a school for the deaf. We would not permit him to learn the sign language. We were determined that he should live a normal life, and associate with normal children, and we stood by that decision, although it cost us many heated debates with school officials.

While he was in high school, he tried an electrical hearing aid, but it was of no value to him; due, we believed, to a condition that was disclosed when the child was six, by Dr. J. Gordon Wilson, of Chicago, when he operated on one side of the boy's head, and discovered that there was no sign of natural hearing equipment.

During his last week in college (eighteen years after the operation), something happened which marked the most important turning-point of his life. Through what seemed to be mere chance, he came into possession of another electrical hearing device, which was sent to him on trial. He was slow about testing it, due to his disappointment with a similar device. Finally he picked the instrument up, and more or less carelessly, placed it on his head, hooked up the battery, and lo! as if by a stroke of magic, his lifelong desire for normal hearing became a reality! For the first time in his life he heard practically as well as any person with normal hearing. "God moves in mysterious ways, His wonders to perform."

Overjoyed because of the Changed World which had been brought to him through his hearing device, he rushed to the telephone, called his mother, and heard her voice perfectly. The next day he plainly heard the voices of his professors in class, for the first time in his life! Previously he could hear them only when they shouted, at short range. He heard the radio. He *heard* the talking pictures. For the first time in his life, he could converse freely with other people, without the necessity of their having to speak loudly. Truly, he had come into possession of a Changed World. We had refused to accept Nature's error, and, by persistent desire, we had induced Nature to correct that error, through the only practical means available.

Desire had commenced to pay dividends, but the victory was not yet complete. The boy still had to find a definite and practical way to convert his handicap into an *equivalent asset.*

Hardly realizing the significance of what had already been accomplished, but intoxicated with the joy of his newly discovered world of sound, he wrote a letter to the manufacturer of the hearing aid, enthusiastically describing his experience. Something in his letter; something, perhaps which was not written on the lines, but back of them; caused the company to invite him to New York. When he arrived, he was escorted through the factory, and while talking with the Chief Engineer, telling him about his Changed World, a hunch, an idea, or an inspiration—call it what you wish—flashed into his mind. It was *this impulse of thought* which converted his affliction into an asset, destined to pay dividends in both money and happiness to thousands for all time to come.

The sum and substance of that impulse of thought was this: It occurred to him that he might be of help to the millions of deafened people who go through life without the benefit of hearing devices, if he could find a way to tell them the story of his Changed World. Then and there, he reached a decision to devote the remainder of his life to rendering useful service to the hard of hearing.

For an entire month, he carried on an intensive research, during which he analyzed the entire marketing system of the manufacturer of the hearing device, and created ways and means of communicating with the hard of hearing all over the world for the purpose of sharing with them his newly discovered Changed World. When this was done, he put in writing a two-year plan, based upon his findings. When he presented the plan to the company, he was instantly given a position, for the purpose of carrying out his ambition.

Little did he dream, when he went to work, that he was destined to bring hope and practical relief to thousands of deafened people who, without his help, would have been doomed forever to deaf mutism.

Shortly after he became associated with the manufacturer of his hearing aid, he invited me to attend a class conducted by his company, for the purpose of teaching deaf mutes to hear, and to speak. I had never heard of such a form of education, therefore I visited the class, skeptical but hopeful that my time would not be entirely wasted. Here I saw a demonstration which gave me a greatly enlarged vision of what I had done to arouse and keep alive in my son's mind the desire for normal hearing. I saw deaf mutes actually being taught to hear and to speak, through application of the self-same principle I had used, more than twenty years previously, in saving my son from deaf mutism.

Thus, through some strange turn of the Wheel of Fate, my son, Blair, and I have been destined to aid in correcting deaf mutism for those as yet unborn, because we are the only living human beings, as far as I know, who have established definitely the fact that deaf mutism can be corrected to the extent of restoring to normal life those who suffer with this affliction. It has been done for one; it will be done for others.

There is no doubt in my mind that Blair would have been a deaf mute all his life, if his mother and I had not managed to shape his mind as we did. The doctor who attended at his birth told us, confidentially, the child might never hear or speak. A few weeks ago, Dr. Irving Voorhees, a noted specialist on such cases, examined Blair very thoroughly. He was astounded when he learned how well my son now hears, and speaks, and said his examination indicated that "theoretically, the boy should not be able to hear at all." But the lad does hear, despite the fact that X-ray pictures show there is no opening in the skull, whatsoever, from where his ears should be to the brain.

When I planted in his mind the desire to hear and talk, and live as a normal person, there went with that impulse some strange influence which caused Nature to become bridge-builder, and span the gulf of silence between his brain and the outer world, by some means which the keenest medical specialists have not been able to interpret. It would be sacrilege for me to even conjecture as to how Nature performed this miracle. It would be unforgivable if I neglected to tell the world as much as I know of the humble part I assumed in the strange experience. It is my duty, and a privilege to say I believe, and not without reason, that nothing is impossible to the person who backs desire with enduring faith.

Verily, a burning desire has devious ways of transmuting itself into its physical equivalent. Blair desired normal hearing; now he has it! He was born with a handicap which might easily have sent one with a less defined desire to the street with a bundle of pencils and a tin cup. That handicap now promises to serve as the medium by which he will render useful service to many millions of hard of hearing, also, to give him useful employment at adequate financial compensation the remainder of his life.

The little "white lies" I planted in his mind when he was a child, by leading him to believe his affliction would become a great asset, which he could capitalize, has justified itself. Verily, there is nothing, right or wrong, which belief, plus burning desire, cannot make real. These qualities are free to everyone.

In all my experience in dealing with men and women who had personal problems, I never handled a single case which more definitely demonstrates the power of desire. Authors sometimes make the mistake of writing of subjects of which they have but superficial, or very elementary, knowledge. It has been my good fortune to have had the privilege of testing the soundness of the power of desire, through the affliction of my own son. Perhaps it was providential that the experience came as it did, for surely no one is better prepared than he to serve as an example of what happens when desire is put to the test. *If Mother Nature bends to the will of desire, is it logical that mere men can defeat a burning desire?*

Strange and imponderable is the power of the human mind! We do not understand the method by which it uses every circumstance, every individual, every physical thing within its reach, as a means of transmuting desire into its physical counterpart. Perhaps science will uncover this secret.

I planted in my son's mind the desire to hear and to speak as any normal person hears and speaks. That desire has now become a reality. I planted in his mind the desire to convert his greatest handicap into his greatest asset. That desire has been realized. The modus operandi by which this astounding result was achieved is not hard to describe. It consisted of three very definite facts. First, I mixed faith with the desire for normal hearing, which I passed on to my son. Second, I communicated my desire to him in every conceivable way available, through persistent, continuous effort, over a period of years. Third, he believed me!

As this chapter was being completed, news came of the death of Mme. Schuman-Heink. One short paragraph in the news dispatch gives the clue to this unusual woman's stupendous success as a singer. I quote the paragraph, because the clue it contains is none other than desire.

Early in her career, Mme. Schuman-Heink visited the director of the Vienna Court Opera, to have him test her voice. But, he did not test it. After taking one look at the awkward and poorly dressed girl, he exclaimed, none too gently: "With such a face, and with no personality at all, how can you ever expect to succeed in opera? My good child, give up the idea. Buy a sewing machine, and go to work. You can never be a singer."

Never is a long time! The director of the Vienna Court Opera knew much about the technique of singing. He knew little about the power of desire, when it assumes the proportion of an obsession. If he had known more of that power, he would not have made the mistake of condemning genius without giving it an opportunity.

Several years ago, one of my business associates became ill. He became worse as time went on, and finally was taken to the hospital for an operation. Just before he was wheeled into the operating room, I took a look at him, and wondered how anyone as thin and emaciated as he could possibly go through a major operation successfully. The doctor warned me that there was little if any chance of my ever seeing him alive again. But that was the doctor's opinion. It was not the opinion of the patient. Just before he was wheeled away, he whispered feebly, "Do not be disturbed, Chief. I will be out of here in a few days." The attending nurse looked at me with pity. But the patient did come through safely. After it was all over, his physician said, "Nothing but his own desire to live saved him. He never would have pulled through if he had not refused to accept the possibility of death."

I believe in the power of desire backed by faith, because I have seen this power lift men from lowly beginnings to places of power and wealth; I have seen it rob the grave of its victims; I have seen it serve as the medium by which men staged a comeback after having been defeated in a hundred different ways; I have seen it provide my own son with a normal, happy, successful life, despite Nature's having sent him into the world without ears.

How can one harness and use the power of desire? This has been answered through this and the subsequent chapters of this book. This message is going out to the world at the end of the longest, and perhaps, the most devastating depression America has ever known. It is reasonable to presume that the message may come to the attention of many who have been wounded by the depression, those who have lost their fortunes, others who have lost their positions, and great numbers who must reorganize their plans and stage a comeback. To all these I wish to convey the thought that all achievement, no matter what may be its nature, or its purpose, must begin with an intense, burning desire for something definite.

Through some strange and powerful principle of "mental chemistry" which she has never divulged, Nature wraps up in the impulse of strong desire "that something" which recognizes no such word as impossible, and accepts no such reality as failure.

CHAPTER 3

FAITH

VISUALIZATION OF AND BELIEF IN ATTAINMENT OF DESIRE

The Second Step Toward Riches

Faith is the head chemist of the mind. When faith is blended with the vibration of thought, the subconscious mind instantly picks up the vibration, translates it into its spiritual equivalent, and transmits it to Infinite Intelligence, as in the case of prayer.

The emotions of faith, love, and sex are the most powerful of all the major positive emotions. When the three are blended, they have the effect of "coloring" the vibration of thought in such a way that it instantly reaches the subconscious mind, where it is changed into its spiritual equivalent, the only form that induces a response from Infinite Intelligence.

Love and faith are psychic, related to the spiritual side of man. Sex is purely biological, and related only to the physical. The mixing, or blending, of these three emotions has the effect of opening a direct line of communication between the finite, thinking mind of man, and Infinite Intelligence.

HOW TO DEVELOP FAITH

There comes, now, a statement which will give a better understanding of the importance the principle of auto-suggestion assumes in the transmutation of desire into its physical, or monetary equivalent; namely, faith is a state of mind which may be induced, or created, by affirmation or repeated instructions to the subconscious mind, through the principle of auto-suggestion.

As an illustration, consider the purpose for which you are, presumably, reading this book. The object is, naturally, to acquire the ability to transmute the intangible thought impulse of desire into its physical counterpart, money. By following the instructions laid down in the chapters on auto-suggestion, and the subconscious mind, as summarized in the chapter on auto-suggestion, you may convince the subconscious mind that you *believe* you will receive that for which you ask, and it will act upon that belief, which your subconscious mind passes back to you in the form of "faith," followed by definite plans for procuring that which you desire.

The method by which one develops faith, where it does not already exist, is extremely difficult to describe, almost as difficult, in fact, as it would be to describe the color of red to a blind man who has never seen color, and has nothing with which to compare what you describe to him. Faith is a state of mind which you may develop at will, after you have mastered the thirteen principles, because it is a state of mind which develops voluntarily, through application and use of these principles.

Repetition of affirmation of orders to your subconscious mind is the only known method of voluntary development of the emotion of faith.

Perhaps the meaning may be made clearer through the following explanation as to the way men sometimes become criminals. Stated in the words of a famous criminologist, "When men first come into contact with crime, they abhor it. If they remain in contact with crime for a time, they become accustomed to it, and endure it. If they remain in contact with it long enough, they finally embrace it, and become influenced by it."

This is the equivalent of saying that any impulse of thought which is repeatedly passed on to the subconscious mind is, finally, accepted and acted upon by the subconscious mind, which proceeds to translate that impulse into its physical equivalent, by the most practical procedure available.

In connection with this, consider again the statement, all thoughts which have been emotionalized (given feeling) and mixed with faith begin immediately to translate themselves into their physical equivalent or counterpart.

The emotions, or the "feeling" portion of thoughts, are the factors which give thoughts vitality, life, and action. The emotions of faith, love, and sex, when mixed with any thought impulse, give it greater action than any of these emotions can do singly.

Not only thought impulses which have been mixed with faith, but those which have been mixed with any of the positive emotions, or any of the negative emotions, may reach and influence the subconscious mind.

From this statement, you will understand that the subconscious mind will translate into its physical equivalent a thought impulse of a negative or destructive nature, just as readily as it will act upon thought impulses of a positive or constructive nature. This accounts for the strange phenomenon which so many millions of people experience, referred to as "misfortune," or "bad luck."

There are millions of people who believe themselves "doomed" to poverty and failure, because of some strange force over which they believe they have no control. They are the creators of their own "misfortunes," because of this negative belief, which is picked up by the subconscious mind, and translated into its physical equivalent.

This is an appropriate place at which to suggest again that you may benefit by passing on to your subconscious mind any desire which you wish translated into its physical or monetary equivalent, in a state of expectancy or belief that the transmutation will actually take place. Your belief, or faith, is the element which determines the action of your subconscious mind. There is nothing to hinder you from "deceiving" your subconscious mind when giving it instructions through auto-suggestion, as I deceived my son's subconscious mind.

To make this "deceit" more realistic, conduct yourself just as you would if you were already in possession of the material thing which you are demanding when you call upon your subconscious mind.

The subconscious mind will transmute into its physical equivalent, by the most direct and practical media available, any order which is given to it in a state of belief, or faith that the order will be carried out.

Surely, enough has been stated to give a starting point from which one may, through experiment and practice, acquire the ability to mix faith with any order given to the subconscious mind. Perfection will come through practice. It *cannot* come by merely *reading* instructions.

If it be true that one may become a criminal by association with crime (and this is a known fact), it is equally true that one may develop faith by voluntarily suggesting to the subconscious mind that one has faith. The mind comes, finally, to take on the nature of the influences which dominate it. Understand this truth, and you will know why it is essential for you to encourage the *positive emotions* as dominating forces of your mind, and discourage—and *eliminate*—negative emotions.

A mind dominated by positive emotions becomes afavorable abode for the state of mind known as faith. A mind so dominated may, at will, give the subconscious mind instructions, which it will accept and act upon immediately.

FAITH IS A STATE OF MIND WHICH MAY BE INDUCED BY AUTO-SUGGESTION

All down the ages, the religionists have admonished struggling humanity to "have faith" in this, that, and the other dogma or creed, but they have failed to tell people how to have faith. They have not stated that "faith is a state of mind, and that it may be induced by self-suggestion."

In language which any normal human being can understand, we will describe all that is known about the principle through which faith may be developed, where it does not already exist.

Have faith in yourself; faith in the Infinite.

Before we begin, you should be reminded again that:

Faith is the "eternal elixir" which gives life, power, and action to the impulse of thought!

The foregoing sentence is worth reading a second time, and a third, and a fourth. It is worth reading aloud!

Faith is the starting point of all accumulation of riches!

Faith is the basis of all "miracles," and all mysteries which cannot be analyzed by the rules of science!

Faith is the only known antidote for failure!

Faith is the element, the "chemical" which, when mixed with prayer, gives one direct communication with Infinite Intelligence.

Faith is the element which transforms the ordinary vibration of thought, created by the finite mind of man, into the spiritual equivalent.

Faith is the only agency through which the cosmic force of Infinite Intelligence can be harnessed and used by man.

Every one of the foregoing statements is capable of proof!

The proof is simple and easily demonstrated. It is wrapped up in the principle of autosuggestion. Let us center our attention, therefore, upon the subject of self-suggestion, and find out what it is, and what it is capable of achieving.

It is a well known fact that one comes, finally, to believe whatever one repeats to one's self, *whether the statement be true or false.* If a man repeats a lie over and over, he will eventually accept the lie as truth. Moreover, he will believe it to be the truth. Every man is what he is because of the dominating thoughts which he permits to occupy his mind. Thoughts which a man deliberately places in his own mind, and encourages with sympathy, and with which he mixes any one or more of the emotions, constitute the motivating forces which direct and control his every movement, act, and deed!

Comes, now, a very significant statement of truth:

Thoughts which are mixed with any of the feelings of emotions constitute a "magnetic" force which attracts, from the vibrations of the ether, other similar or related thoughts. A thought thus "magnetized" with emotion may be compared to a seed which, when planted in fertile soil, germinates, grows, and multiplies itself over and over again, until that which was originally one small seed becomes countless millions of seeds of the same brand!

The ether is a great cosmic mass of eternal forces of vibration. It is made up of both destructive vibrations and constructive vibrations. It carries, at all times, vibrations of fear, poverty, disease, failure, misery; and vibrations of prosperity, health, success, and happiness, just as surely as it carries the sound of hundreds of orchestrations of music, and hundreds of human voices, all of which maintain their own individuality, and means of identification, through the medium of radio.

From the great storehouse of the ether, the human mind is constantly attracting vibrations which harmonize with that which dominates the human mind. Any thought, idea, plan, or purpose which one *holds* in one's mind attracts, from the vibrations of the ether, a host of its relatives, adds these "relatives" to its own force, and grows until it becomes the dominating, motivating master of the individual in whose mind it has been housed.

Now, let us go back to the starting point, and become informed as to how the original seed of an idea, plan, or purpose may be planted in the mind. The information is easily conveyed: any idea, plan, or purpose may be placed in the mind *through repetition of thought.* This is why you are asked to write out a statement of your major purpose, or Definite Chief Aim, commit it to memory, and repeat it, in audible words, day after day, until these vibrations of sound have reached your subconscious mind.

We are what we are because of the vibrations of thought which we pick up and register, through the stimuli of our daily environment.

Resolve to throw off the influences of any unfortunate environment, and to build your own life to order. Taking inventory of mental assets and liabilities, you will discover that your greatest weakness is lack of self-confidence. This handicap can be surmounted, and timidity translated into courage, through the aid of the principle of auto-suggestion. The application of this principle may be made through a simple arrangement of positive thought impulses stated in writing, memorized, and repeated, until they become a part of the working equipment of the subconscious faculty of your mind.

SELF-CONFIDENCE FORMULA

FIRST. I know that I have the ability to achieve the object of my Definite Purpose in life, therefore, I demand of myself persistent, continuous action toward its attainment, and I here and now promise to render such action.

SECOND. I realize the dominating thoughts of my mind will eventually reproduce themselves in outward, physical action, and gradually transform themselves into physical reality, therefore, I will concentrate my thoughts for thirty minutes daily upon the task of thinking of the person I intend to become, thereby creating in my mind a clear mental picture of that person.

THIRD. I know through the principle of auto-suggestion any desire that I persistently hold in my mind will eventually seek expression through some practical means of attaining the object back of it, therefore, I will devote ten minutes daily to demanding of myself the development of self-confidence.

FOURTH. I have clearly written down a description of my Definite Chief Aim in life, and I will never stop trying until I shall have developed sufficient self-confidence for its attainment.

FIFTH. I fully realize that no wealth or position can long endure unless built upon truth and justice, therefore, I will engage in no transaction which does not benefit all whom it affects. I will succeed by attracting to myself the forces I wish to use, and the cooperation of other people. I will induce others to serve me, because of my willingness to serve others. I will eliminate hatred, envy, jealousy, selfishness, and cynicism, by developing love for all humanity, because I know that a negative attitude toward others can never bring me success. I will cause others to believe in me, because I will believe in them, and in myself.

I will sign my name to this formula, commit it to memory, and repeat it aloud once a day, with full faith that it will gradually influence my thoughts and actions so that I will become a self-reliant and successful person.

Back of this formula is a law of Nature which no man has yet been able to explain. It has baffled the scientists of all ages. The psychologists have named this law "auto-suggestion," and let it go at that.

The name by which one calls this law is of little importance. The important fact about it is—it works for the glory and success of mankind, IF it is used constructively. On the other hand, if used destructively, it will destroy just as readily. In this statement may be found a very significant truth; namely, that those who go down in defeat, and end their lives in poverty, misery, and distress, do so because of negative application of the principle of auto-suggestion. The cause may be found in the fact that all impulses of thought have a tendency to clothe themselves in their physical equivalent.

The subconscious mind (the chemical laboratory in which all thought impulses are combined, and made ready for translation into physical reality) makes no distinction between constructive and destructive thought impulses. It works with the material we feed it, through our thought impulses. The subconscious mind will translate into reality a thought driven by fear just as readily as it will translate into reality a thought driven by courage, or faith.

The pages of medical history are rich with illustrations of cases of "suggestive suicide." A man may commit suicide through negative suggestion, just as effectively as by any other means. In a midwestern city, a man by the name of Joseph Grant, a bank official, "borrowed" a large sum of the bank's money, without the consent of the directors. He lost the money through gambling. One afternoon, the Bank Examiner came and began to check the accounts. Grant left the bank, took a room in a local hotel, and when they found him, three days later, he was lying in bed, wailing and moaning, repeating over and over these words, "My God, this will kill me! I cannot stand the disgrace." In a short time he was dead. The doctors pronounced the case one of "mental suicide."

Just as electricity will turn the wheels of industry, and render useful service if used constructively, or snuff out life if wrongly used, so will the law of auto-suggestion lead you to peace and prosperity, or down into the valley of misery, failure, and death, according to your degree of understanding and application of it.

If you fill your mind with fear, doubt, and unbelief in your ability to connect with and use the forces of Infinite Intelligence, the law of auto-suggestion will take this spirit of unbelief and use it as a pattern by which your subconscious mind will translate it into its physical equivalent.

This statement is as true as the statement that two and two are four!

Like the wind which carries one ship East, and another West, the law of auto-suggestion will lift you up or pull you down, according to the way you set your sails of thought.

The law of auto-suggestion, through which any person may rise to altitudes of achievement which stagger the imagination, is well described in the following verse:

If you think *you are beaten, you are,*
If you think *you dare not, you don't*
If you like to win, but you think *you can't,*
It is almost certain you won't.

If you think *you'll lose, you're lost*
For out of the world we find,
Success begins with a fellow's will—
It's all in the state of mind.

If you think *you are outclassed, you are,*
You've got to think *high to rise,*
You've got to be sure of yourself *before*
You can ever win a prize.

Life's battles don't always go
To the stronger or faster man,
But soon or late the man who wins
Is the man WHO THINKS HE CAN*!*

Observe the words which have been emphasized, and you will catch the deep meaning which the poet had in mind.

Somewhere in your make-up (perhaps in the cells of your brain) there lies *sleeping* the seed of achievement which, if aroused and put into action, would carry you to heights such as you may never have hoped to attain.

Just as a master musician may cause the most beautiful strains of music to pour forth from the strings of a violin, so may you arouse the genius which lies asleep in your brain, and cause it to drive you upward to whatever goal you may wish to achieve.

Abraham Lincoln was a failure at everything he tried, until he was well past the age of forty. He was a Mr. Nobody from Nowhere, until a great experience came into his life, aroused the sleeping genius within his heart and brain, and gave the world one of its really great men. That "experience" was mixed with the emotions of sorrow and love. It came to him through Anne Rutledge, the only woman whom he ever truly loved.

It is a known fact that the emotion of love is closely akin to the state of mind known as faith, and this for the reason that love comes very near to translating one's thought impulses into their spiritual equivalent. During his work of research, the author discovered, from the analysis of the lifework and achievements of hundreds of men of outstanding accomplishment, that there was the influence of a woman's love back of nearly every one of them. The emotion of love, in the human heart and brain, creates a favorable field of magnetic attraction, which causes an influx of the higher and finer vibrations which are afloat in the ether.

If you wish evidence of the power of faith, study the achievements of men and women who have employed it. At the head of the list comes the Nazarene. Christianity is the greatest single force which influences the minds of men. The basis of Christianity is faith, no matter how many people may have perverted or misinterpreted the meaning of this great force, and no matter how many dogmas and creeds have been created in its name, which do not reflect its tenets.

The sum and substance of the teachings and the achievements of Christ, which may have been interpreted as "miracles," were nothing more nor less than faith. If there are any such phenomena as "miracles" they are produced only through the state of mind known as faith! Some teachers of religion, and many who call themselves Christians, neither understand nor practice faith.

Let us consider the power of faith, as it is now being demonstrated, by a man who is well known to all of civilization, Mahatma Gandhi, of India. In this man the world has one of the most astounding examples known to civilization of the possibilities of faith. Gandhi wields more potential power than any man living at this time, and this, despite the fact that he has none of the orthodox tools of power, such as money, battle ships, soldiers, and materials of warfare. Gandhi has no money, he has no home, he does not own a suit of clothes, but he does have power. How does he come by that power?

He created it out of his understanding of the principle of faith, and through his ability to transplant that faith into the minds of two hundred million people.

Gandhi has accomplished, through the influence of faith, that which the strongest military power on earth could not, and never will accomplish through soldiers and military equipment. He has accomplished the astounding feat of influencing two hundred million minds to coalesce and move in unison, as a single mind.

What other force on earth, except faith, could do as much?

There will come a day when employees as well as employers will discover the possibilities of faith. That day is dawning. The whole world has had ample opportunity, during the recent business depression, to witness what the lack of faith will do to business.

Surely, civilization has produced a sufficient number of intelligent human beings to make use of this great lesson which the depression has taught the world. During this depression, the world had evidence in abundance that widespread fear will paralyze the wheels of industry and business. Out of this experience will arise leaders in business and industry who will profit by the example which Gandhi has set for the world, and they will apply to business the same tactics which he has used in building the greatest following known in the history of the world. These leaders will come from the rank and file of the unknown men, who now labor in the steel plants, the coal mines, the automobile factories, and in the small towns and cities of America.

Business is due for a reform, make no mistake about this! The methods of the past, based upon economic combinations of force and fear, will be supplanted by the better principles of faith and cooperation. Men who labor will receive more than daily wages; they will receive dividends from the business the same as those who supply the capital for business; but first they must give more to their employers, and stop this bickering and bargaining by force, at the expense of the public. *They must earn the right to dividends!*

Moreover, and this is the most important thing of all—they will be led by leaders who will understand and apply the principles employed by Mahatma Gandhi. Only in this way may leaders get from their followers the spirit of full cooperation which constitutes power in its highest and most enduring form.

This stupendous machine age in which we live, and from which we are just emerging, has taken the soul out of men. Its leaders have driven men as though they were pieces of cold machinery; they were forced to do so by the employees who have bargained, at the expense of all concerned, to *get* and not to *give.* The watchword of the future will be human happiness and contentment, and when this state of mind shall have been attained, the production will take care of itself, more effectively than anything that has ever been accomplished where men did not, and could not, mix faith and individual interest with their labor.

Because of the need for faith and cooperation in operating business and industry, it will be both interesting and profitable to analyze an event which provides an excellent understanding of the method by which industrialists and business men accumulate great fortunes, by *giving* before they try to *get.*

The event chosen for this illustration dates back to 1900, when the United States Steel Corporation was being formed. As you read the story, keep in mind these fundamental facts and you will understand how ideas have been converted into huge fortunes.

First, the huge United States Steel Corporation was born in the mind of Charles M. Schwab, in the form of an idea he created through his imagination! Second, he mixed faith with his idea. Third, he formulated a plan for the transformation of his idea into physical and financial reality. Fourth, he put his plan into action with his famous speech at the University Club. Fifth, he applied, and followed-through on his plan with persistence, and backed it with firm decision until it had been fully carried out. Sixth, he prepared the way for success by a burning desire for success.

If you are one of those who have often wondered how great fortunes are accumulated, this story of the creation of the United States Steel Corporation will be enlightening. If you have any doubt that men can think and grow rich, this story should dispel that doubt, because you can plainly see in the story of the United States Steel the application of a major portion of the thirteen principles described in this book.

This astounding description of the power of an idea was dramatically told by John Lowell, in the *New York World-Telegram,* with whose courtesy it is here reprinted.

A PRETTY AFTER-DINNER SPEECH FOR A BILLION DOLLARS

"When, on the evening of December 12, 1900, some eighty of the nation's financial nobility gathered in the banquet hall of the University Club on Fifth Avenue to do honor to a young man from out of the West, not half a dozen of the guests realized they were to witness the most significant episode in American industrial history.

"J. Edward Simmons and Charles Stewart Smith, their hearts full of gratitude for the lavish hospitality bestowed on them by Charles M. Schwab during a recent visit to Pittsburgh, had arranged the dinner to introduce the thirty-eight-year-old steel man to eastern banking society. But they didn't expect him to stampede the convention. They warned him, in fact, that the bosoms within New York's stuffed shirts would not be responsive to oratory, and that, if he didn't want to bore the Stillmans and Harrimans and Vanderbilts, he had better limit himself to fifteen or twenty minutes of polite vaporings and let it go at that.

"Even John Pierpont Morgan, sitting on the right hand of Schwab as became his imperial dignity, intended to grace the banquet table with his presence only briefly. And so far as the press and public were concerned, the whole affair was of so little moment that no mention of it found its way into print the next day.

"So the two hosts and their distinguished guests ate their way through the usual seven or eight courses. There was little conversation and what there was of it was restrained. Few of the bankers and brokers had met Schwab, whose career had flowered along the banks of the Monongahela, and none knew him well. But before the evening was over, they—and with them Money Master Morgan—were to be swept off their feet, and a billion-dollar baby, the United States Steel Corporation, was to be conceived.

"It is perhaps unfortunate, for the sake of history, that no record of Charlie Schwab's speech at the dinner ever was made. He repeated some parts of it at a later date during a similar meeting of Chicago bankers. And still later, when the Government brought suit to dissolve the Steel Trust, he gave his own version, from the witness stand, of the remarks that stimulated Morgan into a frenzy of financial activity.

"It is probable, however, that it was a 'homely' speech, somewhat ungrammatical (for the niceties of language never bothered Schwab), full of epigram and threaded with wit. But aside from that it had a galvanic force and effect upon the five billions of estimated capital that was represented by the diners. After it was over and the gathering was still under its spell, although Schwab had talked for ninety minutes, Morgan led the orator to a recessed window where, dangling their legs from the high, uncomfortable seat, they talked for an hour more.

"The magic of the Schwab personality had been turned on, full force, but what was more important and lasting was the full-fledged, clear-cut program he laid down for the aggrandizement of Steel. Many other men had tried to interest Morgan in slapping together a Steel Trust after the pattern of the biscuit, wire and hoop, sugar, rubber, whisky, oil or chewing gum combinations. John W. Gates, the gambler, had urged it, but Morgan distrusted him. The Moore boys, Bill and Jim, Chicago stock jobbers who had glued together a match trust and a cracker corporation, had urged it and failed. Elbert H. Gary, the sanctimonious country lawyer, wanted to foster it, but he wasn't big enough to be impressive. Until Schwab's eloquence took J. P. Morgan to the heights from which he could visualize the solid results of the most daring financial undertaking ever conceived, the project was regarded as a delirious dream of easy-money crackpots.

"The financial magnetism that began, a generation ago, to attract thousands of small and sometimes inefficiently managed companies into large and competition-crushing combinations, had become operative in the steel world through the devices of that jovial business pirate, John W. Gates. Gates already had formed the American Steel and Wire Company out of a chain of small concerns, and together with Morgan had created the

Federal Steel Company. The National Tube and American Bridge companies were two more Morgan concerns, and the Moore Brothers had forsaken the match and cookie business to form the 'American' group—Tin Plate, Steel Hoop, Sheet Steel—and the National Steel Company.

"But by the side of Andrew Carnegie's gigantic vertical trust, a trust owned and operated by fifty-three partners, those other combinations were picayune. They might combine to their heart's content but the whole lot of them couldn't make a dent in the Carnegie organization, and Morgan knew it.

"The eccentric old Scot knew it, too. From the magnificent heights of Skibo Castle he had viewed, first with amusement and then with resentment, the attempts of Morgan's smaller companies to cut into his business. When the attempts became too bold, Carnegie's temper was translated into anger and retaliation. He decided to duplicate every mill owned by his rivals. Hitherto, he hadn't been interested in wire, pipe, hoops, or sheet. Instead, he was content to sell such companies the raw steel and let them work it into whatever shape they wanted. Now, with Schwab as his chief and able lieutenant, he planned to drive his enemies to the wall.

"So it was that in the speech of Charles M. Schwab, Morgan saw the answer to his problem of combination. A trust without Carnegie—giant of them all—would be no trust at all, a plum pudding, as one writer said, without the plums.

"Schwab's speech on the night of December 12, 1900, undoubtedly carried the inference, though not the pledge, that the vast Carnegie enterprise could be brought under the Morgan tent. He talked of the world future for steel, of reorganization for efficiency, of specialization, of the scrapping of unsuccessful mills and concentration of effort on the flourishing properties, of economies in the ore traffic, of economies in overhead and administrative departments, of capturing foreign markets.

"More than that, he told the buccaneers among them wherein lay the errors of their customary piracy. Their purposes, he inferred, had been to create monopolies, raise prices, and pay themselves fat dividends out of privilege. Schwab condemned the system in his heartiest manner. The shortsightedness of such a policy, he told his hearers, lay in the fact that it restricted the market in an era when everything cried for expansion. By cheapening the cost of steel, he argued, an ever-expanding market would be created; more uses for steel would be devised, and a goodly portion of the world trade could be captured. Actually, though he did not know it, Schwab was an apostle of modern mass production.

"So, the dinner at the University Club came to an end. Morgan went home, to think about Schwab's rosy predictions. Schwab went back to Pittsburgh to run the steel business for 'Wee Andra Carnegie,' while Gary and the rest went back to their stock tickers, to fiddle around in anticipation of the next move.

"It was not long coming. It took Morgan about one week to digest the feast of reason Schwab had placed before him. When he had assured himself that no financial indigestion was to result, he sent for Schwab—and found that young man rather coy. Mr. Carnegie, Schwab indicated, might not like it if he found his trusted company president had been flirting with the Emperor of Wall Street, the Street upon which Carnegie was resolved never to tread. Then it was suggested by John W. Gates the go-between, that if Schwab 'happened' to be in the Bellevue Hotel in Philadelphia, J. P. Morgan might also 'happen' to be there. When Schwab arrived, however, Morgan was inconveniently ill at his New York home, and so, on the elder man's pressing invitation, Schwab went to New York and presented himself at the door of the financier's library.

"Now certain economic historians have professed the belief that from the beginning to the end of the drama, the stage was set by Andrew Carnegie—that the dinner to Schwab, the famous speech, the Sunday night conference between Schwab and the Money King, were events arranged by the canny Scot. The truth is exactly the opposite. When Schwab was called in to consummate the deal, he didn't even know whether 'the little boss,' as Andrew was called, would so much as listen to an offer to sell, particularly to a group of men whom Andrew regarded as being endowed with something less than holiness. But Schwab did take into the conference with him, in his own handwriting, six sheets of copper-plate figures, representing to his mind the physical worth and the potential earning capacity of every steel company he regarded as an essential star in the new metal firmament.

"Four men pondered over these figures all night. The chief, of course, was Morgan, steadfast in his belief in the Divine Right of Money. With him was his aristocratic partner, Robert Bacon, a scholar and a gentleman. The third was John W. Gates, whom Morgan scorned as a gambler and used as a tool. The fourth was Schwab, who knew more about the processes of making and selling steel than any whole group of men then living. Throughout that conference, the Pittsburgher's figures were never questioned. If he said a company was worth so much, then it was worth that much and no more. He was insistent, too, upon including in the combination only those concerns he nominated. He had conceived a corporation in which there would be no duplication, not even to satisfy the greed of friends who wanted to unload their companies upon the broad Morgan shoulders. Thus he left out, by design, a number of the larger concerns upon which the Walruses and Carpenters of Wall Street had cast hungry eyes.

"When dawn came, Morgan rose and straightened his back. Only one question remained.

"'Do you think you can persuade Andrew Carnegie to sell?' he asked.

"'I can try,' said Schwab.

"'If you can get him to sell, I will undertake the matter,' said Morgan.

"So far so good. But would Carnegie sell? How much would he demand? (Schwab thought about $320,000,000). What would he take payment in? Common or preferred stocks? Bonds? Cash? Nobody could raise a third of a billion dollars in cash.

"There was a golf game in January on the frost-cracking heath of the St. Andrews links in Westchester, with Andrew bundled up in sweaters against the cold, and Charlie talking volubly, as usual, to keep his spirits up. But no word of business was mentioned until the pair sat down in the cozy warmth of the Carnegie cottage hard by. Then, with the same persuasiveness that had hypnotized eighty millionaires at the University Club, Schwab poured out the glittering promises of retirement in comfort, of untold millions to satisfy the old man's social caprices. Carnegie capitulated, wrote a figure on a slip of paper, handed it to Schwab and said, 'All right, that's what we'll sell for.'

"The figure was approximately $400,000,000, and was reached by taking the $320,000,000 mentioned by Schwab as a basic figure, and adding to it $80,000,000 to represent the increased capital value over the previous two years.

"Later, on the deck of a trans-Atlantic liner, the Scotsman said ruefully to Morgan, 'I wish I had asked you for $100,000,000 more.'

"'If you had asked for it, you'd have gotten it,' Morgan told him cheerfully.

"There was an uproar, of course. A British correspondent cabled that the foreign steel world was 'appalled' by the gigantic combination. President Hadley, of Yale, declared that unless trusts were regulated the country might expect 'an emperor in Washington within the next twenty-five years.' But that able stock manipulator, Keene, went at his work of shoving the new stock at the public so vigorously that all the excess water—estimated by some at nearly $600,000,000—was absorbed in a twinkling. So Carnegie had his millions, and the Morgan syndicate had $62,000,000 for all its 'trouble,' and all the 'boys,' from Gates to Gary, had their millions.

"The thirty-eight-year-old Schwab had his reward. He was made president of the new corporation and remained in control until 1930."

The dramatic story of "Big Business" which you have just finished was included in this book because it is a perfect illustration of the method by which *desire can be transmuted into its physical equivalent!*

I imagine some readers will question the statement that a mere, intangible desire can be converted into its physical equivalent. Doubtless some will say, "You cannot convert nothing into something!" The answer is in the story of United States Steel.

That giant organization was created in the mind of one man. The plan by which the organization was provided with the steel mills that gave it financial stability was created in the mind of the same man. His faith, his desire, his imagination, his persistence were the real ingredients that went into United States Steel. The steel mills and mechanical equipment acquired by the corporation, after it had been brought into legal existence, were incidental, but careful analysis will disclose the fact that the appraised value of the properties acquired by the corporation increased in value by an estimated $600,000,000 by the mere transaction which consolidated them under one management.

In other words, Charles M. Schwab's idea, plus the faith with which he conveyed it to the minds of J. P. Morgan and the others, was marketed for a profit of approximately $600,000,000. Not an insignificant sum for a single idea!

What happened to some of the men who took their share of the millions of dollars of profit made by this transaction is a matter with which we are not now concerned. The important feature of the astounding achievement is that it serves as unquestionable evidence of the soundness of the philosophy described in this book, because this philosophy was the warp and the woof of the entire transaction. Moreover, the practicability of the philosophy has been established by the fact that the United States Steel Corporation prospered, and became one of the richest and most powerful corporations in America, employing thousands of people, developing new uses for steel, and opening new markets; thus proving that the $600,000,000 in profit which the Schwab idea produced was earned.

Riches begin in the form of thought!

The amount is limited only by the person in whose mind the thought is put into motion. Faith removes limitations! Remember this when you are ready to bargain with Life for whatever it is that you ask as your price for having passed this way.

Remember, also, that the man who created the United States Steel Corporation was practically unknown at the time. He was merely Andrew Carnegie's "Man Friday" until he gave birth to his famous IDEA. After that he quickly rose to a position of power, fame, and riches.

There are no limitations to the mind except those we *acknowledge*

Both *poverty* and *riches* are the offspring of thought

CHAPTER 4

AUTO-SUGGESTION

THE MEDIUM FOR INFLUENCING THE SUBCONSCIOUS MIND

The Third Step Toward Riches

Auto-suggestion is a term which applies to all suggestions and all self-administered stimuli which reach one's mind through the five senses. Stated in another way, auto-suggestion is self-suggestion. It is the agency of communication between that part of the mind where conscious thought takes place, and that which serves as the seat of action for the subconscious mind.

Through the dominating thoughts which one *permits* to remain in the conscious mind (whether these thoughts be negative or positive, is immaterial), the principle of auto-suggestion voluntarily reaches the subconscious mind and influences it with these thoughts.

No thought, whether it be negative or positive, can enter the subconscious mind without the aid of the principle of auto-suggestion, with the exception of thoughts picked up from the ether. Stated differently, all sense impressions which are perceived through the five senses are stopped by the conscious thinking mind, and may be either passed on to the subconscious mind, or rejected, at will. The conscious faculty serves, therefore, as an outer-guard to the approach of the subconscious.

Nature has so built man that he has absolute control over the material which reaches his subconscious mind, through his five senses, although this is not meant to be construed as a statement that man always exercises this control. In the great majority of instances, he does not exercise it, which explains why so many people go through life in poverty.

Recall what has been said about the subconscious mind resembling a fertile garden spot, in which weeds will grow in abundance if the seeds of more desirable crops are not sown therein. Auto-suggestion is the agency of control through which an individual may voluntarily feed his subconscious mind on thoughts of a creative nature, or, by neglect, permit thoughts of a destructive nature to find their way into this rich garden of the mind.

You were instructed, in the last of the six steps described in the chapter on Desire, to read aloud twice daily the written statement of your desire for money, and to see and feel yourself already in possession of the money! By following these instructions, you communicate the object of your desire directly to your subconscious mind in a spirit of absolute faith. Through repetition of this procedure, you voluntarily create thought habits which are favorable to your efforts to transmute desire into its monetary equivalent.

Go back to these six steps described in chapter two, and read them again, very carefully, before you proceed further. Then (when you come to it), read very carefully the four instructions for the organization of your "Master Mind" group, described in the chapter on Organized Planning. By comparing these two sets of instructions with that which has been stated on auto-suggestion, you, of course, will see that the instructions involve the application of the principle of auto-suggestion.

Remember, therefore, when reading aloud the statement of your desire (through which you are endeavoring to develop a "money consciousness"), that the mere reading of the words is of no consequence—unless you mix emotion, or feeling, with your words. If you repeat a million times the famous Emil Coué formula, "Day by day, in every way, I am getting better and better," without mixing emotion and faith with your words, you will experience no desirable results. Your subconscious mind recognizes and acts upon only thoughts which have been well-mixed with emotion or feeling.

This is a fact of such importance as to warrant repetition in practically every chapter, because the lack of understanding of this is the main reason the majority of people who try to apply the principle of auto-suggestion get no desirable results.

Plain, unemotional words do not influence the subconscious mind. You will get no appreciable results until you learn to reach your subconscious mind with thoughts, or spoken words which have been well emotionalized with belief.

Do not become discouraged if you cannot control and direct your emotions the first time you try to do so. Remember, there is no such possibility as something for nothing. Ability to reach and influence your subconscious mind has its price, and you must pay that price. You cannot cheat, even if you desire to do so. The price of ability to influence your subconscious mind is everlasting persistence in applying the principles described here. You cannot develop the desired ability for a lower price. You, and you alone, must decide whether or not the reward for which you are striving (the "money consciousness") is worth the price you must pay for it in effort.

Wisdom and "cleverness" alone will not attract and retain money except in a few very rare instances, where the law of averages favors the attraction of money through these sources. The method of attracting money described here does not depend upon the law of averages. Moreover, the method plays no favorites. It will work for one person as effectively as it will for another. Where failure is experienced, it is the individual, *not the method,* which has failed. If you try and fail, make another effort, and still another, until you succeed.

Your ability to use the principle of auto-suggestion will depend, very largely, upon your capacity to concentrate upon a given desire until that desire becomes a burning obsession.

When you begin to carry out the instructions in connection with the six steps described in the second chapter, it will be necessary for you to make use of the principle of concentration.

Let us here offer suggestions for the effective use of concentration. When you begin to carry out the first of the six steps, which instructs you to "fix in your own mind the exact amount of money you desire," hold your thoughts on that amount of money by concentration, or fixation of attention, with your eyes closed, until you can actually see the physical appearance of the money. Do this at least once each day. As you go through these exercises, follow the instructions given in the chapter on faith, and see yourself actually in possession of the money!

Here is a most significant fact—the subconscious mind takes any orders given it in a spirit of absolute faith, and acts upon those orders, although the orders often have to be presented *over and over again,* through repetition, before they are interpreted by the subconscious mind. Following the preceding statement, consider the possibility of playing a perfectly legitimate "trick" on your subconscious mind, by making it believe, *because you believe it,* that you must have the amount of money you are visualizing, that this money is already awaiting your claim, that the subconscious mind must hand over to you practical plans for acquiring the money which is yours.

Hand over the thought suggested in the preceding paragraph to your imagination, and see what your imagination can or will do to create practical plans for the accumulation of money through transmutation of your desire.

Do not wait for a definite plan, through which you intend to exchange services or merchandise in return for the money you are visualizing, but begin at once to see yourself in possession of the money, demanding and expecting meanwhile that your subconscious mind will hand over the plan, or plans, you need. Be on the alert for these plans, and when they appear, put them into action immediately. When the plans appear, they will probably "flash" into your mind through the sixth sense, in the form of an "inspiration."

This inspiration may be considered a direct "telegram," or message from Infinite Intelligence. Treat it with respect, and act upon it as soon as you receive it. Failure to do this will be fatal to your success.

In the fourth of the six steps, you were instructed to "Create a definite plan for carrying out your desire, and begin at once to put this plan into action." You should follow this instruction in the manner described in the preceding paragraph. Do not trust to your "reason" when creating your plan for accumulating money through the transmutation of desire. Your reason is faulty. Moreover, your reasoning faculty may be lazy, and, if you depend entirely upon it to serve you, it may disappoint you.

When visualizing the money you intend to accumulate (with closed eyes), *see yourself rendering the service, or delivering the merchandise you intend to give in return for this money. This is important!*

SUMMARY OF INSTRUCTIONS

The fact that you are reading this book is an indication that you earnestly seek knowledge. It is also an indication that you are a student of this subject. If you are only a student, there is a chance that you may learn much that you did not know, but you will learn only by assuming an attitude of humility. If you choose to follow some of the instructions but neglect or refuse to follow others—*you will fail!* To get satisfactory results, you must follow all instructions in a spirit of faith.

The instructions given in connection with the six steps in the second chapter will now be summarized, and blended with the principles covered by this chapter, as follows:

FIRST. Go into some quiet spot (preferably in bed at night) where you will not be disturbed or interrupted, close your eyes, and repeat aloud (so you may hear your own words) the written statement of the amount of money you intend to accumulate, the time limit for its accumulation, and a description of the service or merchandise you intend to give in return for the money. As you carry out these instructions, see yourself already in possession of the money.

For example:—Suppose that you intend to accumulate $50,000 by the first of January, five years hence, that you intend to give personal services in return for the money, in the capacity of a salesman. Your written statement of your purpose should be similar to the following:

"By the first day of January, 19. . , I will have in my possession $50,000, which will come to me in various amounts from time to time during the interim.

"In return for this money I will give the most efficient service of which I am capable, rendering the fullest possible quantity, and the best possible quality of service in the capacity of salesman of . . . (describe the service or merchandise you intend to sell).

"I believe that I will have this money in my possession. My faith is so strong that I can now see this money before my eyes. I can touch it with my hands. It is now awaiting transfer to me at the time and in the proportion that I deliver the service I intend to render in return for it. I am awaiting a plan by which to accumulate this money, and I will follow that plan when it is received."

SECOND. Repeat this program night and morning until you can see (in your imagination) the money you intend to accumulate.

THIRD. Place a written copy of your statement where you can see it night and morning, and read it just before retiring and upon arising until it has been memorized.

Remember, as you carry out these instructions, that you are applying the principle of auto-suggestion, for the purpose of giving orders to your subconscious mind. Remember, also, that your subconscious mind will act only upon instructions which are emotionalized, and handed over to it with "feeling." Faith is the strongest and most productive of the emotions. Follow the instructions given in the chapter on faith.

These instructions may, at first, seem abstract. Do not let this disturb you. Follow the instructions, no matter how abstract or impractical they may, at first, appear to be. The time will soon come, if you do as you have been instructed, *in spirit as well as in act,* when a whole new universe of power will unfold to you.

Scepticism, in connection with all new ideas, is characteristic of all human beings. But if you follow the instructions outlined, your scepticism will soon be replaced by belief, and this, in turn, will soon become crystallized into absolute faith. Then you will have arrived at the point where you may truly say, "I am the master of my fate, I am the captain of my soul!"

Many philosophers have made the statement that man is the master of his own *earthly* destiny, but most of them have failed to say *why* he is the master. The reason that man may be the master of his own earthly status, and especially his financial status, is thoroughly explained in this chapter. Man may become the master of himself, and of his environment, because he has the power to influence his own subconscious mind, and through it, gain the cooperation of Infinite Intelligence.

You are now reading the chapter which represents the keystone to the arch of this philosophy. The instructions contained in this chapter must be understood and applied with persistence if you are to succeed in transmuting desire into money.

The actual performance of transmuting desire into money involves the use of auto-suggestion as an agency by which one may reach, and influence, the subconscious mind. The other principles are simply tools with which to apply auto-suggestion. Keep this thought in mind, and you will, at all times, be conscious of the important part the principle of auto-suggestion is to play in your efforts to accumulate money through the methods described in this book.

Carry out these instructions as though you were a small child. Inject into your efforts something of the faith of a child. The author has been most careful to see that no impractical instructions were included, because of his sincere desire to be helpful.

After you have read the entire book, come back to this chapter, and follow in spirit, and in action, this instruction:

Read the entire chapter aloud once every night, until you become thoroughly convinced that the principle of auto-suggestion is sound, that it will accomplish for you all that has been claimed for it. As you read, *underscore with a pencil* every sentence which impresses you favorably.

Follow the foregoing instruction to the letter and it will open the way for a complete understanding and mastery of the principles of success.

CHAPTER 5

SPECIALIZED KNOWLEDGE

PERSONAL EXPERIENCES OR OBSERVATIONS

The Fourth Step Toward Riches

There are two kinds of knowledge. One is general, the other is specialized. General knowledge, no matter how great in quantity or variety it may be, is of but little use in the accumulation of money. The faculties of the great universities possess, in the aggregate, practically every form of general knowledge known to civilization. *Most of the professors have but little or no money.* They specialize on *teaching* knowledge, but they do not specialize on the organization or the use of knowledge.

Knowledge will not attract money, unless it is organized, and intelligently directed, through practical plans of action, to the definite end of accumulation of money. Lack of understanding of this fact has been the source of confusion to millions of people who falsely believe that "knowledge is power." It is nothing of the sort! Knowledge is only *potential* power. It becomes power only when, and if, it is organized into definite plans of action, and directed to a definite end.

This "missing link" in all systems of education known to civilization today may be found in the failure of educational institutions to teach their students how to organize and use knowledge after they acquire it.

Many people make the mistake of assuming that, because Henry Ford had but little "schooling," he is not a man of "education." Those who make this mistake do not know Henry Ford, nor do they understand the real meaning of the word "educate." That word is derived from the Latin word "educo," meaning to educe, to draw out, to develop from within.

An educated man is not, necessarily, one who has an abundance of general or specialized knowledge. An educated man is one who has so developed the faculties of his mind that he may acquire anything he wants, or its equivalent, without violating the rights of others. Henry Ford comes well within the meaning of this definition.

During the world war, a Chicago newspaper published certain editorials in which, among other statements, Henry Ford was called "an ignorant pacifist." Mr. Ford objected to the statements, and brought suit against the paper for libeling him. When the suit was tried in the Courts, the attorneys for the paper pleaded justification, and placed Mr. Ford, himself, on the witness stand, for the purpose of proving to the jury that he was ignorant. The attorneys asked Mr. Ford a great variety of questions, all of them intended to prove, by his own evidence, that, while he might possess considerable specialized knowledge pertaining to the manufacture of automobiles, he was, in the main, ignorant.

Mr. Ford was plied with such questions as the following:

"Who was Benedict Arnold?" and "How many soldiers did the British send over to America to put down the Rebellion of 1776?" In answer to the last question, Mr. Ford replied, "I do not know the exact number of soldiers the British sent over, but I have heard that it was a considerably larger number than ever went back."

Finally, Mr. Ford became tired of this line of questioning, and in reply to a particularly offensive question, he leaned over, pointed his finger at the lawyer who had asked the question, and said, "If I should really want to answer the foolish question you have just asked, or any of the other questions you have been asking me, let me remind you that I have a row of electric pushbuttons on my desk, and by pushing the right button, I can summon to my aid men who can answer any question I desire to ask concerning the business to which I am devoting most of my efforts. Now, will you kindly tell me, why I should clutter up my mind with general knowledge, for the purpose of being able to answer questions, when I have men around me who can supply any knowledge I require?"

There certainly was good logic to that reply.

That answer floored the lawyer. Every person in the courtroom realized it was the answer not of an ignorant man but of a man of education. Any man is educated who knows where to get knowledge when he needs it, and how to organize that knowledge into definite plans of action. Through the assistance of his "Master Mind" group, Henry Ford had at his command all the specialized knowledge he needed to enable him to become one of the wealthiest men in America. *It was not essential that he have this knowledge in his own mind.* Surely no person who has sufficient inclination and intelligence to read a book of this nature can possibly miss the significance of this illustration.

Before you can be sure of your ability to transmute desire into its monetary equivalent, you will require specialized knowledge of the service, merchandise, or profession which you intend to offer in return for fortune. Perhaps you may need much more specialized knowledge than you have the ability or the inclination to acquire, and if this should be true, you may bridge your weakness through the aid of your "Master Mind" group.

Andrew Carnegie stated that he, personally, knew nothing about the technical end of the steel business; moreover, he did not particularly care to know anything about it. The specialized knowledge which he required for the manufacture and marketing of steel he found available through the individual units of his "Master Mind" group.

The accumulation of great fortunes calls for power, and power is acquired through highly organized and intelligently directed specialized knowledge, but that knowledge does not, necessarily, have to be in the possession of the man who accumulates the fortune.

The preceding paragraph should give hope and encouragement to the man with ambition to accumulate a fortune who has not possessed himself of the necessary "education" to supply such specialized knowledge as he may require. Men sometimes go through life suffering from "inferiority complexes" because they are not men of "education." The man who can organize and direct a "Master Mind" group of men who possess knowledge useful in the accumulation of money is just as much a man of education as any man in the group. Remember this if you suffer from a feeling of inferiority because your schooling has been limited.

Thomas A. Edison had only three months of "schooling" during his entire life. He did not lack education, neither did he die poor.

Henry Ford had less than a sixth grade "schooling" but he has managed to do pretty well by himself, financially.

Specialized knowledge is among the most plentiful, and the cheapest, forms of service which may be had! If you doubt this, consult the payroll of any university.

IT PAYS TO KNOW HOW TO PURCHASE KNOWLEDGE

First of all, decide the sort of specialized knowledge you require, and the purpose for which it is needed. To a large extent your major purpose in life, the goal toward which you are working, will help determine what knowledge you need. With this question settled, your next move requires that you have accurate information concerning dependable sources of knowledge. The more important of these are:

(a) One's own experience and education
(b) Experience and education available through cooperation of others (Master Mind Alliance)
(c) Colleges and universities

(d) Public libraries (through books and periodicals in which may be found all the knowledge organized by civilization)
(e) Special training courses (through night schools and home study schools in particular)

As knowledge is acquired it must be organized and put into use, for a definite purpose, through practical plans. Knowledge has no value except that which can be gained from its application toward some worthy end. This is one reason why college degrees are not valued more highly. They represent nothing but miscellaneous knowledge.

If you contemplate taking additional schooling, first determine the purpose for which you want the knowledge you are seeking, then learn where this particular sort of knowledge can be obtained, from reliable sources.

Successful men, in all callings, never stop acquiring specialized knowledge related to their major purpose, business, or profession. Those who are not successful usually make the mistake of believing that the knowledge acquiring period ends when one finishes school. The truth is that schooling does but little more than to put one in the way of learning how to acquire practical knowledge.

With this Changed World which began at the end of the economic collapse came also astounding changes in educational requirements. The order of the day is specialization! This truth was emphasized by Robert P. Moore, secretary of appointments of Columbia University.

SPECIALISTS MOST SOUGHT

"Particularly sought after by employing companies are candidates who have specialized in some field—business-school graduates with training in accounting and statistics, engineers of all varieties, journalists, architects, chemists, and also outstanding leaders and activity men of the senior class.

"The man who has been active on the campus, whose personality is such that he gets along with all kinds of people and who has done an adequate job with his studies, has a most decided edge over the strictly academic student. Some of these, because of their all-around qualifications, have received several offers of positions, a few of them as many as six.

"In departing from the conception that the 'straight A' student was invariably the one to get the choice of the better jobs, Mr. Moore said that most companies look not only to academic records but to activity records and personalities of the students.

"One of the largest industrial companies, the leader in its field, in writing to Mr. Moore concerning prospective seniors at the college, said:

"'We are interested primarily in finding men who can make exceptional progress in management work. For this reason we emphasize qualities of character, intelligence and personality far more than specific educational background.'"

"APPRENTICESHIP" PROPOSED

"Proposing a system of 'apprenticing' students in offices, stores and industrial occupations during the summer vacation, Mr. Moore asserts that after the first two or three years of college, every student should be asked 'to choose a definite future course and to call a halt if he has been merely pleasantly drifting without purpose through an unspecialized academic curriculum.

"'Colleges and universities must face the practical consideration that all professions and occupations now demand specialists,' he said, urging that educational institutions accept more direct responsibility for vocational guidance."

One of the most reliable and practical sources of knowledge available to those who need specialized schooling is the night schools operated in most large cities. The correspondence schools give specialized training anywhere the U. S. mails go, on all subjects that can be taught by the extension method. One advantage of home study training is the flexibility of the study programme which permits one to study during spare time. Another stupendous advantage of home study training (if the school is carefully chosen) is the fact that most courses offered by home study schools carry with them generous privileges of consultation which can be of priceless value to those needing specialized knowledge. No matter where you live, you can share the benefits.

Anything acquired without effort and without cost is generally unappreciated, often discredited; perhaps this is why we get so little from our marvelous opportunity in public schools. The self-discipline one receives from a definite programme of specialized study makes up, to some extent, for the wasted opportunity when knowledge was available without cost. Correspondence schools are highly organized business institutions. Their tuition fees are so low that they are forced to insist upon prompt payments. Being asked to pay, whether the student makes good grades or poor, has the effect of causing one to follow through with the course when he would otherwise drop it. The correspondence schools have not stressed this point sufficiently, for the truth is that their collection departments constitute the very finest sort of training on decision, promptness, action, and the habit of finishing that which one begins.

I learned this from experience, more than twenty-five years ago. I enrolled for a home study course in advertising. After completing eight or ten lessons I stopped studying, but the school did not stop sending me bills. Moreover, it insisted upon payment, whether I kept up my studies or not. I decided that if I had to pay for the course (which I had legally obligated myself to do), I should complete the lessons and get my money's worth. I felt, at the time, that the collection system of the school was somewhat too well organized, but I learned later in life that it was a valuable part of my training for which no charge had been made. Being forced to pay, I went ahead and completed the course. Later in life I discovered that the efficient collection system of that school had been worth much in the form of money earned, because of the training in advertising I had so reluctantly taken.

We have in this country what is said to be the greatest public school system in the world. We have invested fabulous sums for fine buildings, we have provided convenient transportation for children living in the rural districts so they may attend the best schools, but there is one astounding weakness to this marvelous system—it is free! One of the strange things about human beings is that they value only that which has a price. The free schools of America, and the free public libraries, do not impress people *because they are free.* This is the major reason why so many people find it necessary to acquire additional training after they quit school and go to work. It is also one of the major reasons why employers give greater consideration to employees who take home study courses. They have learned, from experience, that any person who has the ambition to give up a part of his spare time to studying at home has in him those qualities which make for leadership. This recognition is not a charitable gesture—it is sound business judgment upon the part of the employers.

There is one weakness in people for which there is no remedy. It is the universal weakness of lack of ambition! Persons, especially salaried people, who schedule their spare time to provide for home study, seldom remain at the bottom very long. Their action opens the way for the upward climb, removes many obstacles from their path, and gains the friendly interest of those who have the power to put them in the way of opportunity.

The home study method of training is especially suited to the needs of employed people who find, after leaving school, that they must acquire additional specialized knowledge but cannot spare the time to go back to school.

The changed economic conditions prevailing since the depression have made it necessary for thousands of people to find additional or new sources of income. For the majority of these, the solution to their problem may be found only by acquiring specialized knowledge. Many will be forced to change their occupations entirely. When a merchant finds that a certain line of merchandise is not selling, he usually supplants it with another that is in demand. The person whose business is that of marketing personal services must also be an efficient merchant. If his services do not bring adequate returns in one occupation, he must change to another, where broader opportunities are available.

Stuart Austin Wier prepared himself as a Construction Engineer and followed this line of work until the depression limited his market to where it did not give him the income he required. He took inventory of himself, decided to change his profession to law, went back to school, and took special courses by which he prepared himself as a corporation lawyer. Despite the fact the depression had not ended, he completed his training, passed the Bar Examination, and quickly built a lucrative law practice, in Dallas, Texas; in fact, he is turning away clients.

Just to keep the record straight, and to anticipate the alibis of those who will say, "I couldn't go to school because I have a family to support," or "I'm too old," I will add the information that Mr. Wier was past forty and married when he went back to school. Moreover, by carefully selecting highly specialized courses in colleges best prepared to teach the subjects chosen, Mr. Wier completed in two years the work for which the majority of law students require four years. It pays to know how to purchase knowledge!

The person who stops studying merely because he has finished school is forever hopelessly doomed to mediocrity, no matter what may be his calling. The way of success is the way of continuous pursuit of knowledge.

Let us consider a specific instance.

During the depression a salesman in a grocery store found himself without a position. Having had some bookkeeping experience, he took a special course in accounting, familiarized himself with all the latest bookkeeping and office equipment, and went into business for himself. Starting with the grocer for whom he had formerly worked, he made contracts with more than a hundred small merchants to keep their books, at a very nominal monthly fee. His idea was so practical that he soon found it necessary to set up a portable office in a light delivery truck, which he equipped with modern bookkeeping machinery. He now has a fleet of these bookkeeping offices "on wheels" and employs a large staff of assistants, thus providing small merchants with accounting service equal to the best that money can buy, at very nominal cost.

Specialized knowledge plus imagination were the ingredients that went into this unique and successful business. Last year the owner of that business paid an income tax of almost ten times as much as was paid by the merchant for whom he worked when the depression forced upon him a temporary adversity which proved to be a blessing in disguise.

The beginning of this successful business was an idea!

Inasmuch as I had the privilege of supplying the unemployed salesman with that idea, I now assume the further privilege of suggesting another idea which has within it the possibility of even greater income. Also the possibility of rendering useful service to thousands of people who badly need that service.

The idea was suggested by the salesman who gave up selling and went into the business of keeping books on a wholesale basis. When the plan was suggested as a solution of his unemployment problem, he quickly exclaimed, "I like the idea, but I would not know how to turn it into cash." In other words, he complained he would not know how to market his bookkeeping knowledge *after he acquired it.*

So, that brought up another problem which had to be solved. With the aid of a young woman typist, clever at hand lettering, and who could put the story together, a very attractive book was prepared, describing the advantages of the new system of bookkeeping. The pages were neatly typed and pasted in an ordinary scrapbook, which was used as a silent salesman with which the story of this new business was so effectively told that its owner soon had more accounts than he could handle.

There are thousands of people, all over the country, who need the services of a merchandising specialist capable of preparing an attractive brief for use in marketing personal services. The aggregate annual income from such a service might easily exceed that received by the largest employment agency, and the benefits of the service might be made far greater to the purchaser than any to be obtained from an employment agency.

The idea here described was born of necessity, to bridge an emergency which had to be covered, but it did not stop by merely serving one person. The woman who created the idea has a keen imagination. She saw in her newly born brain-child the making of a new profession, one that is destined to render valuable service to thousands of people who need practical guidance in marketing personal services.

Spurred to action by the instantaneous success of her first "prepared plan to market personal services," this energetic woman turned next to the solution of a similar problem for her son, who had just finished college but had been totally unable to find a market for his services. The plan she originated for his use was the finest specimen of merchandising of personal services I have ever seen.

When the plan book had been completed, it contained nearly fifty pages of beautifully typed, properly organized information, telling the story of her son's native ability, schooling, personal experiences, and a great variety of other information too extensive for description. The plan book also contained a complete description of the position her son desired, together with a marvelous word picture of the exact plan he would use in filling the position.

The preparation of the plan book required several weeks' labor, during which time its creator sent her son to the public library almost daily, to procure data needed in selling his services to best advantage. She sent him, also, to all the competitors of his prospective employer, and gathered from them vital information concerning their business methods which was of great value in the formation of the plan he intended to use in filling the position he sought. When the plan had been finished, it contained more than half a dozen very fine suggestions for the use and benefit of the prospective employer. (The suggestions were put into use by the company.)

One may be inclined to ask, "Why go to all this trouble to secure a job?" The answer is straight to the point, also it is dramatic, because it deals with a subject which assumes the proportion of a tragedy with millions of men and women whose sole source of income is personal services.

The answer is, "Doing a thing well never is trouble! The plan prepared by this woman for the benefit of her son helped him get the job for which he applied, at the first interview, at a salary fixed by himself."

Moreover—and this, too, is important—the position did not require the young man to start at the bottom. He began as a junior executive, at an executive's salary.

"Why go to all this trouble?" do you ask.

Well, for one thing, the planned presentation of this young man's application for a position clipped off no less than ten years of time he would have required to get to where he began, had he "started at the bottom and worked his way up."

This idea of starting at the bottom and working one's way up may appear to be sound, but the major objection to it is this—too many of those who begin at the bottom never manage to lift their heads high enough to be seen by opportunity, so they remain at the bottom. It should be remembered, also, that the outlook from the bottom is not so very bright or encouraging. It has a tendency to kill off ambition. We call it "getting into a rut," which means that we accept our fate because we form the habit of daily routine, a habit that finally becomes so strong we cease to try to throw it off. And that is another reason why it pays to start one or two steps above the bottom. By so doing one forms the habit of looking around, of observing how others get ahead, of seeing opportunity, and of embracing it without hesitation.

Dan Halpin is a splendid example of what I mean. During his college days, he was manager of the famous 1930 National Championship Notre Dame football team, when it was under the direction of the late Knute Rockne.

Perhaps he was inspired by the great football coach to aim high, and not mistake temporary defeat for failure, just as Andrew Carnegie, the great industrial leader, inspired his young business lieutenants to set high goals for themselves. At any rate, young Halpin finished college at a mighty unfavorable time, when the depression had made jobs scarce, so, after a fling at investment banking and motion pictures, he took the first opening with a potential future he could find—selling electrical hearing aids on a commission basis. Anyone could start in that sort of job, and Halpin knew it, but it was enough to open the door of opportunity to him.

For almost two years, he continued in a job not to his liking, and he would never have risen above that job if he had not done something about his dissatisfaction. He aimed, first, at the job of Assistant Sales Manager of his company, and got the job. That one step upward placed him high enough above the crowd to enable him to see still greater opportunity; also, it placed him where opportunity could see him.

He made such a fine record selling hearing aids that A. M. Andrews, Chairman of the Board of the Dictograph Products Company, a business competitor of the company for which Halpin worked, wanted to know something about that man Dan Halpin who was taking big sales away from the long established Dictograph Company. He sent for Halpin. When the interview was over, Halpin was the new Sales Manager, in charge of the Acousticon Division. Then, to test young Halpin's metal, Mr. Andrews went away to Florida for three months, leaving him to sink or swim in his new job. He did not sink! Knute Rockne's spirit of "All the world loves a winner, and has no time for a loser," inspired him to put so much into his job that he was recently elected Vice-President of the company, and General Manager of the Acousticon and Silent Radio Division, a job which most men would be proud to earn through ten years of loyal effort. Halpin turned the trick in little more than six months.

It is difficult to say whether Mr. Andrews or Mr. Halpin is more deserving of eulogy, for the reason that both showed evidence of having an abundance of that very rare quality known as imagination. Mr. Andrews deserves credit for seeing in young Halpin a "go-getter" of the highest order. Halpin deserves credit for refusing to compromise with life by accepting and keeping a job he did not want, and that is one of the major points I am trying to emphasize through this entire philosophy—that we rise to high positions or remain at the bottom because of conditions we can control if we desire to control them.

I am also trying to emphasize another point, namely, that both success and failure are largely the results of habit! I have not the slightest doubt that Dan Halpin's close association with the greatest football coach America ever knew planted in his mind the same brand of desire to excel which made the Notre Dame football team world-famous. Truly, there is something to the idea that hero-worship is helpful, provided one worships a winner. Halpin tells me that Rockne was one of the world's greatest leaders of men in all history.

My belief in the theory that business associations are vital factors, both in failure and in success, was recently demonstrated, when my son Blair was negotiating with Dan Halpin for a position. Mr. Halpin offered him a beginning salary of about one half what he could have gotten from a rival company. I brought parental pressure to bear, and induced him to accept the place with Mr. Halpin, because I believe that close association with one who refuses to compromise with circumstances he does not like is an asset that can never be measured in terms of money.

The bottom is a monotonous, dreary, unprofitable place for any person. That is why

I have taken the time to describe how lowly beginnings may be circumvented by proper planning. Also, that is why so much space has been devoted to a description of this new profession, created by a woman who was inspired to do a fine job of planning because she wanted her son to have a favorable "break."

With the changed conditions ushered in by the world economic collapse came also the need for newer and better ways of marketing personal services. It is hard to determine why someone had not previously discovered this stupendous need, in view of the fact that more money changes hands in return for personal services than for any other purpose. The sum paid out monthly, to people who work for wages and salaries, is so huge that it runs into hundreds of millions, and the annual distribution amounts to billions.

Perhaps some will find, in the idea here briefly described, the nucleus of the riches they desire! Ideas with much less merit have been the seedlings from which great fortunes have grown. Woolworth's Five and Ten Cent Store idea, for example, had far less merit, but it piled up a fortune for its creator.

Those seeing opportunity lurking in this suggestion will find valuable aid in the chapter on Organized Planning. Incidentally, an efficient merchandiser of personal services would find a growing demand for his services wherever there are men and women who seek better markets for their services. By applying the Master Mind principle, a few people with suitable talent could form an alliance, and have a paying business very quickly. One would need to be a fair writer, with a flair for advertising and selling, one handy at typing and hand lettering, and one should be a first-class business getter who would let the world know about the service. If one person possessed all these abilities, he might carry on the business alone, until it outgrew him.

The woman who prepared the "Personal Service Sales Plan" for her son now receives requests from all parts of the country for her cooperation in preparing similar plans for others who desire to market their personal services for more money. She has a staff of expert typists, artists, and writers who have the ability to dramatize the case history so effectively that one's personal services can be marketed for much more money than the prevailing wages for similar services. She is so confident of her ability that she accepts, as the major portion of her fee, a percentage of the *increased* pay she helps her clients to earn.

It must not be supposed that her plan merely consists of clever salesmanship by which she helps men and women to demand and receive more money for the same services they formerly sold for less pay. She looks after the interests of the purchaser as well as the seller of personal services, and so prepares her plans that the employer receives full value for the additional money he pays. The method by which she accomplishes this astonishing result is a professional secret which she discloses to no one excepting her own clients.

If you have the imagination, and seek a more profitable outlet for your personal services, this suggestion may be the stimulus for which you have been searching. The idea is capable of yielding an income far greater than that of the "average" doctor, lawyer, or engineer whose education required several years in college. The idea is saleable to those seeking new positions, in practically all positions calling for managerial or executive ability, and those desiring rearrangement of incomes in their present positions.

There is no fixed price for sound ideas!

Back of all ideas is specialized knowledge. Unfortunately, for those who do not find riches in abundance, specialized knowledge is more abundant and more easily acquired than ideas. Because of this very truth, there is a universal demand and an ever-increasing opportunity for the person capable of helping men and women to sell their personal services advantageously. Capability means imagination, the one quality needed to combine specialized knowledge with ideas, in the form of organized plans designed to yield riches.

If you have imagination this chapter may present you with an idea sufficient to serve as the beginning of the riches you desire. Remember, the idea is the main thing. Specialized knowledge may be found just around the corner—any corner!

CHAPTER 6

IMAGINATION

THE WORKSHOP OF THE MIND

The Fifth Step Toward Riches

The imagination is literally the workshop wherein are fashioned all plans created by man. The impulse, the desire, is given shape, form, and action through the aid of the imaginative faculty of the mind.

It has been said that man can create anything which he can imagine.

Of all the ages of civilization, this is the most favorable for the development of the imagination, because it is an age of rapid change. On every hand one may contact stimuli which develop the imagination.

Through the aid of his imaginative faculty, man has discovered, and harnessed, more of Nature's forces during the past fifty years than during the entire history of the human race, previous to that time. He has conquered the air so completely that the birds are a poor match for him in flying. He has harnessed the ether, and made it serve as a means of instantaneous communication with any part of the world. He has analyzed and weighed the sun at a distance of millions of miles, and has determined, through the aid of imagination, the elements of which it consists. He has discovered that his own brain is both a broadcasting and a receiving station for the vibration of thought, and he is beginning now to learn how to make practical use of this discovery. He has increased the speed of locomotion, until he may now travel at a speed of more than three hundred miles an hour. The time will soon come when a man may breakfast in New York, and lunch in San Francisco.

Man's only limitation, within reason, lies in his development and use of his imagination. He has not yet reached the apex of development in the use of his imaginative faculty. He has merely discovered that he has an imagination, and has commenced to use it in a very elementary way.

TWO FORMS OF IMAGINATION

The imaginative faculty functions in two forms. One is known as "synthetic imagination," and the other as "creative imagination."

Synthetic Imagination:—Through this faculty, one may arrange old concepts, ideas, or plans into new combinations. This faculty *creates* nothing. It merely works with the material of experience, education, and observation with which it is fed. It is the faculty used most by the inventor, with the exception of the "genius" who draws upon the creative imagination when he cannot solve his problem through synthetic imagination.

Creative Imagination:—Through the faculty of creative imagination, the finite mind of man has direct communication with Infinite Intelligence. It is the faculty through which "hunches" and "inspirations" are received. It is by this faculty that all basic or new ideas are handed over to man. It is through this faculty that thought vibrations from the minds of others are received. It is through this faculty that one individual may "tune in," or communicate with the subconscious minds of other men.

The creative imagination works automatically, in the manner described in subsequent pages. This faculty functions only when the conscious mind is vibrating at an exceedingly rapid rate, as for example, when the conscious mind is stimulated through the emotion of a *strong desire.*

The creative faculty becomes more alert, more receptive to vibrations from the sources mentioned, in proportion to its development through use. This statement is significant! Ponder over it before passing on.

Keep in mind as you follow these principles that the entire story of how one may convert desire into money cannot be told in one statement. The story will be complete only when one has mastered, assimilated, and begun to make use of all the principles.

The great leaders of business, industry, and finance, and the great artists, musicians, poets, and writers, became great because they developed the faculty of creative imagination.

Both the synthetic and creative faculties of imagination become more alert with use, just as any muscle or organ of the body develops through use.

Desire is only a thought, an impulse. It is nebulous and ephemeral. It is abstract, and of no value, until it has been transformed into its physical counterpart. While the synthetic imagination is the one which will be used most frequently in the process of transforming the impulse of desire into money, you must keep in mind the fact that you may face circumstances and situations which demand use of the creative imagination as well.

Your imaginative faculty may have become weak through inaction. It can be revived and made alert through use. This faculty does not die, though it may become quiescent through lack of use.

Center your attention, for the time being, on the development of the synthetic imagination, because this is the faculty which you will use more often in the process of converting desire into money.

Transformation of the intangible impulse, of desire, into the tangible reality, of money, calls for the use of a plan, or plans. These plans must be formed with the aid of the imagination, and mainly, with the synthetic faculty.

Read the entire book through, then come back to this chapter, and begin at once to put your imagination to work on the building of a plan, or plans, for the transformation of your desire into money. Detailed instructions for the building of plans have been given in almost every chapter. Carry out the instructions best suited to your needs; reduce your plan to writing, if you have not already done so. The moment you complete this, you will have definitely given concrete form to the intangible desire. Read the preceding sentence once more. Read it aloud, very slowly, and as you do so, remember that the moment you reduce the statement of your desire, and a plan for its realization, to writing, you have actually taken the first of a series of steps, which will enable you to convert the thought into its physical counterpart.

The earth on which you live, you, yourself, and every other material thing are the result of evolutionary change, through which microscopic bits of matter have been organized and arranged in an orderly fashion.

Moreover—and this statement is of stupendous importance—this earth, every one of the billions of individual cells of your body, and every atom of matter, *began as an intangible form of energy.*

Desire is thought impulse! Thought impulses are forms of energy. When you begin with the thought impulse, desire, to accumulate money, you are drafting into your service the same "stuff" that Nature used in creating this earth, and every material form in the universe, including the body and brain in which the thought impulses function.

As far as science has been able to determine, the entire universe consists of but two elements—matter and energy.

Through the combination of energy and matter has been created everything perceptible to man, from the largest star which floats in the heavens down to, and including, man himself.

You are now engaged in the task of trying to profit by Nature's method. You are (sincerely and earnestly, we hope) trying to adapt yourself to Nature's laws, by endeavoring to convert desire into its physical or monetary equivalent. You can do it! It has been done before!

You can build a fortune through the aid of laws which are immutable. But, first, you must become familiar with these laws, and learn to use them. Through repetition, and by approaching the description of these principles from every conceivable angle, the author hopes to reveal to you the secret through which every great fortune has been accumulated. Strange and paradoxical as it may seem, the "secret" is not a secret. Nature, herself, advertises it in the earth on which we live, the stars, the planets suspended within our view, in the elements above and around us, in every blade of grass, and every form of life within our vision.

Nature advertises this "secret" in the terms of biology, in the conversion of a tiny cell, so small that it may be lost on the point of a pin, into the human being now reading this line. The conversion of desire into its physical equivalent is, certainly, no more miraculous!

Do not become discouraged if you do not fully comprehend all that has been stated. Unless you have long been a student of the mind, it is not to be expected that you will assimilate all that is in this chapter upon a first reading.

But you will, in time, make good progress.

The principles which follow will open the way for understanding of imagination. Assimilate that which you understand, as you read this philosophy for the first time, then, when you reread and study it, you will discover that something has happened to clarify it, and give you a broader understanding of the whole. Above all, do not stop, nor hesitate in your study of these principles until you have read the book at least three times, for then you will not want to stop.

HOW TO MAKE PRACTICAL USE OF IMAGINATION

Ideas are the beginning points of all fortunes. Ideas are products of the imagination. Let us examine a few well known ideas which have yielded huge fortunes, with the hope that these illustrations will convey definite information concerning the method by which imagination may be used in accumulating riches.

The Enchanted Kettles

Fifty years ago, an old country doctor drove to town, hitched his horse, quietly slipped into a drug store by the back door, and began "dickering" with the young drug clerk.

His mission was destined to yield great wealth to many people. It was destined to bring to the South the most far-flung benefit since the Civil War.

For more than an hour, behind the prescription counter, the old doctor and the clerk talked in low tones. Then the doctor left. He went out to the buggy and brought back a large, old fashioned kettle, a big wooden paddle (used for stirring the contents of the kettle), and deposited them in the back of the store.

The clerk inspected the kettle, reached into his inside pocket, took out a roll of bills, and handed it over to the doctor. The roll contained exactly $500.00—the clerk's entire savings!

The doctor handed over a small slip of paper on which was written a secret formula. The words on that small slip of paper were worth a King's ransom! *But not to the doctor!* Those magic words were needed to start the kettle to boiling, but neither the doctor nor the young clerk knew what fabulous fortunes were destined to flow from that kettle.

The old doctor was glad to sell the outfit for $500.00. The money would pay off his debts, and give him freedom of mind. The clerk was taking a big chance by staking his entire life's savings on a mere scrap of paper and an old kettle! He never dreamed his investment would start a kettle to overflowing with gold that would surpass the miraculous performance of Aladdin's lamp.

What the clerk *really purchased* was an idea!

The old kettle and the wooden paddle and the secret message on a slip of paper were incidental. The strange performance of that kettle began to take place after the new owner mixed with the secret instructions an ingredient of which the doctor knew nothing.

Read this story carefully; give your imagination a test! See if you can discover what it was that the young man added to the secret message which caused the kettle to overflow with gold. Remember, as you read, that this is not a story from *Arabian Nights*. Here you have a story of facts, stranger than fiction, facts which began in the form of an idea.

Let us take a look at the vast fortunes of gold this idea has produced. It has paid, and still pays, huge fortunes to men and women all over the world who distribute the contents of the kettle to millions of people.

The Old Kettle is now one of the world's largest consumers of sugar, thus providing jobs of a permanent nature to thousands of men and women engaged in growing sugar cane, and in refining and marketing sugar.

The Old Kettle consumes, annually, millions of glass bottles, providing jobs to huge numbers of glass workers.

The Old Kettle gives employment to an army of clerks, stenographers, copy writers, and advertising experts throughout the nation. It has brought fame and fortune to scores of artists who have created magnificent pictures describing the product.

The Old Kettle has converted a small Southern city into the business capital of the South, where it now benefits, directly, or indirectly, every business and practically every resident of the city.

The influence of this idea now benefits every civilized country in the world, pouring out a continuous stream of gold to all who touch it.

Gold from the kettle built and maintains one of the most prominent colleges of the South, where thousands of young people receive the training essential for success.

The Old Kettle has done other marvelous things.

All through the world depression, when factories, banks, and business houses were folding up and quitting by the thousands, the owner of this Enchanted Kettle went marching on, *giving continuous employment* to an army of men and women all over the world, and paying out extra portions of gold to those who, long ago, *had faith in the idea.*

If the product of that old brass kettle could talk, it would tell thrilling tales of romance in every language. Romances of love, romances of business, romances of professional men and women who are daily being stimulated by it.

The author is sure of at least one such romance, for he was a part of it, and it all began not far from the very spot on which the drug clerk purchased the Old Kettle. It was here that the author met his wife, and it was she who first told him of the Enchanted Kettle. It was the product of that kettle they were drinking when he asked her to accept him "for better or worse."

Now that you know the content of the Enchanted Kettle is a world famous drink, it is fitting that the author confess that the home city of the drink supplied him with a wife, also that the drink itself provides him with *stimulation of thought without intoxication,* and thereby it serves to give the refreshment of mind which an author must have to do his best work.

Whoever you are, wherever you may live, whatever occupation you may be engaged in, just remember in the future, every time you see the words "Coca-Cola," that its vast empire of wealth and influence grew out of a single idea, and that the mysterious ingredient the drug clerk—Asa Candler—mixed with the secret formula was . . . imagination!

Stop and think of that for a moment.

Remember, also, that the thirteen steps to riches, described in this book, were the media through which the influence of Coca-Cola has been extended to every city, town, village, and cross-roads of the world, and that any idea you may create, as *sound and meritorious* as Coca-Cola, has the possibility of duplicating the stupendous record of this world-wide thirst-killer.

Truly, thoughts are things, and their scope of operation is the world, itself.

What I Would Do If I Had a Million Dollars

This story proves the truth of that old saying "Where there's a will, there's a way." It was told to me by that beloved educator and clergyman, the late Frank W. Gunsaulus, who began his preaching career in the stockyards region of South Chicago.

While Dr. Gunsaulus was going through college, he observed many defects in our educational system, defects which he believed he could correct, if he were the head of a college. His *deepest desire* was to become the directing head of an educational institution in which young men and women would be taught to "learn by doing."

He made up his mind to organize a new college in which he could carry out his ideas, without being handicapped by orthodox methods of education.

He needed a million dollars to put the project across! Where was he to lay his hands on so large a sum of money? That was the question that absorbed most of this ambitious young preacher's thought.

But he couldn't seem to make any progress.

Every night he took that thought to bed with him. He got up with it in the morning. He took it with him everywhere he went. He turned it over and over in his mind until it became a consuming *obsession* with him. A million dollars is a lot of money. He recognized that fact, but he also recognized the truth that *the only limitation is that which one sets up in one's own mind.*

Being a philosopher as well as a preacher, Dr. Gunsaulus recognized, as do all who succeed in life, that definiteness of purpose is the starting point from which one must begin. He recognized, too, that definiteness of purpose takes on animation, life, and power when backed by a burning desire to translate that purpose into its material equivalent.

He knew all these great truths, yet he did not know where, or how to lay his hands on a million dollars. The natural procedure would have been to give up and quit, by saying, "Ah well, my idea is a good one, but I cannot do anything with it, because I never can procure the necessary million dollars." That is exactly what the majority of people would have said, but it is not what Dr. Gunsaulus said. What he said, and what he did, are so important that I now introduce him, and let him speak for himself.

"One Saturday afternoon I sat in my room thinking of ways and means of raising the money to carry out my plans. For nearly two years, I had been thinking, but I *had done nothing but think!*

"The time had come for action!

"I made up my mind, then and there, that I would get the necessary million dollars within a week. How? I was not concerned about that. The main thing of importance was the *decision* to get the money within a specified time, and I want to tell you that the moment I reached a definite decision to get the money within a specified time, a strange feeling of assurance came over me, such as I had never before experienced. Something inside me seemed to say, 'Why didn't you reach that decision a long time ago? The money was waiting for you all the time!'

"Things began to happen in a hurry. I called the newspapers and announced I would preach a sermon the following morning, entitled 'What I would do if I had a Million Dollars.'

"I went to work on the sermon immediately, but I must tell you, frankly, the task was not difficult, because I had been preparing that sermon for almost two years. The spirit back of it was a part of me!

"Long before midnight I had finished writing the sermon. I went to bed and slept with a feeling of confidence, for *I could see myself already in possession of the million dollars.*

"Next morning I arose early, went into the bathroom, read the sermon, then knelt on my knees and asked that my sermon might come to the attention of someone who would supply the needed money.

"While I was praying I again had that feeling of assurance that the money would be forthcoming. In my excitement, I walked out without my sermon, and did not discover the oversight until I was in my pulpit and about ready to begin delivering it.

"It was too late to go back for my notes, and what a blessing that I couldn't go back! Instead, my own subconscious mind yielded the material I needed. When I arose to begin my sermon, I closed my eyes, and spoke with all my heart and soul of my dreams. I not only talked to my audience, but I fancy I talked also to God. I told what I would do with a million dollars if that amount were placed in my hands. I described the plan I had in mind for organizing a great educational institution, where young people would learn to do practical things, and at the same time develop their minds.

"When I had finished and sat down, a man slowly arose from his seat, about three rows from the rear, and made his way toward the pulpit. I wondered what he was going to do. He came into the pulpit, extended his hand, and said, 'Reverend, I liked your sermon. I believe you can do everything you said you would, if you had a million dollars. To prove that I believe in you and your sermon, if you will come to my office tomorrow morning, I will give you the million dollars. My name is Phillip D. Armour.'"

Young Gunsaulus went to Mr. Armour's office and the million dollars was presented to him. With the money, he founded the Armour Institute of Technology.

That is more money than the majority of preachers ever see in an entire lifetime, yet the thought impulse back of the money was created in the young preacher's mind in a fraction of a minute. The necessary million dollars came as a result of an idea. Back of the idea was a DESIRE which young Gunsaulus had been nursing in his mind for almost two years.

Observe this important fact . . . he got the money within thirty-six hours after he reached a definite decision in his own mind to get it, and decided upon a definite plan for getting it!

There was nothing new or unique about young Gunsaulus' vague thinking about a million dollars, and weakly hoping for it. Others before him, and many since his time, have had similar thoughts. But there was something very unique and different about the decision he reached on that memorable Saturday, when he put vagueness into the background, and definitely said, "I will get that money within a week!"

God seems to throw Himself on the side of the man who knows *exactly* what he wants, *if he is determined* to get just that!

Moreover, the principle through which Dr. Gunsaulus got his million dollars is still alive! It is available to you! This universal law is as workable today as it was when the young preacher made use of it so successfully. This book describes, step by step, the thirteen elements of this great law, and suggests how they may be put to use.

Observe that Asa Candler and Dr. Frank Gunsaulus had one characteristic in common. Both knew the astounding truth that ideas can be transmuted into cash through the power of definite purpose, plus definite plans.

If you are one of those who believe that hard work and honesty, alone, will bring riches, perish the thought! It is not true! Riches, when they come in huge quantities, are never the result of hard work! Riches come, if they come at all, in response to definite demands, based upon the application of definite principles, and not by chance or luck.

Generally speaking, an idea is an impulse of thought that impels action, by an appeal to the imagination. All master salesmen know that ideas can be sold where merchandise cannot. Ordinary salesmen do not know this—that is why they are "ordinary."

A publisher of books, which sell for a nickel, made a discovery that should be worth much to publishers generally. He learned that many people buy titles, and not contents of books. By merely changing the name of one book that was not moving, his sales on that book jumped upward more than a million copies. The inside of the book was not changed in any way. He merely ripped off the cover bearing the title that did not sell, and put on a new cover with a title that had "box-office" value.

That, as simple as it may seem, was an idea! It was imagination.

There is no standard price on ideas. The creator of ideas makes his own price, and, if he is smart, gets it.

The moving picture industry created a whole flock of millionaires. Most of them were men who couldn't create ideas—but—they had the imagination to recognize ideas when they saw them.

The next flock of millionaires will grow out of the radio business, which is new and not overburdened with men of keen imagination. The money will be made by those who discover or create new and more meritorious radio programmes and have the imagination to recognize merit, and to give the radio listeners a chance to profit by it.

The sponsor! That unfortunate victim who now pays the cost of all radio "entertainment" soon will become idea conscious, and demand something for his money. The man who beats the sponsor to the draw, and supplies programmes that render useful service, is the man who will become rich in this new industry.

Crooners and light chatter artists who now pollute the air with wisecracks and silly giggles will go the way of all light timbers, and their places will be taken by real artists who interpret carefully planned programmes which have been designed to service the minds of men, as well as provide entertainment.

Here is a wide-open field of opportunity screaming its protest at the way it is being butchered, because of lack of imagination, and begging for rescue at any price. Above all, the thing that radio needs is new ideas!

If this new field of opportunity intrigues you, perhaps you might profit by the suggestion that the successful radio programmes of the future will give more attention to creating "buyer" audiences, and less attention to "listener" audiences. Stated more plainly, the builder of radio programmes who succeeds in the future must find practical ways to convert "listeners" into "buyers." Moreover, the successful producer of radio programmes in the future must key his features so that he can definitely show its effect upon the audience.

Sponsors are becoming a bit weary of buying glib selling talks, based upon statements grabbed out of thin air. They want, and in the future will demand, indisputable proof that the Whoosit programme not only gives millions of people the silliest giggle ever, but that the silly giggler can sell merchandise!

Another thing that might as well be understood by those who contemplate entering this new field of opportunity, radio advertising is going to be handled by an entirely new group of advertising experts, separate and distinct from the old time newspaper and magazine advertising agency men. The old timers in the advertising game *cannot read* the modern radio scripts, because they have been schooled to see ideas. The new radio technique demands men who can interpret ideas from a *written* manuscript in terms of *sound!* It cost the author a year of hard labor, and many thousands of dollars to learn this.

Radio, right now, is about where the moving pictures were when Mary Pickford and her curls first appeared on the screen. There is plenty of room in radio for those who can *produce or recognize* ideas.

If the foregoing comment on the opportunities of radio has not started your idea factory to work, you had better forget it. Your opportunity is in some other field. If the comment intrigued you in the slightest degree, then go further into it, and you may find the one idea you need to round out your career.

Never let it discourage you if you have no experience in radio. Andrew Carnegie knew very little about making steel—I have Carnegie's own word for this—but he made practical use of two of the principles described in this book, and made the steel business yield him a fortune.

The story of practically every great fortune starts with the day when a creator of ideas and a seller of ideas got together and worked in harmony. Carnegie surrounded himself with men who could do all that he could not do—men who created ideas, and men who put ideas into operation—and made himself and the others fabulously rich.

Millions of people go through life hoping for favorable "breaks." Perhaps a favorable break can get one an opportunity, but the safest plan is not to depend upon luck. It was a favorable "break" that gave me the biggest opportunity of my life—*but*—twenty-five years *of determined effort* had to be devoted to that opportunity before it became an asset.

The "break" consisted of my good fortune in meeting and gaining the cooperation of Andrew Carnegie. On that occasion Carnegie planted in my mind the *idea* of organizing the principles of achievement into a philosophy of success. Thousands of people have profited by the discoveries made in the twenty-five years of research, and several fortunes have been accumulated through the application of the philosophy. The beginning was simple. It was an idea which anyone might have developed.

The favorable break came through Carnegie, but what about the determination, definiteness of purpose, and the desire to attain the goal, and the persistent effort of twenty-five years? It was no ordinary desire that survived disappointment, discouragement, temporary defeat, criticism, and the constant reminding of "waste of time." It was a burning desire! An obsession!

When the idea was first planted in my mind by Mr. Carnegie, it was coaxed, nursed, and enticed to *remain alive.* Gradually, the idea became a giant under its own power, and it coaxed, nursed, and drove me. Ideas are like that. First you give life and action and guidance to ideas, then they take on power of their own and sweep aside all opposition.

Ideas are intangible forces, but they have more power than the physical brains that give birth to them. They have the power to live on, after the brain that creates them has returned to dust. For example, take the power of Christianity. That began with a simple idea, born in the brain of Christ. Its chief tenet was "Do unto others as you would have others do unto you." Christ has gone back to the source from whence He came, but His idea goes marching on. Some day, it may grow up, and come into its own, then it will have fulfilled Christ's deepest desire. The idea has been developing for only two thousand years. Give it time!

Success Requires No Explanations

Failure Permits No Alibis

CHAPTER 7

ORGANIZED PLANNING

THE CRYSTALLIZATION OF DESIRE INTO ACTION

The Sixth Step Toward Riches

You have learned that everything man creates or acquires begins in the form of desire, that desire is taken on the first lap of its journey, from the abstract to the concrete, into the workshop of the imagination, where plans for its transition are created and organized.

In chapter two, you were instructed to take six definite, practical steps as your first move in translating the desire for money into its monetary equivalent. One of these steps is the formation of a definite, practical plan, or plans, through which this transformation may be made.

You will now be instructed how to build plans which will be practical, viz:

(a) Ally yourself with a group of as many people as you may need for the creation and carrying out of your plan, or plans, for the accumulation of money—making use of the "Master Mind" principle described in a later chapter. (Compliance with this instruction is *absolutely essential.* Do not neglect it.)

(b) Before forming your "Master Mind" alliance, decide what advantages, and benefits, *you* may offer the individual members of your group, in return for their cooperation. No one will work indefinitely without some form of compensation. No intelligent person will either request or expect another to work without adequate compensation, although this may not always be in the form of money.

(c) Arrange to meet with the members of your "Master Mind" group at least twice a week, and more often if possible, until you have jointly perfected the necessary plan, or plans, for the accumulation of money.

(d) Maintain perfect harmony between yourself and every member of your "Master Mind" group. If you fail to carry out this instruction to the letter, you may expect to meet with failure. The "Master Mind" principle *cannot* obtain where perfect harmony does not prevail.

Keep in mind these facts:—

FIRST. You are engaged in an undertaking of major importance to you. To be sure of success, you must have plans which are faultless.

SECOND. You must have the advantage of the experience, education, native ability, and imagination of other minds. This is in harmony with the methods followed by every person who has accumulated a great fortune.

No individual has sufficient experience, education, native ability, and knowledge to insure the accumulation of a great fortune without the cooperation of other people. Every plan you adopt, in your endeavor to accumulate wealth, should be the joint creation of yourself and every other member of your "Master Mind" group. You may originate your own plans, either in whole or in part, but see that those plans are checked and approved by the members of your "Master Mind" alliance.

If the first plan which you adopt does not work successfully, replace it with a new plan; if this new plan fails to work, replace it in turn with still another, and so on, until you find a plan which does work. Right here is the point at which the majority of men meet with failure, because of their lack of persistence in creating new plans to take the place of those which fail.

The most intelligent man living cannot succeed in accumulating money—nor in any other undertaking—without plans which are practical and workable. Just keep this fact in mind, and remember when your plans fail that temporary defeat is not permanent failure. It may only mean that your plans have not been sound. Build other plans. Start all over again.

Thomas A. Edison "failed" ten thousand times before he perfected the incandescent electric light bulb. That is—he met with *temporary defeat* ten thousand times, before his efforts were crowned with success.

Temporary defeat should mean only one thing—the certain knowledge that there is something wrong with your plan. Millions of men go through life in misery and poverty, because they lack a sound plan through which to accumulate a fortune.

Henry Ford accumulated a fortune, not because of his superior mind, but because he adopted and followed a plan which proved to be sound. A thousand men could be pointed out, each with a better education than Ford's, yet each of whom lives in poverty, because he does not possess the right plan for the accumulation of money.

Your achievement can be no greater than your plans are sound. That may seem to be an axiomatic statement, but it is true. Samuel Insull lost his fortune of over one hundred million dollars. The Insull fortune was built on plans which were sound. The business depression forced Mr. Insull to change his plans; and the change brought "temporary defeat," because his new plans were not sound. Mr. Insull is now an old man; he may, consequently, accept "failure" instead of "temporary defeat," but if his experience turns out to be failure, it will be for the reason that he lacks the fire of persistence to rebuild his plans.

No man is ever whipped, until he quits—*in his own mind.*

This fact will be repeated many times, because it is so easy to "take the count" at the first sign of defeat.

James J. Hill met with temporary defeat when he first endeavored to raise the necessary capital to build a railroad from the East to the West, but he, too, turned defeat into victory *through new plans.*

Henry Ford met with temporary defeat, not only at the beginning of his automobile career, but after he had gone far toward the top. He created new plans, and went marching on to financial victory.

We see men who have accumulated great fortunes, but we often recognize only their triumph, overlooking the temporary defeats which they had to surmount before "arriving."

No follower of this philosophy can reasonably expect to accumulate a fortune without experiencing "temporary defeat." When defeat comes, accept it as a signal that your plans are not sound, rebuild those plans, and set sail once more toward your coveted goal. If you give up before your goal has been reached, you are a "quitter." A quitter never wins—and—a winner never quits. Lift this sentence out, write it on a piece of paper in letters an inch high, and place it where you will see it every night before you go to sleep, and every morning before you go to work.

When you begin to select members for your "Master Mind" group, endeavor to select those who do not take defeat seriously.

Some people foolishly believe that only money can make money. This is not true! Desire, transmuted into its monetary equivalent, through the principles laid down here, is the agency through which money is "made." Money, of itself, is nothing but inert matter. It cannot move, think, or talk, but it can "hear" when a man who desires it calls it to come!

PLANNING THE SALE OF SERVICES

The remainder of this chapter has been given over to a description of ways and means of marketing personal services. The information here conveyed will be of practical help to any person having any form of personal services to market, but it will be of priceless benefit to those who aspire to leadership in their chosen occupations.

Intelligent planning is essential for success in any undertaking designed to accumulate riches. Here will be found detailed instructions to those who must begin the accumulation of riches by selling personal services.

It should be encouraging to know that practically all the great fortunes began in the form of compensation for personal services, or from the sale of ideas. What else, except ideas and personal services, would one not possessed of property have to give in return for riches?

Broadly speaking, there are two types of people in the world. One type is known as leaders, and the other as followers. Decide at the outset whether you intend to become a leader in your chosen calling, or remain a follower. The difference in compensation is vast. The follower cannot reasonably expect the compensation to which a leader is entitled, although many followers make the mistake of expecting such pay.

It is no disgrace to be a follower. On the other hand, it is no credit to remain a follower. Most great leaders began in the capacity of followers. They became great leaders because they were intelligent followers. With few exceptions, the man who cannot follow a leader intelligently cannot become an efficient leader. The man who can follow a leader most efficiently is usually the man who develops into leadership most rapidly. An intelligent follower has many advantages, among them the opportunity to acquire knowledge from his leader.

THE MAJOR ATTRIBUTES OF LEADERSHIP

The following are important factors of leadership:—

1. Unwavering courage based upon knowledge of self, and of one's occupation. No follower wishes to be dominated by a leader who lacks self-confidence and courage. No intelligent follower will be dominated by such a leader very long.
2. Self-control. The man who cannot control himself can never control others. Self-control sets a mighty example for one's followers, which the more intelligent will emulate.
3. A keen sense of justice. Without a sense of fairness and justice, no leader can command and retain the respect of his followers.
4. Definiteness of decision. The man who wavers in his decisions shows that he is not sure of himself. He cannot lead others successfully.
5. Definiteness of plans. The successful leader must plan his work, and *work his plan.* A leader who moves by guesswork, without practical, definite plans, is comparable to a ship without a rudder. Sooner or later he will land on the rocks.

6. The habit of doing more than paid for. One of the penalties of leadership is the necessity of willingness, upon the part of the leader, to do more than he requires of his followers.
7. A pleasing personality. No slovenly, careless person can become a successful leader. Leadership calls for respect. Followers will not respect a leader who does not grade high on all of the factors of a Pleasing Personality.
8. Sympathy and understanding. The successful leader must be in sympathy with his followers. Moreover, he must understand them and their problems.
9. Mastery of detail. Successful leadership calls for mastery of details of the leader's position.
10. Willingness to assume full responsibility. The successful leader must be willing to assume responsibility for the mistakes and the shortcomings of his followers. If he tries to shift this responsibility, he will not remain the leader. If one of his followers makes a mistake, and shows himself incompetent, the leader must consider that it is *he* who failed.
11. Cooperation. The successful leader must understand and *apply* the principle of cooperative effort and be able to induce his followers to do the same. Leadership calls for power, and power calls for cooperation.

There are two forms of Leadership. The first, and by far the most effective, is leadership of consent of, and with the sympathy of, the followers. The second is leadership by force, without the consent and sympathy of the followers.

History is filled with evidences that Leadership by Force cannot endure. The downfall and disappearance of "Dictators" and kings is significant. It means that people will not follow forced leadership indefinitely.

The world has just entered a new era of relationship between leaders and followers, which very clearly calls for new leaders, and a new brand of leadership in business and industry. Those who belong to the old school of Leadership by Force, must acquire an understanding of the new brand of leadership (cooperation) or be relegated to the rank and file of the followers. There is no other way out for them.

The relationship of employer and employee, or of leader and follower, in the future, will be one of mutual cooperation, based upon an equitable division of the profits of business. In the future, the relationship of employer and employee will be more like a partnership than it has been in the past.

Napoleon, Kaiser Wilhelm of Germany, the Czar of Russia, and the King of Spain were examples of Leadership by Force. Their leadership passed. Without much difficulty, one might point to the prototypes of these ex-leaders among the business, financial, and labor leaders of America who have been dethroned or slated to go. *Leadership by Consent* of the followers is the only brand which can endure!

Men may follow the forced leadership temporarily, but they will not do so willingly.

The new brand of leadership will embrace the eleven factors of leadership, described in this chapter, as well as some other factors. The man who makes these the basis of his leadership will find abundant opportunity to lead in any walk of life. The depression was prolonged, largely, because the world lacked leadership of the new brand. At the end of the depression, the demand for leaders who are competent to apply the new methods of leadership has greatly exceeded the supply. Some of the old type of leaders will reform and adapt themselves to the new brand of leadership, but generally speaking, the world will have to look for new timber for its leadership.

This necessity may be your opportunity!

THE 10 MAJOR CAUSES OF FAILURE IN LEADERSHIP

We come now to the major faults of leaders who fail, because it is just as essential to know what not to do as it is to know what to do.

1. Inability to organize details. Efficient leadership calls for ability to organize and to master details. No genuine leader is ever "too busy" to do anything which may be required of him in his capacity as leader. When a man, whether he is a leader or follower, admits that he is "too busy" to change his plans, or to give attention to any emergency, he admits his inefficiency. The successful leader must be the master of all details connected with his position. That means, of course, that he must acquire the habit of relegating details to capable lieutenants.
2. Unwillingness to render humble service. Truly great leaders are willing, when occasion demands, to perform any sort of labor which they would ask another to perform. "The greatest among ye shall be the servant of all" is a truth which all able leaders observe and respect.
3. Expectation of pay for what they "know" instead of what they *do* with that which they know. The world does not pay men for that which they "know." It pays them for what they DO, or induce others to do.
4. Fear of competition from followers. The leader who fears that one of his followers may take his position is practically sure to realize that fear sooner or later. The able leader trains understudies to whom he may delegate, at will, any of the details of his position. Only in this way may a leader multiply himself and prepare himself to be at many places, and give attention to many things at one time. It is an eternal truth that men receive more pay for their ability to get

others to perform than they could possibly earn by their own efforts. An efficient leader may, through his knowledge of his job and the magnetism of his personality, greatly increase the efficiency of others, and induce them to render more service and better service than they could render without his aid.

5. Lack of imagination. Without imagination, the leader is incapable of meeting emergencies, and of creating plans by which to guide his followers efficiently.
6. Selfishness. The leader who claims all the honor for the work of his followers is sure to be met by resentment. The really great leader claims none of the honors. He is contented to see the honors, when there are any, go to his followers, because he knows that most men will work harder for commendation and recognition than they will for money alone.
7. Intemperance. Followers do not respect an intemperate leader. Moreover, intemperance in any of its various forms destroys the endurance and the vitality of all who indulge in it.
8. Disloyalty. Perhaps this should have come at the head of the list. The leader who is not loyal to his trust, and to his associates, those above him, and those below him, cannot long maintain his leadership. Disloyalty marks one as being less than the dust of the earth, and brings down on one's head the contempt he deserves. Lack of loyalty is one of the major causes of failure in every walk of life.
9. Emphasis of the "authority" of leadership. The efficient leader leads by encouraging, and not by trying to instil fear in the hearts of his followers. The leader who tries to impress his followers with his "authority" comes within the category of leadership through force. If a leader is a real leader, he will have no need to advertise that fact except by his conduct—his sympathy, understanding, fairness, and a demonstration that he knows his job.

10. Emphasis of title. The competent leader requires no "title" to give him the respect of his followers. The man who makes too much over his title generally has little else to emphasize. The doors to the office of the real leader are open to all who wish to enter, and his working quarters are free from formality or ostentation.

These are among the more common of the causes of failure in leadership. Any one of these faults is sufficient to induce failure. Study the list carefully if you aspire to leadership, and make sure that you are free of these faults.

SOME FERTILE FIELDS IN WHICH "NEW LEADERSHIP" WILL BE REQUIRED

Before leaving this chapter, your attention is called to a few of the fertile fields in which there has been a decline of leadership, and in which the new type of leader may find an abundance of opportunity.

FIRST. In the field of politics there is a most insistent demand for new leaders, a demand which indicates nothing less than an emergency. The majority of politicians have, seemingly, become high-grade, legalized racketeers. They have increased taxes and debauched the machinery of industry and business until the people can no longer stand the burden.

SECOND. The banking business is undergoing a reform. The leaders in this field have almost entirely lost the confidence of the public. Already the bankers have sensed the need of reform, and they have begun it.

THIRD. Industry calls for new leaders. The old type of leaders thought and moved in terms of dividends instead of thinking and moving in terms of human equations! The future leader in industry, to endure, must regard himself as a quasi-public official whose duty it is to manage his trust in such a way that it will work hardship on no individual, or group of individuals. Exploitation of working men is a thing of the past. Let the man who aspires to leadership in the field of business, industry, and labor remember this.

FOURTH. The religious leader of the future will be forced to give more attention to the temporal needs of his followers, in the solution of their economic and personal problems of the present, and less attention to the dead past, and the yet unborn future.

FIFTH. In the professions of law, medicine, and education, a new brand of leadership, and to some extent, new leaders will become a necessity. This is especially true in the field of education. The leader in that field must, in the future, find ways and means of teaching people how to apply the knowledge they receive in school. He must deal more with practice and less with theory.

SIXTH. New leaders will be required in the field of Journalism. Newspapers of the future, to be conducted successfully, must be divorced from "special privilege" and relieved from the subsidy of advertising. They must cease to be organs of propaganda for the interests which patronize their advertising columns. The type of newspaper which publishes scandal and lewd pictures will eventually go the way of all forces which debauch the human mind.

These are but a few of the fields in which opportunities for new leaders and a new brand of leadership are now available. The world is undergoing a rapid change. This means that the media through which the changes in human habits are promoted must be adapted to the changes. The media here described are the ones which, more than any others, determine the trend of civilization.

WHEN AND HOW TO APPLY FOR A POSITION

The information described here is the net result of many years of experience during which thousands of men and women were helped to market their services effectively. It can, therefore, be relied upon as sound and practical.

MEDIA THROUGH WHICH SERVICES MAY BE MARKETED

Experience has proved that the following media offer the most direct and effective methods of bringing the buyer and seller of personal services together.

1. Employment bureaus. Care must be taken to select only reputable bureaus, the management of which can show adequate records of achievement of satisfactory results. There are comparatively few such bureaus.
2. Advertising in newspapers, trade journals, magazines, and radio. Classified advertising may usually be relied upon to produce satisfactory results in the case of those who apply for clerical or ordinary salaried positions. Display advertising is more desirable in the case of those who seek executive connections, the copy to appear in the section of the paper which is most apt to come to the attention of the class of employer being sought. The copy should be prepared by an expert, who understands how to inject sufficient selling qualities to produce replies.
3. Personal letters of application, directed to particular firms or individuals most apt to need such services as are being offered. Letters should be *neatly*

typed, always, and signed by hand. With the letter should be sent a complete "brief" or outline of the applicant's qualifications. Both the letter of application and the brief of experience or qualifications should be prepared by an expert. (See instructions as to information to be supplied.)

4. Application through personal acquaintances. When possible, the applicant should endeavor to approach prospective employers through some mutual acquaintance. This method of approach is particularly advantageous in the case of those who seek executive connections and do not wish to appear to be "peddling" themselves.
5. Application in person. In some instances, it may be more effective if the applicant offers personally his services to prospective employers, in which event a complete written statement of qualifications for the position should be presented, for the reason that prospective employers often wish to discuss with associates one's record.

INFORMATION TO BE SUPPLIED IN A WRITTEN "BRIEF"

This brief should be prepared as carefully as a lawyer would prepare the brief of a case to be tried in court. Unless the applicant is experienced in the preparation of such briefs, an expert should be consulted, and his services enlisted for this purpose. Successful merchants employ men and women who understand the art and the psychology of advertising to present the merits of their merchandise. One who has personal services for sale should do the same. The following information should appear in the brief:

1. *Education.* State briefly, but definitely, what schooling you have had, and in what subjects you specialized in school, giving the reasons for that specialization.

2. *Experience.* If you have had experience in connection with positions similar to the one you seek, describe it fully; state names and addresses of former employers. Be sure to bring out clearly any special experience you may have had which would equip you to fill the position you seek.
3. *References.* Practically every business firm desires to know all about the previous records, antecedents, etc., of prospective employees who seek positions of responsibility. Attach to your brief photostatic copies of letters from:
   a. Former employers
   b. Teachers under whom you studied
   c. Prominent people whose judgement may be relied upon
4. *Photograph of self.* Attach to your brief a recent, unmounted photograph of yourself.
5. *Apply for a specific position.* Avoid application for a position without describing exactly what particular position you seek. Never apply for "just a position." That indicates you lack specialized qualifications.
6. *State your qualifications* for the particular position for which you apply. Give full details as to the reason you believe you are qualified for the particular position you seek. This is the most important detail of your application. It will determine, more than anything else, what consideration you receive.
7. *Offer to go to work on probation.* In the majority of instances, if you are determined to have the position for which you apply, it will be most effective if you offer to work for a week, or a month, or for a sufficient length of time to enable your prospective employer to judge your value without pay. This may appear to be a radical suggestion, but experience has proved that it seldom fails to win at least a trial. If you are sure of your qualifications, a trial is all you need. Incidentally, such an offer indicates that you have confidence in

your ability to fill the position you seek. It is most convincing. If your offer is accepted, and you make good, more than likely you will be paid for your "probation" period. Make clear the fact that your offer is based upon:

a. Your confidence in your ability to fill the position
b. Your confidence in your prospective employer's decision to employ you after trial
c. Your determination to have the position you seek

8. *Knowledge of your prospective employer's business.* Before applying for a position, do sufficient research in connection with the business to familiarize yourself thoroughly with that business, and indicate in your brief the knowledge you have acquired in this field. This will be impressive, as it will indicate that you have imagination, and a real interest in the position you seek.

Remember that it is not the lawyer who knows the most law but the one who best prepares his case who wins. If your "case" is properly prepared and presented, your victory will have been more than half won at the outset.

Do not be afraid of making your brief too long. Employers are just as much interested in purchasing the services of well-qualified applicants as you are in securing employment. In fact, the success of most successful employers is due, in the main, to their ability to select well-qualified lieutenants. They want all the information available.

Remember another thing: neatness in the preparation of your brief will indicate that you are a painstaking person. I have helped to prepare briefs for clients which were so striking and out of the ordinary that they resulted in the employment of the applicant without a personal interview.

When your brief has been completed, have it neatly bound by an experienced binder, and lettered by an artist, or printer, similar to the following:

BRIEF OF THE QUALIFICATIONS OF

Robert K. Smith

APPLYING FOR THE POSITION OF

Private Secretary to
The President of
THE BLANK COMPANY, INC.

Change names each time brief is shown.

This personal touch is sure to command attention. Have your brief neatly typed or mimeographed on the finest paper you can obtain, and bound with a heavy paper of the book-cover variety; the binder to be changed, and the proper firm name to be inserted, if it is to be shown to more than one company. Your photograph should be pasted on one of the pages of your brief. Follow these instructions to the letter, improving upon them wherever your imagination suggests.

Successful salesmen groom themselves with care. They understand that first impressions are lasting. Your brief is your salesman. Give it a good suit of clothes, so it will stand out in bold contrast to anything your prospective employer ever saw, in the way of an application for a position. If the position you seek is worth having, it is worth going after with care. Moreover, if you sell yourself to an employer in a manner that impresses him with your individuality, you probably will receive more money for your services from the very start than you would if you applied for employment in the usual conventional way.

If you seek employment through an advertising agency or an employment agency, have the agent use copies of your brief in marketing your services. This will help to gain preference for you, both with the agent and the prospective employers.

HOW TO GET THE EXACT POSITION YOU DESIRE

Everyone enjoys doing the kind of work for which he is best suited. An artist loves to work with paints, a craftsman with his hands, a writer loves to write. Those with less definite talents have their preferences for certain fields of business and industry. If America does anything well, it offers a full range of occupations: tilling the soil, manufacturing, marketing, and the professions.

FIRST. Decide exactly what kind of a job you want. If the job doesn't already exist, perhaps you can create it.

SECOND. Choose the company, or individual, for whom you wish to work.

THIRD. Study your prospective employer as to policies, personnel, and chances of advancement.

FOURTH. By analysis of yourself, your talents, and capabilities, figure what you can offer, and plan ways and means of giving advantages, services, developments, ideas that *you believe* you can successfully deliver.

FIFTH. Forget about "a job." Forget whether or not there is an opening. Forget the usual routine of "have you got a job for me?" Concentrate on what *you can give.*

SIXTH. Once you have your plan in mind, arrange with an experienced writer to put it on paper in neat form, and in full detail.

SEVENTH. Present it to the *proper person with authority* and he will do the rest. Every company is looking for men who can give something of value, whether it be ideas, services, or "connections." Every company has room for the man who has a definite plan of action which is to the advantage of that company.

This line of procedure may take a few days or weeks of extra time, but the difference in income, in advancement, and in gaining recognition will save years of hard work at small pay. It has many advantages, the main one being that it will often save from one to five years of time in reaching a chosen goal.

Every person who starts or "gets in" half way up the ladder does so by deliberate and careful planning (excepting, of course, the Boss' son).

THE NEW WAY OF MARKETING SERVICES

"JOBS" ARE NOW "PARTNERSHIPS"

Men and women who market their services to best advantage in the future must recognize the stupendous change which has taken place in connection with the relationship between employer and employee.

In the future, the "Golden Rule," and not the "Rule of Gold," will be the dominating factor in the marketing of merchandise as well as personal services. The future relationship between employers and their employees will be more in the nature of a partnership consisting of:

a. The employer
b. The employee
c. The public they serve

This new way of marketing personal services is called new for many reasons; first, both the employer and the employee of the future will be considered as fellow-employees whose business it will be to serve the public efficiently. In times past, employers and employees have bartered among themselves, driving the best bargains they could with one another, not considering that in the final analysis they were, in reality, bargaining at the expense of the third party, the public they served.

The depression served as a mighty protest from an injured public, whose rights had been trampled upon in every direction by those who were clamoring for individual advantages and profits. When the debris of the depression shall have been cleared away, and business shall have been once again restored to balance, both employers and employees will recognize that they are no longer privileged to drive bargains at the expense of those whom they serve. The real employer of the future will be the public. This should be kept uppermost in mind by every person seeking to market personal services effectively.

Nearly every railroad in America is in financial difficulty. Who does not remember the day when, if a citizen enquired at the ticket office, the time of departure of a train, he was abruptly referred to the bulletin board instead of being politely given the information?

The street car companies have experienced a "change of times" also. There was a time not so very long ago when street car conductors took pride in giving argument to passengers. Many of the street car tracks have been removed and passengers ride on a bus, whose driver is "the last word in politeness."

All over the country street car tracks are rusting from abandonment, or have been taken up. Wherever street cars are still in operation, passengers may now ride without argument, and one may even hail the car in the middle of the block, and the motorman will obligingly pick him up.

How times have changed! That is just the point I am trying to emphasize. Times have changed! Moreover, the change is reflected not merely in railroad offices and on street cars, but in other walks of life as well. The "public-be-damned" policy is now passé. It has been supplanted by the "we-are-obligingly-at-your-service, sir" policy.

The bankers have learned a thing or two during this rapid change which has taken place during the past few years. Impoliteness on the part of a bank official or bank employee today is as rare as it was conspicuous a dozen years ago. In the years past, some bankers (not all of them, of course) carried an atmosphere of austerity which gave every would-be borrower a chill when he even thought of approaching his banker for a loan.

The thousands of bank failures during the depression had the effect of removing the mahogany doors behind which bankers formerly barricaded themselves. They now sit at desks in the open, where they may be seen and approached at will by any depositor, or by anyone who wishes to see them, and the whole atmosphere of the bank is one of courtesy and understanding.

It used to be customary for customers to have to stand and wait at the corner grocery until the clerks were through passing the time of day with friends, and the proprietor had finished making up his bank deposit, before being waited upon. Chain stores, managed by courteous men who do everything in the way of service, short of shining the customer's shoes, have pushed the old-time merchants into the background. Time marches on!

"Courtesy" and "Service" are the watch-words of merchandising today, and apply to the person who is marketing personal services even more directly than to the employer whom he serves, because, in the final analysis, both the employer and his employee are employed by the public they serve. If they fail to serve well, they pay by the loss of their privilege of serving.

We can all remember the time when the gas-meter reader pounded on the door hard enough to break the panels. When the door was opened, he pushed his way in, uninvited, with a scowl on his face which plainly said, "What the hell did you keep me waiting for?" All that has undergone a change. The meter-man now conducts himself as a gentleman who is "delighted-to-be-at-your-service-sir." Before the gas companies learned that their scowling meter-men were accumulating liabilities never to be cleared away, the polite salesmen of oil burners came along and did a land office business.

During the depression, I spent several months in the anthracite coal region of Pennsylvania, studying conditions which all but destroyed the coal industry. Among several very significant discoveries was the fact that greed on the part of operators and their employees was the chief cause of the loss of business for the operators, and loss of jobs for the miners.

Through the pressure of a group of overzealous labor leaders, representing the employees, and the greed for profits on the part of the operators, the anthracite business suddenly dwindled. The coal operators and their employees drove sharp bargains with one another, adding the cost of the "bargaining" to the price of the coal, until, finally, they discovered they had built up a wonderful business for the manufacturers of oil burning outfits and the producers of crude oil.

"The wages of sin is death!" Many have read this in the Bible, but few have discovered its meaning. Now, and for several years, the entire world has been listening by force to a sermon which might well be called "Whatsoever a man soweth, that shall he also reap."

Nothing as widespread and effective as the depression could possibly be "just a coincidence." Behind the depression was a cause. Nothing ever happens without a cause. In the main, the cause of the depression is traceable directly to the worldwide habit of trying to reap without sowing.

This should not be mistaken to mean that the depression represents a crop which the world is being forced to reap without having sown. The trouble is that the world *sowed the wrong sort of seed.* Any farmer knows he cannot sow the seed of thistles, and reap a harvest of grain. Beginning at the outbreak of the world war, the people of the world began to sow the seed of service inadequate in both quality and quantity. Nearly everyone was engaged in the pastime of trying to get without giving.

These illustrations are brought to the attention of those who have personal services to market, to show that we are where we are, and what we are, because of *our own conduct!* If there is a principle of cause and effect, which controls business, finance, and transportation, this same principle controls individuals and determines their economic status.

WHAT IS YOUR "QQS" RATING?

The causes of success in marketing services effectively and permanently have been clearly described. Unless those causes are studied, analyzed, understood, and applied, no man can market his services effectively and permanently. Every person must be his own salesman of personal services. The quality and the quantity of service rendered, and the spirit in which it is rendered, determine to a large extent the price and the duration of employment. To market personal services effectively (which means a permanent market, at a satisfactory price, under pleasant conditions), one must adopt and follow the "QQS" formula, which means that quality, plus quantity, plus the proper spirit of cooperation, equals perfect salesmanship of service. Remember the "QQS" formula, but do more—apply it as a habit!

Let us analyze the formula to make sure we understand exactly what it means.

1. *Quality* of service shall be construed to mean the performance of every detail, in connection with your position, in the most efficient manner possible, with the object of greater efficiency always in mind.
2. *Quantity* of service shall be understood to mean the habit of rendering all the service of which you are capable, at all times, with the purpose of increasing the amount of service rendered as greater skill is developed through practice and experience. Emphasis is again placed on the word "habit."
3. *Spirit* of service shall be construed to mean the habit of agreeable, harmonious conduct which will induce cooperation from associates and fellow employees.

Adequacy of quality and quantity of service is not sufficient to maintain a permanent market for your services. The conduct, or the spirit in which you deliver service, is a strong determining factor in connection with both the price you receive and the duration of employment.

Andrew Carnegie stressed this point more than others in connection with his description of the factors which lead to success in the marketing of personal services. He emphasized again, and again, the necessity for harmonious conduct. He stressed the fact that he would not retain any man, no matter how great a quantity, or how efficient the quality of his work, *unless* he worked in a spirit of harmony. Mr. Carnegie insisted upon men being agreeable. To prove that he placed a high value upon this quality, he permitted many men *who conformed to his standards* to become very wealthy. Those who did not conform had to make room for others.

The importance of a pleasing personality has been stressed because it is a factor which enables one to render service in the proper spirit. If one has a personality which pleases, and renders service in a spirit of harmony, these assets often make up for deficiencies in both the quality and the quantity of service one renders. Nothing, however, can be successfully substituted for pleasing conduct.

THE CAPITAL VALUE OF YOUR SERVICES

The person whose income is derived entirely from the sale of personal services is no less a merchant than the man who sells commodities, and it might well be added, such a person is subject to exactly the same rules of conduct as the merchant who sells merchandise.

This has been emphasized because the majority of people who live by the sale of personal services make the mistake of considering themselves free from the rules of conduct, and the responsibilities attached to those who are engaged in marketing commodities.

The new way of marketing services has practically forced both employer and employee into partnership alliances, through which both take into consideration the rights of the third party, the public they serve.

The day of the "go-getter" has passed. He has been supplanted by the "go-giver." High-pressure methods in business finally blew the lid off. There will never be the need to put the lid back on, because, in the future, business will be conducted by methods that will require no pressure.

The actual capital value of your brains may be determined by the amount of income you can produce (by marketing your services). A fair estimate of the capital value of your services may be made by multiplying your annual income by sixteen and two-thirds, as it is reasonable to estimate that your annual income represents 6% of your capital value. Money rents for 6% per annum. Money is worth no more than brains. It is often worth much less.

Competent "brains," if effectively marketed, represent a much more desirable form of capital than that which is required to conduct a business dealing in commodities, because "brains" are a form of capital which cannot be permanently depreciated through depressions, nor can this form of capital be stolen or spent. Moreover, the money which is essential for the conduct of business is as worthless as a sand dune, until it has been mixed with efficient "brains."

THE THIRTY MAJOR CAUSES OF FAILURE

HOW MANY OF THESE ARE HOLDING YOU BACK?

Life's greatest tragedy consists of men and women who earnestly try, and fail! The tragedy lies in the overwhelmingly large majority of people who fail, as compared to the few who succeed.

I have had the privilege of analyzing several thousand men and women, 98% of whom were classed as "failures." There is something radically wrong with a civilization, and a system of education, which permit 98% of the people to go through life as failures. But I did not write this book for the purpose of moralizing on the rights and wrongs of the world; that would require a book a hundred times the size of this one.

My analysis work proved that there are thirty major reasons for failure, and thirteen major principles through which people accumulate fortunes. In this chapter, a description of the thirty major causes of failure will be given. As you go over the list, check yourself by it, point by point, for the purpose of discovering how many of these causes-of-failure stand between you and success.

1. Unfavorable hereditary background. There is but little, if anything, which can be done for people who are born with a deficiency in brain power. This philosophy offers but one method of bridging this weakness—through the aid of the Master Mind. Observe with profit, however, that this is the only one of the thirty causes of failure which may not be *easily corrected* by any individual.
2. Lack of a well-defined purpose in life. There is no hope of success for the person who does not have a central purpose, or *definite goal*, at which to aim. Ninety-eight out of every hundred of those whom I have analyzed had no such aim. Perhaps this was the major cause of their failure.
3. Lack of ambition to aim above mediocrity. We offer no hope for the person who is so indifferent as not to want to get ahead in life, and who is not willing to pay the price.
4. Insufficient education. This is a handicap which may be overcome with comparative ease. Experience has proven that the best-educated people are often those who are known as "self-made," or self-educated. It takes more than a

college degree to make one a person of education. Any person who is educated is one who has learned to get whatever he wants in life without violating the rights of others. Education consists not so much of knowledge, but of knowledge effectively and persistently applied. Men are paid not merely for what they know, but more particularly for what they do with that which they know.

5. Lack of self-discipline. Discipline comes through self-control. This means that one must control all negative qualities. Before you can control conditions, you must first control yourself. Self-mastery is the hardest job you will ever tackle. If you do not conquer self, you will be conquered by self. You may see at one and the same time both your best friend and your greatest enemy by stepping in front of a mirror.
6. Ill health. No person may enjoy outstanding success without good health. Many of the causes of ill health are subject to mastery and control. These, in the main are:
   a. Overeating of foods not conducive to health
   b. Wrong habits of thought; giving expression to negatives
   c. Wrong use of, and over indulgence in, sex
   d. Lack of proper physical exercise
   e. An inadequate supply of fresh air, due to improper breathing
7. Unfavorable environmental influences during childhood. "As the twig is bent, so shall the tree grow." Most people who have criminal tendencies acquire them as the result of bad environment, and improper associates during childhood.
8. Procrastination. This is one of the most common causes of failure. "Old Man Procrastination" stands within the shadow of every human being, waiting his opportunity to spoil one's chances of success. Most of us go through life as

failures, because we are waiting for the "time to be right" to start doing something worthwhile. Do not wait. The time will never be "just right." Start where you stand, and work with whatever tools you may have at your command, and better tools will be found as you go along.

9. Lack of persistence. Most of us are good "starters" but poor "finishers" of everything we begin. Moreover, people are prone to give up at the first signs of defeat. There is no substitute for persistence. The person who makes persistence his watch-word discovers that "Old Man Failure" finally becomes tired, and makes his departure. Failure cannot cope with persistence.
10. Negative personality. There is no hope of success for the person who repels people through a negative personality. Success comes through the application of power, and power is attained through the cooperative efforts of other people. A negative personality will not induce cooperation.
11. Lack of controlled sexual urge. Sex energy is the most powerful of all the stimuli which move people into action. Because it is the most powerful of the emotions, it must be controlled, through transmutation, and converted into other channels.
12. Uncontrolled desire for "something for nothing." The gambling instinct drives millions of people to failure. Evidence of this may be found in a study of the Wall Street crash of '29, during which millions of people tried to make money by gambling on stock margins.
13. Lack of a well-defined power of decision. Men who succeed reach decisions promptly, and change them, if at all, very slowly. Men who fail reach decisions, if at all, very slowly, and change them frequently, and quickly. Indecision and procrastination are twin brothers. Where one is found, the other

may usually be found also. Kill off this pair before they completely "hog-tie" you to the treadmill of failure.

14. One or more of the six basic fears. These fears have been analyzed for you in a later chapter. They must be mastered before you can market your services effectively.
15. Wrong selection of a mate in marriage. This a most common cause of failure. The relationship of marriage brings people intimately into contact. Unless this relationship is harmonious, failure is likely to follow. Moreover, it will be a form of failure that is marked by misery and unhappiness, destroying all signs of ambition.
16. Over-caution. The person who takes no chances generally has to take whatever is left when others are through choosing. Over-caution is as bad as under-caution. Both are extremes to be guarded against. Life itself is filled with the element of chance.
17. Wrong selection of associates in business. This is one of the most common causes of failure in business. In marketing personal services, one should use great care to select an employer who will be an inspiration, and who is, himself, intelligent and successful. We emulate those with whom we associate most closely. Pick an employer who is worth emulating.
18. Superstition and prejudice. Superstition is a form of fear. It is also a sign of ignorance. Men who succeed keep open minds and are afraid of nothing.
19. Wrong selection of a vocation. No man can succeed in a line of endeavor which he does not like. The most essential step in the marketing of personal services is that of selecting an occupation into which you can throw yourself wholeheartedly.

20. Lack of concentration of effort. The "jack-of-all-trades" seldom is good at any. Concentrate all of your efforts on one definite chief aim.
21. The habit of indiscriminate spending. The spend-thrift cannot succeed, mainly because he stands eternally in fear of poverty. Form the habit of systematic saving by putting aside a definite percentage of your income. Money in the bank gives one a very safe foundation of courage when bargaining for the sale of personal services. Without money, one must take what one is offered, and be glad to get it.
22. Lack of enthusiasm. Without enthusiasm one cannot be convincing. Moreover, enthusiasm is contagious, and the person who has it, under control, is generally welcome in any group of people.
23. Intolerance. The person with a "closed" mind on any subject seldom gets ahead. Intolerance means that one has stopped acquiring knowledge. The most damaging forms of intolerance are those connected with religious, racial, and political differences of opinion.
24. Intemperance. The most damaging forms of intemperance are connected with eating, strong drink, and sexual activities. Overindulgence in any of these is fatal to success.
25. Inability to cooperate with others. More people lose their positions and their big opportunities in life because of this fault than for all other reasons combined. It is a fault which no well-informed business man or leader will tolerate.
26. Possession of power that was not acquired through self effort. (Sons and daughters of wealthy men, and others who inherit money which they did not earn.) Power in the hands of one who did not acquire it gradually is often fatal to success. Quick riches are more dangerous than poverty.

27. Intention dishonesty. There is no substitute for honesty. One may be temporarily dishonest by force of circumstances over which one has no control, without permanent damage. But, there is no hope for the person who is dishonest by choice. Sooner or later, his deeds will catch up with him, and he will pay by loss of reputation, and perhaps even loss of liberty.
28. Egotism and vanity. These qualities serve as red lights which warn others to keep away. They are fatal to success.
29. Guessing instead of thinking. Most people are too indifferent or lazy to acquire facts with which to think accurately. They prefer to act on "opinions" created by guesswork or snap-judgments.
30. Lack of capital. This is a common cause of failure among those who start out in business for the first time, without sufficient reserve of capital to absorb the shock of their mistakes, and to carry them over until they have established a reputation.
31. Under this, name any particular cause of failure from which you have suffered that has not been included in the foregoing list.

In these thirty major causes of failure is found a description of the tragedy of life, which obtains for practically every person who tries and fails. It will be helpful if you can induce someone who knows you well to go over this list with you, and help to analyze you by the thirty causes of failure. It may be beneficial if you try this alone. Most people cannot see themselves as others see them. You may be one who cannot.

The oldest of admonitions is "Man, know thyself!" If you market merchandise successfully, you must know the merchandise. The same is true in marketing personal services. You should know all of your weaknesses in order that you may either bridge them or eliminate them entirely. You should know your strength in order that you may call attention to it when selling your services. You can know yourself only through *accurate* analysis.

The folly of ignorance in connection with self was displayed by a young man who applied to the manager of a well-known business for a position. He made a very good impression until the manager asked him what salary he expected. He replied that he had no fixed sum in mind *(lack of a definite aim).* The manager then said, "We will pay you all you are worth, after we try you out for a week."

"I will not accept it," the applicant replied, "because I am getting more than that where I am now employed."

Before you even start to negotiate for a readjustment of your salary in your present position, or to seek employment elsewhere, be sure that you are worth more than you now receive.

It is one thing to want money—everyone wants more—but it is something entirely different to be worth more! Many people mistake their wants for their just dues. Your financial requirements or wants have nothing whatever to do with your worth. Your value is established entirely by your ability to render useful service or your capacity to induce others to render such service.

TAKE INVENTORY OF YOURSELF

28 QUESTIONS YOU SHOULD ANSWER

Annual self-analysis is an essential in the effective marketing of personal services, as is annual inventory in merchandising. Moreover, the yearly analysis should disclose a decrease in faults, and an increase in virtues. One goes ahead, stands still, or goes backward in life. One's object should be, of course, to go ahead. Annual self-analysis will disclose whether advancement has been made, and if so, how much. It will also disclose any backward steps one may have made. The effective marketing of personal services requires one to move forward even if the progress is slow.

Your annual self-analysis should be made at the end of each year, so you can include in your New Year's Resolutions any improvements which the analysis indicates should be made. Take this inventory by asking yourself the following questions, and by checking your answers with the aid of someone who will not permit you to deceive yourself as to their accuracy.

Self-Analysis Questionnaire for Personal Inventory

1. Have I attained the goal which I established as my objective for this year? (You should work with a definite yearly objective to be attained as a part of your major life objective.)
2. Have I delivered service of the best possible quality of which I was capable, or could I have improved any part of this service?
3. Have I delivered service in the greatest possible quantity of which I was capable?
4. Has the spirit of my conduct been harmonious, and cooperative at all times?
5. Have I permitted the habit of procrastination to decrease my efficiency and if so, to what extent?
6. Have I improved my personality, and if so, in what ways?
7. Have I been persistent in following my plans through to completion?
8. Have I reached decisions promptly and definitely on all occasions?
9. Have I permitted any one or more of the six basic fears to decrease my efficiency?
10. Have I been either "over-cautious," or "under-cautious"?

11. Has my relationship with my associates in work been pleasant, or unpleasant? If it has been unpleasant, has the fault been partly, or wholly mine?
12. Have I dissipated any of my energy through lack of concentration of effort?
13. Have I been open-minded and tolerant in connection with all subjects?
14. In what way have I improved my ability to render service?
15. Have I been intemperate in any of my habits?
16. Have I expressed, either openly or secretly, any form of egotism?
17. Has my conduct toward my associates been such that it has induced them to respect me?
18. Have my opinions and decisions been based upon guesswork, or accuracy of analysis and thought?
19. Have I followed the habit of budgeting my time, my expenses, and my income, and have I been conservative in these budgets?
20. How much time have I devoted to unprofitable effort which I might have used to better advantage?
21. How may I re-budget my time, and change my habits so I will be more efficient during the coming year?
22. Have I been guilty of any conduct which was not approved by my conscience?
23. In what ways have I rendered more service and better service than I was paid to render?
24. Have I been unfair to anyone, and if so, in what way?
25. If I had been the purchaser of my own services for the year, would I be satisfied with my purchase?
26. Am I in the right vocation, and if not, why not?
27. Has the purchaser of my services been satisfied with the service I have rendered, and if not, why not?

28. What is my present rating on the fundamental principles of success? (Make this rating fairly, and frankly, and have it checked by someone who is courageous enough to do it accurately.)

Having read and assimilated the information conveyed through this chapter, you are now ready to create a practical plan for marketing your personal services. In this chapter will be found an adequate description of every principle essential in planning the sale of personal services, including the major attributes of leadership; the most common causes of failure in leadership; a description of the fields of opportunity for leadership; the main causes of failure in all walks of life, and the important questions which should be used in self-analysis.

This extensive and detailed presentation of accurate information has been included, because it will be needed by all who must begin the accumulation of riches by marketing personal services. Those who have lost their fortunes, and those who are just beginning to earn money, have nothing but personal services to offer in return for riches, therefore it is essential that they have available the practical information needed to market services to best advantage.

The information contained in this chapter will be of great value to all who aspire to attain leadership in any calling. It will be particularly helpful to those aiming to market their services as business or industrial executives.

Complete assimilation and understanding of the information here conveyed will be helpful in marketing one's own services, and it will also help one to become more analytical and capable of judging people. The information will be priceless to personnel directors, employment managers, and other executives charged with the selection of employees, and the maintenance of efficient organizations. If you doubt this statement, test its soundness by answering in writing the twenty-eight self-analysis questions. That might be both interesting and profitable, even though you do not doubt the soundness of the statement.

WHERE AND HOW ONE MAY FIND OPPORTUNITIES TO ACCUMULATE RICHES

Now that we have analyzed the principles by which riches may be accumulated, we naturally ask, "where may one find favorable opportunities to apply these principles?" Very well, let us take inventory and see what the United States of America offer the person seeking riches, great or small.

To begin with, let us remember, *all of us,* that we live in a country where *every law-abiding citizen enjoys freedom of thought and freedom of deed unequaled anywhere in the world.* Most of us have never taken inventory of the advantages of this freedom. We have never compared our unlimited freedom with the curtailed freedom in other countries.

Here we have freedom of thought, freedom in the choice and enjoyment of education, freedom in religion, freedom in politics, freedom in the choice of a business, profession or occupation, freedom to accumulate and own without molestation, *all the property we can accumulate,* freedom to choose our place of residence, freedom in marriage, freedom through equal opportunity to all races, freedom of travel from one state to another, freedom in our choice of foods, and freedom to *aim for any station in life for which we have prepared ourselves,* even for the presidency of the United States.

We have other forms of freedom, but this list will give a bird's eye view of the most important, which constitute opportunity of the highest order. This advantage of freedom is all the more conspicuous because the United States is the only country guaranteeing to every citizen, whether native born or naturalized, so broad and varied a list of freedoms.

Next, let us recount some of the blessings which our widespread freedom has placed within our hands. Take the average American family for example (meaning, the family of average income) and sum up the benefits available to every member of the family, in this land of opportunity and plenty!

a. Food. Next to freedom of thought and deed come food, clothing, and shelter, the three basic necessities of life.

Because of our universal freedom the average American family has available, at its very door, the choicest selection of food to be found anywhere in the world, and at prices within its financial range.

A family of two, living in the heart of Times Square district of New York City, far removed from the source of production of foods, took careful inventory of the cost of a simple breakfast, with this astonishing result:

ARTICLES OF FOOD;	COST AT THE BREAKFAST TABLE:
Grape Fruit Juice (From Florida)	02
Rippled Wheat Breakfast food (Kansas Farm)	02
Tea (From China)	02
Bananas (From South America)	02½
Toasted Bread (From Kansas Farm)	01
Fresh Country Eggs (From Utah)	07
Sugar (From Cuba, or Utah)	00½
Butter and Cream (From New England)	03
GRAND TOTAL	20

It is not very difficult to obtain food in a country where two people can have breakfast consisting of all they want or need for a dime apiece! Observe that this simple breakfast was gathered, by some strange form of magic (?) from China, South America, Utah, Kansas and the New England States, and delivered on the breakfast table, ready for consumption, in the very heart of the most crowded city in America, at a cost well within the means of the most humble laborer.

The cost included all federal, state and city taxes! (Here is a fact the politicians did not mention when they were crying out to the voters to throw their opponents out of office because the people were being taxed to death.)

b. Shelter. This family lives in a comfortable apartment, heated by steam, lighted with electricity, with gas for cooking, all for $65.00 a month. In a smaller city, or a more sparsely settled part of New York City, the same apartment could be had for as low as $20.00 a month.

The toast they had for breakfast in the food estimate was toasted on an electric toaster, which cost but a few dollars; the apartment is cleaned with a vacuum sweeper that is run by electricity. Hot and cold water is available, at all times, in the kitchen and the bathroom. The food is kept cool in a refrigerator that is run by electricity. The wife curls her hair, washes her clothes and irons them with easily operated electrical equipment, on power obtained by sticking a plug in the wall. The husband shaves with an electric shaver, and they receive entertainment from all over the world, twenty-four hours a day, if they want it, without cost, by merely turning the dial of their radio.

There are other conveniences in this apartment, but the foregoing list will give a fair idea of some of the concrete evidences of the freedom we, of America, enjoy. *(And this is neither political nor economic propaganda.)*

c. Clothing. Anywhere in the United States, the woman of average clothing requirements can dress very comfortably and neatly for less than $200.00 a year, and the average man can dress for the same, or less.

Only the three basic necessities of food, clothing, and shelter have been mentioned. The average American citizen has other privileges and advantages available in return for modest effort, not exceeding eight hours per day of labor. Among these is the privilege of automobile transportation, with which one can go and come at will, at very small cost.

The average American has security of property rights not found in any other country in the world. He can place his surplus money in a bank with the assurance that his government will protect it, and make good to him if the bank fails. If an American citizen wants to travel from one state to another he needs no passport, no one's permission. He may go when he pleases, and return at will. Moreover, he may travel by train, private automobile, bus, airplane, or ship, as his pocketbook permits. In Germany, Russia, Italy, and most of the other European and Oriental countries, the people cannot travel with so much freedom, and at so little cost.

THE "MIRACLE" THAT HAS PROVIDED THESE BLESSINGS

We often hear politicians proclaiming the freedom of America, when they solicit votes, but seldom do they take the time or devote sufficient effort to the analysis of the source or nature of this "freedom." Having no axe to grind, no grudge to express, no ulterior motives to be carried out, I have the privilege of going into a frank analysis of that mysterious, abstract, greatly misunderstood "something" which gives to every citizen of America more blessings, more opportunities to accumulate wealth, more freedom of every nature, than may be found in any other country.

I have the right to analyze the source and nature of this unseen power, because I know, and have known for more than a quarter of a century, many of the men who organized that power, and many who are now responsible for its maintenance.

The name of this mysterious benefactor of mankind is capital!

Capital consists not alone of money, but more particularly of highly organized, intelligent groups of men who plan ways and means of using money efficiently for the good of the public, and profitably to themselves.

These groups consist of scientists, educators, chemists, inventors, business analysts, publicity men, transportation experts, accountants, lawyers, doctors, and both men and women who have highly specialized knowledge in all fields of industry and business. They pioneer, experiment, and blaze trails in new fields of endeavor. They support colleges, hospitals, public schools, build good roads, publish newspapers, pay most of the cost of government, and take care of the multitudinous detail essential to human progress. Stated briefly, the capitalists are the brains of civilization, because they supply the entire fabric of which all education, enlightenment and human progress consists.

Money, without brains, always is dangerous. Properly used, it is the most important essential of civilization. The simple breakfast here described could not have been delivered to the New York family at a dime each, *or at any other price,* if organized capital had not provided the machinery, the ships, the railroads, and the huge armies of trained men to operate them.

Some slight idea of the importance of organized capital may be had by trying to imagine yourself burdened with the responsibility of collecting, without the aid of capital, and delivering to the New York City family, the simple breakfast described.

To supply the tea, you would have to make a trip to China or India, both a very long way from America. Unless you are an excellent swimmer, you would become rather tired before making the round trip. Then, too, another problem would confront you. What would you use for money, even if you had the physical endurance to swim the ocean?

To supply the sugar, you would have to take another long swim to Cuba, or a long walk to the sugar beet section of Utah. But even then, you might come back without the sugar, because organized effort and money are necessary to produce sugar, to say nothing of what is required to refine, transport, and deliver it to the breakfast table anywhere in the United States.

The eggs, you could deliver easily enough from the barn yards near New York City, but you would have a very long walk to Florida and return, before you could serve the two glasses of grapefruit juice.

You would have another long walk, to Kansas, or one of the other wheat growing states, when you went after the four slices of wheat bread.

The Rippled Wheat Biscuits would have to be omitted from the menu, because they would not be available except through the labor of a trained organization of men and suitable machinery, all of which call for capital.

While resting, you could take off for another little swim down to South America, where you would pick up a couple of bananas, and on your return, you could take a short walk to the nearest farm having a dairy and pick up some butter and cream. Then your New York City family would be ready to sit down and enjoy breakfast, and *you could collect your two dimes for your labor!*

Seems absurd, doesn't it? Well, the procedure described would be the only possible way these simple items of food could be delivered to the heart of New York City, if we had no capitalistic system.

The sum of money required for the building and maintenance of the railroads and steam ships used in the delivery of that simple breakfast is so huge that it staggers one's imagination. It runs into hundreds of millions of dollars, not to mention the armies of trained employees required to man the ships and trains. But, transportation is only a part of the requirements of modern civilization in capitalistic America. Before there can be anything to haul, something must be grown from the ground, or manufactured and prepared for market. This calls for more millions of dollars for equipment, machinery, boxing, marketing, and for the wages of millions of men and women.

Steam ships and railroads do not spring up from the earth and function automatically. They come in response to the call of civilization, through the labor and ingenuity and organizing ability of men who have imagination, faith, enthusiasm, decision, persistence! These men are known as capitalists. They are motivated by the desire to build, construct, achieve, render useful service, earn profits and accumulate riches. And, because they render service without which there would be no civilization, they put themselves in the way of great riches.

Just to keep the record simple and understandable, I will add that these capitalists are the selfsame men of whom most of us have heard soap-box orators speak. They are the same men to whom radicals, racketeers, dishonest politicians and grafting labor leaders refer as "the predatory interests," or "Wall Street."

I am not attempting to present a brief for or against any group of men or any system of economics. I am not attempting to condemn collective bargaining when I refer to "grafting labor leaders," nor do I aim to give a clean bill of health to all individuals known as capitalists.

The purpose of this book—*a purpose to which I have faithfully devoted over a quarter of a century*—is to present to all who want the knowledge, the most dependable philosophy through which individuals may accumulate riches in whatever amounts they desire.

I have here analyzed the economic advantages of the capitalistic system for the two-fold purpose of showing:

1. that all who seek riches must recognize and adapt themselves to the system that controls all approaches to fortunes, large or small, and
2. to present the side of the picture opposite to that being shown by politicians and demagogues who deliberately becloud the issues they bring up, by referring to organized capital as if it were something poisonous.

This is a capitalistic country, it was developed through the use of capital, and we who claim the right to partake of the blessings of freedom and opportunity, we who seek to accumulate riches here, may as well know that neither riches nor opportunity would be available to us if organized capital had not provided these benefits.

For more than twenty years it has been a somewhat popular and growing pastime for radicals, self-seeking politicians, racketeers, crooked labor leaders, and on occasion religious leaders, to take pot-shots at "Wall Street, the money changers, and big business."

The practice became so general that we witnessed during the business depression, the unbelievable sight of high government officials lining up with the cheap politicians, and labor leaders, with the openly avowed purpose of throttling the system which has made Industrial America the richest country on earth. The line-up was so general and so well organized that it prolonged the worst depression America has ever known. It cost millions of men their jobs, because those jobs were inseparably a part of the industrial and capitalistic system which form the very backbone of the nation.

During this unusual alliance of government officials and self-seeking individuals who were endeavoring to profit by declaring "open season" on the American system of industry, a certain type of labor leader joined forces with the politicians and offered to deliver voters in return for legislation designed to permit men to take riches away from industry by organized force of numbers, instead of the better method of giving a fair day's work for a fair day's pay.

Millions of men and women throughout the nation are still engaged in this popular pastime of trying to get without giving. Some of them are lined up with labor unions, where they demand shorter hours and more pay! Others do not take the trouble to work at all. They demand government relief and are getting it. Their idea of their rights of freedom was demonstrated in New York City, where violent complaint was registered with the Postmaster, by a group of "relief beneficiaries," because the Postmen awakened them at 7:30 a.m. to deliver Government relief checks. They demanded that the time of delivery be set up to 10:00 o'clock.

If you are one of those who believe that riches can be accumulated by the mere act of men who organize themselves into groups and demand more pay for less service, if you are one of those who demand Government relief without early morning disturbance when the money is delivered to you, if you are one of those who believe in trading their votes to politicians in return for the passing of laws which permit the raiding of the public treasury, you may rest securely on your belief, with certain knowledge that no one will disturb you, because this is a free country where every man may think as he pleases, where nearly everybody can live with but little effort, where many may live well without doing any work whatsoever.

However, you should know the full truth concerning this freedom of which so many people boast, and so few understand. As great as it is, as far as it reaches, as many privileges as it provides, it does not, and cannot bring riches without effort.

There is but one dependable method of accumulating, and legally holding riches, and that is by rendering useful service. No system has ever been created by which men can legally acquire riches through mere force of numbers, or without giving in return an equivalent value of one form or another.

There is a principle known as the law of economics! This is more than a theory. It is a law no man can beat.

Mark well the name of the principle, and remember it, because it is far more powerful than all the politicians and political machines. It is above and beyond the control of all the labor unions. It cannot be swayed, nor influenced nor bribed by racketeers or self-appointed leaders in any calling. Moreover, it has an all-seeing eye, and a perfect system of bookkeeping, in which it keeps an accurate account of the transactions of every human being engaged in the business of trying to get without giving. Sooner or later its auditors come around, look over the records of individuals both great and small, and demand an accounting.

"Wall Street, Big Business, Capital Predatory Interests," or whatever name you choose to give the system which has given us American Freedom, represents a group of men who understand, respect, and adapt themselves to this powerful law of economics! Their financial continuation depends upon their respecting the law.

Most people living in America like this country, its capitalistic system and all. I must confess I know of no better country, where one may find greater opportunities to accumulate riches. Judging by their acts and deeds, there are some in this country who do not like it. That, of course is their privilege; if they do not like this country, its capitalistic system, its boundless opportunities, *they have the privilege of clearing out!* Always there are other countries, such as Germany, Russia, and Italy, where one may try one's hand at enjoying freedom, and accumulating riches providing one is not too particular.

America provides all the freedom and all the opportunity to accumulate riches that any honest person may require. When one goes hunting for game, one selects hunting grounds where game is plentiful. When seeking riches, the same rule would naturally obtain.

If it is riches you are seeking, do not overlook the possibilities of a country whose citizens are so rich that women, alone, spend over two hundred million dollars annually for lip-sticks, rouge and cosmetics. Think twice, you who are seeking riches, before trying to destroy the Capitalistic System of a country whose citizens spend over fifty million dollars a year for greeting cards, with which to express their appreciation of their freedom!

If it is money you are seeking, consider carefully a country that spends hundreds of millions of dollars annually for cigarettes, the bulk of the income from which goes to only four major companies engaged in supplying this national builder of "nonchalance" and "quiet nerves."

By all means give plenty of consideration to a country whose people spend annually more than fifteen million dollars for the privilege of seeing moving pictures, and toss in a few additional millions for liquor, narcotics, and other less potent soft drinks and giggle-waters.

Do not be in too big a hurry to get away from a country whose people willingly, even eagerly, hand over millions of dollars annually for football, baseball, and prize fights.

And, by all means, stick by a country whose inhabitants give up more than a million dollars a year for chewing gum, and another million for safety razor blades.

Remember, also, that this is but the beginning of the available sources for the accumulation of wealth. Only a few of the luxuries and non-essentials have been mentioned. But, remember that the business of producing, transporting, and marketing these few items of merchandise gives regular employment to many millions of men and women, who receive for their services many millions of dollars monthly, and spend it freely for both the luxuries and the necessities.

Especially remember, that back of all this exchange of merchandise and personal services may be found an abundance of opportunity to accumulate riches. Here our American Freedom comes to one's aid. There is nothing to stop you, or anyone from engaging in any portion of the effort necessary to carry on these businesses. If one has superior talent, training, experience, one may accumulate riches in large amounts. Those not so fortunate may accumulate smaller amounts. Anyone may earn a living in return for a very nominal amount of labor.

So—there you are!

Opportunity has spread its wares before you. Step up to the front, select what you want, create your plan, put the plan into action, and follow through with persistence. "Capitalistic" America will do the rest. You can depend upon this much—capitalistic America insures every person the opportunity to render useful service, and to collect riches in proportion to the value of the service.

The "System" denies no one this right, but it does not, and cannot, promise something for nothing, because the system, itself, is irrevocably controlled by the law of economics which neither recognizes nor tolerates for long, getting without giving.

The law of economics was passed by Nature! There is no Supreme Court to which violators of this law may appeal. The law hands out both penalties for its violation, and appropriate rewards for its observance, *without interference or the possibility of interference by any human being.* The law cannot be repealed. It is as fixed as the stars in the heavens, and subject to, and a part of the same system that controls the stars.

May one refuse to adapt one's self to the law of economics?

Certainly! This is a free country, where all men are born with equal rights, including the privilege of ignoring the law of economics.

What happens then?

Well, nothing happens until large numbers of men join forces for the avowed purpose of ignoring the law, and taking what they want by force. *Then comes the dictator, with well-organized firing squads and machine guns!*

We have not yet reached that stage in America! But we have heard all we want to know about how the system works. Perhaps we shall be fortunate enough not to demand personal knowledge of so gruesome a reality. Doubtless we shall prefer to continue with our freedom of speech, freedom of deed and freedom to render useful service in return for riches.

The practice, by Government officials of extending to men and women the privilege of raiding the public treasury in return for votes, sometimes results in election, but as night follows day, the final payoff comes; when every penny wrongfully used must be repaid with compound interest on compound interest. If those who make the grab are not forced to repay, the burden falls on their children, and their children's children, "even unto the third and fourth generations." There is no way to avoid the debt.

Men can, and sometimes do, form themselves into groups for the purpose of crowding wages up, and working hours down. There is a point beyond which they cannot go. It is the point at which the law of economics steps in, and the sheriff gets both the employer and the employees.

For six years, from 1929 to 1935, the people of America, both rich and poor, barely missed seeing the Old Man Economics hand over to the sheriff all the businesses, and industries and banks. It was not a pretty sight! It did not increase our respect for mob psychology through which men cast reason to the winds and start trying to get without giving.

We who went through those six discouraging years, when fear was in the saddle, and faith was on the ground, cannot forget how ruthlessly the law of economics exacted its toll from both rich and poor, weak and strong, old and young. We shall not wish to go through another such experience.

These observations are not founded upon short-time experience. They are the result of twenty-five years of careful analysis of the methods of both the most successful and the most unsuccessful men America has known.

CHAPTER 8

DECISION

THE MASTERY OF PROCRASTINATION

The Seventh Step Toward Riches

Accurate analysis of over 25,000 men and women who had experienced failure disclosed the fact that lack of decision was near the head of the list of the thirty major causes of failure. This is no mere statement of a theory—it is a fact.

Procrastination, the opposite of decision, is a common enemy which practically every man must conquer.

You will have an opportunity to test your capacity to reach *quick* and *definite* decisions when you finish reading this book, and are ready to begin putting into action the principles which it describes.

Analysis of several hundred people who had accumulated fortunes well beyond the million dollar mark disclosed the fact that *every one of them* had the habit of reaching decisions promptly, and of changing these decisions slowly, if, and when they were changed. People who fail to accumulate money, *without exception,* have the habit of reaching decisions, if at all, very *slowly,* and *of changing these decisions quickly and often.*

One of Henry Ford's most outstanding qualities is his *habit* of reaching decisions quickly and definitely, and changing them slowly. This quality is so pronounced in

Mr. Ford, that it has given him the reputation of being obstinate. It was this quality which prompted Mr. Ford to continue to manufacture his famous Model "T" (the world's ugliest car), when all of his advisors, and many of the purchasers of the car, were urging him to change it.

Perhaps, Mr. Ford delayed too long in making the change, but the other side of the story is, that Mr. Ford's firmness of decision yielded a huge fortune, before the change in model became *necessary.* There is but little doubt that Mr. Ford's habit of definiteness of decision assumes the proportion of obstinacy, but this quality is preferable to slowness in reaching decisions and quickness in changing them.

The majority of people who fail to accumulate money sufficient for their needs, are, generally, easily influenced by the "opinions" of others. They permit the newspapers and the "gossiping" neighbors to do their "thinking" for them. "Opinions" are the cheapest commodities on earth. Everyone has a flock of opinions ready to be wished upon anyone who will accept them. If you are influenced by "opinions" when you reach decisions, you will not succeed in any undertaking, much less in that of transmuting your own desire into money.

If you are influenced by the opinions of others, you will have no desire of your own.

Keep your own counsel, when you begin to put into practice the principles described here, by *reaching your own decisions* and following them. Take no one into your confidence, except the members of your "Master Mind" group, and be very sure in your selection of this group, that you choose only those who will be in complete sympathy and harmony with your purpose.

Close friends and relatives, while not meaning to do so, often handicap one through "opinions" and sometimes through ridicule, which is meant to be humorous. Thousands of men and women carry inferiority complexes with them all through life, because some well-meaning, but ignorant person destroyed their confidence through "opinions" or ridicule.

You have a brain and mind of your own. Use it, and reach your own decisions. If you need facts or information from other people, to enable you to reach decisions, as you probably will in many instances; acquire these facts or secure the information you need quietly, without disclosing your purpose.

It is characteristic of people who have but a smattering or a veneer of knowledge to try to give the impression that they have much knowledge. Such people generally do too much talking, and too little listening. Keep your eyes and ears wide open—and your mouth closed, if you wish to acquire the habit of prompt decision. Those who talk too much do little else. If you talk more than you listen, you not only deprive yourself of many opportunities to accumulate useful knowledge, but you also disclose your plans and purposes to people who will take great delight in defeating you, because they envy you.

Remember, also, that every time you open your mouth in the presence of a person who has an abundance of knowledge, you display to that person, your exact stock of knowledge, or your lack of it! Genuine wisdom is usually conspicuous through *modesty and silence.*

Keep in mind the fact that every person with whom you associate is, like yourself, seeking the opportunity to accumulate money. If you talk about your plans too freely, you may be surprised when you learn that some other person has beaten you to your goal by putting into action ahead of you, the plans of which you talked unwisely.

Let one of your first decisions be to keep a closed mouth and open ears and eyes.

As a reminder to yourself to follow this advice, it will be helpful if you copy the following epigram in large letters and place it where you will see it daily.

"Tell the world what you intend to do, but first show it."

This is the equivalent of saying that "deeds, and not words, are what count most."

FREEDOM OR DEATH ON A DECISION

The value of decisions depends upon the courage required to render them. The great decisions, which served as the foundation of civilization, were reached by assuming great risks, which often meant the possibility of death.

Lincoln's decision to issue his famous Proclamation of Emancipation, which gave freedom to the colored people of America, was rendered with full understanding that his act would turn thousands of friends and political supporters against him. He knew, too, that the carrying out of that proclamation would mean death to thousands of men on the battlefield. In the end, it cost Lincoln his life. That required courage.

Socrates' decision to drink the cup of poison, rather than compromise in his personal belief, was a decision of courage. It turned Time ahead a thousand years, and gave to people then unborn, the right to freedom of thought and of speech.

The decision of Gen. Robert E. Lee, when he came to the parting of the way with the Union, and took up the cause of the South, was a decision of courage, for he well knew that it might cost him his own life, that it would surely cost the lives of others.

But, the greatest decision of all time, as far as any American citizen is concerned, was reached in Philadelphia, July 4, 1776, when fifty-six men signed their names to a document, which they well knew would bring freedom to all Americans, or *leave every one of the fifty-six hanging from a gallows!*

You have heard of this famous document, but you may not have drawn from it the great lesson in personal achievement it so plainly taught.

We all remember the date of this momentous decision, but few of us realize what courage that decision required. We remember our history, as it was taught; we remember dates, and the names of the men who fought; we remember Valley Forge, and Yorktown; we remember George Washington, and Lord Cornwallis. But we know little of the real forces back of these names, dates, and places. We know still less of that intangible power, which insured us freedom *long before Washington's armies reached Yorktown.*

We read the history of the Revolution, and falsely imagine that George Washington was the Father of our Country, that it was he who won our freedom, while the truth is—Washington was only an accessory after the fact, because victory for his armies had been insured long before Lord Cornwallis surrendered. This is not intended to rob Washington of any of the glory he so richly merited. Its purpose, rather, is to give greater attention to the astounding power that was the real cause of his victory.

It is nothing short of tragedy that the writers of history have missed, entirely, even the slightest reference to the irresistible power, which gave birth and freedom to the nation destined to set up new standards of independence for all the peoples of the earth. I say it is a tragedy, because it is the selfsame power which must be used by every individual who surmounts the difficulties of Life, and forces Life to pay the price asked.

Let us briefly review the events which gave birth to this power. The story begins with an incident in Boston, March 5, 1770. British soldiers were patroling the streets, by their presence, openly threatening the citizens. The colonists resented armed men marching in their midst. They began to express their resentment openly, hurling stones as well as epithets, at the marching soldiers, until the commanding officer gave orders, "Fix bayonets. . . . Charge!"

The battle was on. It resulted in the death and injury of many. The incident aroused such resentment that the Provincial Assembly (made up of prominent colonists) called a meeting for the purpose of taking definite action. Two of the members of that Assembly were John Hancock, and Samuel Adams—long live their names! They spoke up courageously, and declared that a move must be made to eject all British soldiers from Boston.

Remember this—a decision, in the minds of two men, might properly be called the beginning of the freedom which we of the United States now enjoy. Remember, too, that the decision of these two men called for faith, and courage, because it was dangerous.

Before the Assembly adjourned, Samuel Adams was appointed to call on the Governor of the Province, Hutchinson, and demand the withdrawal of the British troops.

The request was granted, the troops were removed from Boston, but the incident was not closed. It had caused a situation destined to change the entire trend of civilization. Strange, is it not, how the great changes, such as the American Revolution, and the world war, often have their beginnings in circumstances which seem unimportant? It is interesting, also, to observe that these important changes usually begin in the form of a definite decision in the minds of a relatively small number of people. Few of us know the history of our country well enough to realize that John Hancock, Samuel Adams, and Richard Henry Lee (of the Province of Virginia) were the real Fathers of our Country.

Richard Henry Lee became an important factor in this story by reason of the fact that he and Samuel Adams communicated frequently (by correspondence), sharing freely their fears and their hopes concerning the welfare of the people of their Provinces. From this practice, Adams conceived the idea that a mutual exchange of letters between the thirteen Colonies might help to bring about the coordination of effort so badly needed in connection with the solution of their problems. Two years after the clash with the soldiers in Boston (March '72), Adams presented this idea to the Assembly, in the form of a motion that a Correspondence Committee be established among the Colonies, with definitely appointed correspondents in each Colony, "for the purpose of friendly cooperation for the betterment of the Colonies of British America."

Mark well this incident! It was the beginning of the organization of the far-flung power destined to give freedom to you, and to me. The Master Mind had already been organized. It consisted of Adams, Lee, and Hancock. "I tell you further, that if two of you agree upon the earth concerning anything for which you ask, it will come to you from My Father, who is in Heaven."

The Committee of Correspondence was organized. Observe that this move provided the way for increasing the power of the Master Mind by adding to it men from all the Colonies. Take notice that this procedure constituted the first organized planning of the disgruntled Colonists.

In union there is strength! The citizens of the Colonies had been waging disorganized warfare against the British soldiers, through incidents similar to the Boston riot, but nothing of benefit had been accomplished. Their individual grievances had not been consolidated under one Master Mind. No group of individuals had put their hearts, minds, souls, and bodies together in one definite decision to settle their difficulty with the British once and for all, until Adams, Hancock, and Lee got together.

Meanwhile, the British were not idle. They, too, were doing some planning and "Master-Minding" on their own account, with the advantage of having back of them money, and organized soldiery.

The Crown appointed Gage to supplant Hutchinson as the Governor of Massachusetts. One of the new Governor's first acts was to send a messenger to call on Samuel Adams, for the purpose of endeavoring to stop his opposition—by fear.

We can best understand the spirit of what happened by quoting the conversation between Col. Fenton (the messenger sent by Gage) and Adams.

Col. Fenton: "I have been authorized by Governor Gage, to assure you, Mr. Adams, that the Governor has been empowered to confer upon you such benefits as would be satisfactory [endeavor to win Adams by promise of bribes] upon the condition that you engage to cease in your opposition to the measures of the government. It is the Governor's advice to you, Sir, not to incur the further displeasure of his majesty. Your conduct has been such as makes you liable to penalties of an Act of Henry VIII, by which persons can be sent to England for trial for treason, or misprision of treason, at the discretion of a governor of a province. But, by changing your political course, you will not only receive great personal advantages, but you will make your peace with the King."

Samuel Adams had the choice of two decisions. He could cease his opposition, and receive personal bribes, or he could continue, and run the risk of being hanged!

Clearly, the time had come when Adams was *forced* to reach *instantly,* a decision which could have cost his life. The majority of men would have found it difficult to reach such a decision. The majority would have sent back an evasive reply, but not Adams! He insisted upon Col. Fenton's word of honor, that the Colonel would deliver to the Governor the answer exactly as Adams would give it to him.

Adams' answer, "Then you may tell Governor Gage that I trust I have long since made my peace with the King of Kings. No personal consideration shall induce me to abandon the righteous cause of my Country. And, tell Governor Gage it is the advice of Samuel Adams to him, no longer to insult the feelings of an exasperated people."

Comment as to the character of this man seems unnecessary. It must be obvious to all who read this astounding message that its sender possessed loyalty of the highest order. *This is important.* (Racketeers and dishonest politicians have prostituted the honor for which such men as Adams died.)

When Governor Gage received Adams' caustic reply, he flew into a rage, and issued a proclamation which read, "I do, hereby, in his majesty's name, offer and promise his most gracious pardon to all persons who shall forthwith lay down their arms, and return to the duties of peaceable subjects, excepting only from the benefit of such pardon, Samuel Adams and John Hancock, whose offences are of too flagitious a nature to admit of any other consideration but that of condign punishment."

As one might say, in modern slang, Adams and Hancock were "on the spot!" The threat of the irate Governor forced the two men to reach another decision, equally as dangerous. They hurriedly called a secret meeting of their staunchest followers. (Here the Master Mind began to take on momentum.) After the meeting had been called to order, Adams locked the door, placed the key in his pocket, and informed all present that it was imperative that a Congress of the Colonists be organized, and that no man should leave the room until the decision for such a congress had been reached.

Great excitement followed. Some weighed the possible consequences of such radicalism (Old Man Fear). Some expressed grave doubt as to the wisdom of so *definite a decision* in defiance of the Crown. Locked in that room were two men immune to Fear, blind to the possibility of Failure. Hancock and Adams. Through the influence of their minds, the others were induced to agree that, through the Correspondence Committee, arrangements should be made for a meeting of the First Continental Congress, to be held in Philadelphia, September 5, 1774.

Remember this date. It is more important than July 4, 1776. If there had been no DECISION to hold a Continental Congress, there could have been no signing of the Declaration of Independence.

Before the first meeting of the new Congress, another leader, in a different section of the country was deep in the throes of publishing a "Summary View of the Rights of British America." He was Thomas Jefferson, of the Province of Virginia, whose relationship to Lord Dunmore (representative of the Crown in Virginia) was as strained as that of Hancock and Adams with their Governor.

Shortly after his famous Summary of Rights was published, Jefferson was informed that he was subject to prosecution for high treason against his majesty's government. Inspired by the threat, one of Jefferson's colleagues, Patrick Henry, boldly spoke his mind, concluding his remarks with a sentence which shall remain forever a classic, *"If this be treason, then make the most of it."*

It was such men as these who, without power, without authority, without military strength, without money, sat in solemn consideration of the destiny of the colonies, beginning at the opening of the First Continental Congress, and continuing at intervals for two years—until on June 7, 1776, Richard Henry Lee arose, addressed the Chair, and to the startled Assembly made this motion:

"Gentlemen, I make the motion that these United Colonies are, and of right ought to be free and independent states, that they be absolved from all allegiance to the British Crown, and that all political connection between them and the state of Great Britain is, and ought to be totally dissolved."

Lee's astounding motion was discussed fervently, and at such length that he began to lose patience. Finally, after days of argument, he again took the floor, and declared, in a clear, firm voice, "Mr. President, we have discussed this issue for days. It is the only course for us to follow. Why, then Sir, do we longer delay? Why still deliberate? Let this happy day give birth to an American Republic. Let her arise, not to devastate and to conquer, but to reestablish the reign of peace, and of law. The eyes of Europe are fixed upon us. She demands of us a living example of freedom, that may exhibit a contrast, in the felicity of the citizen, to the ever increasing tyranny."

Before his motion was finally voted upon, Lee was called back to Virginia, because of serious family illness, but before leaving, he placed his cause in the hands of his friend, Thomas Jefferson, who promised to fight until favorable action was taken. Shortly thereafter, the President of the Congress (Hancock) appointed Jefferson as Chairman of a Committee to draw up a Declaration of Independence.

Long and hard the Committee labored, on a document which would mean, when accepted by the Congress, that every man who signed it, would be signing his own death warrant, should the Colonies lose in the fight with Great Britain, which was sure to follow.

The document was drawn, and on June 28, the original draft was read before the

Congress. For several days it was discussed, altered, and made ready. On July 4, 1776, Thomas Jefferson stood before the Assembly, and fearlessly read the most momentous decision ever placed upon paper.

"When in the course of human events it is necessary for one people to dissolve the political bands which have connected them with another, and to assume, among the powers of the earth, the separate and equal station to which the laws of Nature, and of Nature's God entitle them, a decent respect to the opinions of mankind requires that they should declare the causes which impel them to the separation. . . ."

When Jefferson finished, the document was voted upon, accepted, and signed by the fifty-six men, every one staking his own life upon his decision to write his name. By that decision came into existence a nation destined to bring to mankind forever, the privilege of making decisions.

By decisions made in a similar spirit of Faith, and only by such decisions, can men solve their personal problems, and win for themselves high estates of material and spiritual wealth. Let us not forget this!

Analyze the events which led to the Declaration of Independence, and be convinced that this nation, which now holds a position of commanding respect and power among all nations of the world, was born of a decision created by a Master Mind, consisting of fifty-six men. Note well, the fact that it was their decision which insured the success of Washington's armies, because the *spirit* of that decision was in the heart of every soldier who fought with him, and served as a spiritual power which recognizes no such thing as failure.

Note, also (with great personal benefit) that the power which gave this nation its freedom, is the self-same power that must be used by every individual who becomes self-determining. This power is made up of the principles described in this book. It will not be difficult to detect, in the story of the Declaration of Independence, at least six of these principles: desire, decision, faith, persistence, the Master Mind, and organized planning.

Throughout this philosophy will be found the suggestion that thought, backed by strong desire, has a tendency to transmute itself into its physical equivalent. Before passing on, I wish to leave with you the suggestion that one may find in this story, and in the story of the organization of the United States Steel Corporation, a perfect description of the method by which thought makes this astounding transformation.

In your search for the secret of the method, do not look for a miracle, because you will not find it. You will find only the eternal laws of Nature. These laws are available to every person who has the faith and the courage to use them. They may be used to bring freedom to a nation, or to accumulate riches. There is no charge save the time necessary to understand and appropriate them.

Those who reach decisions promptly and definitely know what they want, and generally get it. The leaders in every walk of life decide quickly, and firmly. That is the major reason why they are leaders. The world has the habit of making room for the man whose words and actions show that he knows where he is going.

Indecision is a habit which usually begins in youth. The habit takes on permanency as the youth goes through graded school, high school, and even through college, without definiteness of purpose. The major weakness of all educational systems is that they neither teach nor encourage the habit of definite decision.

It would be beneficial if no college would permit the enrollment of any student, unless and until the student declared his major purpose in matriculating. It would be of still greater benefit, if every student who enters the graded schools were compelled to accept training in the habit of decision, and forced to pass a satisfactory examination on this subject before being permitted to advance in the grades.

The habit of indecision acquired because of the deficiencies of our school systems, goes with the student into the occupation he chooses . . . if . . . in fact, he chooses his occupation. Generally, the youth just out of school seeks any job that can be found. He takes the first place he finds, because he has fallen into the habit of indecision. Ninety-eight out of every hundred people working for wages today are in the positions they hold, because they lacked the definiteness of decision to plan a definite position, and the knowledge of how to choose an employer.

Definiteness of decision always requires courage, sometimes very great courage. The fifty-six men who signed the Declaration of Independence staked their lives on the decision to affix their signatures to that document. The person who reaches a definite decision to procure the particular job, and make life pay the price he asks, does not stake his life on that decision; he stakes his economic freedom. Financial independence, riches, desirable business and professional positions are not within reach of the person who neglects or refuses to expect, plan, and demand these things. The person who desires riches in the same spirit that Samuel Adams desired freedom for the Colonies, is sure to accumulate wealth.

In the chapter on Organized Planning, you will find complete instructions for marketing every type of personal services. You will find also detailed information on how to choose the employer you prefer, and the particular job you desire. These instructions will be of no value to you unless you definitely decide to organize them into a plan of action.

CHAPTER 9

PERSISTENCE

THE SUSTAINED EFFORT NECESSARY TO INDUCE FAITH

The Eighth Step Toward Riches

Persistence is an essential factor in the procedure of transmuting desire into its monetary equivalent. The basis of persistence is the power of will.

Will-power and desire, when properly combined, make an irresistible pair. Men who accumulate great fortunes are generally known as cold-blooded, and sometimes ruthless. Often they are misunderstood. What they have is will-power, which they mix with persistence, and place back of their desires to *insure* the attainment of their objectives.

Henry Ford has been generally misunderstood to be ruthless and cold-blooded. This misconception grew out of Ford's habit of following through in all of his plans with persistence.

The majority of people are ready to throw their aims and purposes overboard, and give up at the first sign of opposition or misfortune. A few carry on despite all opposition, until they attain their goal. These few are the Fords, Carnegies, Rockefellers, and Edisons.

There may be no heroic connotation to the word "persistence," but the quality is to the character of man what carbon is to steel.

The building of a fortune, generally, involves the application of the entire thirteen factors of this philosophy. These principles must be understood; they must be applied with persistence by all who accumulate money.

If you are following this book with the intention of applying the knowledge it conveys, your first test as to your persistence will come when you begin to follow the six steps described in the second chapter. Unless you are one of the two out of every hundred who already have a definite goal at which you are aiming, and a definite plan for its attainment, you may read the instructions, and then pass on with your daily routine, and never comply with those instructions.

The author is checking you up at this point, because lack of persistence is one of the major causes of failure. Moreover, experience with thousands of people has proved that lack of persistence is a weakness common to the majority of men. It is a weakness which may be overcome by effort. The ease with which lack of persistence may be conquered will depend *entirely* upon the intensity of one's desire.

The starting point of all achievement is desire. Keep this constantly in mind. Weak desires bring weak results, just as a small amount of fire makes a small amount of heat. If you find yourself lacking in persistence, this weakness may be remedied by building a stronger fire under your desires.

Continue to read through to the end, then go back to chapter two, and start *immediately* to carry out the instructions given in connection with the six steps. The eagerness with which you follow these instructions will indicate clearly, how much, or how little you really desire to accumulate money. If you find that you are indifferent, you may be sure that you have not yet acquired the "money consciousness" which you must possess, before you can be sure of accumulating a fortune.

Fortunes gravitate to men whose minds have been prepared to "attract" them, just as surely as water gravitates to the ocean. In this book may be found all the stimuli necessary to "attune" any normal mind to the vibrations which will attract the object of one's desires.

If you find you are weak in persistence, center your attention upon the instructions contained in the chapter on "Power"; surround yourself with a "Master Mind" group, and through the cooperative efforts of the members of this group, you can develop persistence. You will find additional instructions for the development of persistence in the chapters on auto-suggestion, and the subconscious mind. Follow the instructions outlined in these chapters until your habit nature hands over to your subconscious mind, a clear picture of the object of your desire. From that point on, you will not be handicapped by lack of persistence.

Your subconscious mind works continuously, while you are awake, and while you are asleep.

Spasmodic, or occasional effort to apply the rules will be of no value to you. To get results, you must apply all of the rules until their application becomes a fixed habit with you. In no other way can you develop the necessary "money consciousness."

Poverty is attracted to the one whose mind is favorable to it, as money is attracted to him whose mind has been deliberately prepared to attract it, and through the same laws. Poverty consciousness will voluntarily seize the mind which is not occupied with the money consciousness. A poverty consciousness develops without *conscious* application of habits favorable to it. The money consciousness must be created to order, unless one is born with such a consciousness.

Catch the full significance of the statements in the preceding paragraph, and you will understand the importance of persistence in the accumulation of a fortune. Without persistence, you will be defeated, even before you start. With persistence you will win.

If you have ever experienced a nightmare, you will realize the value of persistence. You are lying in bed, half awake, with a feeling that you are about to smother. You are unable to turn over, or to move a muscle. You realize that you must begin to regain control over your muscles. Through persistent effort of will-power, you finally manage to move the fingers of one hand. By continuing to move your fingers, you extend your control to the muscles of one arm, until you can lift it. Then you gain control of the other arm in the same manner. You finally gain control over the muscles of one leg, and then extend it to the other leg. Then—with one supreme effort of will—you regain complete control over your muscular system, and "snap" out of your nightmare. The trick has been turned step by step.

You may find it necessary to "snap" out of your mental inertia, through a similar procedure, moving slowly at first, then increasing your speed, until you gain complete control over your will. Be persistent no matter how slowly you may, at first, have to move. With persistence will come success.

If you select your "Master Mind" group with care, you will have in it, at least one person who will aid you in the development of persistence. Some men who have accumulated great fortunes, did so because of necessity. They developed the habit of persistence, because they were so closely driven by circumstances, that they *had to become persistent.*

There is no substitute for persistence! It cannot be supplanted by any other quality! Remember this, and it will hearten you, in the beginning, when the going may seem difficult and slow.

Those who have cultivated the habit of persistence seem to enjoy insurance against failure. No matter how many times they are defeated, they finally arrive up toward the top of the ladder. Sometimes it appears that there is a hidden Guide whose duty is to test men through all sorts of discouraging experiences. Those who pick themselves up after defeat and keep on trying, arrive; and the world cries, "Bravo! I knew you could do it!" The hidden Guide lets no one enjoy great achievement without passing the persistence test. Those who can't take it, simply do not make the grade.

Those who can "take it" are bountifully rewarded for their persistence. They receive, as their compensation, whatever goal they are pursuing. That is not all! They receive something infinitely more important than material compensation—the knowledge that "every failure brings with it the seed of an equivalent advantage."

There are exceptions to this rule; a few people know from experience the soundness of persistence. They are the ones who have not accepted defeat as being anything more than temporary. They are the ones whose desires are so persistently applied that defeat is finally changed into victory. We who stand on the side-lines of Life see the overwhelmingly large number who go down in defeat, never to rise again. We see the few who take the punishment of defeat *as an urge to greater effort.* These, fortunately, never learn to accept Life's reverse gear. But what we do not see, what most of us never suspect of existing, is the silent but irresistible power which comes to the rescue of those who fight on in the face of discouragement. If we speak of this power at all we call it persistence, and let it go at that. One thing we all know, if one does not possess persistence, one does not achieve noteworthy success in any calling.

As these lines are being written, I look up from my work, and see before me, less than a block away, the great mysterious "Broadway," the "Graveyard of Dead Hopes," and the "Front Porch of Opportunity." From all over the world people have come to Broadway, seeking fame, fortune, power, love, or whatever it is that human beings call success. Once in a great while someone steps out from the long procession of seekers, and the world hears that another person has mastered Broadway. But Broadway is not easily nor quickly conquered. She acknowledges talent, recognizes genius, pays off in money, only *after* one has refused to quit.

Then we know he has discovered the secret of how to conquer Broadway. The secret is always inseparably attached to one word, persistence!

The secret is told in the struggle of Fannie Hurst, whose persistence conquered the Great White Way. She came to New York in 1915, to convert writing into riches. The conversion did not come quickly, but it came. For four years Miss Hurst learned about

"The Sidewalks of New York" from first hand experience. She spent her days laboring, and her nights hoping. When hope grew dim, she did not say, "All right Broadway, you win!" She said, "Very well, Broadway, you may whip some, but not me. I'm going to force you to give up."

One publisher *(The Saturday Evening Post)* sent her *thirty-six* rejection slips, before she "broke the ice" and got a story across. The average writer, like the "average" in other walks of life, would have given up the job when the first rejection slip came. She pounded the pavements for four years to the tune of the publisher's "no," because she was determined to win.

Then came the "payoff." The spell had been broken, the unseen Guide had tested Fannie Hurst, and she could take it. From that time on publishers made a beaten path to her door. Money came so fast she hardly had time to count it. Then the moving picture men discovered her, and money came not in small change, but in floods. The moving picture rights to her latest novel, *Great Laughter,* brought $100,000.00, said to be the highest price ever paid for a story before publication. Her royalties from the sale of the book probably will run much more.

Briefly, you have a description of what persistence is capable of achieving. Fannie Hurst is no exception. Wherever men and women accumulate great riches, you may be sure they first acquired persistence. Broadway will give any beggar a cup of coffee and a sandwich, but it demands persistence of those who go after the big stakes.

Kate Smith will say "amen" when she reads this. For years she sang, without money, and without price, before any microphone she could reach. Broadway said to her, "Come and get it, if you can take it." She did take it until one happy day Broadway got tired and said, "Aw, what's the use? You don't know when you're whipped, so name your price, and go to work in earnest." Miss Smith named her price! It was plenty. Away up in figures so high that one week's salary is far more than most people make in a whole year.

Verily it pays to be persistent!

And here is an encouraging statement which carries with it a suggestion of great significance—thousands of singers who excel Kate Smith are walking up and down Broadway looking for a "break"—without success. Countless others have come and gone; many of them sang well enough, but they failed to make the grade because they lacked the courage to keep on keeping on, until Broadway became tired of turning them away.

Persistence is a state of mind, therefore it can be cultivated. Like all states of mind, persistence is based upon definite causes, among them these:—

a. Definiteness of purpose. Knowing what one wants is the first and, perhaps, the most important step toward the development of persistence. A strong motive forces one to surmount many difficulties.
b. Desire. It is comparatively easy to acquire and to maintain persistence in pursuing the object of intense desire.
c. Self-reliance. Belief in one's ability to carry out a plan encourages one to follow the plan through with persistence. (Self-reliance can be developed through the principle described in the chapter on auto-suggestion.)
d. Definiteness of plans. Organized plans, even though they may be weak and entirely impractical, encourage persistence.
e. Accurate knowledge. Knowing that one's plans are sound, based upon experience or observation, encourages persistence; "guessing" instead of "knowing" destroys persistence.
f. Co-operation. Sympathy, understanding, and harmonious cooperation with others tend to develop persistence.
g. Will-power. The habit of concentrating one's thoughts upon the building of plans for the attainment of a definite purpose, leads to persistence.

h. Habit. Persistence is the direct result of habit. The mind absorbs and becomes a part of the daily experiences upon which it feeds. Fear, the worst of all enemies, can be effectively cured *by forced repetition of acts of courage.* Everyone who has seen active service in war knows this.

Before leaving the subject of persistence, take inventory of yourself, and determine in what particular, if any, you are lacking in this essential quality. Measure yourself courageously, point by point, and see how many of the eight factors of persistence you lack. The analysis may lead to discoveries that will give you a new grip on yourself.

SYMPTOMS OF LACK OF PERSISTENCE

Here you will find the real enemies which stand between you and noteworthy achievement. Here you will find not only the "symptoms" indicating weakness of persistence, but also the deeply seated subconscious causes of this weakness. Study the list carefully, and face yourself squarely if you really wish to know who you are, and what you are capable of doing. These are the weaknesses which must be mastered by all who accumulate riches.

1. Failure to recognize and to clearly define exactly what one wants.
2. Procrastination, with or without cause. (Usually backed up with a formidable array of alibis and excuses.)
3. Lack of interest in acquiring specialized knowledge.
4. Indecision, the habit of "passing the buck" on all occasions, instead of facing issues squarely. (Also backed by alibis.)
5. The habit of relying upon alibis instead of creating definite plans for the solution of problems.

6. Self-satisfaction. There is but little remedy for this affliction, and no hope for those who suffer from it.
7. Indifference, usually reflected in one's readiness to compromise on all occasions, rather than meet opposition and fight it.
8. The habit of blaming others for one's mistakes, and accepting unfavorable circumstances as being unavoidable.
9. Weakness of desire, due to neglect in the choice of motives that impel action.
10. Willingness, even eagerness, to quit at the first sign of defeat. (Based upon one or more of the six basic fears.)
11. Lack of organized plans, placed in writing where they may be analyzed.
12. The habit of neglecting to move on ideas, or to grasp opportunity when it presents itself.
13. Wishing instead of willing.
14. The habit of compromising with poverty instead of aiming at riches. General absence of ambition to *be,* to *do,* and to *own.*
15. Searching for all the short-cuts to riches, trying to get without giving a fair equivalent, usually reflected in the habit of gambling, endeavoring to drive "sharp" bargains.
16. Fear of criticism, failure to create plans and to put them into action, because of what other people will think, do, or say. This enemy belongs at the head of the list, because it generally exists in one's subconscious mind, where its presence is not recognized. (See the Six Basic Fears in a later chapter.)

Let us examine some of the symptoms of the Fear of Criticism. The majority of people permit relatives, friends, and the public at large to so influence them that they cannot live their own lives, because they fear criticism.

Huge numbers of people make mistakes in marriage, stand by the bargain, and go through life miserable and unhappy, because they fear criticism which may follow if they correct the mistake. (Anyone who has submitted to this form of fear knows the irreparable damage it does, by destroying ambition, self-reliance, and the desire to achieve.)

Millions of people neglect to acquire belated educations, after having left school, because they fear criticism.

Countless numbers of men and women, both young and old, permit relatives to wreck their lives in the name of duty, because they fear criticism. (Duty does not require any person to submit to the destruction of his personal ambitions and the right to live his own life in his own way.)

People refuse to take chances in business, because they fear the criticism which may follow if they fail. *The fear of criticism in such cases is stronger than the desire for success.*

Too many people refuse to set high goals for themselves, or even neglect selecting a career, because they fear the criticism of relatives and "friends" who may say "Don't aim so high, people will think you are crazy."

When Andrew Carnegie suggested that I devote twenty years to the organization of a philosophy of individual achievement my first impulse of thought was fear of what people might say. The suggestion set up a goal for me, far out of proportion to any I had ever conceived. As quick as a flash, my mind began to create alibis and excuses, all of them traceable to the inherent fear of criticism. Something inside of me said, "You can't do it—the job is too big, and requires too much time—what will your relatives think of you?—how will you earn a living?—no one has ever organized a philosophy of success, what right have you to believe you can do it?—who are you, anyway, to aim so high?—remember your humble birth—what do you know about philosophy—people will think you are crazy—(and they did)—why hasn't some other person done this before now?"

These, and many other questions flashed into my mind, and demanded attention. It seemed as if the whole world had suddenly turned its attention to me with the purpose of ridiculing me into giving up all desire to carry out Mr. Carnegie's suggestion.

I had a fine opportunity, then and there, to kill off ambition before it gained control of me. Later in life, after having analyzed thousands of people, I discovered that most ideas are stillborn, and need the breath of life injected into them through definite plans of immediate action. The time to nurse an idea is at the time of its birth. Every minute it lives gives it a better chance of surviving. The fear of criticism is at the bottom of the destruction of most ideas which never reach the planning and action stage.

Many people believe that material success is the result of favorable "breaks." There is an element of ground for the belief, but those depending entirely upon luck are nearly always disappointed, because they overlook another important factor which must be present before one can be sure of success. It is the knowledge with which favorable "breaks" can be made to order.

During the depression, W. C. Fields, the comedian, lost all his money, and found himself without income, without a job, and his means of earning a living (vaudeville) no longer existed. Moreover, he was past sixty, when many men consider themselves "old." He was so eager to stage a comeback that he offered to work without pay, in a new field (movies). In addition to his other troubles, he fell and injured his neck. To many that would have been the place to give up and quit. But Fields was persistent. He knew that if he carried on he would get the "breaks" sooner or later, and he did get them, but not by chance.

Marie Dressler found herself down and out, with her money gone, with no job, when she was about sixty. She, too, went after the "breaks," and got them. Her persistence brought an astounding triumph late in life, long beyond the age when most men and women are done with ambition to achieve.

Eddie Cantor lost his money in the 1929 stock crash, but he still had his persistence and his courage. With these, plus two prominent eyes, he exploited himself back into an income of $10,000 a week! Verily, if one has persistence, one can get along very well without many other qualities.

The only "break" anyone can afford to rely upon is a self-made "break." These come through the application of persistence. The starting point is definiteness of purpose.

Examine the first hundred people you meet, ask them what they want most in life, and ninety-eight of them will not be able to tell you. If you press them for an answer, some will say—security, many will say—money, a few will say—happiness, others will say—fame and power, and still others will say—social recognition, ease in living, ability to sing, dance, or write, but none of them will be able to define these terms, or give the slightest indication of a plan by which they hope to attain these vaguely expressed wishes. Riches do not respond to wishes. They respond only to definite plans, backed by definite desires, through constant persistence.

HOW TO DEVELOP PERSISTENCE

There are four simple steps which lead to the habit of persistence. They call for no great amount of intelligence, no particular amount of education, and but little time or effort. The necessary steps are:—

1. A definite purpose backed by burning desire for its fulfillment.
2. A definite plan, expressed in continuous action.
3. A mind closed tightly against all negative and discouraging influences, including negative suggestions of relatives, friends and acquaintances.
4. A friendly alliance with one or more persons who will encourage one to follow through with both plan and purpose.

These four steps are essential for success in all walks of life. The entire purpose of the thirteen principles of this philosophy is to enable one to take these four steps as a matter of *habit*.

These are the steps by which one may control one's economic destiny.
They are the steps that lead to freedom and independence of thought.
They are the steps that lead to riches, in small or great quantities.
They lead the way to power, fame, and worldly recognition.
They are the four steps which guarantee favorable "breaks."
They are the steps that convert dreams into physical realities.
They lead, also, to the mastery of fear, discouragement, indifference.

There is a magnificent reward for all who learn to take these four steps. It is the privilege of writing one's own ticket, and of making Life yield whatever price is asked.

I have no way of knowing the facts, but I venture to conjecture that Mrs. Wallis Simpson's great love for a man was not accidental, nor the result of favorable "breaks" alone. There was a burning desire, and careful searching at every step of the way. Her first duty was to love. What is the greatest thing on earth? The Master called it love—not man made rules, criticism, bitterness, slander, or political "marriages," but love.

She knew what she wanted, not after she met the Prince of Wales, but long before that. Twice when she had failed to find it, she had the courage to continue her search. "To thine own self be true, and it must follow, as the night the day, thou canst not then be false to any man."

Her rise from obscurity was of the slow, progressive, persistent order, but it was sure! She triumphed over unbelievably long odds; and, no matter who you are, or what you may think of Wallis Simpson, or the king who gave up his Crown for her love, she is an astounding example of applied persistence, an instructor on the rules of self-determination, from whom the entire world might profitably take lessons.

When you think of Wallis Simpson, think of one who knew what she wanted, and shook the greatest empire on earth to get it. Women who complain that this is a man's world, that women do not have an equal chance to win, owe it to themselves to study carefully the life of this unusual woman, who, at an age which most women consider "old," captured the affections of the most desirable bachelor in the entire world.

And what of King Edward? What lesson may we learn from his part in the world's greatest drama of recent times? Did he pay too high a price for the affections of the woman of his choice?

Surely no one but he can give the correct answer.

The rest of us can only conjecture. This much we know, the king came into the world without his own consent. He was born to great riches, without requesting them. He was persistently sought in marriage; politicians and statesmen throughout Europe tossed dowagers and princesses at his feet. Because he was the first born of his parents, he inherited a crown, which he did not seek, and perhaps did not desire. For more than forty years he was not a free agent, could not live his life in his own way, had but little privacy, and finally assumed duties inflicted upon him when he ascended the throne.

Some will say, "With all these blessings, King Edward should have found peace of mind, contentment, and joy of living."

The truth is that back of all the privileges of a crown, all the money, the fame, and the power inherited by King Edward, there was an emptiness which could be filled only by love.

His greatest desire was for love. Long before he met Wallis Simpson, he doubtless felt this great universal emotion tugging at the strings of his heart, beating upon the door of his soul, and crying out for expression.

And when he met a kindred spirit, crying out for this same Holy privilege of expression, he recognized it, and without fear or apology, opened his heart and bade it enter. All the scandalmongers in the world cannot destroy the beauty of this international drama, through which two people found love, and had the courage to face open criticism, renounce all else to give it *holy* expression.

King Edward's decision to give up the Crown of the world's most powerful empire, for the privilege of going the remainder of the way through life with the woman of his choice, was a decision that required courage. The decision also had a price, but who has the right to say the price was too great? Surely not He who said, "He among you who is without sin, let him cast the first stone."

As a suggestion to any evil-minded person who chooses to find fault with the Duke of Windsor, because his desire was for love, and for openly declaring his love for Wallis Simpson, and giving up his throne for her, let it be remembered that the open declaration was not essential. He could have followed the custom of clandestine liaison which has prevailed in Europe for centuries, without giving up either his throne, or the woman of his choice, and there would have been no complaint from either church or laity. But this unusual man was built of sterner stuff. His love was clean. It was deep and sincere. It represented the one thing which above all else he truly desired, therefore, he took what he wanted, and paid the price demanded.

If Europe had been blessed with more rulers with the human heart and the traits of honesty of ex-king Edward, for the past century, that unfortunate hemisphere now seething with greed, hate, lust, political connivance, and threats of war, would have a different and a better story to tell. A story in which Love and not Hate would rule.

In the words of Stuart Austin Wier we raise our cup and drink this toast to ex-king Edward and Wallis Simpson:

"Blessed is the man who has come to know that our muted thoughts are our sweetest thoughts.

"Blessed is the man who, from the blackest depths, can see the luminous figure of love, and seeing, sing; and singing, say: 'Sweeter far than uttered lays are the thoughts I have of you.'"

In these words would we pay tribute to the two people who, more than all others of modern times, have been the victims of criticism and the recipients of abuse, because they found Life's greatest treasure, and claimed it.*

Most of the world will applaud the Duke of Windsor and Wallis Simpson, because of their persistence in searching until they found life's greatest reward. All of us can profit by following their example in our own search for that which we demand of life.

What mystical power gives to men of persistence the capacity to master difficulties? Does the quality of persistence set up in one's mind some form of spiritual, mental or chemical activity which gives one access to supernatural forces? Does Infinite Intelligence throw *itself* on the side of the person who still fights on, after the battle has been lost, with the whole world on the opposing side?

These and many other similar questions have arisen in my mind as I have observed men like Henry Ford, who started at scratch, and built an Industrial Empire of huge proportions, with little else in the way of a beginning but persistence. Or, Thomas A. Edison, who, with less than three months of schooling, became the world's leading inventor and

* Mrs. Simpson read and approved this analysis.

converted persistence into the talking machine, the moving picture machine, and the incandescent light, to say nothing of half a hundred other useful inventions.

I had the happy privilege of analyzing both Mr. Edison and Mr. Ford, year by year, over a long period of years, and therefore, the opportunity to study them at close range, so I speak from actual knowledge when I say that I found no quality save persistence, in either of them, that even remotely suggested the major source of their stupendous achievements.

As one makes an impartial study of the prophets, philosophers, "miracle" men, and religious leaders of the past, one is drawn to the inevitable conclusion that persistence, concentration of effort, and definiteness of purpose, were the major sources of their achievements.

Consider, for example, the strange and fascinating story of Mohammed; analyze his life, compare him with men of achievement in this modern age of industry and finance, and observe how they have one outstanding trait in common, persistence!

If you are keenly interested in studying the strange power which gives potency to persistence, read a biography of Mohammed, especially the one by Essad Bey. This brief review of that book, by Thomas Sugrue, in the *Herald-Tribune,* will provide a preview of the rare treat in store for those who take the time to read the entire story of one of the most astounding examples of the power of persistence known to civilization.

THE LAST GREAT PROPHET

REVIEWED BY THOMAS SUGRUE

"Mohammed was a prophet, but he never performed a miracle. He was not a mystic; he had no formal schooling; he did not begin his mission until he was forty. When he announced that he was the Messenger of God, bringing word of the true religion, he was ridiculed and labeled a lunatic. Children tripped him and women threw filth upon him.

He was banished from his native city, Mecca, and his followers were stripped of their worldly goods and sent into the desert after him. When he had been preaching ten years he had nothing to show for it but banishment, poverty and ridicule. Yet before another ten years had passed, he was dictator of all Arabia, ruler of Mecca, and the head of a New World religion which was to sweep to the Danube and the Pyrenees before exhausting the impetus he gave it. That impetus was three-fold: the power of words, the efficacy of prayer and man's kinship with God.

"His career never made sense. Mohammed was born to impoverished members of a leading family of Mecca. Because Mecca, the crossroads of the world, home of the magic stone called the Caaba, great city of trade and the center of trade routes, was unsanitary, its children were sent to be raised in the desert by Bedouins. Mohammed was thus nurtured, drawing strength and health from the milk of nomad, vicarious mothers. He tended sheep and soon hired out to a rich widow as leader of her caravans. He traveled to all parts of the Eastern World, talked with many men of diverse beliefs and observed the decline of Christianity into warring sects. When he was twenty-eight, Khadija, the widow, looked upon him with favor, and married him. Her father would have objected to such a marriage, so she got him drunk and held him up while he gave the paternal blessing. For the next twelve years Mohammed lived as a rich and respected and very shrewd trader. Then he took to wandering in the desert, and one day he returned with the first verse of the Koran and told Khadija that the archangel Gabriel had appeared to him and said that he was to be the Messenger of God.

"The Koran, the revealed word of God, was the closest thing to a miracle in Mohammed's life. He had not been a poet; he had no gift of words. Yet the verses of the Koran, as he received them and recited them to the faithful, were better than any verses which the professional poets of the tribes could produce. This, to the Arabs, was a miracle. To them the gift of words was the greatest gift, the poet was all-powerful. In addition the

Koran said that all men were equal before God, that the world should be a democratic state Islam. It was this political heresy, plus Mohammed's desire to destroy all the 360 idols in the courtyard of the Caaba, which brought about his banishment. The idols brought the desert tribes to Mecca, and that meant trade. So the business men of Mecca, the capitalists, of which he had been one, set upon Mohammed. Then he retreated to the desert and demanded sovereignty over the world.

"The rise of Islam began. Out of the desert came a flame which would not be extinguished—a democratic army fighting as a unit and prepared to die without wincing. Mohammed had invited the Jews and Christians to join him; for he was not building a new religion. He was calling all who believed in one God to join in a single faith. If the Jews and Christians had accepted his invitation Islam would have conquered the world. They didn't. They would not even accept Mohammed's innovation of humane warfare. When the armies of the prophet entered Jerusalem not a single person was killed because of his faith. When the crusaders entered the city, centuries later, not a Moslem man, woman, or child was spared. But the Christians did accept one Moslem idea—the place of learning, the university."

CHAPTER 10

POWER OF THE MASTER MIND

THE DRIVING FORCE

The Ninth Step Toward Riches

Power is essential for success in the accumulation of money. Plans are inert and useless, without sufficient power to translate them into action. This chapter will describe the method by which an individual may attain and apply power.

Power may be defined as "organized and intelligently directed knowledge." Power, as the term is here used, refers to organized effort, sufficient to enable an individual to transmute desire into its monetary equivalent. Organized effort is produced through the coordination of effort of two or more people, who work toward a definite end, in a spirit of harmony.

Power is required for the accumulation of money! Power is necessary for the retention of money after it has been accumulated!

Let us ascertain how power may be acquired. If power is "organized knowledge," let us examine the sources of knowledge:

a. Infinite Intelligence. This source of knowledge may be contacted through the procedure described in another chapter, with the aid of Creative Imagination.

b. Accumulated experience. The accumulated experience of man (or that portion of it which has been organized and recorded) may be found in any well-equipped public library. An important part of this accumulated experience is taught in public schools and colleges, where it has been classified and organized.
c. Experiment and research. In the field of science, and in practically every other walk of life, men are gathering, classifying, and organizing new facts daily. This is the source to which one must turn when knowledge is not available through "accumulated experience." Here, too, the Creative Imagination must often be used.

Knowledge may be acquired from any of the foregoing sources. It may be converted into power by organizing it into definite plans and by expressing those plans in terms of action.

Examination of the three major sources of knowledge will readily disclose the difficulty an individual would have, if he depended upon his efforts alone, in assembling knowledge and expressing it through definite plans in terms of action. If his plans are comprehensive, and if they contemplate large proportions, he must, generally, induce others to cooperate with him, before he can inject into them the necessary element of power.

GAINING POWER THROUGH THE "MASTER MIND"

The "Master Mind" may be defined as: "Coordination of knowledge and effort, in a spirit of harmony, between two or more people, for the attainment of a definite purpose."

No individual may have great power without availing himself of the "Master Mind." In a preceding chapter, instructions were given for the creation of plans for the purpose of translating desire into its monetary equivalent. If you carry out these instructions with persistence and intelligence, and use discrimination in the selection of your "Master Mind" group, your objective will have been halfway reached, even before you begin to recognize it.

So you may better understand the "intangible" potentialities of power available to you, through a properly chosen "Master Mind" group, we will here explain the two characteristics of the Master Mind principle, one of which is economic in nature, and the other psychic. The economic feature is obvious. Economic advantages may be created by any person who surrounds himself with the advice, counsel, and personal cooperation of a group of men who are willing to lend him wholehearted aid, in a spirit of perfect harmony. This form of cooperative alliance has been the basis of nearly every great fortune. Your understanding of this great truth may definitely determine your financial status.

The psychic phase of the Master Mind principle is much more abstract, much more difficult to comprehend, because it has reference to the spiritual forces with which the human race, as a whole, is not well acquainted. You may catch a significant suggestion from this statement: "No two minds ever come together without, thereby, creating a third, invisible, intangible force which may be likened to a third mind."

Keep in mind the fact that there are only two known elements in the whole universe, energy and matter. It is a well-known fact that matter may be broken down into units of molecules, atoms, and electrons. There are units of matter which may be isolated, separated, and analyzed.

Likewise, there are units of energy.

The human mind is a form of energy, a part of it being spiritual in nature. When the minds of two people are coordinated in a spirit of harmony, the spiritual units of energy of each mind form an affinity, which constitutes the "psychic" phase of the Master Mind.

The Master Mind principle, or rather the economic feature of it, was first called to my attention by Andrew Carnegie, over twenty-five years ago. Discovery of this principle was responsible for the choice of my life's work.

Mr. Carnegie's Master Mind group consisted of a staff of approximately fifty men, with whom he surrounded himself, for the definite purpose of manufacturing and marketing steel. He attributed his entire fortune to the power he accumulated through this "Master Mind."

Analyze the record of any man who has accumulated a great fortune, and many of those who have accumulated modest fortunes, and you will find that they have either consciously, or unconsciously employed the "Master Mind" principle.

Great power can be accumulated through no other principle!

Energy is Nature's universal set of building blocks, out of which she constructs every material thing in the universe, including man, and every form of animal and vegetable life. Through a process which only Nature completely understands, she translates energy into matter.

Nature's building blocks are available to man, in the energy involved in thinking! Man's brain may be compared to an electric battery. It absorbs energy from the ether, which permeates every atom of matter, and fills the entire universe.

It is a well-known fact that a group of electric batteries will provide more energy than a single battery. It is also a well-known fact that an individual battery will provide energy in proportion to the number and capacity of the cells it contains.

The brain functions in a similar fashion. This accounts for the fact that some brains are more efficient than others, and leads to this significant statement—a group of brains coordinated (or connected) in a spirit of harmony will provide more thought-energy than a single brain, just as a group of electric batteries will provide more energy than a single battery.

Through this metaphor it becomes immediately obvious that the Master Mind principle holds the secret of the power wielded by men who surround themselves with other men of brains.

There follows, now, another statement which will lead still nearer to an understanding of the psychic phase of the Master Mind principle: When a group of individual brains are coordinated and function in harmony, the increased energy created through that alliance becomes available to every individual brain in the group.

It is a well-known fact that Henry Ford began his business career under the handicap of poverty, illiteracy, and ignorance. It is an equally well-known fact that, within the inconceivably short period of ten years, Mr. Ford mastered these three handicaps, and that within twenty-five years he made himself one of the richest men in America. Connect with this fact, the additional knowledge that Mr. Ford's most rapid strides became noticeable, from the time he became a personal friend of Thomas A. Edison, and you will begin to understand what the influence of one mind upon another can accomplish. Go a step further, and consider the fact that Mr. Ford's most outstanding achievements began from the time that he formed the acquaintances of Harvey Firestone, John Burroughs, and Luther Burbank (each a man of great brain capacity) and you will have further evidence that power may be produced through friendly alliance of minds.

There is little if any doubt that Henry Ford is one of the best-informed men in the business and industrial world. The question of his wealth needs no discussion. Analyze Mr. Ford's intimate personal friends, some of whom have already been mentioned, and you will be prepared to understand the following statement:—

"Men take on the nature and the habits and the power of thought of those with whom they associate in a spirit of sympathy and harmony."

Henry Ford whipped poverty, illiteracy, and ignorance by allying himself with great minds, whose vibrations of thought he absorbed into his own mind. Through his association with Edison, Burbank, Burroughs, and Firestone, Mr. Ford added to his own brain power, the sum and substance of the intelligence, experience, knowledge, and spiritual forces of these four men. Moreover, he appropriated, and made use of the Master Mind principle through the methods of procedure described in this book.

This principle is available to you!

We have already mentioned Mahatma Gandhi. Perhaps the majority of those who have heard of Gandhi look upon him as merely an eccentric little man, who goes around without formal wearing apparel, and makes trouble for the British Government.

In reality, Gandhi is not eccentric, but he is the most powerful man now living. (Estimated by the number of his followers and their faith in their leader.) Moreover, he is probably the most powerful man who has ever lived. His power is passive, but it is real.

Let us study the method by which he attained his stupendous power. It may be explained in a few words. He came by power through inducing over two hundred million people to coordinate, with mind and body, in a spirit of harmony, for a definite purpose.

In brief, Gandhi has accomplished a miracle, for it is a miracle when two hundred million people can be induced—not forced—to cooperate in a spirit of harmony, for a limitless time. If you doubt that this is a miracle, try to induce any two people to cooperate in a spirit of harmony for *any length of time.*

Every man who manages a business knows what a difficult matter it is to get employees to work together in a spirit even remotely resembling harmony.

The list of the chief sources from which power may be attained is, as you have seen, headed by Infinite Intelligence. When two or more people coordinate in a spirit of harmony, and work toward a definite objective, they place themselves in position, through that alliance, to absorb power directly from the great universal storehouse of Infinite Intelligence. This is the greatest of all sources of power. It is the source to which the genius turns. It is the source to which every great leader turns (whether he may be conscious of the fact or not).

The other two major sources from which the knowledge, necessary for the accumulation of power, may be obtained are no more reliable than the five senses of man. The senses are not always reliable. Infinite Intelligence does not err.

In subsequent chapters, the methods by which Infinite Intelligence may be most readily contacted will be adequately described.

This is not a course on religion. No fundamental principle described in this book should be interpreted as being intended to interfere either directly, or indirectly, with any man's religious habits. This book has been confined, exclusively, to instructing the reader how to transmute the definite purpose of desire for money, into its monetary equivalent.

Read, *think,* and meditate as you read. Soon, the entire subject will unfold, and you will see it in perspective. You are now seeing the detail of the individual chapters.

Money is as shy and elusive as the "old time" maiden. It must be wooed and won by methods not unlike those used by a determined lover, in pursuit of the girl of his choice. And, coincidental as it is, the power used in the "wooing" of money is not greatly different from that used in wooing a maiden. That power, when successfully used in the pursuit of money must be mixed with faith. It must be mixed with desire. It must be mixed with persistence. It must be applied through a plan, and that plan must be set into action.

When money comes in quantities known as "the big money," it flows to the one who accumulates it, as easily as water flows downhill. There exists a great unseen stream of power, which may be compared to a river; except that one side flows in one direction, carrying all who get into that side of the stream, onward and upward to wealth—and the other side flows in the opposite direction, carrying all who are unfortunate enough to get into it (and not able to extricate themselves from it), downward to misery and poverty.

Every man who has accumulated a great fortune has recognized the existence of this stream of life. It consists of one's thinking process. The positive emotions of thought form the side of the stream which carries one to fortune. The negative emotions form the side which carries one down to poverty.

This carries a thought of stupendous importance to the person who is following this book with the object of accumulating a fortune.

If you are in the side of the stream of power which leads to poverty, this may serve as an oar, by which you may propel yourself over into the other side of the stream. It can serve you only through application and use. Merely reading, and passing judgment on it, either one way or another, will in no way benefit you.

Some people undergo the experience of alternating between the positive and negative sides of the stream, being at times on the positive side, and at times on the negative side. The Wall Street crash of '29 swept millions of people from the positive to the negative side of the stream. These millions are struggling, some of them in desperation and fear, to get back to the positive side of the stream. This book was written especially for those millions.

Poverty and riches often change places. The Crash taught the world this truth, although the world will not long remember the lesson. Poverty may, and generally does, voluntarily take the place of riches. When riches take the place of poverty, the change is usually brought about through well-conceived and carefully executed PLANS. Poverty needs no plan. It needs no one to aid it, because it is bold and ruthless. Riches are shy and timid. They have to be "attracted."

Anybody can wish for riches, and most people do, but only a few know that a definite plan, plus a burning desire for wealth, are the only dependable means of accumulating wealth.

CHAPTER 11

THE MYSTERY OF SEX TRANSMUTATION

The Tenth Step Toward Riches

The meaning of the word "transmute" is, in simple language, "the changing, or transferring of one element, or form of energy, into another."

The emotion of sex brings into being a state of mind.

Because of ignorance on the subject, this state of mind is generally associated with the physical, and because of improper influences, to which most people have been subjected, in acquiring knowledge of sex, things essentially physical have highly biased the mind.

The emotion of sex has back of it the possibility of three constructive potentialities, they are:—

1. The perpetuation of mankind.
2. The maintenance of health (as a therapeutic agency, it has no equal).
3. The transformation of mediocrity into genius through transmutation.

Sex transmutation is simple and easily explained. It means the switching of the mind from thoughts of physical expression, to thoughts of some other nature.

Sex desire is the most powerful of human desires. When driven by this desire, men develop keenness of imagination, courage, will-power, persistence, and creative ability unknown to them at other times. So strong and impelling is the desire for sexual contact that men freely run the risk of life and reputation to indulge it. When harnessed, and redirected along other lines, this motivating force maintains all of its attributes of keenness of imagination, courage, etc., which may be used as powerful creative forces in literature, art, or in any other profession or calling, including, of course, the accumulation of riches.

The transmutation of sex energy calls for the exercise of will-power, to be sure, but the reward is worth the effort. The desire for sexual expression is inborn and natural. The desire cannot, and should not be submerged or eliminated. But it should be given an outlet through forms of expression which enrich the body, mind, and spirit of man. If not given this form of outlet, through transmutation, it will seek outlets through purely physical channels.

A river may be dammed, and its water controlled for a time, but eventually, it will force an outlet. The same is true of the emotion of sex. It may be submerged and controlled for a time, but its very nature causes it to be ever seeking means of expression. If it is not transmuted into some creative effort it will find a less worthy outlet.

Fortunate, indeed, is the person who has discovered how to give sex emotion an outlet through some form of creative effort, for he has, by that discovery, lifted himself to the status of a genius.

Scientific research has disclosed these significant facts:

1. The men of greatest achievement are men with highly developed sex natures; men who have learned the art of sex transmutation.
2. The men who have accumulated great fortunes and achieved outstanding recognition in literature, art, industry, architecture, and the professions, were motivated by the influence of a woman.

The research from which these astounding discoveries were made went back through the pages of biography and history for more than two thousand years. Wherever there was evidence available in connection with the lives of men and women of great achievement, it indicated most convincingly that they possessed highly developed sex natures.

The emotion of sex is an "irresistible force," against which there can be no such opposition as an "immovable body," When driven by this emotion, men become gifted with a super power for action. Understand this truth, and you will catch the significance of the statement that sex transmutation will lift one to the status of a genius.

The emotion of sex contains the secret of creative ability.

Destroy the sex glands, whether in man or beast, and you have removed the major source of action. For proof of this, observe what happens to any animal after it has been castrated. A bull becomes as docile as a cow after it has been altered sexually. Sex alteration takes out of the male, whether man or beast, all the fight that was in him. Sex alteration of the female has the same effect.

THE TEN MIND STIMULI

The human mind responds to stimuli, through which it may be "keyed up" to high rates of vibration, known as enthusiasm, creative imagination, intense desire, etc. The stimuli to which the mind responds most freely are:—

1. The desire for sex expression
2. Love
3. A burning desire for fame, power, or financial gain, money
4. Music
5. Friendship between either those of the same sex, or those of the opposite sex

6. A Master Mind alliance based upon the harmony of two or more people who ally themselves for spiritual or temporal advancement
7. Mutual suffering, such as that experienced by people who are persecuted
8. Auto-suggestion
9. Fear
10. Narcotics and alcohol

The desire for sex expression comes at the head of the list of stimuli, which most effectively "step-up" the vibrations of the mind and start the "wheels" of physical action. Eight of these stimuli are natural and constructive. Two are destructive. The list is here presented for the purpose of enabling you to make a comparative study of the major sources of mind stimulation. From this study, it will be readily seen that the emotion of sex is, by great odds, the most intense and powerful of all mind stimuli.

This comparison is necessary as a foundation for proof of the statement that transmutation of sex energy may lift one to the status of a genius. Let us find out what constitutes a genius.

Some wiseacre has said that a genius is a man who "wears long hair, eats queer food, lives alone, and serves as a target for the joke makers." A better definition of a genius is "a man who has discovered how to increase the vibrations of thought to the point where he can freely communicate with sources of knowledge not available through the ordinary rate of vibration of thought."

The person who thinks will want to ask some questions concerning this definition of genius. The first question will be, "How may one communicate with sources of knowledge which are not available through the ordinary rate of vibration of thought?"

The next question will be, "Are there known sources of knowledge which are available only to genii, and if so, what are these sources, and exactly how may they be reached?"

We shall offer proof of the soundness of some of the more important statements made in this book—or at least we shall offer evidence through which you may secure your own proof through experimentation, and in doing so, we shall answer both of these questions.

"GENIUS" IS DEVELOPED THROUGH THE SIXTH SENSE

The reality of a "sixth sense" has been fairly well established. This sixth sense is "Creative Imagination." The faculty of creative imagination is one which the majority of people never use during an entire lifetime, and if used at all, it usually happens by mere accident. A relatively small number of people use, with deliberation and purpose aforethought, the faculty of creative imagination. Those who use this faculty voluntarily, and with understanding of its functions, are genii.

The faculty of creative imagination is the direct link between the finite mind of man and Infinite Intelligence. All so-called revelations, referred to in the realm of religion, and all discoveries of basic or new principles in the field of invention take place through the faculty of creative imagination.

When ideas or concepts flash into one's mind, through what is popularly called a "hunch," they come from one or more of the following sources:—

1. Infinite Intelligence
2. One's subconscious mind, wherein is stored every sense impression and thought impulse which ever reached the brain through any of the five senses

3. From the mind of some other person who has just released the thought, or picture of the idea or concept, through conscious thought, or
4. From the other person's subconscious storehouse.

There are no other known sources from which "inspired" ideas or "hunches" may be received.

The creative imagination functions best when the mind is vibrating (due to some form of mind stimulation) at an exceedingly high rate. That is, when the mind is functioning at a rate of vibration higher than that of ordinary, normal thought.

When brain action has been stimulated, through one or more of the ten mind stimulants, it has the effect of lifting the individual far above the horizon of ordinary thought, and permits him to envision distance, scope, and quality of thoughts not available on the lower plane, such as that occupied while one is engaged in the solution of the problems of business and professional routine.

When lifted to this higher level of thought, through any form of mind stimulation, an individual occupies, relatively, the same position as one who has ascended in an airplane to a height from which he may see over and beyond the horizon line which limits his vision, while on the ground. Moreover, while on this higher level of thought, the individual is not hampered or bound by any of the stimuli which circumscribe and limit his vision while wrestling with the problems of gaining the three basic necessities of food, clothing, and shelter. He is in a world of thought in which the ordinary, work-a-day thoughts have been as effectively removed as are the hills and valleys and other limitations of physical vision, when he rises in an airplane.

While on this exalted plane of thought, the creative faculty of the mind is given freedom for action. The way has been cleared for the sixth sense to function; it becomes receptive to ideas which could not reach the individual under any other circumstances. The "sixth sense" is the faculty which marks the difference between a genius and an ordinary individual.

The creative faculty becomes more alert and receptive to vibrations, originating outside the individual's subconscious mind, the more this faculty is used, and the more the individual relies upon it, and makes demands upon it for thought impulses. This faculty can be cultivated and developed only through use.

That which is known as one's "conscience" operates entirely through the faculty of the sixth sense.

The great artists, writers, musicians, and poets become great, because they acquire the habit of relying upon the "still small voice" which speaks from within, through the faculty of creative imagination. It is a fact well known to people who have "keen" imaginations that their best ideas come through so-called "hunches."

There is a great orator who does not attain to greatness, until he closes his eyes and begins to rely entirely upon the faculty of Creative Imagination. When asked why he closed his eyes just before the climaxes of his oratory, he replied, "I do it, because, then I speak through ideas which come to me from within."

One of America's most successful and best-known financiers followed the habit of closing his eyes for two or three minutes before making a decision. When asked why he did this, he replied, "With my eyes closed, I am able to draw upon a source of superior intelligence."

The late Dr. Elmer R. Gates, of Chevy Chase, Maryland, created more than two hundred useful patents, many of them basic, through the process of cultivating and using the creative faculty. His method is both significant and interesting to one interested in attaining to the status of genius, in which category Dr. Gates, unquestionably belonged. Dr. Gates was one of the really great, though less publicized scientists of the world.

In his laboratory, he had what he called his "personal communication room." It was practically sound proof, and so arranged that all light could be shut out. It was equipped with a small table, on which he kept a pad of writing paper. In front of the table, on the wall, was an electric pushbutton, which controlled the lights. When Dr. Gates desired to draw upon the forces available to him through his Creative Imagination, he would go into this room, seat himself at the table, shut off the lights, and concentrate upon the known factors of the invention on which he was working, remaining in that position until ideas began to "flash" into his mind in connection with the unknown factors of the invention.

On one occasion, ideas came through so fast that he was forced to write for almost three hours. When the thoughts stopped flowing, and he examined his notes, he found they contained a minute description of principles which had not a parallel among the known data of the scientific world. Moreover, the answer to his problem was intelligently presented in those notes. In this manner Dr. Gates completed over two hundred patents, which had been begun, but not completed, by "half-baked" brains. Evidence of the truth of this statement is in the United States Patent Office.

Dr. Gates earned his living by "sitting for ideas" for individuals and corporations. Some of the largest corporations in America paid him substantial fees, by the hour, for "sitting for ideas."

The reasoning faculty is often faulty, because it is largely guided by one's accumulated experience. Not all knowledge, which one accumulates through "experience," is accurate. Ideas received through the creative faculty are much more reliable, for the reason that they come from sources more reliable than any which are available to the reasoning faculty of the mind.

The major difference between the genius and the ordinary "crank" inventor may be found in the fact that the genius works through his faculty of creative imagination, while the "crank" knows nothing of this faculty. The scientific inventor (such as Mr.

Edison, and Dr. Gates) makes use of both the synthetic and the creative faculties of imagination.

For example, the scientific inventor, or "genius," begins an invention by organizing and combining the known ideas, or principles accumulated through experience, through the synthetic faculty (the reasoning faculty). If he finds this accumulated knowledge to be insufficient for the completion of his invention, he then draws upon the sources of knowledge available to him through his *creative* faculty. The method by which he does this varies with the individual, but this is the sum and substance of his procedure:

1. He stimulates his mind so that it vibrates on a higher-than-average plane, using one or more of the ten mind stimulants or some other stimulant of his choice.
2. He concentrates upon the known factors (the finished part) of his invention, and creates in his mind a perfect picture of unknown factors (the unfinished part) of his invention. He holds this picture in mind until it has been taken over by the subconscious mind, then relaxes by clearing his mind of all thought, and waits for his answer to "flash" into his mind.

Sometimes the results are both definite and immediate. At other times, the results are negative, depending upon the state of development of the "sixth sense," or creative faculty.

Mr. Edison tried out more than ten thousand different combinations of ideas through the synthetic faculty of his imagination before he "tuned in" through the creative faculty, and got the answer which perfected the incandescent light. His experience was similar when he produced the talking machine.

There is plenty of reliable evidence that the faculty of creative imagination exists.

This evidence is available through accurate analysis of men who have become leaders in their respective callings, without having had extensive educations. Lincoln was a notable example of a great leader who achieved greatness, through the discovery, and use of his faculty of creative imagination. He discovered, and began to use this faculty as the result of the stimulation of love which he experienced after he met Anne Rutledge, a statement of the highest significance, in connection with the study of the source of genius.

The pages of history are filled with the records of great leaders whose achievements may be traced directly to the influence of women who aroused the creative faculties of their minds, through the stimulation of sex desire. Napoleon Bonaparte was one of these. When inspired by his first wife, Josephine, he was irresistible and invincible. When his "better judgment" or reasoning faculty prompted him to put Josephine aside, he began to decline. His defeat and St. Helena were not far distant.

If good taste would permit, we might easily mention scores of men, well known to the American people, who climbed to great heights of achievement under the stimulating influence of their wives, only to drop back to destruction after money and power went to their heads, and they put aside the old wife for a new one. Napoleon was not the only man to discover that sex influence, *from the right source,* is more powerful than any substitute of expediency, which may be created by mere reason.

The human mind responds to stimulation!

Among the greatest, and most powerful of these stimuli is the urge of sex. When harnessed and transmuted, this driving force is capable of lifting men into that higher sphere of thought which enables them to master the sources of worry and petty annoyance which beset their pathway on the lower plane.

Unfortunately, only the genii have made the discovery. Others have accepted the experience of sex urge, without discovering one of its major potentialities—a fact which accounts for the great number of "others" as compared to the limited number of genii.

For the purpose of refreshing the memory, in connection with the facts available from the biographies of certain men, we here present the names of a few men of outstanding achievement, each of whom was known to have been of a highly sexed nature. The genius which was theirs, undoubtedly found its source of power in transmuted sex energy:

George Washington	Thomas Jefferson
Napoleon Bonaparte	Elbert Hubbard
William Shakespeare	Elbert H. Gary
Abraham Lincoln	Oscar Wilde
Ralph Waldo Emerson	Woodrow Wilson
Robert Burns	John H. Patterson
Andrew Jackson	Enrico Caruso

Your own knowledge of biography will enable you to add to this list. Find, if you can, a single man, in all history of civilization, who achieved outstanding success in any calling, who was not driven by a well-developed sex nature.

If you do not wish to rely upon biographies of men not now living, take inventory of those whom you know to be men of great achievement, and see if you can find one among them who is not highly sexed.

Sex energy is the creative energy of all genii. *There never has been, and never will be a great leader, builder, or artist lacking in this driving force of sex.*

Surely no one will misunderstand these statements to mean that all who are highly sexed are genii! Man attains to the status of a genius only when, and if, he stimulates his mind so that it draws upon the forces available, through the creative faculty of the imagination. Chief among the stimuli with which this "stepping up" of the vibrations may be produced is sex energy. The mere *possession of* this energy is not sufficient to produce a genius. The energy must be *transmuted* from desire for physical contact, into some other form of desire and action, before it will lift one to the status of a genius.

Far from becoming genii, because of great sex desires, the majority of men *lower* themselves, through misunderstanding and misuse of this great force, to the status of the lower animals.

WHY MEN SELDOM SUCCEED BEFORE FORTY

I discovered, from the analysis of over 25,000 people, that men who succeed in an outstanding way, seldom do so before the age of forty, and more often they do not strike their real pace until they are well beyond the age of fifty. This fact was so astounding that it prompted me to go into the study of its cause most carefully, carrying the investigation over a period of more than twelve years.

This study disclosed the fact that the major reason why the majority of men who succeed do not begin to do so before the age of forty to fifty, is their tendency to dissipate their energies through over indulgence in physical expression of the emotion of sex. The majority of men *never* learn that the urge of sex has other possibilities, which far transcend in importance, that of mere physical expression. The majority of those who make this discovery, do so *after having wasted many years* at a period when the sex energy is at its height, prior to the age of forty-five to fifty. This usually is followed by noteworthy achievement.

The lives of many men up to, and sometimes well past the age of forty, reflect a continued dissipation of energies, which could have been more profitably turned into better channels. Their finer and more powerful emotions are sown wildly to the four winds. Out of this habit of the male, grew the term, "sowing his wild oats."

The desire for sexual expression is by far the strongest and most impelling of all the human emotions, and for this very reason this desire, when *harnessed and transmuted* into action, other than that of physical expression, may raise one to the status of a genius.

One of America's most able business men frankly admitted that his attractive secretary was responsible for most of the plans he created. He admitted that her presence lifted him to heights of creative imagination, such as he could experience under no other stimulus.

One of the most successful men in America owes most of his success to the influence of a very charming young woman, who has served as his source of inspiration for more than twelve years. Everyone knows the man to whom this reference is made, but not everyone knows the real source of his achievements.

History is not lacking in examples of men who attained to the status of genii, as the result of the use of artificial mind stimulants in the form of alcohol and narcotics. Edgar Allan Poe wrote the "Raven" while under the influence of liquor, "dreaming dreams that mortal never dared to dream before." James Whitcomb Riley did his best writing while under the influence of alcohol. Perhaps it was thus he saw "the ordered intermingling of the real and the dream, the mill above the river, and the mist above the stream." Robert Burns wrote best when intoxicated, "For Auld Lang Syne, my dear, we'll take a cup of kindness yet, for Auld Lang Syne."

But let it be remembered that many such men have destroyed themselves in the end. Nature has prepared her own potions with which men may safely stimulate their minds so they vibrate on a plane that enables them to tune in to fine and rare thoughts which come from—no man knows where! No satisfactory substitute for Nature's stimulants has ever been found.

It is a fact well known to psychologists that there is a very close relationship between sex desires and spiritual urges—a fact which accounts for the peculiar behavior of people who participate in the orgies known as religious "revivals," common among the primitive types.

The world is ruled, and the destiny of civilization is established, by the human emotions. People are influenced in their actions, not by reason so much as by "feelings." The creative faculty of the mind is set into action entirely by emotions, and *not by cold reason.* The most powerful of all human emotions is that of sex. There are other mind stimulants, some of which have been listed, but no one of them, nor all of them combined, can equal the driving power of sex.

A mind stimulant is any influence which will either temporarily, or permanently, increase the vibrations of thought. The ten major stimulants, described, are those most commonly resorted to. Through these sources one may commune with Infinite Intelligence, or enter, at will, the storehouse of the subconscious mind, either one's own, or that of another person, a procedure *which is all there is of genius.*

A teacher, who has trained and directed the efforts of more than 30,000 sales people, made the astounding discovery that highly sexed men are the most efficient salesmen. The explanation is, that the factor of personality known as "personal magnetism" is nothing more nor less than sex energy. Highly sexed people always have a plentiful supply of magnetism. Through cultivation and understanding, this vital force may be drawn upon and used to great advantage in the relationships between people. This energy may be communicated to others through the following media:

1. The hand-shake. The touch of the hand indicates, instantly, the presence of magnetism, or the lack of it.
2. The tone of voice. Magnetism, or sex energy, is the factor with which the voice may be colored, or made musical and charming.
3. Posture and carriage of the body. Highly sexed people move briskly, and with grace and ease.
4. The vibrations of thought. Highly sexed people mix the emotion of sex with

their thoughts, or may do so at will, and in that way, may influence those around them.

5. Body adornment. People who are highly sexed are usually very careful about their personal appearance. They usually select clothing of a style becoming to their personality, physique, complexion, etc.

When employing salesmen, the more capable sales manager looks for the quality of personal magnetism as the *first requirement* of a salesman. People who lack sex energy will never become enthusiastic nor inspire others with enthusiasm, and enthusiasm is one of the most important requisites in salesmanship, no matter what one is selling.

The public speaker, orator, preacher, lawyer, or salesman who is lacking in sex energy is a "flop," as far as being able to influence others is concerned. Couple with this the fact, that most people can be influenced only through an appeal to their emotions, and you will understand the importance of sex energy as a part of the salesman's native ability. Master salesmen attain the status of mastery in selling, because they, either consciously, or unconsciously, *transmute* the energy of sex into sales enthusiasm! In this statement may be found a very practical suggestion as to the actual meaning of sex transmutation.

The salesman who knows how to take his mind off the subject of sex, and direct it in sales effort with as much enthusiasm and determination as he would apply to its original purpose, has acquired the art of sex transmutation, whether he knows it or not. The majority of salesmen who transmute their sex energy do so without being in the least aware of what they are doing, or how they are doing it.

Transmutation of sex energy calls for more will-power than the average person cares to use for this purpose. Those who find it difficult to summon will-power sufficient for transmutation, may gradually acquire this ability. Though this requires will-power, the reward for the practice is more than worth the effort.

The entire subject of sex is one with which the majority of people appear to be unpardonably ignorant. The urge of sex has been grossly misunderstood, slandered, and burlesqued by the ignorant and the evil minded, for so long that the very word sex is seldom used in polite society. Men and women who are known to be blessed—yes, blessed—with highly sexed natures, are usually looked upon as being people who will bear watching. Instead of being called blessed, they are usually called cursed.

Millions of people, even in this age of enlightenment, have inferiority complexes which they developed because of this false belief that a highly sexed nature is a curse. These statements, of the virtue of sex energy, should not be construed as justification for the libertine. The emotion of sex is a virtue only when used intelligently, and with discrimination. It may be misused, and often is, to such an extent that it debases, instead of enriches, both body and mind. The better use of this power is the burden of this chapter.

It seemed quite significant to the author, when he made the discovery that practically every great leader, whom he had the privilege of analyzing, was a man whose achievements were largely inspired by a woman. In many instances, the "woman in the case" was a modest, self-denying wife, of whom the public had heard but little or nothing. In a few instances, the source of inspiration has been traced to the "other woman." Perhaps such cases may not be entirely unknown to you.

Intemperance in sex habits is just as detrimental as intemperance in habits of drinking and eating. In this age in which we live, an age which began with the world war, intemperance in habits of sex is common. This orgy of indulgence may account for the shortage of great leaders. No man can avail himself of the forces of his creative imagination, while dissipating them. Man is the only creature on earth which violates Nature's purpose in this connection. Every other animal indulges its sex nature in moderation, and with purpose which harmonizes with the laws of nature. Every other animal responds to the call of sex only in "season." Mans inclination is to declare "open season."

Every intelligent person knows that stimulation in excess, through alcoholic drink and narcotics, is a form of intemperance which destroys the vital organs of the body, including the brain. Not every person knows, however, that over indulgence in sex expression may become a habit as destructive and as detrimental to creative effort as narcotics or liquor.

A sex-mad man is not essentially different than a dope-mad man! Both have lost control over their faculties of reason and will-power. Sexual over-indulgence may not only destroy reason and will-power, but it may also lead to either temporary or permanent insanity. Many cases of hypochondria (imaginary illness) grow out of habits developed in ignorance of the true function of sex.

From these brief references to the subject, it may be readily seen that ignorance on the subject of sex transmutation forces stupendous penalties upon the ignorant on the one hand, and withholds from them equally stupendous benefits, on the other.

Widespread ignorance on the subject of sex is due to the fact that the subject has been surrounded with mystery and beclouded by dark silence. The conspiracy of mystery and silence has had the same effect upon the minds of young people that the psychology of prohibition had. The result has been increased curiosity, and desire to acquire more knowledge on this "verboten" subject; and to the shame of all lawmakers, and most physicians—by training best qualified to educate youth on that subject—information has not been easily available.

Seldom does an individual enter upon highly creative effort in any field of endeavor before the age of forty. The average man reaches the period of his greatest capacity to create between forty and sixty. These statements are based upon analysis of thousands of men and women who have been carefully observed. They should be encouraging to those who fail to arrive before the age of forty, and to those who become frightened at the approach of "old age," around the forty-year mark. The years between forty and fifty are, as a rule, the most fruitful. Man should approach this age, not with fear and trembling, but with hope and eager anticipation.

If you want evidence that most men do not begin to do their best work before the age of forty, study the records of the most successful men known to the American people, and you will find it. Henry Ford had not "hit his pace" of achievement until he had passed the age of forty. Andrew Carnegie was well past forty before he began to reap the reward of his efforts. James J. Hill was still running a telegraph key at the age of forty. His stupendous achievements took place after that age. Biographies of American industrialists and financiers are filled with evidence that the period from forty to sixty is the most productive age of man.

Between the ages of thirty and forty, man begins to learn (if he ever learns) the art of sex transmutation. This discovery is generally accidental, and more often than otherwise, the man who makes it is totally unconscious of his discovery. He may observe that his powers of achievement have increased around the age of thirty-five to forty, but in most cases, he is not familiar with the cause of this change; that Nature begins to harmonize the emotions of love and sex in the individual, between the ages of thirty and forty, so that he may draw upon these great forces, and apply them jointly as stimuli to action.

Sex, alone, is a mighty urge to action, but its forces are like a cyclone—they are often uncontrollable. When the emotion of love begins to mix itself with the emotion of sex, the result is calmness of purpose, poise, accuracy of judgment, and balance. What person, who has attained to the age of forty, is so unfortunate as to be unable to analyze these statements, and to corroborate them by his own experience?

When driven by his desire to please a woman, based solely upon the emotion of sex, a man may be, and usually is, capable of great achievement, but his actions may be disorganized, distorted, and totally destructive. When driven by his desire to please a woman, based upon the motive of sex alone, a man may steal, cheat, and even commit murder. But when the emotion of love is mixed with the emotion of sex, that same man will guide his actions with more sanity, balance, and reason.

Criminologists have discovered that the most hardened criminals can be reformed through the influence of a woman's *love.* There is no record of a criminal having been reformed solely through the sex influence. These facts are well known, but their cause is not. Reformation comes, if at all, through the *heart,* or the emotional side of man, *not* through his head, or reasoning side. Reformation means, "a change of heart." It does not mean a "change of head." A man may, because of reason, make certain changes in his personal conduct to avoid the consequences of undesirable effects, but genuine reformation comes only through a change of heart—through a desire to change.

Love, romance, and sex are all emotions capable of driving men to heights of super achievement. Love is the emotion which serves as a safety valve, and insures balance, poise, and constructive effort. When combined, these three emotions may lift one to an altitude of a genius. There are genii, however, who know but little of the emotion of love. Most of them may be found engaged in some form of action which is destructive, or at least, not based upon justice and fairness toward others. If good taste would permit, a dozen genii could be named in the field of industry and finance, who ride ruthlessly over the rights of their fellow men. They seem totally lacking in conscience. The reader can easily supply his own list of such men.

The emotions are states of mind. Nature has provided man with a "chemistry of the mind" which operates in a manner similar to the principles of chemistry of matter. It is a well-known fact that, through the aid of chemistry of matter, a chemist may create a deadly poison by mixing certain elements, none of which are—in themselves—harmful in the right proportions. The emotions may, likewise, be combined so as to create a deadly poison. The emotions of sex and jealousy, when mixed, may turn a person into an insane beast.

The presence of any one or more of the destructive emotions in the human mind, through the chemistry of the mind, sets up a poison which may destroy one's sense of justice and fairness. In extreme cases, the presence of any combination of these emotions in the mind may destroy one's reason.

The road to genius consists of the development, control, and use of sex, love, and romance. Briefly, the process may be stated as follows:

Encourage the presence of these emotions as the dominating thoughts in one's mind, and discourage the presence of all the destructive emotions. The mind is a creature of habit. It thrives upon the *dominating* thoughts fed it. Through the faculty of will-power, one may discourage the presence of any emotion, and encourage the presence of any other. Control of the mind, through the power of will, is not difficult. Control comes from persistence, and habit. The secret of control lies in understanding the process of transmutation. When any negative emotion presents itself in one's mind, it can be transmuted into a positive, or constructive emotion, by the simple procedure of changing one's thoughts.

There is no other road to genius than through voluntary self effort! A man may attain to great heights of financial or business achievement, solely by the driving force of sex energy, but history is filled with evidence that he may, and usually does, carry with him certain traits of character which rob him of the ability to either hold or enjoy his fortune. This is worthy of analysis, thought, and meditation, for it states a truth, the knowledge of which may be helpful to women as well as men. Ignorance of this has cost thousands of people their privilege of happiness, even though they possessed riches.

The emotions of love and sex leave their unmistakable marks upon the features. Moreover, these signs are so visible, that all who wish may read them. The man who is driven by the storm of passion, based upon sex desires alone, plainly advertises that fact to the entire world, by the expression of his eyes, and the lines of his face. The emotion of love, when mixed with the emotion of sex, softens, modifies, and beautifies the facial expression. No character analyst is needed to tell you this—you may observe it for yourself.

The emotion of love brings out, and develops, the artistic and the aesthetic nature of man. It leaves its impress upon one's very soul, even after the fire has been subdued by time and circumstance.

Memories of love never pass. They linger, guide, and influence long after the source of stimulation has faded. There is nothing new in this. Every person, who has been moved by genuine love, knows that it leaves enduring traces upon the human heart. The effect of love endures, because love is spiritual in nature. The man who cannot be stimulated to great heights of achievement by love, is hopeless—he is dead, though he may seem to live.

Even the memories of love are sufficient to lift one to a higher plane of creative effort. The major force of love may spend itself and pass away, like a fire which has burned itself out, but it leaves behind indelible marks as evidence that it passed that way. Its departure often prepares the human heart for a still greater love.

Go back into your yesterdays, at times, and bathe your mind in the beautiful memories of past love. It will soften the influence of the present worries and annoyances. It will give you a source of escape from the unpleasant realities of life, and maybe—who knows?—your mind will yield to you, during this temporary retreat into the world of fantasy, ideas, or plans which may change the entire financial or spiritual status of your life.

If you believe yourself unfortunate, because you have "loved and lost," perish the thought. One who has loved truly, can never lose entirely. Love is whimsical and temperamental. Its nature is ephemeral, and transitory. It comes when it pleases, and goes away without warning. Accept and enjoy it while it remains, but spend no time worrying about its departure. Worry will never bring it back.

Dismiss, also, the thought that love never comes but once. Love may come and go, times without number, but there are no two love experiences which affect one in just the same way. There may be, and there usually is, one love experience which leaves a deeper imprint on the heart than all the others, but all love experiences are beneficial, except to the person who becomes resentful and cynical when love makes its departure.

There should be no disappointment over love, and there would be none if people understood the difference between the emotions of love and sex. The major difference is that love is spiritual, while sex is biological. No experience, which touches the human heart with a spiritual force, can possibly be harmful, except through ignorance, or jealousy.

Love is, without question, life's greatest experience. It brings one into communion with Infinite Intelligence. When mixed with the emotions of romance and sex, it may lead one far up the ladder of creative effort. The emotions of love, sex, and romance are sides of the eternal triangle of achievement-building genius. Nature creates genii through no other force.

Love is an emotion with many sides, shades, and colors. The love which one feels for parents, or children is quite different from that which one feels for one's sweetheart. The one is mixed with the emotion of sex, while the other is not.

The love which one feels in true friendship is not the same as that felt for one's sweetheart, parents, or children, but it, too, is a form of love.

Then, there is the emotion of love for things inanimate, such as the love of Nature's handiwork. But the most intense and burning of all these various kinds of love is that experienced in the blending of the emotions of love and sex. Marriages, not blessed with the eternal affinity of love, properly balanced and proportioned, with sex, cannot be happy ones—and seldom endure. Love, alone, will not bring happiness in marriage, nor will sex alone. When these two beautiful emotions are blended, marriage may bring about a state of mind, closest to the spiritual that one may ever know on this earthly plane.

When the emotion of romance is added to those of love and sex, the obstructions between the finite mind of man and Infinite Intelligence are removed. Then a genius has been born!

What a different story is this, than those usually associated with the emotion of sex. Here is an interpretation of the emotion which lifts it out of the commonplace, and makes of it potter's clay in the hands of God, from which He fashions all that is beautiful and inspiring. It is an interpretation which would, when properly understood, bring harmony out of the chaos which exists in too many marriages. The disharmonies often expressed in the form of nagging may usually be traced to *lack of knowledge* on the subject of sex. Where love, romance and the proper understanding of the emotion and function of sex abide, there is no disharmony between married people.

Fortunate is the husband whose wife understands the true relationship between the emotions of love, sex, and romance. When motivated by this holy triumvirate, no form of labor is burdensome, because even the most lowly form of effort takes on the nature of a labor of love.

It is a very old saying that "a man's wife may either make him or break him," but the reason is not always understood. The "making" and "breaking" is the result of the wife's understanding, or lack of understanding of the emotions of love, sex, and romance.

Despite the fact that men are polygamous, by the very nature of their biological inheritance, it is true that no woman has as great an influence on a man as his wife, unless he is married to a woman totally unsuited to his nature. If a woman permits her husband to lose interest in her, and become more interested in other women, it is usually because of her ignorance, or indifference toward the subjects of sex, love, and romance. This statement presupposes, of course, that genuine love once existed between a man and his wife. The facts are equally applicable to a man who permits his wife's interest in him to die.

Married people often bicker over a multitude of trivialities. If these are analyzed accurately, the real cause of the trouble will often be found to be indifference, or ignorance on these subjects.

Man's greatest motivating force is his desire to please woman! The hunter who excelled during prehistoric days, before the dawn of civilization, did so, because of his desire to appear great in the eyes of woman. Man's nature has not changed in this respect. The "hunter" of today brings home no skins of wild animals, but he indicates his desire for her favor by supplying fine clothes, motor cars, and wealth. Man has the same desire to please woman that he had before the dawn of civilization. The only thing that has changed, is his method of pleasing. Men who accumulate large fortunes, and attain to great heights of power and fame, do so, mainly, to satisfy their *desire to please women.* Take women out of their lives, and great wealth would be useless to most men. *It is this inherent desire of man to please woman, which gives woman the power to make or break a man.*

The woman who understands man's nature and tactfully caters to it, need have no fear of competition from other women. Men may be "giants" with indomitable will-power when dealing with other men, but they are easily managed by the women of their choice.

Most men will not admit that they are easily influenced by the women they prefer, because it is in the nature of the male to want to be recognized as the stronger of the species. Moreover, the intelligent woman recognizes this "manly trait" and very wisely makes no issue of it.

Some men know that they are being influenced by the women of their choice—their wives, sweethearts, mothers or sisters—but they tactfully refrain from rebelling against the influence because they are intelligent enough to know that no man is happy or complete without the modifying influence of the right woman. The man who does not recognize this important truth deprives himself of the power which has done more to help men achieve success than all other forces combined.

CHAPTER 12

THE SUBCONSCIOUS MIND

THE CONNECTING LINK

The Eleventh Step Toward Riches

The subconscious mind consists of a field of consciousness, in which every impulse of thought that reaches the objective mind through any of the five senses, is classified and recorded, and from which thoughts may be recalled or withdrawn as letters may be taken from a filing cabinet.

It receives, and files, sense impressions or thoughts, regardless of their nature. You may voluntarily plant in your subconscious mind any plan, thought, or purpose which you desire to, translate into its physical or monetary equivalent. The subconscious acts first on the dominating desires which have been mixed with emotional feeling, such as faith.

Consider this in connection with the instructions given in the chapter on desire, for taking the six steps there outlined, and the instructions given in the chapter on the building and execution of plans, and you will understand the importance of the thought conveyed.

The subconscious mind works day and night. Through a method of procedure, unknown to man, the subconscious mind draws upon the forces of Infinite Intelligence for the power with which it voluntarily transmutes one's desires into their physical equivalent, making use, always of the most practical media by which this end may be accomplished.

You cannot *entirely* control your subconscious mind, but you can voluntarily hand over to it any plan, desire, or purpose which you wish transformed into concrete form. Read, again, instructions for using the subconscious mind, in the chapter on autosuggestion.

There is plenty of evidence to support the belief that the subconscious mind is the connecting link between the finite mind of man and Infinite Intelligence. It is the intermediary through which one may draw upon the forces of Infinite Intelligence at will. It, alone, contains the secret process by which mental impulses are modified and changed into their spiritual equivalent. It, alone, is the medium through which prayer may be transmitted to the source capable of answering prayer.

The possibilities of creative effort connected with the subconscious mind are stupendous and imponderable. They inspire one with awe.

I never approach the discussion of the subconscious mind without a feeling of littleness and inferiority due, perhaps, to the fact that man's entire stock of knowledge on this subject is so pitifully limited. The very fact that the subconscious mind is the medium of communication between the thinking mind of man and Infinite Intelligence is, of itself, a thought which almost paralyzes one's reason.

After you have accepted, as a reality, the existence of the subconscious mind, and understand its possibilities, as a medium for transmuting your desires into their physical or monetary equivalent, you will comprehend the full significance of the instructions given in the chapter on desire. You will also understand why you have been repeatedly admonished to make your desires clear, and to reduce them to writing. You will also understand the necessity of persistence in carrying out instructions.

The thirteen principles are the stimuli with which you acquire the ability to reach, and to influence your subconscious mind. Do not become discouraged, if you cannot do this upon the first attempt. Remember that the subconscious mind may be voluntarily directed *only through habit,* under the directions given in the chapter on faith. You have not yet had time to master faith. Be patient. Be persistent.

A good many statements in the chapters on faith and auto-suggestion will be repeated here, for the benefit of your subconscious mind. Remember, your subconscious mind functions voluntarily, *whether you make any effort to influence it or not.* This, naturally, suggests to you that thoughts of fear and poverty, and all negative thoughts serve as stimuli to your subconscious mind, *unless,* you master these impulses and give it more desirable food upon which it may feed.

The subconscious mind will not remain idle! If you fail to plant desires in your subconscious mind, it will feed upon the thoughts which reach it as the *result of your neglect.* We have already explained that thought impulses, both negative and positive are reaching the subconscious mind continuously, from the four sources which were mentioned in the chapter on Sex Transmutation.

For the present, it is sufficient if you remember that you are living *daily,* in the midst of all manner of thought impulses which are reaching your subconscious mind, without your knowledge. Some of these impulses are negative, some are positive. You are now engaged in trying to help shut off the flow of negative impulses, and to aid in voluntarily influencing your subconscious mind, through positive impulses of desire.

When you achieve this, you will possess the key which unlocks the door to your subconscious mind. Moreover, you will control that door so completely, that no undesirable thought may influence your subconscious mind.

Everything which man creates begins in the form of a thought impulse. Man can create nothing which he does not first conceive in thought. Through the aid of the imagination, thought impulses may be assembled into plans. The imagination, when under control, may be used for the creation of plans or purposes that lead to success in one's chosen occupation.

All thought impulses, intended for transmutation into their physical equivalent, voluntarily planted in the subconscious mind, must pass through the imagination, and be mixed with faith. The "mixing" of faith with a plan, or purpose, intended for submission to the subconscious mind, may be done only through the imagination.

From these statements, you will readily observe that voluntary use of the subconscious mind calls for coordination and application of all the principles.

Ella Wheeler Wilcox gave evidence of her understanding of the power of the subconscious mind when she wrote:

You never can tell what a thought will do
In bringing you hate or love—
For thoughts are things, and their airy wings
Are swifter than carrier doves.
They follow the law of the universe—
Each thing creates its kind,
And they speed O'er the track to bring you back
Whatever went out from your mind.

Mrs. Wilcox understood the truth, that thoughts which go out from one's mind, also imbed themselves deeply in one's subconscious mind, where they serve as a magnet, pattern, or blueprint by which the subconscious mind is influenced while translating them into their physical equivalent. Thoughts are truly things, for the reason that every material thing begins in the form of thought-energy.

The subconscious mind is more susceptible to influence by impulses of thought mixed with "feeling" or emotion, than by those originating solely in the reasoning portion of the mind. In fact, there is much evidence to support the theory, that only emotionalized thoughts have any action influence upon the subconscious mind. It is a well-known fact that emotion or feeling rules the majority of people. If it is true that the subconscious mind responds more quickly to, and is influenced more readily by thought impulses which are well mixed with emotion, it is essential to become familiar with the more important of the emotions. There are seven major positive emotions, and seven major negative emotions. The negatives *voluntarily* inject themselves into the thought impulses, which insure passage into the subconscious mind. The positives must be injected, through the principle of auto-suggestion, into the thought impulses which an individual wishes to pass on to his subconscious mind. (Instructions have been given in the chapter on auto-suggestion.)

These emotions, or feeling impulses, may be likened to yeast in a loaf of bread, because they constitute the action element, which transforms thought impulses from the passive to the active state. Thus may one understand why thought impulses, which have been well mixed with emotion, are acted upon more readily than thought impulses originating in "cold reason."

You are preparing yourself to influence and control the "inner audience" of your subconscious mind, in order to hand over to it the desire for money, which you wish transmuted into its monetary equivalent. It is essential, therefore, that you understand the method of approach to this "inner audience." You must speak its language, or it will not heed your call. It understands best the language of emotion or feeling. Let us, therefore describe here the seven major positive emotions, and the seven major negative emotions, so that you may draw upon the positives, and avoid the negatives, when giving instructions to your subconscious mind.

THE SEVEN MAJOR POSITIVE EMOTIONS

The emotion of DESIRE
The emotion of FAITH
The emotion of LOVE
The emotion of SEX
The emotion of ENTHUSIASM
The emotion of ROMANCE
The emotion of HOPE

There are other positive emotions, but these are the seven most powerful, and the ones most commonly used in creative effort. Master these seven emotions (they can be mastered only by use) and the other positive emotions will be at your command when you need them. Remember, in this connection, that you are studying a book which is intended to help you develop a "money consciousness" *by filling your mind with positive emotions.* One does not become money conscious by filling one's mind with negative emotions.

THE SEVEN MAJOR NEGATIVE EMOTIONS

(TO BE AVOIDED)

The emotion of FEAR
The emotion of JEALOUSY
The emotion of HATRED
The emotion of REVENGE
The emotion of GREED

The emotion of SUPERSTITION
The emotion of ANGER

Positive and negative emotions cannot occupy the mind at the same time. One or the other must dominate. It is your responsibility to make sure that positive emotions constitute the dominating influence of your mind. Here the law of habit will come to your aid. *Form the habit* of applying and using the positive emotions! Eventually, they will dominate your mind so completely, that the negatives *cannot enter it.*

Only by following these instructions literally, and continuously, can you gain control over your subconscious mind. The presence of a single negative in your conscious mind is sufficient to *destroy* all chances of constructive aid from your subconscious mind.

If you are an observing person, you must have noticed that most people resort to prayer only after everything else has failed! Or else they pray by a ritual of meaningless words. And because it is a fact that most people who pray, do so only after everything else has failed, they go to prayer with their minds filled with fear and doubt, *which are the emotions the subconscious mind acts upon,* and passes on to Infinite Intelligence. Likewise, that is the emotion which Infinite Intelligence receives, and acts upon.

If you pray for a thing, but have fear as you pray, that you may not receive it, or that your prayer will not be acted upon by Infinite Intelligence, your prayer *will have been in vain.*

Prayer does, sometimes, result in the realization of that for which one prays. If you have ever had the experience of receiving that for which you prayed, go back in your memory, and recall your actual state of mind, while you were praying, and you will know, for sure, that the theory here described is more than a theory.

The time will come when the schools and educational institutions of the country will teach the "science of prayer." Moreover, then prayer may be, and will be reduced to a science. When that time comes (it will come as soon as mankind is ready for it, and demands it), no one will approach the Universal Mind in a state of fear, for the very good reason that there will be no such emotion as fear. Ignorance, superstition, and false teaching will have disappeared, and man will have attained his true status as a child of Infinite Intelligence. A few have already attained this blessing.

If you believe this prophesy is far-fetched, take a look at the human race in retrospect. Less than a hundred years ago, men believed the lightning to be evidence of the wrath of God, and feared it. Now, thanks to the power of faith, men have harnessed the lightning and made it turn the wheels of industry. Much less than a hundred years ago, men believed the space between the planets to be nothing but a great void, a stretch of dead nothingness. Now, thanks to this same power of faith, men know that far from being either dead or a void, the space between the planets is very much alive, that it is the highest form of vibration known, excepting, perhaps, the vibration of thought. Moreover, men know that this living, pulsating, vibratory energy which permeates every atom of matter, and fills every niche of space, connects every human brain with every other human brain.

What reason have men to believe that this same energy does not connect every human brain with Infinite Intelligence?

There are no toll-gates between the finite mind of man and Infinite Intelligence. The communication costs nothing except Patience, Faith, Persistence, Understanding, and a sincere desire to communicate. Moreover, the approach can be made only by the individual himself. Paid prayers are worthless. Infinite Intelligence does no business by proxy. You either go direct, or you do not communicate.

You may buy prayer books and repeat them until the day of your doom, without avail. Thoughts which you wish to communicate to Infinite Intelligence, must undergo transformation, such as can be given only through your own subconscious mind.

The method by which you may communicate with Infinite Intelligence is very similar to that through which the vibration of sound is communicated by radio. If you understand the working principle of radio, you of course, know that sound cannot be communicated through the ether until it has been "stepped up," or changed into a rate of vibration which the human ear cannot detect. The radio sending station picks up the sound of the human voice, and "scrambles," or modifies it by stepping up the vibration millions of times. Only in this way, can the vibration of sound be communicated through the ether. After this transformation has taken place, the ether "picks up" the energy (which originally was in the form of vibrations of sound) carries that energy to radio receiving stations, and these receiving sets "step" that energy back down to its original rate of vibration so it is recognized as sound.

The subconscious mind is the intermediary, which translates one's prayers into terms which Infinite Intelligence can recognize, presents the message, and brings back the answer in the form of a definite plan or idea for procuring the object of the prayer. Understand this principle, and you will know why mere words read from a prayer book cannot, and will never serve as an agency of communication between the mind of man and Infinite Intelligence.

Before your prayer will reach Infinite Intelligence (a statement of the author's theory only), it probably is transformed from its original thought vibration into terms of spiritual vibration. Faith is the only known agency which will give your thoughts a spiritual nature. Faith and fear make poor bedfellows. *Where one is found, the other cannot exist.*

CHAPTER 13

THE BRAIN

A BROADCASTING AND RECEIVING STATION FOR THOUGHT

The Twelfth Step Toward Riches

More than twenty years ago, the author, working in conjunction with the late Dr. Alexander Graham Bell, and Dr. Elmer R. Gates, observed that every human brain is both a broadcasting and receiving station for the vibration of thought.

Through the medium of the ether, in a fashion similar to that employed by the radio broadcasting principle, every human brain is capable of picking up vibrations of thought which are being released by other brains.

In connection with the statement in the preceding paragraph, compare, and consider the description of the Creative Imagination, as outlined in the chapter on Imagination. The Creative Imagination is the "receiving set" of the brain, which receives thoughts, released by the brains of others. It is the agency of communication between one's conscious, or reasoning mind, and the four sources from which one may receive thought stimuli.

When stimulated, or "stepped up" to a high rate of vibration, the mind becomes more receptive to the vibration of thought which reaches it through the ether from outside sources. This "stepping up" process takes place through the positive emotions, or the negative emotions. Through the emotions, the vibrations of thought may be increased.

Vibrations of an exceedingly high rate are the only vibrations picked up and carried, by the ether, from one brain to another. Thought is energy travelling at an exceedingly high rate of vibration. Thought, which has been modified or "stepped up" by any of the major emotions, vibrates at a much higher rate than ordinary thought, and it is this type of thought which passes from one brain to another, through the broadcasting machinery of the human brain.

The emotion of sex stands at the head of the list of human emotions, as far as intensity and driving force are concerned. The brain which has been stimulated by the emotion of sex, vibrates at a much more rapid rate than it does when that emotion is quiescent or absent.

The result of sex transmutation is the increase of the rate of vibration of thoughts to such a pitch that the Creative Imagination becomes highly receptive to ideas, which it picks up from the ether. On the other hand, when the brain is vibrating at a rapid rate, it not only attracts thoughts and ideas released by other brains through the medium of the ether, but it gives to one's own thoughts that "feeling" which is essential before those thoughts will be picked up and acted upon by one's subconscious mind.

Thus, you will see that the broadcasting principle is the factor through which you mix feeling, or emotion with your thoughts and pass them on to your subconscious mind.

The subconscious mind is the "sending station" of the brain, through which vibrations of thought are broadcast. The Creative Imagination is the "receiving set," through which the vibrations of thought are picked up from the ether.

Along with the important factors of the subconscious mind, and the faculty of the Creative Imagination, which constitute the sending and receiving sets of your mental broadcasting machinery, consider now the principle of auto-suggestion, which is the medium by which you may put into operation your "broadcasting" station.

Through the instructions described in the chapter on auto-suggestion, you were definitely informed of the method by which desire may be transmuted into its monetary equivalent.

Operation of your mental "broadcasting" station is a comparatively simple procedure. You have but three principles to bear in mind, and to apply, when you wish to use your broadcasting station—the subconscious mind, creative imagination, and auto-suggestion. The stimuli through which you put these three principles into action have been described—the procedure begins with desire.

GREATEST FORCES ARE "INTANGIBLE"

The depression brought the world to the very border-line of understanding of the forces which are intangible and unseen. Through the ages which have passed, man has depended too much upon his physical senses, and has limited his knowledge to physical things, which he could see, touch, weigh, and measure.

We are now entering the most marvelous of all ages—an age which will teach us something of the intangible forces of the world about us. Perhaps we shall learn, as we pass through this age, that the "other self" is more powerful than the physical self we see when we look into a mirror.

Sometimes men speak lightly of the intangibles—the things which they cannot perceive through any of their five senses, and when we hear them, it should remind us that *all of us are controlled by forces which are unseen and intangible.*

The whole of mankind has not the power to cope with, nor to control the intangible force wrapped up in the rolling waves of the oceans. Man has not the capacity to understand the intangible force of gravity, which keeps this little earth suspended in mid-air, and keeps man from falling from it, much less the power to control that force. Man is entirely subservient to the intangible force which comes with a thunder storm, and he is just as helpless in the presence of the intangible force of electricity—nay, he does not even know what electricity is, where it comes from, or what is its purpose!

Nor is this by any means the end of man's ignorance in connection with things unseen and intangible. He does not understand the intangible force (and intelligence) wrapped up in the soil of the earth—*the force which provides him with every morsel of food he eats, every article of clothing he wears, every dollar he carries in his pockets.*

THE DRAMATIC STORY OF THE BRAIN

Last, but not least, man, with all of his boasted culture and education, understands little or nothing of the intangible force (the greatest of all the intangibles) of *thought.* He knows but little concerning the physical brain, and its vast network of intricate machinery through which the power of thought is translated into its material equivalent, but he is now entering an age which shall yield enlightenment on the subject. Already men of science have begun to turn their attention to the study of this stupendous thing called a brain, and, while they are still in the kindergarten stage of their studies, they have uncovered enough knowledge to know that the central switchboard of the human brain, the number of lines which connect the brain cells one with another, equal the figure one, followed by fifteen million ciphers.

"The figure is so stupendous," said Dr. C. Judson Herrick, of the University of Chicago, "that astronomical figures dealing with hundreds of millions of light years, become insignificant by comparison. . . . It has been determined that there are from 10,000,000,000 to 14,000,000,000 nerve cells in the human cerebral cortex, and we know that these are arranged in definite patterns. These arrangements are not haphazard. They are orderly. Recently developed methods of electro-physiology draw off action currents from very precisely located cells, or fibers with micro-electrodes, amplify them with radio tubes, and record potential differences to a millionth of a volt."

It is inconceivable that such a network of intricate machinery should be in existence for the sole purpose of carrying on the physical functions incidental to growth and maintenance of the physical body. Is it not likely that the same system, which gives billions of brain cells the media for communication one with another, provides, also the means of communication with other intangible forces?

After this book had been written, just before the manuscript went to the publisher, there appeared in the *New York Times* an editorial showing that at least one great university, and one intelligent investigator in the field of mental phenomena, are carrying on an organized research through which conclusions have been reached that parallel many of those described in this and the following chapter. The editorial briefly analyzed the work carried on by Dr. Rhine, and his associates at Duke University, viz:—

WHAT IS "TELEPATHY"?

"A month ago we cited on this page some of the remarkable results achieved by Professor Rhine and his associates in Duke University from more than a hundred thousand tests to determine the existence of 'telepathy' and 'clairvoyance.' These results were summarized in the first two articles in *Harpers Magazine.* In the second which has now appeared, the author, E. H. Wright, attempts to summarize what has been learned, or what it seems reasonable to infer, regarding the exact nature of these 'extrasensory' modes of perception.

"The actual existence of telepathy and clairvoyance now seems to some scientists enormously probable as the result of Rhine's experiments. Various percipients were asked to name as many cards in a special pack as they could without looking at them and without other sensory access to them. About a score of men and women were discovered who could regularly name so many of the cards correctly that 'there was not one chance in many a million million of their having done their feats by luck or accident.'

"But how did they do them? These powers, assuming that they exist, do not seem to be sensory. There is no known organ for them. The experiments worked just as well at distances of several hundred miles as they did in the same room. These facts also dispose, in Mr. Wright's opinion, of the attempt to explain telepathy or clairvoyance through any physical theory of radiation. All known forms of radiant energy decline inversely as the square of the distance traversed. Telepathy and clairvoyance do not. But they do vary through physical causes as our other mental powers do. Contrary to widespread opinion, they do not improve when the percipient is asleep or half-asleep, but, on the contrary, when he is most wide-awake and alert. Rhine discovered that a narcotic will invariably lower a percipient's score, while a stimulant will always send it higher. The most reliable performer apparently cannot make a good score unless he tries to do his best.

"One conclusion that Wright draws with some confidence is that telepathy and clairvoyance are really one and the same gift. That is, the faculty that 'sees' a card face down on a table seems to be exactly the same one that 'reads' a thought residing only in another mind. There are several grounds for believing this. So far, for example, the two gifts have been found in every person who enjoys either of them. In every one so far the two have been of equal vigor, almost exactly. Screens, walls, distances, have no effect at all on either. Wright advances from this conclusion to express what he puts forward as no more than the mere 'hunch' that other extrasensory experiences, prophetic dreams, premonitions of disaster, and the like, may also prove to be part of the same faculty. The reader is not asked to accept any of these conclusions unless he finds it necessary, but the evidence that Rhine has piled up must remain impressive."

In view of Dr. Rhine's announcement in connection with the conditions under which the mind responds to what he terms "extrasensory" modes of perception, I now feel privileged to add to his testimony by stating that my associates and I have discovered what we believe to be the ideal conditions under which the mind can be stimulated so that the sixth sense described in the next chapter can be made to function in a practical way.

The conditions to which I refer consist of a close working alliance between myself and two members of my staff. Through experimentation and practice, we have discovered how to stimulate our minds (by applying the principle used in connection with the "Invisible Counselors" described in the next chapter) so that we can, by a process of blending our three minds into one, find the solution to a great variety of personal problems which are submitted by my clients.

The procedure is very simple. We sit down at a conference table, clearly state the nature of the problem we have under consideration, then begin discussing it. Each contributes whatever thoughts that may occur. The strange thing about this method of mind stimulation is that it places each participant in communication with unknown sources of knowledge definitely outside his own experience.

If you understand the principle described in the chapter on the Master Mind, you of course recognize the round-table procedure here described as being a practical application of the Master Mind.

This method of mind stimulation, through harmonious discussion of definite subjects, between three people, illustrates the simplest and most practical use of the Master Mind.

By adopting and following a similar plan any student of this philosophy may come into possession of the famous Carnegie formula briefly described in the introduction. If it means nothing to you at this time, mark this page and read it again after you have finished the last chapter.

The "depression" was a blessing in disguise. It reduced the whole world to a new starting point that gives every one a new opportunity.

CHAPTER 14

THE SIXTH SENSE

THE DOOR TO THE TEMPLE OF WISDOM

The Thirteenth Step Toward Riches

The "thirteenth" principle is known as the sixth sense, through which Infinite Intelligence may, and will communicate voluntarily, without any effort from, or demands by, the individual.

This principle is the apex of the philosophy. It can be assimilated, understood, and applied only by first mastering the other twelve principles.

The sixth sense is that portion of the subconscious mind which has been referred to as the Creative Imagination. It has also been referred to as the "receiving set" through which ideas, plans, and thoughts flash into the mind. The "flashes" are sometimes called "hunches" or "inspirations."

The sixth sense defies description! It cannot be described to a person who has not mastered the other principles of this philosophy, because such a person has no knowledge, and no experience with which the sixth sense may be compared. Understanding of the sixth sense comes only by meditation through mind development *from within*. The sixth sense probably is the medium of contact between the finite mind of man and Infinite

Intelligence, and for this reason, *it is a mixture of both the mental and the spiritual.* It is believed to be the point at which the mind of man contacts the Universal Mind.

After you have mastered the principles described in this book, you will be prepared to accept as truth a statement which may, otherwise, be incredible to you, namely:

Through the aid of the sixth sense, you will be warned of impending dangers in time to avoid them, and notified of opportunities in time to embrace them.

There comes to your aid, and to do your bidding, with the development of the sixth sense, a "guardian angel" who will open to you at all times the door to the Temple of Wisdom.

Whether or not this is a statement of truth, you will never know, except by following the instructions described in the pages of this book, or some similar method of procedure.

The author is not a believer in, nor an advocate of "miracles," for the reason that he has enough knowledge of Nature to understand that Nature *never deviates from her established laws.* Some of her laws are so incomprehensible that they produce what appear to be "miracles." The sixth sense comes as near to being a miracle as anything I have ever experienced, and it appears so, only because I do not understand the method by which this principle is operated.

This much the author does know—that there is a power, or a First Cause, or an Intelligence, which permeates every atom of matter, and embraces every unit of energy perceptible to man—that this Infinite Intelligence converts acorns into oak trees, causes water to flow down hill in response to the law of gravity, follows night with day, and winter with summer, each maintaining its proper place and relationship to the other. This Intelligence may, through the principles of this philosophy, be induced to aid in transmuting desires into concrete, or material form. The author has this knowledge, because he has experimented with it—and has experienced it.

Step by step, through the preceding chapters, you have been led to this, the last principle. If you have mastered each of the preceding principles, you are now prepared to accept, *without being skeptical,* the stupendous claims made here. If you have not mastered the other principles, you must do so before you may determine, definitely, whether or not the claims made in this chapter are fact or fiction.

While I was passing through the age of "hero-worship" I found myself trying to imitate those whom I most admired. Moreover, I discovered that the element of faith, with which I endeavored to imitate my idols, gave me great capacity to do so quite successfully.

I have never entirely divested myself of this habit of hero-worship, although I have passed the age commonly given over to such. My experience has taught me that the next best thing to being truly great, is to emulate the great, by feeling and action, as nearly as possible.

Long before I had ever written a line for publication, or endeavored to deliver a speech in public, I followed the habit of reshaping my own character, by trying to imitate the nine men whose lives and life-works had been most impressive to me. These nine men were Emerson, Paine, Edison, Darwin, Lincoln, Burbank, Napoleon, Ford, and Carnegie. Every night, over a long period of years, I held an imaginary Council meeting with this group whom I called my "Invisible Counselors."

The procedure was this. Just before going to sleep at night, I would shut my eyes, and see, in my imagination, this group of men seated with me around my Council Table. Here I had not only an opportunity to sit among those whom I considered to be great, but I actually dominated the group, by serving as the Chairman.

I had a very definite purpose in indulging my imagination through these nightly meetings. My purpose was to rebuild my own character so it would represent a composite of the characters of my imaginary counselors. Realizing, as I did, early in life, that I had to overcome the handicap of birth in an environment of ignorance and superstition, I deliberately assigned myself the task of voluntary rebirth through the method here described.

BUILDING CHARACTER THROUGH AUTO-SUGGESTION

Being an earnest student of psychology, I knew, of course, that all men have become what they are, because of their dominating thoughts and desires. I knew that every deeply seated desire has the effect of causing one to seek outward expression through which that desire may be transmuted into reality. I knew that self-suggestion is a powerful factor in building character, that it is, in fact, the sole principle through which character is built.

With this knowledge of the principles of mind operation, I was fairly well armed with the equipment needed in rebuilding my character. In these imaginary Council meetings I called on my Cabinet members for the knowledge I wished each to contribute, addressing myself to each member in audible words, as follows:—

"Mr. Emerson, I desire to acquire from you the marvelous understanding of Nature which distinguished your life. I ask that you make an impress upon my subconscious mind, of whatever qualities you possessed, which enabled you to understand and adapt yourself to the laws of Nature. I ask that you assist me in reaching and drawing upon whatever sources of knowledge are available to this end.

"Mr. Burbank, I request that you pass on to me the knowledge which enabled you to so harmonize the laws of Nature that you caused the cactus to shed its thorns, and become an edible food. Give me access to the knowledge which enabled you to make two blades of grass grow where but one grew before, and helped you to blend the coloring of the flowers with more splendor and harmony, for you, alone, have successfully gilded the lily.

"Napoleon, I desire to acquire from you, by emulation, the marvelous ability you possessed to inspire men, and to arouse them to greater and more determined spirit of action. Also to acquire the spirit of enduring faith, which enabled you to turn defeat into victory, and to surmount staggering obstacles. Emperor of Fate, King of Chance, Man of Destiny, I salute you!

"Mr. Paine, I desire to acquire from you the freedom of thought and the courage and clarity with which to express convictions, which so distinguished you!

"Mr. Darwin, I wish to acquire from you the marvelous patience, and ability to study cause and effect, without bias or prejudice, so exemplified by you in the field of natural science.

"Mr. Lincoln, I desire to build into my own character the keen sense of justice, the untiring spirit of patience, the sense of humor, the human understanding, and the tolerance, which were your distinguishing characteristics.

"Mr. Carnegie, I am already indebted to you for my choice of a life-work, which has brought me great happiness and peace of mind. I wish to acquire a thorough understanding of the principles of *organized effort,* which you used so effectively in the building of a great industrial enterprise.

"Mr. Ford, you have been among the most helpful of the men who have supplied much of the material essential to my work. I wish to acquire your spirit of persistence, the determination, poise, and self-confidence which have enabled you to master poverty, organize, unify, and simplify human effort, so I may help others to follow in your footsteps.

"Mr. Edison, I have seated you nearest to me, at my right, because of the personal cooperation you have given me, during my research into the causes of success and failure. I wish to acquire from you the marvelous spirit of faith, with which you have uncovered so many of Natures secrets, the spirit of unremitting toil with which you have so often wrested victory from defeat."

My method of addressing the members of the imaginary Cabinet would vary, according to the traits of character in which I was, for the moment, most interested in acquiring. I studied the records of their lives with painstaking care. After some months of this nightly procedure, I was astounded by the discovery that these imaginary figures became, apparently *real.*

Each of these nine men developed individual characteristics, which surprised me. For example, Lincoln developed the habit of always being late, then walking around in solemn parade. When he came, he walked very slowly, with his hands clasped behind him, and once in a while, he would stop as he passed, and rest his hand, momentarily, upon my shoulder. He always wore an expression of seriousness upon his face. Rarely did I see him smile. The cares of a sundered nation made him grave.

That was not true of the others. Burbank and Paine often indulged in witty repartee which seemed, at times, to shock the other members of the Cabinet. One night Paine suggested that I prepare a lecture on "The Age of Reason," and deliver it from the pulpit of a church which I formerly attended. Many around the table laughed heartily at the suggestion. Not Napoleon! He drew his mouth down at the corners and groaned so loudly that all turned and looked at him with amazement. To him the church was but a pawn of the State, not to be reformed, but to be used, as a convenient inciter to mass activity by the people.

On one occasion Burbank was late. When he came, he was excited with enthusiasm, and explained that he had been late, because of an experiment he was making, through which he hoped to be able to grow apples on any sort of tree. Paine chided him by reminding him that it was an apple which started all the trouble between man and woman. Darwin chuckled heartily as he suggested that Paine should watch out for little serpents, when he went into the forest to gather apples, as they had the habit of growing into big snakes. Emerson observed—"No serpents, no apples," and Napoleon remarked, "No apples, no state!"

Lincoln developed the habit of always being the last one to leave the table after each meeting. On one occasion, he leaned across the end of the table, his arms folded, and remained in that position for many minutes. I made no attempt to disturb him. Finally, he lifted his head slowly, got up and walked to the door, then turned around, came back, and laid his hand on my shoulder and said, "My boy, you will need much courage if you remain steadfast in carrying out your purpose in life. But remember, when difficulties overtake you, the common people have common sense. Adversity will develop it."

One evening Edison arrived ahead of all the others. He walked over and seated himself at my left, where Emerson was accustomed to sit, and said, "You are destined to witness the discovery of the secret of life. When the time comes, you will observe that life consists of great swarms of energy, or entities, each as intelligent as human beings *think* themselves to be. These units of life group together like hives of bees, and remain together until they disintegrate, *through lack of harmony.* These units have differences of opinion, the same as human beings, and often fight among themselves. These meetings which you are conducting will be very helpful to you. They will bring to your rescue some of the same units of life which served the members of your Cabinet, during their lives. These units are eternal. They never die! Your own thoughts and desires serve as the magnet which attracts units of life, from the great ocean of life out there. Only the friendly units are attracted—the ones which harmonize with the nature of your desires."

The other members of the Cabinet began to enter the room. Edison got up, and slowly walked around to his own seat. Edison was still living when this happened. It impressed me so greatly that I went to see him, and told him about the experience. He smiled broadly, and said, "Your dream was more a reality than you may imagine it to have been." He added no further explanation to his statement.

These meetings became so realistic that I became fearful of their consequences, and discontinued them for several months. The experiences were so uncanny, I was afraid if I continued them I would lose sight of the fact that the meetings were purely *experiences of my imagination.*

Some six months after I had discontinued the practice I was awakened one night, or thought I was, when I saw Lincoln standing at my bedside. He said, "The world will soon need your services. It is about to undergo a period of chaos which will cause men and women to lose faith, and become panic stricken. Go ahead with your work and complete your philosophy. That is your mission in life. If you neglect it, for any cause whatsoever, you will be reduced to a primal state, and be compelled to retrace the cycles through which you have passed during thousands of years."

I was unable to tell, the following morning, whether I had dreamed this, or had actually been awake, and I have never since found out which it was, but I do know that the dream, if it were a dream, was so vivid in my mind the next day that I resumed my meetings the following night.

At our next meeting, the members of my Cabinet all filed into the room together, and stood at their accustomed places at the Council Table, while Lincoln raised a glass and said, "Gentlemen, let us drink a toast to a friend who has returned to the fold."

After that, I began to add new members to my Cabinet, until now it consists of more than fifty, among them Christ, St. Paul, Galileo, Copernicus, Aristotle, Plato, Socrates, Homer, Voltaire, Bruno, Spinoza, Drummond, Kant, Schopenhauer, Newton, Confucius, Elbert Hubbard, Brann, Ingersoll, Wilson, and William James.

This is the first time that I have had the courage to mention this. Heretofore, I have remained quiet on the subject, because I knew, from my own attitude in connection with such matters, that I would be misunderstood if I described my unusual experience. I have been emboldened now to reduce my experience to the printed page, because I am now less concerned about what "they say" than I was in the years that have passed. One of the blessings of maturity is that it sometimes brings one greater courage to be truthful, regardless of what those who do not understand may think or say.

Lest I be misunderstood, I wish here to state most emphatically, that I still regard my Cabinet meetings as being purely imaginary, but I feel entitled to suggest that, while the members of my Cabinet may be purely fictional, and the meetings existent only in my own imagination, they have led me into glorious paths of adventure, rekindled an appreciation of true greatness, encouraged creative endeavor, and emboldened the expression of honest thought.

Somewhere in the cell-structure of the brain, is located an organ which receives vibrations of thought ordinarily called "hunches." So far, science has not discovered where this organ of the sixth sense is located, but this is not important. The fact remains that human beings do receive accurate knowledge, through sources other than the physical senses. Such knowledge, generally, is received when the mind is under the influence of extraordinary stimulation. Any emergency which arouses the emotions, and causes the heart to beat more rapidly than normal may, and generally does, bring the sixth sense into action. Anyone who has experienced a near accident while driving, knows that on such occasions, the sixth sense often comes to one's rescue, and aids, by split seconds, in avoiding the accident.

These facts are mentioned preliminary to a statement of fact which I shall now make, namely, that during my meetings with the "Invisible Counselors" I find my mind most receptive to ideas, thoughts, and knowledge which reach me through the sixth sense. I can truthfully say that I owe entirely to my "Invisible Counselors" full credit for such ideas, facts, or knowledge as I received through "inspiration."

On scores of occasions, when I have faced emergencies, some of them so grave that my life was in jeopardy, I have been miraculously guided past these difficulties through the influence of my "Invisible Counselors."

My original purpose in conducting Council meetings with imaginary beings was solely that of impressing my own subconscious mind, through the principle of auto-suggestion, with certain characteristics which I desired to acquire. In more recent years, my experimentation has taken on an entirely different trend. I now go to my imaginary counselors with every difficult problem which confronts me and my clients. The results are often astonishing, although I do not depend entirely on this form of counsel.

You, of course, have recognized that this chapter covers a subject with which a majority of people are not familiar. The sixth sense is a subject that will be of great interest and benefit to the person whose aim is to accumulate vast wealth, but it need not claim the attention of those whose desires are more modest.

Henry Ford undoubtedly understands and makes practical use of the sixth sense. His vast business and financial operations make it necessary for him to understand and use this principle. The late Thomas A. Edison understood and used the sixth sense in connection with the development of inventions, especially those involving basic patents, in connection with which he had no human experience and no accumulated knowledge to guide him, as was the case while he was working on the talking machine, and the moving picture machine.

Nearly all great leaders, such as Napoleon, Bismarck, Joan of Arc, Christ, Buddha, Confucius, and Mohammed, understood, and probably made use of the sixth sense almost continuously. The major portion of their greatness consisted of their knowledge of this principle.

The sixth sense is not something that one can take off and put on at will. Ability to use this great power comes slowly, through application of the other principles outlined in this book. Seldom does any individual come into workable knowledge of the sixth sense before the age of forty. More often the knowledge is not available until one is well past fifty, and this, for the reason that the spiritual forces, with which the sixth sense is so closely related, do not mature and become usable except through years of meditation, self-examination, and serious thought.

No matter who you are, or what may have been your purpose in reading this book, you can profit by it without understanding the principle described in this chapter. This is especially true if your major purpose is that of accumulation of money or other material things.

The chapter on the sixth sense was included, because the book is designed for the purpose of presenting a complete philosophy by which individuals may unerringly guide themselves in attaining whatever they ask of life. The starting point of all achievement is desire. The finishing point is that brand of knowledge which leads to understanding—understanding of self, understanding of others, understanding of the laws of Nature, recognition and understanding of happiness.

This sort of understanding comes in its fullness only through familiarity with, and use of the principle of the sixth sense, hence that principle had to be included as a part of this philosophy, for the benefit of those who demand more than money.

Having read the chapter, you must have observed that while reading it, you were lifted to a high level of mental stimulation. Splendid! Come back to this again a month from now, read it once more, and observe that your mind will soar to a still-higher level of stimulation. Repeat this experience from time to time, giving no concern as to how much or how little you learn at the time, and eventually you will find yourself in possession of a power that will enable you to throw off discouragement, master fear, overcome procrastination, and draw freely upon your imagination. Then you will have felt the touch of that unknown "something" which has been the moving spirit of every truly great thinker, leader, artist, musician, writer, statesman. Then you will be in position to transmute your desires into their physical or financial counterpart as easily as you may lie down and quit at the first sign of opposition.

FAITH VS. FEAR!

Previous chapters have described how to develop faith, through auto-suggestion, desire and the subconscious. The next chapter presents detailed instructions for the mastery of fear.

Here will be found a full description of the six fears which are the cause of all discouragement, timidity, procrastination, indifference, indecision, and the lack of ambition, self-reliance, initiative, self-control, and enthusiasm.

Search yourself carefully as you study these six enemies, as they may exist only in your subconscious mind, where their presence will be hard to detect.

Remember, too, as you analyze the "Six Ghosts of Fear," that they are nothing but ghosts because they exist only in one's mind.

Remember, also, that ghosts—creations of uncontrolled imagination—have caused most of the damage people have done to their own minds, therefore, ghosts can be as dangerous as if they lived and walked on the earth in physical bodies.

The Ghost of the Fear of Poverty, which seized the minds of millions of people in 1929, was so real that it caused the worst business depression this country has ever known. Moreover, this particular ghost still frightens some of us out of our wits.

CHAPTER 15

HOW TO OUTWIT THE SIX GHOSTS OF FEAR

Take Inventory of Yourself, As You Read This Closing Chapter, and Find Out How Many of the "Ghosts" Are Standing in Your Way

Before you can put any portion of this philosophy into successful use, your mind must be prepared to receive it. The preparation is not difficult. It begins with study, analysis, and understanding of three enemies which you shall have to clear out. These are indecision, doubt, and fear!

The sixth sense will never function while these three negatives, or any of them remain in your mind. The members of this unholy trio are closely related; where one is found, the other two are close at hand.

Indecision is the seedling of fear! Remember this, as you read. Indecision crystallizes into doubt; the two blend and become fear! The "blending" process often is slow. This is one reason why these three enemies are so dangerous. They germinate and grow *without their presence being observed.*

The remainder of this chapter describes an end which must be attained before the philosophy, as a whole, can be put into practical use. It also analyzes a condition which has, but lately, reduced huge numbers of people to poverty, and it states a truth which must be understood by all who accumulate riches, whether measured in terms of money or a state of mind of far greater value than money.

The purpose of this chapter is to turn the spotlight of attention upon the cause and the cure of the six basic fears. Before we can master an enemy, we must know its name, its habits, and its place of abode. As you read, analyze yourself carefully, and determine which, if any, of the six common fears have attached themselves to you.

Do not be deceived by the habits of these subtle enemies. Sometimes they remain hidden in the subconscious mind, where they are difficult to locate, and still more difficult to eliminate.

THE SIX BASIC FEARS

There are six basic fears, with some combination of which every human suffers at one time or another. Most people are fortunate if they do not suffer from the entire six. Named in the order of their most common appearance, they are:—

The fear of POVERTY
The fear of CRITICISM
The fear of ILL HEALTH
} at the bottom of most of one's worries

The fear of LOSS OF LOVE OF SOMEONE
The fear of OLD AGE
The fear of DEATH

All other fears are of minor importance; they can be grouped under these six headings.

The prevalence of these fears, as a curse to the world, runs in cycles. For almost six years, while the depression was on, we floundered in the cycle of fear of poverty. During the world war, we were in the cycle of fear of death. Just following the war, we were in the cycle of fear of ill health, as evidenced by the epidemic of disease which spread itself all over the world.

Fears are nothing more than states of mind. One's state of mind is subject to control and direction. Physicians, as everyone knows, are less subject to attack by disease than ordinary laymen, for the reason that physicians do not fear disease. Physicians, without fear or hesitation, have been known to physically contact hundreds of people, daily, who were suffering from such contagious diseases as small-pox, without becoming infected. Their immunity against the disease consisted, largely, if not solely, in their absolute lack of fear.

Man can create nothing which he does not first conceive in the form of an impulse of thought. Following this statement, comes another of still greater importance, namely man's thought impulses begin immediately to translate themselves into their physical equivalent, whether those thoughts are voluntary or involuntary. Thought impulses which are picked up through the ether, by mere chance (thoughts which have been released by other minds) may determine one's financial, business, professional, or social destiny just as surely as do the thought impulses which one creates by intent and design.

We are here laying the foundation for the presentation of a fact of great importance to the person who does not understand why some people appear to be "lucky" while others of equal or greater ability, training, experience, and brain capacity, seem destined to ride with misfortune. This fact may be explained by the statement that *every human being has the ability to completely control his own mind,* and with this control, obviously, every person may open his mind to the tramp thought impulses which are being released by other brains, or close the doors tightly and admit only thought impulses of his own choice.

Nature has endowed man with absolute control over but one thing, and that is thought. This fact, coupled with the additional fact that everything which man creates begins in the form of a thought, leads one very near to the principle by which fear may be mastered.

If it is true that all thought has a tendency to clothe itself in its physical equivalent (and this is true, beyond any reasonable room for doubt), it is equally true that thought impulses of fear and poverty cannot be translated into terms of courage and financial gain.

The people of America began to think of poverty, following the Wall Street crash of 1929. Slowly, but surely that mass thought was crystallized into its physical equivalent, which was known as a "depression." This had to happen; it is in conformity with the laws of Nature.

THE FEAR OF POVERTY

There can be no compromise between poverty and riches! The two roads that lead to poverty and riches travel in opposite directions. If you want riches, you must refuse to accept any circumstance that leads toward poverty. (The word "riches" is here used in its broadest sense, meaning financial, spiritual, mental and material estates.) The starting point of the path that leads to riches is desire. In chapter two, you received full instructions for the proper use of desire. In this chapter, on fear, you have complete instructions for preparing your mind to make practical use of desire.

Here, then, is the place to give yourself a challenge which will definitely determine how much of this philosophy you have absorbed. Here is the point at which you can turn prophet and foretell, accurately, what the future holds in store for you. If, after reading this chapter, you are willing to accept poverty, you may as well make up your mind to receive poverty. This is one decision you cannot avoid.

If you demand riches, determine what form, and how much will be required to satisfy you. You know the road that leads to riches. You have been given a road map which, if followed, will keep you on that road. If you neglect to make the start, or stop before you arrive, no one will be to blame but you. This responsibility is yours. No alibi will save you from accepting the responsibility if you now fail or refuse to demand riches of Life, because the acceptance calls for but one thing—incidentally, the only thing you can control—and that is a state of mind. A state of mind is something that one assumes. It cannot be purchased; it must be created.

Fear of poverty is a state of mind, nothing else! But it is sufficient to destroy one's chances of achievement in any undertaking, a truth which became painfully evident during the depression.

This fear paralyzes the faculty of reason, destroys the faculty of imagination, kills off self-reliance, undermines enthusiasm, discourages initiative, leads to uncertainty of purpose, encourages procrastination, wipes out enthusiasm and makes self-control an impossibility. It takes the charm from one's personality, destroys the possibility of accurate thinking, diverts concentration of effort; it masters persistence, turns the will-power into nothingness, destroys ambition, beclouds the memory and invites failure in every conceivable form; it kills love and assassinates the finer emotions of the heart, discourages friendship and invites disaster in a hundred forms, leads to sleeplessness, misery and unhappiness—and all this despite the obvious truth that we live in a world of over-abundance of everything the heart could desire, with nothing standing between us and our desires, excepting lack of a definite purpose.

The Fear of Poverty is, without doubt, the most destructive of the six basic fears. It has been placed at the head of the list, because it is the most difficult to master. Considerable courage is required to state the truth about the origin of this fear, and still greater courage to accept the truth after it has been stated. The fear of poverty grew out of man's inherited tendency to prey upon his fellow man economically. Nearly all animals lower than man are motivated by instinct, but their capacity to "think" is limited, therefore, they prey upon one another physically. Man, with his superior sense of intuition, with the capacity to think and to reason, does not eat his fellow man bodily, he gets more satisfaction out of "eating" him financially. Man is so avaricious that every conceivable law has been passed to safeguard him from his fellow man.

Of all the ages of the world, of which we know anything, the age in which we live seems to be one that is outstanding because of man's money-madness. A man is considered less than the dust of the earth, unless he can display a fat bank account; but if he has money—never mind how he acquired it—he is a "king" or a "big shot"; he is above the law, he rules in politics, he dominates in business, and the whole world about him bows in respect when he passes.

Nothing brings man so much suffering and humility as poverty! Only those who have experienced poverty understand the full meaning of this.

It is no wonder that man *fears* poverty. Through a long line of inherited experiences man has learned, for sure, that some men cannot be trusted, where matters of money and earthly possessions are concerned. This is a rather stinging indictment, the worst part of it being that it is true.

The majority of marriages are motivated by the wealth possessed by one, or both of the contracting parties. It is no wonder, therefore, that the divorce courts are busy.

So eager is man to possess wealth that he will acquire it in whatever manner he can—through legal methods if possible— through other methods if necessary or expedient.

Self-analysis may disclose weaknesses which one does not like to acknowledge. This form of examination is essential to all who demand of Life more than mediocrity and poverty. Remember, as you check yourself point by point, that you are both the court and the jury, the prosecuting attorney and the attorney for the defense, and that you are the plaintiff and the defendant, also, that you are on trial. Face the facts squarely. Ask yourself definite questions and demand direct replies. When the examination is over, you will know more about yourself. If you do not feel that you can be an impartial judge in this self-examination, call upon someone who knows you well to serve as judge while you cross-examine yourself. You are after the truth. *Get it, no matter at what cost, even though it may temporarily embarrass you!*

The majority of people, if asked what they fear most, would reply, "I fear nothing." The reply would be inaccurate, because few people realize that they are bound, handicapped, whipped spiritually and physically through some form of fear. So subtle and deeply seated is the emotion of fear that one may go through life burdened with it, never recognizing its presence. Only a courageous analysis will disclose the presence of this universal enemy. When you begin such an analysis, search deeply into your character. Here is a list of the symptoms for which you should look:

Symptoms of the Fear of Poverty

INDIFFERENCE. Commonly expressed through lack of ambition; willingness to tolerate poverty; acceptance of whatever compensation life may offer without protest; mental and physical laziness; lack of initiative, imagination, enthusiasm and self-control

INDECISION. The habit of permitting others to do one's thinking. Staying "on the fence."

DOUBT. Generally expressed through alibis and excuses designed to cover up, explain away, or apologize for one's failures, sometimes expressed in the form of envy of those who are successful, or by criticising them.

WORRY. Usually expressed by finding fault with others, a tendency to spend beyond one's income, neglect of personal appearance, scowling and frowning;

intemperance in the use of alcoholic drink, sometimes through the use of narcotics; nervousness, lack of poise, self-consciousness and lack of self-reliance.

OVER-CAUTION. The habit of looking for the negative side of every circumstance, thinking and talking of possible failure instead of concentrating upon the means of succeeding. Knowing all the roads to disaster, but never searching for the plans to avoid failure. Waiting for "the right time" to begin putting ideas and plans into action, until the waiting becomes a permanent habit. Remembering those who have failed, and forgetting those who have succeeded. Seeing the hole in the doughnut, but overlooking the doughnut. Pessimism, leading to indigestion, poor elimination, auto-intoxication, bad breath and bad disposition.

PROCRASTINATION. The habit of putting off until tomorrow that which should have been done last year. Spending enough time in creating alibis and excuses to have done the job. This symptom is closely related to over-caution, doubt and worry. Refusal to accept responsibility when it can be avoided. Willingness to compromise rather than put up a stiff fight. Compromising with difficulties instead of harnessing and using them as stepping stones to advancement. Bargaining with Life for a penny, instead of demanding prosperity, opulence, riches, contentment and happiness. Planning what to do if and when overtaken by failure, instead of burning all bridges and making retreat impossible. Weakness of, and often total lack of self-confidence, definiteness of purpose, self-control, initiative, enthusiasm, ambition, thrift and sound reasoning ability. Expecting poverty instead of demanding riches. Association with those who accept poverty instead of seeking the company of those who demand and receive riches.

MONEY TALKS!

Some will ask, "Why did you write a book about money? Why measure riches in dollars, alone?" Some will believe, and rightly so, that there are other forms of riches more desirable than money. Yes, there are riches which cannot be measured in terms of dollars, but there are millions of people who will say, "Give me all the money I need, and I will find everything else I want."

The major reason why I wrote this book on how to get money is the fact that the world has but lately passed through an experience that left millions of men and women paralyzed with the fear of poverty. What this sort of fear does to one was well described by Westbrook Pegler, in the *New York World-Telegram*, viz:

"Money is only clam shells or metal discs or scraps of paper, and there are treasures of the heart and soul which money cannot buy, but most people, being broke, are unable to keep this in mind and sustain their spirits. When a man is down and out and on the street, unable to get any job at all, something happens to his spirit which can be observed in the droop of his shoulders, the set of his hat, his walk and his gaze. He cannot escape a feeling of inferiority among people with regular employment, even though he knows they are definitely not his equals in character, intelligence or ability.

"These people—even his friends—feel, on the other hand, a sense of superiority and regard him, perhaps unconsciously, as a casualty. He may borrow for a time, but not enough to carry on in his accustomed way, and he cannot continue to borrow very long. But borrowing in itself, when a man is borrowing merely to live, is a depressing experience, and the money lacks the power of earned money to revive his spirits. Of course, none of this applies to bums or habitual ne'er-do-wells, but only to men of normal ambitions and self-respect.

WOMEN CONCEAL DESPAIR

"Women in the same predicament must be different. We somehow do not think of women at all in considering the down-and-outers. They are scarce in the breadlines, they rarely are seen begging on the streets, and they are not recognizable in crowds by the same plain signs which identify busted men. Of course, I do not mean the shuffling hags of the city streets who are the opposite number of the confirmed male bums. I mean reasonably young, decent and intelligent women. There must be many of them, but their despair is not apparent. Maybe they kill themselves.

"When a man is down and out he has time on his hands for brooding. He may travel miles to see a man about a job and discover that the job is filled or that it is one of those jobs with no base pay but only a commission on the sale of some useless knickknack which nobody would buy except out of pity. Turning that down, he finds himself back on the street with nowhere to go but just anywhere. So he walks and walks. He gazes into store windows at luxuries which are not for him, and feels inferior and gives way to people who stop to look with an active interest. He wanders into the railroad station or puts himself down in the library to ease his legs and soak up a little heat, but that isn't looking for a job, so he gets going again. He may not know it, but his aimlessness would give him away even if the very lines of his figure did not. He may be well dressed in the clothes left over from the days when he had a steady job, but the clothes cannot disguise the droop.

MONEY MAKES DIFFERENCE

"He sees thousands of other people, bookkeepers or clerks or chemists or wagon hands, busy at their work and envies them from the bottom of his soul. They have their independence, their self-respect and manhood, and he simply cannot convince himself that he is a good man, too, though he argue it out and arrive at a favorable verdict hour after hour.

"It is just money which makes this difference in him. With a little money he would be himself again.

"Some employers take the most shocking advantage of people who are down and out. The agencies hang out little colored cards offering miserable wages to busted men—$12 a week, $15 a week. A $17 a week job is a plum, and anyone with $25 a week to offer does not hang the job in front of an agency on a colored card. I have a want ad clipped from a local paper demanding a clerk, a good, clean penman, to take telephone orders for a sandwich shop from 11 a.m. to 2 p.m. for $8 a month—not $8 a week but $8 a month. The ad says also, 'State religion.' Can you imagine the brutal effrontery of anyone who demands a good, clean penman for 11 cents an hour inquiring into the victim's religion? But that is what busted people are offered."

THE FEAR OF CRITICISM

Just how man originally came by this fear, no one can state definitely, but one thing is certain—he has it in a highly developed form. Some believe that this fear made its appearance about the time that politics became a "profession." Others believe it can be traced to the age when women first began to concern themselves with "styles" in wearing apparel.

This author, being neither a humorist nor a prophet, is inclined to attribute the basic fear of criticism to that part of man's inherited nature which prompts him not only to take away his fellow man's goods and wares, but to justify his action by criticism of his fellow man's character. It is a well-known fact that a thief will criticise the man from whom he steals—that politicians seek office, not by displaying their own virtues and qualifications, but by attempting to besmirch their opponents.

The fear of criticism takes on many forms, the majority of which are petty and trivial. Baldheaded men, for example, are bald for no other reason than their fear of criticism. Heads become bald because of the tight-fitting bands of hats which cut off the circulation from the roots of the hair. Men wear hats, not because they actually need them, but mainly because "everyone is doing it." The individual falls into line and does likewise, lest some other individual criticise him. Women seldom have bald heads, or even thin hair, because they wear hats which fit their heads loosely, the only purpose of the hats being adornment.

But, it must not be supposed that women are free from the fear of criticism. If any woman claims to be superior to man with reference to this fear, ask her to walk down the street wearing a hat of the vintage of 1890.

The astute manufacturers of clothing have not been slow to capitalize on this basic fear of criticism, with which all mankind has been cursed. Every season the styles in many articles of wearing apparel change. Who establishes the styles? Certainly not the purchaser of clothing, but the manufacturer. Why does he change the styles so often? The answer is obvious. He changes the styles so he can sell more clothes.

For the same reason the manufacturers of automobiles (with a few rare and very sensible exceptions) change styles of models every season. No man wants to drive an automobile which is not of the latest style, although the older model may actually be the better car.

We have been describing the manner in which people behave under the influence of fear of criticism as applied to the small and petty things of life. Let us now examine human behavior when this fear affects people in connection with the more important events of human relationship. Take for example practically any person who has reached the age of "mental maturity" (from thirty-five to forty years of age, as a general average), and if you could read the secret thoughts of his mind, you would find a very decided disbelief in most of the fables taught by the majority of the dogmatists and theologians a few decades back.

Not often, however, will you find a person who has the courage to openly state his belief on this subject. Most people will, if pressed far enough, tell a lie rather than admit that they do not believe the stories associated with that form of religion which held people in bondage prior to the age of scientific discovery and education.

Why does the average person, even in this day of enlightenment, shy away from denying his belief in the fables which were the basis of most of the religions a few decades ago? The answer is, "because of the fear of criticism." Men and women have been burned at the stake for daring to express disbelief in ghosts. It is no wonder we have inherited a consciousness which makes us fear criticism. The time was, and not so far in the past, when criticism carried severe punishments — it still does in some countries.

The fear of criticism robs man of his initiative, destroys his power of imagination, limits his individuality, takes away his self-reliance, and does him damage in a hundred other ways. Parents often do their children irreparable injury by criticising them. The mother of one of my boyhood chums used to punish him with a switch almost daily, always completing the job with the statement, "You'll land in the penitentiary before you are twenty." He was sent to a Reformatory at the age of seventeen.

Criticism is the one form of service, of which everyone has too much. Everyone has a stock of it which is handed out, gratis, whether called for or not. One's nearest relatives often are the worst offenders. It should be recognized as a crime (in reality it is a crime of the worst nature) for any parent to build inferiority complexes in the mind of a child, through unnecessary criticism. Employers who understand human nature, get the best there is in men, not by criticism, but by constructive suggestion. Parents may accomplish the same results with their children. Criticism will plant fear in the human heart, or resentment, but it will not build love or affection.

Symptoms of the Fear of Criticism

This fear is almost as universal as the fear of poverty, and its effects are just as fatal to personal achievement, mainly because this fear destroys initiative, and discourages the use of imagination. The major symptoms of the fear are:

SELF-CONSCIOUSNESS. Generally expressed through nervousness, timidity in conversation and in meeting strangers, awkward movement of the hands and limbs, shifting of the eyes.

LACK OF POISE. Expressed through lack of voice control, nervousness in the presence of others, poor posture of body, poor memory.

PERSONALITY. Lacking in firmness of decision, personal charm, and ability to express opinions definitely. The habit of sidestepping issues instead of meeting them squarely. Agreeing with others without careful examination of their opinions.

INFERIORITY COMPLEX. The habit of expressing self-approval by word of mouth and by actions, as a means of covering up a feeling of inferiority. Using "big words" to impress others (often without knowing the real meaning of the words). Imitating others in dress, speech and manners. Boasting of imaginary achievements. This sometimes gives a surface appearance of a feeling of superiority.

EXTRAVAGANCE. The habit of trying to "keep up with the Joneses," spending beyond one's income.

LACK OF INITIATIVE. Failure to embrace opportunities for self-advancement, fear to express opinions, lack of confidence in one's own ideas, giving evasive answers to questions asked by superiors, hesitancy of manner and speech, deceit in both words and deeds.

LACK OF AMBITION. Mental and physical laziness, lack of self-assertion, slowness in reaching decisions, easily influenced by others, the habit of criticising others behind their backs and flattering them to their faces, the habit of accepting defeat without protest, quitting an undertaking when opposed by others, suspicious of other people without cause, lacking in tactfulness of manner and speech, unwillingness to accept the blame for mistakes.

THE FEAR OF ILL HEALTH

This fear may be traced to both physical and social heredity. It is closely associated, as to its origin, with the causes of fear of Old Age and the fear of Death, because it leads one closely to the border of "terrible worlds" of which man knows not, but concerning which he has been taught some discomforting stories. The opinion is somewhat general, also, that certain unethical people engaged in the business of "selling health" have had not a little to do with keeping alive the fear of ill health.

In the main, man fears ill health because of the terrible pictures which have been planted in his mind of what may happen if death should overtake him. He also fears it because of the economic toll which it may claim.

A reputable physician estimated that 75% of all people who visit physicians for professional service are suffering with hypochondria (imaginary illness). It has been shown most convincingly that the fear of disease, even where there is not the slightest cause for fear, often produces the physical symptoms of the disease feared.

Powerful and mighty is the human mind! It builds or it destroys.

Playing upon this common weakness of fear of ill health, dispensers of patent medicines have reaped fortunes. This form of imposition upon credulous humanity became so prevalent some twenty years ago that *Colliers' Weekly Magazine* conducted a bitter campaign against some of the worst offenders in the patent medicine business.

During the "flu" epidemic which broke out during the world war, the mayor of New York City took drastic steps to check the damage which people were doing themselves through their inherent fear of ill health. He called in the newspaper men and said to them, "Gentlemen, I feel it necessary to ask you not to publish any *scare headlines* concerning the 'flu' epidemic. Unless you cooperate with me, we will have a situation which we cannot control." The newspapers quit publishing stories about the "flu," and within one month the epidemic had been successfully checked.

Through a series of experiments conducted some years ago, it was proved that people may be made ill by suggestion. We conducted this experiment by causing three acquaintances to visit the "victims," each of whom asked the question, "What ails you? You look terribly ill." The first questioner usually provoked a grin, and a nonchalant "Oh, nothing, I'm all right," from the victim. The second questioner usually was answered with the statement, "I don't know exactly, but I do feel badly." The third questioner was usually met with the frank admission that the victim was actually feeling ill.

Try this on an acquaintance if you doubt that it will make him uncomfortable, but do not carry the experiment too far. There is a certain religious sect whose members take vengeance upon their enemies by the "hexing" method. They call it "placing a spell" on the victim.

There is overwhelming evidence that disease sometimes begins in the form of negative thought impulse. Such an impulse may be passed from one mind to another, by suggestion, or created by an individual in his own mind.

A man who was blessed with more wisdom than this incident might indicate, once said, "When anyone asks me how I feel, I always want to answer by knocking him down."

Doctors send patients into new climates for their health, because a change of "mental attitude" is necessary. The seed of fear of ill health lives in every human mind. Worry, fear, discouragement, disappointment in love and business affairs, cause this seed to germinate and grow. The recent business depression kept the doctors on the run, because every form of negative thinking may cause ill health.

Disappointments in business and in love stand at the head of the list of causes of fear of ill health. A young man suffered a disappointment in love which sent him to a hospital. For months he hovered between life and death. A specialist in suggestive therapeutics was called in. The specialist changed nurses, placing him in charge of a very *charming young woman* who began (by pre-arrangement with the doctor) to make love to him the first day of her arrival on the job. Within three weeks the patient was discharged from the hospital, still suffering, but with an entirely different malady. He was in love again. The remedy was a hoax, but the patient and the nurse were later married. Both are in good health at the time of this writing.

Symptoms of the Fear of Ill Health

The symptoms of this almost universal fear are:

AUTO-SUGGESTION. The habit of negative use of self-suggestion by looking for, and expecting to find the symptoms of all kinds of disease. "Enjoying" imaginary illness and speaking of it as being real. The habit of trying all "fads" and "isms" recommended by others as having therapeutic value. Talking to others of operations, accidents and other forms of illness. Experimenting with diets, physical exercises, reducing systems, without professional guidance. Trying home remedies, patent medicines and "quack" remedies.

HYPOCHONDRIA. The habit of talking of illness, concentrating the mind upon disease, and expecting its appearance until a nervous break occurs. Nothing that comes in bottles can cure this condition. It is brought on by negative thinking and nothing but positive thought can effect a cure. Hypochondria (a medical term for imaginary disease) is said to do as much damage on occasion, as the disease one fears might do. Most so-called cases of "nerves" come from imaginary illness.

EXERCISE. Fear of ill health often interferes with proper physical exercise, and results in over-weight, by causing one to avoid outdoor life.

SUSCEPTIBILITY. Fear of ill health breaks down Nature's body resistance, and creates a favorable condition for any form of disease one may contact. The fear of ill health often is related to the fear of Poverty, especially in the case of the hypochondriac, who constantly worries about the possibility of having to pay doctor's bills, hospital bills, etc. This type of person spends much time preparing for sickness, talking about death, saving money for cemetery lots, and burial expenses, etc.

SELF-CODDLING. The habit of making a bid for sympathy, using imaginary illness as the lure. (People often resort to this trick to avoid work.) The habit of feigning illness to cover plain laziness, or to serve as an alibi for lack of ambition.

INTEMPERANCE. The habit of using alcohol or narcotics to destroy pains such as headaches, neuralgia, etc., instead of eliminating the cause.

The habit of reading about illness and worrying over the possibility of being stricken by it. The habit of reading patent medicine advertisements.

THE FEAR OF LOSS OF LOVE

The original source of this inherent fear needs but little description, because it obviously grew out of man's polygamous habit of stealing his fellow man's mate, and his habit of taking liberties with her whenever he could.

Jealousy, and other similar forms of dementia praecox grow out of man's inherited fear of the loss of love of someone. This fear is the most painful of all the six basic fears. It probably plays more havoc with the body and mind than any of the other basic fears, as it often leads to permanent insanity.

The fear of the loss of love probably dates back to the stone age, when men stole women by brute force. They continue to steal females, but their technique has changed. Instead of force, they now use persuasion, the promise of pretty clothes, motor cars, and other "bait" much more effective than physical force. Man's habits are the same as they were at the dawn of civilization, but he expresses them differently.

Careful analysis has shown that women are more susceptible to this fear than men. This fact is easily explained. Women have learned, from experience, that men are polygamous by nature, that they are not to be trusted in the hands of rivals.

Symptoms of the Fear of Loss of Love

The distinguishing symptoms of this fear are:—

> JEALOUSY. The habit of being suspicious of friends and loved ones without any reasonable evidence of sufficient grounds. (Jealousy is a form of dementia praecox which sometimes becomes violent without the slightest cause.) The habit of

accusing wife or husband of infidelity without grounds. General suspicion of everyone, absolute faith in no one.

FAULT FINDING. The habit of finding fault with friends, relatives, business associates and loved ones upon the slightest provocation, or without any cause whatsoever.

GAMBLING. The habit of gambling, stealing, cheating, and otherwise taking hazardous chances to provide money for loved ones, with the belief that love can be bought. The habit of spending beyond one's means, or incurring debts, to provide gifts for loved ones, with the object of making a favorable showing. Insomnia, nervousness, lack of persistence, weakness of will, lack of self-control, lack of self-reliance, bad temper.

THE FEAR OF OLD AGE

In the main, this fear grows out of two sources. First, the thought that old age may bring with it poverty. Secondly, and by far the most common source of origin, from false and cruel teachings of the past which have been too well mixed with "fire and brimstone," and other bogies cunningly designed to enslave man through fear.

In the basic fear of old age, man has two very sound reasons for his apprehension—one growing out of his distrust of his fellow man, who may seize whatever worldly goods he may possess, and the other arising from the terrible pictures of the world beyond, which were planted in his mind, through social heredity before he came into full possession of his mind.

The possibility of ill health, which is more common as people grow older, is also a contributing cause of this common fear of old age. Eroticism also enters into the cause of the fear of old age, as no man cherishes the thought of diminishing sex attraction.

The most common cause of fear of old age is associated with the possibility of poverty. "Poorhouse" is not a pretty word. It throws a chill into the mind of every person who faces the possibility of having to spend his declining years on a poor farm.

Another contributing cause of the fear of old age is the possibility of loss of freedom and independence, as old age may bring with it the loss of both physical and economic freedom.

Symptoms of the Fear of Old Age

The commonest symptoms of this fear are:

The tendency to slow down and develop an inferiority complex at the age of mental maturity, around the age of forty, falsely believing oneself to be "slipping" be-cause of age. (The truth is that man's most useful years, mentally and spiritually, are those between forty and sixty.)

The habit of speaking apologetically of one's self as "being old" merely because one has reached the age of forty, or fifty, instead of reversing the rule and expressing gratitude for having reached the age of wisdom and understanding.

The habit of killing off initiative, imagination, and self-reliance by falsely believing one's self too old to exercise these qualities. The habit of the man or woman of forty dress-ing with the aim of trying to appear much younger, and affecting mannerisms of youth; thereby inspiring ridicule by both friends and strangers.

THE FEAR OF DEATH

To some this is the cruelest of all the basic fears. The reason is obvious. The terrible pangs of fear associated with the thought of death, in the majority of cases, may be charged directly to religious fanaticism. So-called "heathen" are less afraid of death than the more "civilized." For hundreds of millions of years man has been asking the still-unanswered questions, "whence" and "whither." Where did I come from, and where am I going?

During the darker ages of the past, the more cunning and crafty were not slow to offer the answer to these questions, for a price. Witness, now, the major source of origin of the fear of death.

"Come into my tent, embrace my faith, accept my dogmas, and I will give you a ticket that will admit you straightaway into heaven when you die," cries a leader of sectarianism. "Remain out of my tent," says the same leader, "and may the devil take you and burn you throughout eternity."

Eternity is a long time. Fire is a terrible thing. The thought of eternal punishment, with fire, not only causes man to fear death, it often causes him to lose his reason. It destroys interest in life and makes happiness impossible.

During my research, I reviewed a book entitled A *Catalogue of the Gods,* in which were listed the *30,000 gods* which man has worshiped. Think of it! Thirty thousand of them, represented by everything from a crawfish to a man. It is little wonder that men have become frightened at the approach of death.

While the religious leader may not be able to provide safe conduct into heaven, nor, by lack of such provision, allow the unfortunate to descend into hell, the possibility of the latter seems so terrible that the very thought of it lays hold of the imagination in such a realistic way that it paralyzes reason, and sets up the fear of death.

In truth, no man knows, and no man has ever known, what heaven or hell is like, nor does any man know if either place actually exists. This very lack of positive knowledge opens the door of the human mind to the charlatan so he may enter and control that mind with his stock of legerdemain and various brands of pious fraud and trickery.

The fear of death is not as common now as it was during the age when there were no great colleges and universities. Men of science have turned the spotlight of truth upon the world, and this truth is rapidly freeing men and women from this terrible fear of death. The young men and young women who attend the colleges and universities are not easily impressed by "fire" and "brimstone." Through the aid of biology, astronomy, geology, and other related sciences, the fears of the dark ages which gripped the minds of men and destroyed their reason have been dispelled.

Insane asylums are filled with men and women who have gone mad, because of the fear of death.

This fear is useless. Death will come, no matter what anyone may think about it. Accept it as a necessity, and pass the thought out of your mind. It must be a necessity, or it would not come to all. Perhaps it is not as bad as it has been pictured.

The entire world is made up of only two things, energy and matter. In elementary physics we learn that neither matter nor energy (the only two realities known to man) can be created or destroyed. Both matter and energy can be transformed, but neither can be destroyed.

Life is energy, if it is anything. If neither energy nor matter can be destroyed, of course life cannot be destroyed. Life, like other forms of energy, may be passed through various processes of transition, or change, but it cannot be destroyed. Death is mere transition.

If death is not mere change, or transition, then nothing comes after death except a long, eternal, peaceful sleep, and sleep is nothing to be feared. Thus you may wipe out, forever, the fear of Death.

Symptoms of the Fear of Death

The general symptoms of this fear are:—

> The habit of thinking about dying instead of making the most of life, due, generally, to lack of purpose, or lack of a suitable occupation. This fear is more prevalent among the aged, but sometimes the more youthful are victims of it. The greatest of all remedies for the fear of death is a burning desire for achievement, backed by useful service to others. A busy person seldom has time to think about dying. He finds life too thrilling to worry about death. Sometimes the fear of death is closely associated with the Fear of Poverty, where one's death would leave loved ones poverty-stricken. In other cases, the fear of death is caused by illness and the consequent breaking down of physical body resistance. The commonest causes of the fear of death are: ill-health, poverty, lack of appropriate occupation, disappointment over love, insanity, religious fanaticism.

OLD MAN WORRY

Worry is a state of mind based upon fear. It works slowly, but persistently. It is insidious and subtle. Step by step it "digs itself in" until it paralyzes one's reasoning faculty, destroys self-confidence and initiative. Worry is a form of sustained fear caused by indecision, therefore it is a state of mind which can be controlled.

An unsettled mind is helpless. Indecision makes an unsettled mind. Most individuals lack the will-power to reach decisions promptly, and to stand by them after they have been made, even during normal business conditions. During periods of economic unrest (such as the world recently experienced), the individual is handicapped, not alone by his inherent nature to be slow at reaching decisions, but he is influenced by the indecision of others around him who have created a state of "mass indecision."

During the depression the whole atmosphere, all over the world, was filled with "Fearenza" and "Worryitis," the two mental disease germs which began to spread themselves after the Wall Street frenzy in 1929. There is only one known antidote for these germs; it is the habit of prompt and firm decision. Moreover, it is an antidote which every individual must apply for himself.

We do not worry over conditions, once we have reached a decision to follow a definite line of action. I once interviewed a man who was to be electrocuted two hours later. The condemned man was the calmest of some eight men who were in the death-cell with him. His calmness prompted me to ask him how it felt to know that he was going into eternity in a short while. With a smile of confidence on his face, he said, "It feels fine. Just think, brother, my troubles will soon be over. I have had nothing but trouble all my life. It has been a hardship to get food and clothing. Soon I will not need these things. I have felt fine ever since I learned for certain that I must die. I made up my mind then, to accept my fate in good spirit."

As he spoke he devoured a dinner of proportions sufficient for three men, eating every mouthful of the food brought to him, and apparently enjoying it as much as if no disaster awaited him. Decision gave this man resignation to his fate! Decision can also prevent one's acceptance of undesired circumstances.

The six basic fears become translated into a state of worry, through indecision. Relieve yourself, forever of the fear of death, by reaching a decision to accept death as an inescapable event. Whip the fear of poverty by reaching a decision to get along with whatever wealth you can accumulate without worry. Put your foot upon the neck of the fear of criticism by reaching a decision not to worry about what other people think, do, or say. Eliminate the fear of old age by reaching a decision to accept it, not as a handicap, but as a great blessing which carries with it wisdom, self-control, and understanding not known to youth. Acquit yourself of the fear of ill health by the decision to forget symptoms. Master the fear of loss of love by reaching a decision to get along without love, if that is necessary.

Kill the habit of worry, in all its forms, by reaching a general, blanket decision that nothing which life has to offer is worth the price of worry. With this decision will come poise, peace of mind, and calmness of thought which will bring happiness.

A man whose mind is filled with fear not only destroys his own chances of intelligent action, but, he transmits these destructive vibrations to the minds of all who come into contact with him, and destroys, also, their chances.

Even a dog or a horse knows when its master lacks courage; moreover, a dog or a horse will pick up the vibrations of fear thrown off by its master, and behave accordingly. Lower down the line of intelligence in the animal kingdom, one finds this same capacity to pick up the vibrations of fear. A honey-bee immediately senses fear in the mind of a person—for reasons unknown, a bee will sting the person whose mind is releasing vibrations of fear, much more readily than it will molest the person whose mind registers no fear.

The vibrations of fear pass from one mind to another just as quickly and as surely as the sound of the human voice passes from the broadcasting station to the receiving set of a radio—and by the self-same medium.

Mental telepathy is a reality. Thoughts pass from one mind to another, voluntarily, whether or not this fact is recognized by either the person releasing the thoughts, or the persons who pick up those thoughts.

The person who gives expression, by word of mouth, to negative or destructive thoughts is practically certain to experience the results of those words in the form of a destructive "kick-back." The release of destructive thought impulses, alone, without the aid of words, produces also a "kick-back" in more ways than one. First of all, and perhaps most important to be remembered, the person who releases thoughts of a destructive nature must suffer damage through the breaking down of the faculty of creative imagination. Secondly, the presence in the mind of any destructive emotion develops a negative personality which repels people, and often converts them into antagonists. The third source of damage to the person who entertains or releases negative thoughts, lies in this significant fact—these thought-impulses are not only damaging to others, but they imbed themselves in the subconscious mind of the person releasing them, and there become a part of his character.

One is never through with a thought, merely by releasing it. When a thought is released, it spreads in every direction, through the medium of the ether, but it also plants itself *permanently* in the subconscious mind of *the person releasing it.*

Your business in life is presumably to achieve success. To be successful, you must find peace of mind, acquire the material needs of life, and above all, attain happiness. All of these evidences of success begin in the form of thought impulses.

You may control your own mind; you have the power to feed it whatever thought impulses you choose. With this privilege goes also the responsibility of using it constructively. You are the master of your own earthly destiny just as surely as you have the power to control your own thoughts. You may influence, direct, and eventually control your own environment, making your life what you want it to be—or, you may neglect to exercise the privilege which is yours, to make your life to order, thus casting yourself upon the broad sea of "Circumstance" where you will be tossed hither and yon, like a chip on the waves of the ocean.

THE DEVIL'S WORKSHOP

THE SEVENTH BASIC EVIL

In addition to the Six Basic Fears, there is another evil by which people suffer. It constitutes a rich soil in which the seeds of failure grow abundantly. It is so subtle that its presence often is not detected. This affliction cannot properly be classed as a fear. It is more deeply seated and more often fatal than all of the six fears. For want of a better name, let us call this evil susceptibility to negative influences.

Men who accumulate great riches always protect themselves against this evil! The poverty stricken never do! Those who succeed in any calling must prepare their minds to resist the evil. If you are reading this philosophy for the purpose of accumulating riches, you should examine yourself very carefully, to determine whether you are susceptible to negative influences. If you neglect this self-analysis, you will forfeit your right to attain the object of your desires.

Make the analysis searching. After you read the questions prepared for this self-analysis, hold yourself to a strict accounting in your answers. Go at the task as carefully as you would search for any other enemy you knew to be awaiting you in ambush and deal with your own faults as you would with a more tangible enemy.

You can easily protect yourself against highway robbers, because the law provides organized cooperation for your benefit, but the "seventh basic evil" is more difficult to master, because it strikes when you are not aware of its presence, when you are asleep, and while you are awake. Moreover, its weapon is intangible, because it consists of merely—a state of mind. This evil is also dangerous because it strikes in as many different forms as there are human experiences. Sometimes it enters the mind through the well-meant words of one's own relatives. At other times, it bores from within, through one's own mental attitude. Always it is as deadly as poison, even though it may not kill as quickly.

How to Protect Yourself Against Negative Influences

To protect yourself against negative influences, whether of your own making, or the result of the activities of negative people around you, recognize that you have a will-power, and put it into constant use, until it builds a wall of immunity against negative influences in your own mind.

Recognize the fact that you, and every other human being, are, by nature, lazy, indifferent, and susceptible to all suggestions which harmonize with your weaknesses.

Recognize that you are, by nature, susceptible to all the six basic fears, and set up habits for the purpose of counteracting all these fears.

Recognize that negative influences often work on you through your subconscious mind, therefore they are difficult to detect, and keep your mind closed against all people who depress or discourage you in any way.

Clean out your medicine chest, throw away all pill bottles, and stop pandering to colds, aches, pains and imaginary illness.

Deliberately seek the company of people who influence you to think and act for yourself.

Do not expect troubles as they have a tendency not to disappoint.

Without doubt, the most common weakness of all human beings is the habit of leaving their minds open to the negative influence of other people. This weakness is all the more damaging, because most people do not recognize that they are cursed by it, and many who acknowledge it, neglect or refuse to correct the evil until it becomes an uncontrollable part of their daily habits.

To aid those who wish to see themselves as they really are, the following list of questions has been prepared. Read the questions and state your answers aloud, so you can hear your own voice. This will make it easier for you to be truthful with yourself.

Self-Analysis Test Questions

Do you complain often of "feeling bad," and if so, what is the cause?

Do you find fault with other people at the slightest provocation?

Do you frequently make mistakes in your work, and if so, why?

Are you sarcastic and offensive in your conversation?

Do you deliberately avoid the association of anyone, and if so, why?

Do you suffer frequently with indigestion? If so, what is the cause?

Does life seem futile and the future hopeless to you? If so, why?

Do you like your occupation? If not, why?

Do you often feel self-pity, and if so why?

Are you envious of those who excel you?

To which do you devote most time, thinking of success, or of failure?

Are you gaining or losing self-confidence as you grow older?

Do you learn something of value from all mistakes? Are you permitting some relative or acquaintance to worry you? If so, why?

Are you sometimes "in the clouds" and at other times in the depths of despondency?

Who has the most inspiring influence upon you? What is the cause?

Do you tolerate negative or discouraging influences which you can avoid?

Are you careless of your personal appearance? If so, when and why?

Have you learned how to "drown your troubles" by being too busy to be annoyed by them?

Would you call yourself a "spineless weakling" if you permitted others to do your thinking for you?

Do you neglect internal bathing until auto-intoxication makes you ill-tempered and irritable?

How many preventable disturbances annoy you, and why do you tolerate them?

Do you resort to liquor, narcotics, or cigarettes to "quiet your nerves"? If so, why do you not try will-power instead?

Does anyone "nag" you, and if so, for what reason?

Do you have a definite major purpose, and if so, what is it, and what plan have you for achieving it?

Do you suffer from any of the Six Basic Fears? If so, which ones?

Have you a method by which you can shield yourself against the negative influence of others?

Do you make deliberate use of auto-suggestion to make your mind positive?

Which do you value most, your material possessions, or your privilege of controlling your own thoughts?

Are you easily influenced by others, against your own judgment?

Has today added anything of value to your stock of knowledge or state of mind?

Do you face squarely the circumstances which make you unhappy, or sidestep the responsibility?

Do you analyze all mistakes and failures and try to profit by them or, do you take the attitude that this is not your duty?

Can you name three of your most damaging weaknesses? What are you doing to correct them?

Do you encourage other people to bring their worries to you for sympathy?

Do you choose, from your daily experiences, lessons or influences which aid in your personal advancement?

Does your presence have a negative influence on other people as a rule?

What habits of other people annoy you most?

Do you form your own opinions or permit yourself to be influenced by other people?

Have you learned how to create a mental state of mind with which you can shield yourself against all discouraging influences?

Does your occupation inspire you with faith and hope?

Are you conscious of possessing spiritual forces of sufficient power to enable you to keep your mind free from all forms of fear?

Does your religion help you to keep your own mind positive?

Do you feel it your duty to share other people's worries? If so, why?

If you believe that "birds of a feather flock together" what have you learned about yourself by studying the friends whom you attract?

What connection, if any, do you see between the people with whom you associate most closely, and any unhappiness you may experience?

Could it be possible that some person whom you consider to be a friend is, in reality, your worst enemy, because of his negative influence on your mind?

By what rules do you judge who is helpful and who is damaging to you?

Are your intimate associates mentally superior or inferior to you?

How much time out of every twenty-four hours do you devote to:

a. your occupation
b. sleep
c. play and relaxation
d. acquiring useful knowledge
e. plain waste

Who among your acquaintances,

a. encourages you most

b. cautions you most

c. discourages you most

d. helps you most in other ways

What is your greatest worry? Why do you tolerate it?

When others offer you free, unsolicited advice, do you accept it without question, or analyze their motive?

What, above all else, do you most desire? Do you intend to acquire it? Are you willing to subordinate all other desires for this one? How much time daily do you devote to acquiring it?

Do you change your mind often? If so, why?

Do you usually finish everything you begin?

Are you easily impressed by other people's business or professional titles, college degrees, or wealth? Are you easily influenced by what other people think or say of you?

Do you cater to people because of their social or financial status?

Whom do you believe to be the greatest person living? In what respect is this person superior to yourself?

How much time have you devoted to studying and answering these questions? (At least one day is necessary for the analysis and the answering of the entire list.)

If you have answered all these questions truthfully, you know more about yourself than the majority of people. Study the questions carefully, come back to them once each week for several months, and be astounded at the amount of additional knowledge of great value to yourself, you will have gained by the simple method of answering the questions truthfully. If you are not certain concerning the answers to some of the questions, seek the counsel of those who know you well, especially those who have no motive in flattering you, and see yourself through their eyes. The experience will be astonishing.

You have absolute control over but one thing, and that is your thoughts. This is the most significant and inspiring of all facts known to man! It reflects man's Divine nature. This Divine prerogative is the sole means by which you may control your own destiny. If you fail to control your own mind, you may be sure you will control nothing else.

If you must be careless with your possessions, let it be in connection with material things. *Your mind is your spiritual estate!* Protect and use it with the care to which Divine Royalty is entitled. You were given a will-power for this purpose.

Unfortunately, there is no legal protection against those who, either by design or ignorance, poison the minds of others by negative suggestion. This form of destruction should be punishable by heavy legal penalties, because it may and often does destroy one's chances of acquiring material things which are protected by law.

Men with negative minds tried to convince Thomas A. Edison that he could not build a machine that would record and reproduce the human voice, "because" they said, "no one else had ever produced such a machine." Edison did not believe them. He knew that the mind could produce anything the mind could conceive and believe, and that knowledge was the thing that lifted the great Edison above the common herd.

Men with negative minds told F. W. Woolworth he would go "broke" trying to run a store on five and ten cent sales. He did not believe them. He knew that he could do anything, within reason, if he backed his plans with faith. Exercising his right to keep other men's negative suggestions out of his mind, he piled up a fortune of more than a hundred million dollars.

Men with negative minds told George Washington he could not hope to win against the vastly superior forces of the British, but he exercised his Divine right to believe, therefore this book was published under the protection of the Stars and Stripes, while the name of Lord Cornwallis has been all but forgotten.

Doubting Thomases scoffed scornfully when Henry Ford tried out his first crudely built automobile on the streets of Detroit. Some said the thing never would become practical. Others said no one would pay money for such a contraption. Ford said, "I'll belt the earth with dependable motor cars," and he did! His decision to trust his own judgment has already piled up a fortune far greater than the next five generations of his descendants can squander. For the benefit of those seeking vast riches, let it be remembered that practically the sole difference between Henry Ford and a majority of the more than one hundred thousand men who work for him, is this—Ford has a mind and controls it, the others have minds which they do not try to control.

Henry Ford has been repeatedly mentioned, because he is an astounding example of what a man with a mind of his own, and a will to control it, can accomplish. His record knocks the foundation from under that time-worn alibi, "I never had a chance." Ford never had a chance, either, but he created an opportunity and backed it with persistence until it made him richer than Croesus.

Mind control is the result of self-discipline and habit. You either control your mind or it controls you. There is no halfway compromise. The most practical of all methods for controlling the mind is the habit of keeping it busy with a definite purpose, backed by a definite plan. Study the record of any man who achieves noteworthy success, and you will observe that he has control over his own mind, moreover, that he exercises that control and directs it toward the attainment of definite objectives. Without this control, success is not possible.

"FIFTY-SEVEN" FAMOUS ALIBIS

BY OLD MAN IF

People who do not succeed have one distinguishing trait in common. They know *all the reasons for failure,* and have what they believe to be airtight alibis to explain away their own lack of achievement.

Some of these alibis are clever, and a few of them are justifiable by the facts. But alibis cannot be used for money. The world wants to know only one thing—have you achieved success?

A character analyst compiled a list of the most commonly used alibis. As you read the list, examine yourself carefully, and determine how many of these alibis, if any, are your own property. Remember, too, the philosophy presented in this book makes every one of these alibis obsolete.

IF I didn't have a wife and family . . .
IF I had enough "pull" . . .
IF I had money . . .
IF I had a good education . . .
IF I could get a job . . .
IF I had good health . . .
IF I only had time . . .
IF times were better . . .
IF other people understood me . . .
IF conditions around me were only different . . .
IF I could live my life over again . . .

IF I did not fear what "they" would say . . .
IF I had been given a chance . . .
IF I now had a chance . . .
IF other people didn't "have it in for me" . . .
IF nothing happens to stop me . . .
IF I were only younger . . .
IF I could only do what I want. . .
IF I had been born rich . . .
IF I could meet "the right people" . . .
IF I had the talent that some people have . . .
IF I dared assert myself. . .
IF I only had embraced past opportunities . . .
IF people didn't get on my nerves . . .
IF I didn't have to keep house and look after the children . . .
IF I could save some money . . .
IF the boss only appreciated me . . .
IF I only had somebody to help me . . .
IF my family understood me . . .
IF I lived in a big city . . .
IF I could just get started . . .
IF I were only free . . .
IF I had the personality of some people . . .
IF I were not so fat . . .
IF my talents were known . . .
IF I could just get a "break" . . .

IF I could only get out of debt . . .
IF I hadn't failed . . .
IF I only knew how . . .
IF everybody didn't oppose me . . .
IF I didn't have so many worries . . .
IF I could marry the right person . . .
IF people weren't so dumb . . .
IF my family were not so extravagant . . .
IF I were sure of myself. . .
IF luck were not against me . . .
IF I had not been born under the wrong star . . .
IF it were not true that "what is to be will be" . . .
IF I did not have to work so hard . . .
IF I hadn't lost my money . . .
IF I lived in a different neighborhood . . .
IF I didn't have a "past" . . .
IF I only had a business of my own . . .
IF other people would only listen to me . . .
IF ★ ★ ★ and this is the greatest of them all ★ ★ ★

I had the courage to see myself as I really am, I would *find out what is wrong with me, and correct it,* then I might have a chance to profit by my mistakes and learn something from the experience of others, for I know that there is something wrong with me, or I would now be where *I would have been if* I had spent more time analyzing my weaknesses, and less time building alibis to cover them.

Building alibis with which to explain away failure is a national pastime. The habit is as old as the human race, and *is fatal to success!* Why do people cling to their pet alibis? The answer is obvious. They defend their alibis because they create them! A man's alibi is the child of his own imagination. It is human nature to defend one's own brainchild.

Building alibis is a deeply rooted habit. Habits are difficult to break, especially when they provide justification for something we do. Plato had this truth in mind when he said, "The first and best victory is to conquer self. To be conquered by self is, of all things, the most shameful and vile."

Another philosopher had the same thought in mind when he said, "It was a great surprise to me when I discovered that most of the ugliness I saw in others, was but a reflection of my own nature."

"It has always been a mystery to me," said Elbert Hubbard, "why people spend so much time deliberately fooling themselves by creating alibis to cover their weaknesses. If used differently, this same time would be sufficient to cure the weakness, then no alibis would be needed."

In parting, I would remind you that "Life is a checkerboard, and the player opposite you is time. If you hesitate before moving, or neglect to move promptly, your men will be wiped off the board by time. You are playing against a partner who will not tolerate indecision!"

Previously you may have had a logical excuse for not having forced Life to come through with whatever you asked, but that alibi is now obsolete, because you are in possession of the Master Key that unlocks the door to Life's bountiful riches.

The Master Key is intangible, but it is powerful! It is the privilege of creating, *in your own mind,* a burning desire for a definite form of riches. There is no penalty for the use of the Key, but there is a price you must pay if you do not use it. The price is failure. There is a reward of stupendous proportions if you put the Key to use. It is the satisfaction that comes to all who *conquer self and force Life to pay whatever is asked.*

The reward is worthy of your effort. Will you make the start and be convinced?

"If we are related," said the immortal Emerson, "we shall meet." In closing, may I borrow his thought, and say, "If we are related, we have, through these pages, met."

AS A MAN THINKETH

BY JAMES ALLEN

1903

They themselves are makers of themselves.

Mind is the Master power that moulds and makes,

And Man is Mind, and evermore he takes

The tool of Thought, and, shaping what he wills,

Brings forth a thousand joys, a thousand ills:—

He thinks in secret and it comes to pass:

Environment is but his looking-glass.

FOREWORD

This little volume (the result of meditation and experience) is not intended as an exhaustive treatise on the much-written-upon subject of the power of thought. It is suggestive rather than explanatory, its object being to stimulate men and women to the discovery and perception of the truth that—

"They themselves are makers of themselves"

by virtue of the thoughts which they choose and encourage; that mind is the master weaver, both of the inner garment of character and the outer garment of circumstance, and that, as they may have hitherto woven in ignorance and pain they may now weave in enlightenment and happiness.

James Allen
Broad Park Avenue
Ilfracombe, England

CONTENTS

THOUGHT AND CHARACTER

The aphorism, "As a man thinketh in his heart so is he," not only embraces the whole of a man's being, but is so comprehensive as to reach out to every condition and circumstance of his life. A man is literally *what he thinks,* his character being the complete sum of all his thoughts.

As the plant springs from, and could not be without, the seed, so every act of a man springs from the hidden seeds of thought, and could not have appeared without them. This applies equally to those acts called "spontaneous" and "unpremeditated" as to those which are deliberately executed.

Act is the blossom of thought, and joy and suffering are its fruits; thus does a man garner in the sweet and bitter fruitage of his own husbandry.

"Thought in the mind hath made us. What we are
By thought was wrought and built. If a man's mind
Hath evil thoughts, pain comes on him as comes
The wheel the ox behind. . . .

. . . If one endure
In purity of thought, joy follows him
As his own shadow—sure."

Man is a growth by law, and not a creation by artifice, and cause and effect is as absolute and undeviating in the hidden realm of thought as in the world of visible and material things. A noble and Godlike character is not a thing of favor or chance, but is the natural result of continued effort in right thinking, the effect of long-cherished association with Godlike thoughts. An ignoble and bestial character, by the same process, is the result of the continued harboring of groveling thoughts.

Man is made or unmade by himself; in the armory of thought he forges the weapons by which he destroys himself; he also fashions the tools with which he builds for himself heavenly mansions of joy and strength and peace. By the right choice and true application of thought, man ascends to the Divine Perfection; by the abuse and wrong application of thought, he descends below the level of the beast. Between these two extremes are all the grades of character, and man is their maker and master.

Of all the beautiful truths pertaining to the soul which have been restored and brought to light in this age, none is more gladdening or fruitful of divine promise and confidence than this—that man is the master of thought, the molder of character, and the maker and shaper of condition, environment, and destiny.

As a being of Power, Intelligence, and Love, and the lord of his own thoughts, man holds the key to every situation, and contains within himself that transforming and regenerative agency by which he may make himself what he wills.

Man is always the master, even in his weakest and most abandoned state; but in his weakness and degradation he is the foolish master who misgoverns his "household." When he begins to reflect upon his condition, and to search diligently for the Law upon which his being is established, he then becomes the wise master, directing his energies with intelligence, and fashioning his thoughts to fruitful issues. Such is the *conscious* master, and man can only thus become by discovering *within himself* the laws of thought; which discovery is totally a matter of application, self-analysis, and experience.

Only by much searching and mining are gold and diamonds obtained, and man can find every truth connected with his being if he will dig deep into the mine of his soul; and that he is the maker of his character, the molder of his life, and the builder of his destiny, he may unerringly prove, if he will watch, control, and alter his thoughts, tracing their effects upon himself, upon others, and upon his life and circumstances, linking cause and effect by patient practice and investigation, and utilizing his every experience, even to the most trivial, everyday occurrence, as a means of obtaining that knowledge of himself which is Understanding, Wisdom, Power. In this direction, as in no other, is the law absolute that "He that seeketh findeth; and to him that knocketh it shall be opened"; for only by patience, practice, and ceaseless importunity can a man enter the Door of the Temple of Knowledge.

EFFECT OF THOUGHT ON CIRCUMSTANCES

A man's mind may be likened to a garden, which may be intelligently cultivated or allowed to run wild; but whether cultivated or neglected, it must, and will, *bring forth*. If no useful seeds are *put* into it, then an abundance of useless weed seeds will *fall* therein, and will continue to produce their kind.

Just as a gardener cultivates his plot, keeping it free from weeds, and growing the flowers and fruits which he requires, so may a man tend the garden of his mind, weeding out all the wrong, useless, and impure thoughts, and cultivating toward perfection the flowers and fruits of right, useful, and pure thoughts. By pursuing this process, a man sooner or later discovers that he is the master gardener of his soul, the director of his life. He also reveals, within himself, the laws of thought, and understands, with ever-increasing accuracy, how the thought forces and mind elements operate in the shaping of his character, circumstances, and destiny.

Thought and character are one, and as character can only manifest and discover itself through environment and circumstance, the outer conditions of a person's life will always be found to be harmoniously related to his inner state. This does not mean that a man's circumstances at any given time are an indication of his *entire* character, but that those circumstances are so intimately connected with some vital thought element within himself that, for the time being, they are indispensable to his development.

Every man is where he is by the law of his being; the thoughts which he has built into his character have brought him there, and in the arrangement of his life there is no element of chance, but all is the result of a law which cannot err. This is just as true of those who feel "out of harmony" with their surroundings as of those who are contented with them.

As a progressive and evolving being, man is where he is that he may learn that he may grow; and as he learns the spiritual lesson which any circumstance contains for him, it passes away and gives place to other circumstances.

Man is buffered by circumstances so long as he believes himself to be the creature of outside conditions, but when he realizes that he is a creative power, and that he may command the hidden soil and seeds of his being out of which circumstances grow, he then becomes the rightful master of himself.

That circumstances *grow* out of thought every man knows who has for any length of time practiced self-control and self-purification, for he will have noticed that the alteration in his circumstances has been in exact ratio with his altered mental condition. So true is this that when a man earnestly applies himself to remedy the defects in his character, and makes swift and marked progress, he passes rapidly through a succession of vicissitudes.

The soul attracts that which it secretly harbors; that which it loves, and also that which it fears; it reaches the height of its cherished aspirations; it falls to the level of its unchastened desires—and circumstances are the means by which the soul receives its own.

Every thought seed sown or allowed to fall into the mind, and to take root there, produces its own, blossoming sooner or later into act, and bearing its own fruitage of opportunity and circumstance. Good thoughts bear good fruit, bad thoughts bad fruit.

The outer world of circumstance shapes itself to the inner world of thought, and both pleasant and unpleasant external conditions are factors which make for the ultimate good of the individual. As the reaper of his own harvest, man learns both by suffering and bliss.

Following the inmost desires, aspirations, thoughts, by which he allows himself to be dominated (pursuing the will-o'-the-wisps of impure imaginings or steadfastly walking the highway of strong and high endeavor), a man at last arrives at their fruition and fulfillment in the outer conditions of his life. The laws of growth and adjustment everywhere obtain.

A man does not come to the almshouse or the jail by the tyranny of fate or circumstance, but by the pathway of groveling thoughts and base desires. Nor does a pure-minded man fall suddenly into crime by stress of any mere external force; the criminal thought had long been secretly fostered in the heart, and the hour of opportunity revealed its gathered power. Circumstance does not make the man; it reveals him to himself. No such conditions can exist as descending into vice and its attendant sufferings apart from vicious inclinations, or ascending into virtue and its pure happiness without the continued cultivation of virtuous aspirations; and man, therefore, as the lord and master of thought, is the maker of himself, the shaper and author of environment. Even at birth the soul comes to its own, and through every step of its earthly pilgrimage it attracts those combinations of conditions which reveal itself, which are the reflections of its own purity and impurity, its strength and weakness.

Men do not attract that which they *want,* but that which they *are.* Their whims, fancies, and ambitions are thwarted at every step, but their inmost thoughts and desires are fed with their own food, be it foul or clean. The "divinity that shapes our ends" is in ourselves; it is our very self. Man is manacled only by himself: thought and action are the jailers of Fate—they imprison, being base; they are also the angels of Freedom—they liberate, being noble. Not what he wishes and prays for does a man get, but what he justly earns. His wishes and prayers are only gratified and answered when they harmonize with his thoughts and actions.

In the light of this truth, what, then, is the meaning of "fighting against circumstances"? It means that a man is continually revolting against an *effect* without, while all the time he is nourishing and preserving its *cause* in his heart. That cause may take the form of a conscious vice or an unconscious weakness; but whatever it is, it stubbornly retards the efforts of its possessor, and thus calls aloud for remedy.

Men are anxious to improve their circumstances, but are unwilling to improve themselves; they therefore remain bound. The man who does not shrink from self-crucifixion can never fail to accomplish the object upon which his heart is set. This is as true of earthly as of heavenly things. Even the man whose sole object is to acquire wealth must be prepared to make great personal sacrifices before he can accomplish his object; and how much more so he who would realize a strong and well-poised life?

Here is a man who is wretchedly poor. He is extremely anxious that his surroundings and home comforts should be improved, yet all the time he shirks his work, and considers he is justified in trying to deceive his employer on the ground of the insufficiency of his wages. Such a man does not understand the simplest rudiments of those principles which are the basis of true prosperity, and is not only totally unfitted to rise out of his wretchedness, but is actually attracting to himself a still deeper wretchedness by dwelling in, and acting out, indolent, deceptive, and unmanly thoughts.

Here is a rich man who is the victim of a painful and persistent disease as the result of gluttony. He is willing to give large sums of money to get rid of it, but he will not sacrifice his gluttonous desires. He wants to gratify his taste for rich and unnatural viands and have his health as well. Such a man is totally unfit to have health, because he has not yet learned the first principles of a healthy life.

Here is an employer of labor who adopts crooked measures to avoid paying the regulation wage, and, in the hope of making larger profits, reduces the wages of his workpeople. Such a man is altogether unfitted for prosperity, and when he finds himself bankrupt, both as regards reputation and riches, he blames circumstances, not knowing that he is the sole author of his condition.

I have introduced these three cases merely as illustrative of the truth that man is the causer (though nearly always unconsciously) of his circumstances, and that, while aiming at a good end, he is continually frustrating its accomplishment by encouraging thoughts and desires which cannot possibly harmonize with that end. Such cases could be multiplied and varied almost indefinitely, but this is not necessary, as the reader can, if he so resolves, trace the action of the laws of thought in his own mind and life, and until this is done, mere external facts cannot serve as a ground of reasoning.

Circumstances, however, are so complicated, thought is so deeply rooted, and the conditions of happiness vary so vastly with individuals, that a man's *entire* soul condition (although it may be known to himself) cannot be judged by another from the external aspect of his life alone. A man may be honest in certain directions, yet suffer privations; a man may be dishonest in certain directions, yet acquire wealth; but the conclusion usually formed that the one man fails *because of his particular honesty,* and that the other prospers *because of his particular dishonesty,* is the result of a superficial judgment, which assumes that the dishonest man is almost totally corrupt, and the honest man almost entirely virtuous. In the light of a deeper knowledge and wider experience, such judgment is found to be erroneous. The dishonest man may have some admirable virtues which the other does not possess; and the honest man obnoxious vices which are absent in the other. The honest man reaps the good results of his honest thoughts and acts; he also brings upon himself the sufferings which his vices produce. The dishonest man likewise garners his own suffering and happiness.

It is pleasing to human vanity to believe that one suffers because of one's virtue; but not until a man has extirpated every sickly, bitter, and impure thought from his mind, and washed every sinful stain from his soul, can he be in a position to know and declare that his sufferings are the result of his good, and not of his bad qualities; and on the way to, yet long before he has reached, that supreme perfection, he will have found, working in his mind and life, the Great Law which is absolutely just, and which cannot, therefore, give good for evil, evil for good. Possessed of such knowledge, he will then know, looking back upon his past ignorance and blindness, that his life is, and always was, justly ordered, and that all his past experiences, good and bad, were the equitable outworking of his evolving, yet unevolved self.

Good thoughts and actions can never produce bad results; bad thoughts and actions can never produce good results. This is but saying that nothing can come from corn but corn, nothing from nettles but nettles. Men understand this law in the natural world, and work with it; but few understand it in the mental and moral world (though its operation there is just as simple and undeviating), and they, therefore, do not coöperate with it.

Suffering is *always* the effect of wrong thought in some direction. It is an indication that the individual is out of harmony with himself, with the Law of his being. The sole and supreme use of suffering is to purify, to burn out all that is useless and impure. Suffering ceases for him who is pure. There could be no object in burning gold after the dross had been removed, and a perfectly pure and enlightened being could not suffer.

The circumstances which a man encounters with suffering are the result of his own mental inharmony. The circumstances which a man encounters with blessedness are the result of his own mental harmony. Blessedness, not material possessions, is the measure of right thought; wretchedness, not lack of material possessions, is the measure of wrong thought. A man may be cursed and rich; he may be blessed and poor. Blessedness and riches are only joined together when the riches are rightly and wisely used; and the poor man only descends into wretchedness when he regards his lot as a burden unjustly imposed.

Indigence and indulgence are the two extremes of wretchedness. They are both equally unnatural and the result of mental disorder. A man is not rightly conditioned until he is a happy, healthy, and prosperous being; and happiness, health, and prosperity are the result of a harmonious adjustment of the inner with the outer, of the man with his surroundings.

A man only begins to be a man when he ceases to whine and revile, and commences to search for the hidden justice which regulates his life. And as he adapts his mind to that regulating factor, he ceases to accuse others as the cause of his condition, and builds himself up in strong and noble thoughts; ceases to kick against circumstances, but begins to *use* them as aids to his more rapid progress, and as a means of discovering the hidden powers and possibilities within himself.

Law, not confusion, is the dominating principle in the universe; justice, not injustice, is the soul and substance of life; and righteousness, not corruption, is the molding and moving force in the spiritual government of the world. This being so, man has but to right himself to find that the universe is right; and during the process of putting himself right, he will find that as he alters his thoughts toward things, and other people, things and other people will alter toward him.

The proof of this truth is in every person, and it therefore admits of easy investigation by systematic introspection and self-analysis. Let a man radically alter his thoughts, and he will be astonished at the rapid transformation it will effect in the material conditions of his life. Men imagine that thought can be kept secret, but it cannot; it rapidly crystallizes into habit, and habit solidifies into circumstance. Bestial thoughts crystallize into habits of drunkenness and sensuality, which solidify into circumstances of destitution and disease: impure thoughts of every kind crystallize into enervating and confusing habits, which solidify into distracting and adverse circumstances: thoughts of fear, doubt, and indecision crystallize into weak, unmanly, and irresolute habits, which solidify into circumstances of failure, indigence, and slavish dependence: lazy thoughts crystallize into habits of uncleanliness and dishonesty, which solidify into circumstances of foulness and beggary: hateful and condemnatory thoughts crystallize into habits of accusation and violence, which solidify into circumstances of injury and persecution: selfish thoughts of all kinds crystallize into habits of self-seeking, which solidify into circumstances more or less distressing. On the other hand, beautiful thoughts of all kinds crystallize into habits of grace and kindliness, which solidify into genial and sunny circumstances: pure thoughts crystallize into habits of temperance and self-control, which solidify into circumstances of repose and peace: thoughts of courage, self-reliance, and decision crystallize into manly habits, which solidify into circumstances of success, plenty, and freedom: energetic thoughts crystallize into habits of cleanliness and industry, which solidify into circumstances of pleasantness: gentle and forgiving thoughts crystallize into habits of gentleness, which solidify into protective and preservative circumstances: loving and unselfish thoughts crystallize into habits of self-forgetfulness for others, which solidify into circumstances of sure and abiding prosperity and true riches.

A particular train of thought persisted in, be it good or bad, cannot fail to produce its results on the character and circumstances. A man cannot *directly* choose his circumstances, but he can choose his thoughts, and so indirectly, yet surely, shape his circumstances.

Nature helps every man to the gratification of the thoughts which he most encourages, and opportunities are presented which will most speedily bring to the surface both the good and evil thoughts.

Let a man cease from his sinful thoughts, and all the world will soften toward him, and be ready to help him; let him put away his weakly and sickly thoughts, and lo! opportunities will spring up on every hand to aid his strong resolves; let him encourage good thoughts, and no hard fate shall bind him down to wretchedness and shame. The world is your kaleidoscope, and the varying combinations of colors which at every succeeding moment it presents to you are the exquisitely adjusted pictures of your evermoving thoughts.

"You will be what you will to be;
Let failure find its false content
In that poor word, 'environment,'
But spirit scorns it, and is free.

"It masters time, it conquers space;
It cows that boastful trickster, Chance,
And bids the tyrant Circumstance
Uncrown, and fill a servant's place.

"The human Will, that force unseen,
The offspring of a deathless Soul,

Can hew a way to any goal,
Though walls of granite intervene.

"Be not impatient in delay,
But wait as one who understands;
When spirit rises and commands,
The gods are ready to obey."

EFFECT OF THOUGHT ON HEALTH AND THE BODY

The body is the servant of the mind. It obeys the operations of the mind, whether they be deliberately chosen or automatically expressed. At the bidding of unlawful thoughts the body sinks rapidly into disease and decay; at the command of glad and beautiful thoughts it becomes clothed with youthfulness and beauty.

Disease and health, like circumstances, are rooted in thought. Sickly thoughts will express themselves through a sickly body. Thoughts of fear have been known to kill a man as speedily as a bullet, and they are continually killing thousands of people just as surely though less rapidly. The people who live in fear of disease are the people who get it. Anxiety quickly demoralizes the whole body, and lays it open to the entrance of disease; while impure thoughts, even if not physically indulged, will soon shatter the nervous system.

Strong, pure, and happy thoughts build up the body in vigor and grace. The body is a delicate and plastic instrument, which responds readily to the thoughts by which it is impressed, and habits of thought will produce their own effects, good or bad, upon it.

Men will continue to have impure and poisoned blood so long as they propagate unclean thoughts. Out of a clean heart comes a clean life and a clean body. Out of a defiled mind proceeds a defiled life and a corrupt body. Thought is the font of action, life, and manifestation; make the fountain pure, and all will be pure.

Change of diet will not help a man who will not change his thoughts. When a man makes his thoughts pure, he no longer desires impure food.

Clean thoughts make clean habits. The so-called saint who does not wash his body is not a saint. He who has strengthened and purified his thoughts does not need to consider the malevolent microbe.

If you would perfect your body, guard your mind. If you would renew your body, beautify your mind. Thoughts of malice, envy, disappointment, despondency, rob the body of its health and grace. A sour face does not come by chance; it is made by sour thoughts. Wrinkles that mar are drawn by folly, passion, pride.

I know a woman of ninety-six who has the bright, innocent face of a girl. I know a man well under middle age whose face is drawn into inharmonious contours. The one is the result of a sweet and sunny disposition; the other is the outcome of passion and discontent.

As you cannot have a sweet and wholesome abode unless you admit the air and sunshine freely into your rooms, so a strong body and a bright, happy, or serene countenance can only result from the free admittance into the mind of thoughts of joy and good will and serenity.

On the faces of the aged there are wrinkles made by sympathy; others by strong and pure thought, and others are carved by passion: who cannot distinguish them? With those who have lived righteously, age is calm, peaceful, and softly mellowed, like the setting sun. I have recently seen a philosopher on his deathbed. He was not old except in years. He died as sweetly and peacefully as he had lived.

There is no physician like cheerful thought for dissipating the ills of the body; there is no comforter to compare with good will for dispersing the shadows of grief and sorrow. To live continually in thoughts of ill will, cynicism, suspicion, and envy, is to be confined in a self-made prison hole. But to think well of all, to be cheerful with all, to patiently learn to find the good in all—such unselfish thoughts are the very portals of heaven; and to dwell day by day in thoughts of peace toward every creature will bring abounding peace to their possessor.

THOUGHT AND PURPOSE

Until thought is linked with purpose there is no intelligent accomplishment. With the majority the bark of thought is allowed to "drift" upon the ocean of life. Aimlessness is a vice, and such drifting must not continue for him who would steer clear of catastrophe and destruction.

They who have no central purpose in their life fall an easy prey to petty worries, fears, troubles, and self-pityings, all of which are indications of weakness, which lead, just as surely as deliberately planned sins (though by a different route), to failure, unhappiness, and loss, for weakness cannot persist in a power-evolving universe.

A man should conceive of a legitimate purpose in his heart, and set out to accomplish it. He should make this purpose the centralizing point of his thoughts. It may take the form of a spiritual ideal, or it may be a worldly object, according to his nature at the time being; but whichever it is, he should steadily focus his thought forces upon the object which he has set before him. He should make this purpose his supreme duty, and should devote himself to its attainment, not allowing his thoughts to wander away into ephemeral fancies, longings, and imaginings. This is the royal road to self-control and true concentration of thought. Even if he fails again and again to accomplish his purpose (as he necessarily must until weakness is overcome), the *strength of character gained* will be the measure of his *true* success, and this will form a new starting point for future power and triumph.

Those who are not prepared for the apprehension of a *great* purpose, should fix the thoughts upon the faultless performance of their duty, no matter how insignificant their task may appear. Only in this way can the thoughts be gathered and focused, and resolution and energy be developed, which being done, there is nothing which may not be accomplished.

The weakest soul, knowing its own weakness, and believing this truth—*that strength can only be developed by effort and practice,* will, thus believing, at once begin to exert itself, and, adding effort to effort, patience to patience, and strength to strength, will never cease to develop, and will at last grow divinely strong.

As the physically weak man can make himself strong by careful and patient training, so the man of weak thoughts can make them strong by exercising himself in right thinking.

To put away aimlessness and weakness, and to begin to think with purpose, is to enter the ranks of those strong ones who only recognize failure as one of the pathways to attainment; who make all conditions serve them, and who think strongly, attempt fearlessly, and accomplish masterfully.

Having conceived of his purpose, a man should mentally mark out a *straight* pathway to its achievement, looking neither to the right nor the left. Doubts and fears should be rigorously excluded; they are disintegrating elements which break up the straight line of effort, rendering it crooked, ineffectual, useless. Thoughts of doubt and fear never accomplish anything, and never can. They always lead to failure. Purpose, energy, power to do, and all strong thoughts cease when doubt and fear creep in.

The will to do springs from the knowledge that we *can* do. Doubt and fear are the great enemies of knowledge, and he who encourages them, who does not slay them, thwarts himself at every step.

He who has conquered doubt and fear has conquered failure. His every thought is allied with power, and all difficulties are bravely met and wisely overcome. His purposes are seasonably planted, and they bloom and bring forth fruit which does not fall prematurely to the ground.

Thought allied fearlessly to purpose becomes creative force: he who *knows* this is ready to become something higher and stronger than a mere bundle of wavering thoughts and fluctuating sensations; he who *does* this has become the conscious and intelligent wielder of his mental powers.

THE THOUGHT-FACTOR IN ACHIEVEMENT

All that a man achieves and all that he fails to achieve is the direct result of his own thoughts. In a justly ordered universe, where loss of equipoise would mean total destruction, individual responsibility must be absolute. A man's weakness and strength, purity and impurity, are his own, and not another man's; they are brought about by himself, and not by another; and they can only be altered by himself, never by another. His condition is also his own, and not another man's. His suffering and his happiness are evolved from within. As he thinks, so he is; as he continues to think, so he remains.

A strong man cannot help a weaker unless that weaker is *willing* to be helped, and even then the weak man must become strong of himself; he must, by his own efforts, develop the strength which he admires in another. None but himself can alter his condition.

It has been usual for men to think and to say, "Many men are slaves because one is an oppressor; let us hate the oppressor." Now, however, there is among an increasing few a tendency to reverse this judgment, and to say, "One man is an oppressor because many are slaves; let us despise the slaves." The truth is that oppressor and slave are coöperators in ignorance, and, while seeming to afflict each other, are in reality afflicting themselves. A perfect Knowledge perceives the action of law in the weakness of the oppressed and the misapplied power of the oppressor; a perfect Love, seeing the suffering which both states entail, condemns neither; a perfect Compassion embraces both oppressor and oppressed.

He who has conquered weakness, and has put away all selfish thoughts, belongs neither to oppressor nor oppressed. He is free.

A man can only rise, conquer, and achieve by lifting up his thoughts. He can only remain weak, and abject, and miserable by refusing to lift up his thoughts.

Before a man can achieve anything, even in worldly things, he must lift his thoughts above slavish animal indulgence. He may not, in order to succeed, give up *all* animality and selfishness, by any means; but a portion of it must, at least, be sacrificed. A man whose first thought is bestial indulgence could neither think clearly nor plan methodically; he could not find and develop his latent resources, and would fail in any undertaking. Not having commenced manfully to control his thoughts, he is not in a position to control affairs and to adopt serious responsibilities. He is not fit to act independently and stand alone. But he is limited only by the thoughts which he chooses.

There can be no progress, no achievement without sacrifice, and a man's worldly success will be in the measure that he sacrifices his confused animal thoughts, and fixes his mind on the development of his plans, and the strengthening of his resolution and self-reliance. And the higher he lifts his thoughts, the more manly, upright, and righteous he becomes, the greater will be his success, the more blessed and enduring will be his achievements.

The universe does not favor the greedy, the dishonest, the vicious, although on the mere surface it may sometimes appear to do so; it helps the honest, the magnanimous, the virtuous. All the great Teachers of the ages have declared this in varying forms, and to prove and know it a man has but to persist in making himself more and more virtuous by lifting up his thoughts.

Intellectual achievements are the result of thought consecrated to the search for knowledge, or for the beautiful and true in life and nature. Such achievements may be sometimes connected with vanity and ambition, but they are not the outcome of those characteristics; they are the natural outgrowth of long and arduous effort, and of pure and unselfish thoughts.

Spiritual achievements are the consummation of holy aspirations. He who lives constantly in the conception of noble and lofty thoughts, who dwells upon all that is pure and unselfish, will, as surely as the sun reaches its zenith and the moon its full, become wise and noble in character, and rise into a position of influence and blessedness.

Achievement, of whatever kind, is the crown of effort, the diadem of thought. By the aid of self-control, resolution, purity, righteousness, and well-directed thought a man ascends; by the aid of animality, indolence, impurity, corruption, and confusion of thought a man descends.

A man may rise to high success in the world, and even to lofty altitudes in the spiritual realm, and again descend into weakness and wretchedness by allowing arrogant, selfish, and corrupt thoughts to take possession of him.

Victories attained by right thought can only be maintained by watchfulness. Many give way when success is assured, and rapidly fall back into failure.

All achievements, whether in the business, intellectual, or spiritual world, are the result of definitely directed thought, are governed by the same law and are of the same method; the only difference lies in *the object of attainment.*

He who would accomplish little must sacrifice little; he who would achieve much must sacrifice much; he who would attain highly must sacrifice greatly.

VISIONS AND IDEALS

The dreamers are the saviors of the world. As the visible world is sustained by the invisible, so men, through all their trials and sins and sordid vocations, are nourished by the beautiful visions of their solitary dreamers. Humanity cannot forget its dreamers; it cannot let their ideals fade and die; it lives in them; it knows them as the *realities* which it shall one day see and know.

Composer, sculptor, painter, poet, prophet, sage, these are the makers of the afterworld, the architects of heaven. The world is beautiful because they have lived; without them, laboring humanity would perish.

He who cherishes a beautiful vision, a lofty ideal in his heart, will one day realize it. Columbus cherished a vision of another world, and he discovered it; Copernicus fostered the vision of a multiplicity of worlds and a wider universe, and he revealed it; Buddha beheld the vision of a spiritual world of stainless beauty and perfect peace, and he entered into it.

Cherish your visions; cherish your ideals; cherish the music that stirs in your heart, the beauty that forms in your mind, the loveliness that drapes your purest thoughts, for out of them will grow all delightful conditions, all heavenly environment; of these, if you but remain true to them, your world will at last be built.

To desire is to obtain; to aspire is to achieve. Shall man's basest desires receive the fullest measure of gratification, and his purest aspirations starve for lack of sustenance? Such is not the Law: such a condition of things can never obtain: "Ask and receive."

Dream lofty dreams, and as you dream, so shall you become. Your Vision is the promise of what you shall one day be; your Ideal is the prophecy of what you shall at last unveil.

The greatest achievement was at first and for a time a dream. The oak sleeps in the acorn; the bird waits in the egg; and in the highest vision of the soul a waking angel stirs. Dreams are the seedlings of realities.

Your circumstances may be uncongenial, but they shall not long remain so if you but perceive an Ideal and strive to reach it. You cannot travel *within* and stand still *without*. Here is a youth hard pressed by poverty and labor; confined long hours in an unhealthy workshop; unschooled, and lacking all the arts of refinement. But he dreams of better things: he thinks of intelligence, of refinement, of grace and beauty. He conceives of, mentally builds up, an ideal condition of life; the vision of a wider liberty and a larger scope takes possession of him; unrest urges him to action, and he utilizes all his spare time and means, small though they are, to the development of his latent powers and resources. Very soon so altered has his mind become that the workshop can no longer hold him. It has become so out of harmony with his mentality that it falls out of his life as a garment is cast aside, and, with the growth of opportunities which fit the scope of his expanding powers, he passes out of it forever. Years later we see this youth as a full-grown man. We find him a master of certain forces of the mind which he wields with world-wide influence and almost unequaled power. In his hands he holds the cords of gigantic responsibilities; he speaks, and lo! lives are changed; men and women hang upon his words and remold their characters, and, sunlike, he becomes the fixed and luminous center around which innumerable destinies revolve. He has realized the Vision of his youth. He has become one with his Ideal.

And you, too, youthful reader, will realize the Vision (not the idle wish) of your heart, be it base or beautiful, or a mixture of both, for you will always gravitate toward that which you, secretly, most love. Into your hands will be placed the exact results of your own thoughts; you will receive that which you earn; no more, no less. Whatever your present environment may be, you will fall, remain, or rise with your thoughts, your Vision, your Ideal. You will become as small as your controlling desire; as great as your dominant aspiration: in the beautiful words of Stanton Kirkham Davis, "You may be keeping accounts, and presently you shall walk out of the door that for so long has seemed to you the barrier of your ideals, and shall find yourself before an audience—the pen still behind your ear, the ink stains on your fingers—and then and there shall pour out the torrent of your inspiration. You may be driving sheep, and you shall wander to the city—bucolic and open mouthed; shall wander under the intrepid guidance of the spirit into the studio of the master, and after a time he shall say, 'I have nothing more to teach you.' And now you have become the master, who did so recently dream of great things while driving sheep. You shall lay down the saw and the plane to take upon yourself the regeneration of the world."

The thoughtless, the ignorant, and the indolent, seeing only the apparent effects of things and not the things themselves, talk of luck, of fortune, and chance. Seeing a man grow rich, they say, "How lucky he is!" Observing another become intellectual, they exclaim, "How highly favored he is!" And noting the saintly character and wide influence of another, they remark, "How chance aids him at every turn!" They do not see the trials and failures and struggles which these men have voluntarily encountered in order to gain their experience; have no knowledge of the sacrifices they have made, of the undaunted efforts they have put forth, of the faith they have exercised, that they might overcome the apparently insurmountable, and realize the Vision of their heart. They do not know the darkness and the heartaches; they only see the light and joy, and call it "luck"; do not see the long and arduous journey, but only behold the pleasant goal, and call it "good fortune"; do not understand the process, but only perceive the result, and call it "chance."

In all human affairs there are *efforts,* and there are *results,* and the strength of the effort is the measure of the result. Chance is not. "Gifts," powers, material, intellectual, and spiritual possessions are the fruits of effort; they are thoughts completed, objects accomplished, visions realized.

The Vision that you glorify in your mind, the Ideal that you enthrone in your heart—this you will build your life by, this you will become.

SERENITY

Calmness of mind is one of the beautiful jewels of wisdom. It is the result of long and patient effort in self-control. Its presence is an indication of ripened experience, and of a more than ordinary knowledge of the laws and operations of thought.

A man becomes calm in the measure that he understands himself as a thought-evolved being, for such knowedge necessitates the understanding of others as the result of thought, and as he develops a right understanding, and sees more and more clearly the internal relations of things by the action of cause and effect, he ceases to fuss and fume and worry and grieve, and remains poised, steadfast, serene.

The calm man, having learned how to govern himself, knows how to adapt himself to others; and they, in turn, reverence his spiritual strength, and feel that they can learn of him and rely upon him. The more tranquil a man becomes, the greater is his success, his influence, his power for good. Even the ordinary trader will find his business prosperity increase as he develops a greater self-control and equanimity, for people will always prefer to deal with a man whose demeanor is strongly equable.

The strong, calm man is always loved and revered. He is like a shade-giving tree in a thirsty land, or a sheltering rock in a storm. "Who does not love a tranquil heart, a sweet-tempered, balanced life? It does not matter whether it rains or shines, or what changes come to those possessing these blessings, for they are always sweet, serene, and calm. That exquisite poise of character which we call serenity is the last lesson of culture; it is the flowering of life, the fruitage of the soul. It is precious as wisdom, more to be desired than gold—yea, than even fine gold. How insignificant mere money-seeking looks in comparison with a serene life—a life that dwells in the ocean of Truth, beneath the waves, beyond the reach of tempests, in the Eternal Calm!

"How many people we know who sour their lives, who ruin all that is sweet and beautiful by explosive tempers, who destroy their poise of character, and make bad blood! It is a question whether the great majority of people do not ruin their lives and mar their happiness by lack of self-control. How few people we meet in life who are well-balanced, who have that exquisite poise which is characteristic of the finished character!"

Yes, humanity surges with uncontrolled passion, is tumultuous with ungoverned grief, is blown about by anxiety and doubt. Only the wise man, only he whose thoughts are controlled and purified, makes the winds and the storms of the soul obey him.

Tempest-tossed souls, wherever ye may be, under whatsoever conditions ye may live, know this—in the ocean of life the isles of Blessedness are smiling, and the sunny shore of your ideal awaits your coming. Keep your hand firmly upon the helm of thought. In the bark of your soul reclines the commanding Master; He does but sleep; wake Him. Self-control is strength; Right Thought is mastery; Calmness is power. Say unto your heart, "Peace, be still!"

THE POWER OF YOUR SUBCONSCIOUS MIND

By Joseph Murphy

1963

CONTENTS

HOW THIS BOOK CAN WORK MIRACLES IN YOUR LIFE

I have seen miracles happen to men and women in all walks of life all over the world. Miracles will happen to you, too—when you begin using the magic power of your subconscious mind. This book is designed to teach you that your habitual thinking and imagery mold, fashion, and create your destiny; for as a man thinketh in his subconscious mind, so is he.

DO YOU KNOW THE ANSWERS?

Why is one man sad and another man happy? Why is one man joyous and prosperous and another man poor and miserable? Why is one man fearful and anxious and another full of faith and confidence? Why does one man have a beautiful, luxurious home while another man lives out a meager existence in a slum? Why is one man a great success and another an abject failure? Why is one speaker outstanding and immensely popular and another mediocre and unpopular? Why is one man a genius in his work or profession while the other man toils and moils all his life without doing or accomplishing anything worthwhile? Why is one man healed of a so-called incurable disease and another isn't? Why is it so many good, kind religious people suffer the tortures of the damned in their mind and body? Why is it many immoral and irreligious people succeed and prosper and enjoy radiant health? Why is one woman happily married and her sister very unhappy and frustrated? Is there an answer to these questions in the workings of your conscious and subconscious minds? There most certainly is.

REASON FOR WRITING THIS BOOK

It is for the express purpose of answering and clarifying the above questions and many others of a similar nature that motivated me to write this book. I have endeavored to explain the great fundamental truths of your mind in the simplest language possible. I believe that it is perfectly possible to explain the basic, foundational, and fundamental laws of life and of your mind in ordinary everyday language. You will find that the language of this book is that used in your daily papers, current periodicals, in your business offices, in your home, and in the daily workshop. I urge you to study this book and apply the techniques outlined therein; and as you do, I feel absolutely convinced that you will lay hold of a miracle-working power that will lift you up from confusion, misery, melancholy, and failure, and guide you to your true place, solve your difficulties, sever you from emotional and physical bondage, and place you on the royal road to freedom, happiness, and peace of mind. This miracle-working power of your subconscious mind can heal you of your sickness, make you vital and strong again. In learning how to use your inner powers, you will open the prison door of fear and enter into a life described by Paul as the glorious liberty of the sons of God.

RELEASING THE MIRACLE-WORKING POWER

A personal healing will ever be the most convincing evidence of our subconscious powers. Over forty-two years ago I resolved a malignancy—in medical terminology it was called a sarcoma—by using the healing power of my subconscious mind which created me and still maintains and governs all my vital functions. The technique I applied is elaborated on in this book, and I feel sure that it will help others to trust the same Infinite Healing Presence lodged in the subconscious depths of all men. Through the kindly offices of my doctor friend, I suddenly realized that it was natural to assume that the Creative Intelligence which made all my organs, fashioned my body, and started my heart, could heal its own handiwork. The ancient proverb says, "The doctor dresses the wound and God heals it."

WONDERS HAPPEN WHEN YOU PRAY EFFECTIVELY

Scientific prayer is the harmonious interaction of the conscious and subconscious levels of mind scientifically directed for a specific purpose. This book will teach you the scientific way to tap the realm of infinite power within you enabling you to get what you really want in life. You desire a happier, fuller, and richer life. Begin to use this miracle-working power and smooth your way in daily affairs, solve business problems, and bring harmony in family relationships. Be sure that you read this book several times. The many chapters will show you how this wonderful power works, and how you can draw out the hidden inspiration and wisdom that is within you. Learn the simple techniques of impressing the subconscious mind. Follow the new scientific way in tapping the infinite storehouse. Read this book carefully, earnestly, and lovingly. Prove to yourself the amazing way it can help you. It could be and I believe it will be the turning point of your life.

EVERYBODY PRAYS

Do you know how to pray effectively? How long is it since you prayed as part of your everyday activities? In an emergency, in time of danger or trouble, in illness, and when death lurks, prayers pour forth—your own and friends'. Just read your daily newspaper. It is reported that prayers are being offered up all over the nation for a child stricken with a so-called incurable ailment, for peace among nations, for a group of miners trapped in a flooded mine. Later it is reported that when rescued, the miners said that they prayed while waiting for rescue; an airplane pilot says that he prayed as he made a successful emergency landing. Certainly, prayer is an ever-present help in time of trouble; but you do not have to wait for trouble to make prayer an integral and constructive part of your life. The dramatic answers to prayer make headlines and are the subject of testimonies to the effectiveness of prayer. What of the many humble prayers of children, the simple thanksgiving of grace at the table daily, the faithful devotions wherein the individual seeks only communion with God? My work with people has made it necessary for me to study the various approaches to prayer. I have experienced the power of prayer in my own life, and I have talked and worked with many people who also have enjoyed the help of prayer. The problem usually is how to tell others how to pray. People who are in trouble have difficulty in thinking and acting reasonably. They need an easy formula to follow, an obviously workable pattern that is simple and specific. Often they must be led to approach the emergency.

UNIQUE FEATURE OF THIS BOOK

The unique feature of this book is its down-to-earth practicality. Here you are presented with simple, usable techniques and formulas which you can easily apply in your workaday world. I have taught these simple processes to men and women all over the world, and recently over a thousand men and women of all religious affiliations attended a special class in Los Angeles where I presented the highlights of what is offered in the pages of this book. Many came from distances of two hundred miles for each class lesson. The special features of this book will appeal to you because they show you why oftentimes you get the opposite of what you prayed for and reveal to you the reasons why. People have asked me in all parts of the world and thousands of times, "Why is it I have prayed and prayed and got no answer?" In this book you will find the reasons for this common complaint. The many ways of impressing the subconscious mind and getting the right answers make this an extraordinarily valuable book and an ever-present help in time of trouble.

WHAT DO YOU BELIEVE?

It is not the thing believed in that brings an answer to man's prayer; the answer to prayer results when the individual's subconscious mind responds to the mental picture or thought in his mind. This law of belief is operating in all religions of the world and is the reason why they are psychologically true. The Buddhist, the Christian, the Moslem, and the Hebrew all may get answers to their prayers, not because of the particular creed, religion, affiliation, ritual, ceremony, formula, liturgy, incantation, sacrifices, or offerings, but solely because of belief or mental acceptance and receptivity about that for which they pray. The law of life is the law of belief, and belief could be summed up briefly as a thought in your mind. As a man thinks, feels, and believes, so is the condition of his mind, body, and circumstances. A technique, a methodology based on an understanding of what you are doing and why you are doing it will help you to bring about a subconscious embodiment of all the good things of life. Essentially, answered prayer is the realization of your heart's desire.

DESIRE IS PRAYER

Everyone desires health, happiness, security, peace of mind, true expression, but many fail to achieve clearly defined results. A university professor admitted to me recently, "I know that if I changed my mental pattern and redirected my emotional life, my ulcers would not recur, but I do not have any technique, process, or modus operandi. My mind wanders back and forth on my many problems, and I feel frustrated, defeated, and unhappy." This professor had a desire for perfect health; he needed a knowledge of the way his mind worked which would enable him to fulfill his desire. By practicing the healing methods outlined in this book, he became whole and perfect.

THERE IS ONE MIND COMMON TO ALL INDIVIDUAL MEN (EMERSON)

The miracle-working powers of your subconscious mind existed before you and I were born, before any church or world existed. The great eternal truths and principles of life antedate all religions. It is with these thoughts in mind that I urge you in the following chapters to lay hold of this wonderful, magical, transforming power which will bind up mental and physical wounds, proclaim liberty to the fear-ridden mind, and liberate you completely from the limitations of poverty, failure, misery, lack, and frustration. All you have to do is unite mentally and emotionally with the good you wish to embody, and the creative powers of your subconscious will respond accordingly. Begin now, today, let wonders happen in your life! Keep on, keeping on until the day breaks and the shadows flee away.

CHAPTER ONE

THE TREASURE HOUSE WITHIN YOU

Infinite riches are all around you if you will open your mental eyes and behold the treasure house of infinity within you. There as a gold mine within you from which you can extract everything you need to live life gloriously, joyously, and abundantly.

Many are sound asleep because they do not know about this gold mine of infinite intelligence and boundless love within themselves. Whatever you want, you can draw forth. A magnetized piece of steel will lift about twelve times its own weight, and if you demagnetize this same piece of steel, it will not even lift a feather. Similarly, there are two types of men. There is the magnetized man who is full of confidence and faith. He knows that he is born to win and to succeed. Then, there is the type of man who is demagnetized. He is full of fears and doubts. Opportunities come, and he says, "I might fail; I might lose my money; people will laugh at me." This type of man will not get very far in life because, if he is afraid to go forward, he will simply stay where he is. Become a magnetized man and discover the master secret of the ages.

THE MASTER SECRET OF THE AGES

What, in your opinion, is the master secret of the ages? The secret of atomic energy? Thermonuclear energy? The neutron bomb? Interplanetary travel? No—not any of these. Then, what is this master secret? Where can one find it, and how can it be contacted and brought into action? The answer is extraordinarily simple. This secret is the marvelous, miracle-working power found in your own subconscious mind, the last place that most people would seek it.

THE MARVELOUS POWER OF YOUR SUBCONSCIOUS

You can bring into your life more power, more wealth, more health, more happiness, and more joy by learning to contact and release the hidden power of your subconscious mind.

You need not acquire this power; you already possess it. But, you want to learn how to use it; you want to understand it so that you can apply it in all departments of your life.

As you follow the simple techniques and processes set forth in this book, you can gain the necessary knowledge and understanding. You can be inspired by a new light, and you can generate a new force enabling you to realize your hopes and make all your dreams come true. Decide now to make your life grander, greater, richer, and nobler than ever before.

Within your subconscious depths lie infinite wisdom, infinite power, and infinite supply of all that is necessary, which is waiting for development and expression. Begin now to recognize these potentialities of your deeper mind, and they will take form in the world without.

The infinite intelligence within your subconscious mind can reveal to you everything you need to know at every moment of time and point of space provided you are open-minded and receptive. You can receive new thoughts and ideas enabling you to bring forth new inventions, make new discoveries, or write books and plays. Moreover, the infinite intelligence in your subconscious can impart to you wonderful kinds of knowledge of an original nature. It can reveal to you and open the way for perfect expression and true place in your life.

Through the wisdom of your subconscious mind you can attract the ideal companion, as well as the right business associate or partner. It can find the right buyer for your home, and provide you with all the money you need, and the financial freedom to be, to do, and to go as your heart desires.

It is your right to discover this inner world of thought, feeling, and power, of light, love, and beauty. Though invisible, its forces are mighty. Within your subconscious mind you will find the solution for every problem, and the cause for every effect. Because you can draw out the hidden powers, you come into actual possession of the power and wisdom necessary to move forward in abundance, security, joy, and dominion.

I have seen the power of the subconscious lift people up out of crippled states, making them whole, vital, and strong once more, and free to go out into the world to experience happiness, health, and joyous expression. There is a miraculous healing power in your subconscious that can heal the troubled mind and the broken heart. It can open the prison door of the mind and liberate you. It can free you from all kinds of material and physical bondage.

NECESSITY OF A WORKING BASIS

Substantial progress in any field of endeavor is impossible in the absence of a working basis which is universal in its application. You can become skilled in the operation of your subconscious mind. You can practice its powers with a certainty of results in exact proportion to your knowledge of its principles and to your application of them for definite specific purposes and goals you wish to achieve.

Being a former chemist, I would like to point out that if you combine hydrogen and oxygen in the proportions of two atoms of the former to one of the latter, water will be the result. You are very familiar with the fact that one atom of oxygen and one atom of carbon will produce carbon monoxide, a poisonous gas. But, if you add another atom of oxygen, you will get carbon dioxide, a harmless gas, and so on throughout the vast realm of chemical compounds.

You must not think that the principles of chemistry, physics, and mathematics differ from the principles of your subconscious mind. Let us consider a generally accepted principle: "Water seeks its own level." This is a universal principle which is applicable to water everywhere.

Consider another principle: "Matter expands when heated." This is true anywhere, at any time, and under all circumstances. You can heat a piece of steel, and it will expand regardless whether the steel is found in China, England, or India. It is a universal truth that matter expands when heated. It is also a universal truth that whatever you impress on your subconscious mind is expressed on the screen of space as condition, experience, and event.

Your prayer is answered because your subconscious mind is principle, and by principle I mean the way a thing works. For example, the principle of electricity is that it works from a higher to a lower potential. You do not change the principle of electricity when you use it, but by co-operating with nature, you can bring forth marvelous inventions and discoveries which bless humanity in countless ways.

Your subconscious mind is principle and works according to the law of belief. You must know what belief is, why it works, and how it works. Your Bible says in a simple, clear, and beautiful way: *Whosoever shall say unto this mountain, Be thou removed, and be thou cast into the sea; and shall not doubt in his heart, but shall believe that those things which he saith shall come to pass; he shall have whatsoever he saith.* MARK 11:23.

The law of your mind is the law of belief. This means to believe in the way your mind works, to believe in belief itself. The belief of your mind is the thought of your mind—that is simple—just that and nothing else.

All your experiences, events, conditions, and acts are the reactions of your subconscious mind to your thoughts. Remember, it is not the thing believed in, but the belief in your own mind which brings about the result. Cease believing in the false beliefs, opinions, superstitions, and fears of mankind. Begin to believe in the eternal verities and truths of life which never change. Then, you will move onward, upward, and Godward.

Whoever reads this book and applies the principles of the subconscious mind herein set forth, will be able to pray scientifically and effectively for himself and for others. Your prayer is answered according to the universal law of action and reaction. Thought is incipient action. The reaction is the response from your subconscious mind which corresponds with the nature of your thought. Busy your mind with the concepts of harmony, health, peace, and good will, and wonders will happen in your life.

THE DUALITY OF MIND

You have only one mind, but your mind possesses two distinctive characteristics. The line of demarcation between the two is well known to all thinking men and women today. The two functions of your mind are essentially unlike. Each is endowed with separate and distinct attributes and powers. The nomenclature generally used to distinguish the two functions of your mind is as follows: The objective and subjective mind, the conscious and subconscious mind, the waking and sleeping mind, the surface self and the deep self, the voluntary mind and the involuntary mind, the male and the female, and many other terms. You will find the terms "conscious" and "subconscious" used to represent the dual nature of your mind throughout this book.

THE CONSCIOUS AND SUBCONSCIOUS MINDS

An excellent way to get acquainted with the two functions of your mind is to look upon your own mind as a garden. You are a gardener, and you are planting seeds (thoughts) in your subconscious mind all day long, based on your habitual thinking. As you sow in your subconscious mind, so shall you reap in your body and environment.

Begin now to sow thoughts of peace, happiness, right action, good will, and prosperity. Think quietly and with interest on these qualities and accept them fully in your conscious reasoning mind. Continue to plant these wonderful seeds (thoughts) in the garden of your mind, and you will reap a glorious harvest. Your subconscious mind may be likened to the soil which will grow all kinds of seeds, good or bad. *Do men gather grapes of thorns, or figs of thistles?* Every thought is, therefore, a cause, and every condition is an effect. For this reason, it is essential that you take charge of your thoughts so as to bring forth only desirable conditions.

When your mind thinks correctly, when you understand the truth, when the thoughts deposited in your subconscious mind are constructive, harmonious, and peaceful, the magic working power of your subconscious will respond and bring about harmonious conditions, agreeable surroundings, and the best of everything. When you begin to control your thought processes, you can apply the powers of your subconscious to any problem or difficulty. In other words, you will actually be consciously co-operating with the infinite power and omnipotent law which governs all things.

Look around you wherever you live and you will notice that the vast majority of mankind lives in the world without; the more enlightened men are intensely interested in the world within. Remember, it is the world within, namely, your thoughts, feelings, and imagery that makes your world without. It is, therefore, the only creative power, and everything which you find in your world of expression has been created by you in the inner world of your mind consciously or unconsciously.

A knowledge of the interaction of your conscious and subconscious minds will enable you to transform your whole life. In order to change external conditions, you must change the cause. Most men try to change conditions and circumstances by working with conditions and circumstances. To remove discord, confusion, lack, and limitation, you must remove the cause, and the cause is the way you are using your conscious mind. In other words, the way you are thinking and picturing in your mind.

You are living in a fathomless sea of infinite riches. Your subconscious is very sensitive to your thoughts. Your thoughts form the mold or matrix through which the infinite intelligence, wisdom, vital forces, and energies of your subconscious flow. The practical application of the laws of your mind as illustrated in each chapter of this book will cause you to experience abundance for poverty, wisdom for superstition and ignorance, peace for pain, joy for sadness, light for darkness, harmony for discord, faith and confidence for fear, success for failure, and freedom from the law of averages. Certainly, there can be no more wonderful blessing than these from a mental, emotional, and material standpoint.

Most of the great scientists, artists, poets, singers, writers, and inventors have a deep understanding of the workings of the conscious and subconscious minds.

One time Caruso, the great operatic tenor, was struck with stage fright. He said his throat was paralyzed due to spasms caused by intense fear which constricted the muscles of his throat. Perspiration poured copiously down his face. He was ashamed because in a few minutes he had to go out on the stage, yet he was shaking with fear and trepidation. He said, "They will laugh at me. I can't sing." Then he shouted in the presence of those behind the stage, "The Little Me wants to strangle the Big Me within."

He said to the Little Me, "Get out of here, the Big Me wants to sing through me."

By the Big Me, he meant the limitless power and wisdom of his subconscious mind, and he began to shout, "Get out, get out, the Big Me is going to sing!"

His subconscious mind responded, releasing the vital forces within him. When the call came, he walked out on the stage and sang gloriously and majestically, enthralling the audience.

It is obvious to you now that Caruso must have understood the two levels of mind—the conscious or rational, and the subconscious or irrational level. Your subconscious mind is reactive and responds to the nature of your thoughts. When your conscious mind (the Little Me) is full of fear, worry and anxiety, the negative emotions engendered in your subconscious mind (the Big Me) are released and flood the conscious mind with a sense of panic, foreboding, and despair. When this happens, you can, like Caruso, speak affirmatively and with a deep sense of authority to the irrational emotions generated in your deeper mind as follows: "Be still, be quiet, I am in control, you must obey me, you are subject to my command, you cannot intrude where you do not belong."

It is fascinating and intensely interesting to observe how you can speak authoritatively and with conviction to the irrational movement of your deeper self bringing silence, harmony, and peace to your mind. The subconscious is subject to the conscious mind, and that is why it is called subconscious or subjective.

OUTSTANDING DIFFERENCES AND MODES OF OPERATION

You will perceive the main differences by the following illustrations: The conscious mind is like the navigator or captain at the bridge of a ship. He directs the ship and signals orders to men in the engine room, who in turn control all the boilers, instruments, gauges, etc. The men in the engine room do not know where they are going; they follow orders. They would go on the rocks if the man on the bridge issued faulty or wrong instructions based on his findings with the compass, sextant, or other instruments. The men in the engine room obey him because he is in charge and issues orders which are automatically obeyed. Members of the crew do not talk back to the captain; they simply carry out orders.

The captain is the master of his ship, and his decrees are carried out. Likewise, your conscious mind is the captain and the master of your ship, which represents your body, environment, and all your affairs. Your subconscious mind takes the orders you give it based upon what your conscious mind believes and accepts as true.

When you repeatedly say to people, "I can't afford it," then your subconscious mind takes you at your word and sees to it that you will not be in a position to purchase what you want. As long as you persist in saying, "I can't afford that car, that trip to Europe, that home, that fur coat or ermine wrap," you can rest assured that your subconscious mind will follow your orders, and you will go through life experiencing the lack of all these things.

Last Christmas Eve a beautiful young university student looked at an attractive and rather expensive traveling bag in a store window. She was going home to Buffalo, New York, for the holidays. She was about to say, "I can't afford that bag," when she recalled something she had heard at one of my lectures which was, "Never finish a negative statement; reverse it immediately, and wonders will happen in your life."

She said, "That bag is mine. It is for sale. I accept it mentally, and my subconscious sees to it that I receive it."

At eight o'clock Christmas Eve her fiancé presented her with a bag exactly the same as the one she had looked at and mentally identified herself with at ten o'clock the same morning. She had filled her mind with the thought of expectancy and released the whole thing to her deeper mind which has the "know-how" of accomplishment.

This young girl, a student at the University of Southern California, said to me, "I didn't have the money to buy that bag, but now I know where to find money and all the things I need, and that is in the treasure house of eternity within me."

Another simple illustration is this: When you say, "I do not like mushrooms," and the occasion subsequently comes that you are served mushrooms in sauces or salads, you will get indigestion because your subconscious mind says to you, "The boss (your conscious mind) does not like mushrooms." This is an amusing example of the outstanding differences and modes of operation of your conscious and subconscious minds.

A woman may say, "I wake up at three o'clock, if I drink coffee at night." Whenever she drinks coffee, her subconscious mind nudges her, as if to say, "The boss wants you to stay awake tonight."

Your subconscious mind works twenty-four hours a day and makes provisions for your benefit, pouring all the fruit of your habitual thinking into your lap.

HOW HER SUBCONSCIOUS RESPONDED

A woman wrote me a few months ago as follows: "I am seventy-five years old, a widow with a grown family. I was living alone and on a pension. I heard your lectures on the powers of the subconscious mind wherein you said that ideas could be conveyed to the subconscious mind by repetition, faith, and expectancy.

"I began to repeat frequently with feeling, 'I am wanted. I am happily married to a kind, loving, and spiritual-minded man. I am secure!'

"I kept on doing this many times a day for about two weeks, and one day at the corner drugstore I was introduced to a retired pharmacist. I found him to be kind, understanding, and very religious. He was a perfect answer to my prayer. Within a week he proposed to me, and now we are on our honeymoon in Europe. I know that the intelligence within my subconscious mind brought both of us together in divine order."

This woman discovered that the treasure house was within her. Her prayer was felt as true in her heart, and her affirmation sank down by osmosis into her subconscious mind, which is the creative medium. The moment she succeeded in bringing about a subjective embodiment, her subconscious mind brought about the answer through the law of attraction. Her deeper mind, full of wisdom and intelligence, brought both of them together in divine order.

Be sure that you think on *whatsoever things are true, whatsoever things are honest, whatsoever things are just, whatsoever things are pure, whatsoever things are lovely, whatsoever things are of good report; if there be any virtue, and if there be any praise, think on these things.* PHIL. 4:8.

BRIEF SUMMARY OF IDEAS WORTH REMEMBERING

1. The treasure house is within you. Look within for the answer to your heart's desire.
2. The great secret possessed by the great men of all ages was their ability to contact and release the powers of their subconscious mind. You can do the same.
3. Your subconscious has the answer to all problems. If you suggest to your subconscious prior to sleep, "I want to get up at 6 A.M.," it will awaken you at that exact time.
4. Your subconscious mind is the builder of your body and can heal you. Lull yourself to sleep every night with the idea of perfect health, and your subconscious, being your faithful servant, will obey you.
5. Every thought is a cause, and every condition is an effect.
6. If you want to write a book, write a wonderful play, give a better talk to your audience, convey the idea lovingly and feelingly to your subconscious mind, and it will respond accordingly.

7. You are like a captain navigating a ship. He must give the right orders, and likewise, you must give the right orders (thoughts and images) to your subconscious mind which controls and governs all your experiences.
8. Never use the terms "I can't afford it" and "I can't do this." Your subconscious mind takes you at your word and sees to it that you do not have the money or the ability to do what you want to do. Affirm, "I can do all things through the power of my subconscious mind."
9. The law of life is the law of belief. A belief is a thought in your mind. Do not believe in things to harm or hurt you. Believe in the power of your subconscious to heal, inspire, strengthen, and prosper you. According to your belief is it done unto you.
10. Change your thoughts, and you change your destiny.

CHAPTER TWO

HOW YOUR OWN MIND WORKS

You have a mind, and you should learn how to use it. There are two levels of your mind—the conscious or rational level, and the subconscious or irrational level. You think with your conscious mind, and whatever you habitually think sinks down into your subconscious mind, which creates according to the nature of your thoughts. Your subconscious mind is the seat of your emotions and is the creative mind. If you think good, good will follow; if you think evil, evil will follow. This is the way your mind works.

The main point to remember is once the subconscious mind accepts an idea, it begins to execute it. It is an interesting and subtle truth that the law of the subconscious mind works for good and bad ideas alike. This law, when applied in a negative way, is the cause of failure, frustration, and unhappiness. However, when your habitual thinking is harmonious and constructive, you experience perfect health, success, and prosperity.

Peace of mind and a healthy body are inevitable when you begin to think and feel in the right way. Whatever you claim mentally and feel as true, your subconscious mind will accept and bring forth into your experience. The only thing necessary for you to do is to get your subconscious mind to accept your idea, and the law of your own subconscious mind will bring forth the health, peace, or the position you desire. You give the command or decree, and your subconscious will faithfully reproduce the idea impressed upon it. The law of your mind is this: You will get a reaction or response from your subconscious mind according to the nature of the thought or idea you hold in your conscious mind.

Psychologists and psychiatrists point out that when thoughts are conveyed to your subconscious mind, impressions are made in the brain cells. As soon as your subconscious accepts any idea, it proceeds to put it into effect immediately. It works by association of ideas and uses every bit of knowledge that you have gathered in your lifetime to bring about its purpose. It draws on the infinite power, energy, and wisdom within you. It lines up all the laws of nature to get its way. Sometimes it seems to bring about an immediate solution to your difficulties, but at other times it may take days, weeks, or longer. . . . *Its ways are past finding out.*

CONSCIOUS AND SUBCONSCIOUS TERMS DIFFERENTIATED

You must remember that these are not two minds. They are merely two spheres of activity within one mind. Your conscious mind is the reasoning mind. It is that phase of mind which chooses. For example, you choose your books, your home, and your partner in life. You make all your decisions with your conscious mind. On the other hand, without any conscious choice on your part, your heart is kept functioning automatically, and the process of digestion, circulation, and breathing are carried on by your subconscious mind through processes independent of your conscious control.

Your subconscious mind accepts what is impressed upon it or what you consciously believe. It does not reason things out like your conscious mind, and it does not argue with you controversially. Your subconscious mind is like the soil which accepts any kind of seed, good or bad. Your thoughts are active and might be likened unto seeds. Negative, destructive thoughts continue to work negatively in your subconscious mind, and in due time will come forth into outer experience which corresponds with them.

Remember, your subconscious mind does not engage in proving whether your thoughts are good or bad, true or false, but it responds according to the nature of your thoughts or suggestions. For example, if you consciously assume something as true, even though it may be false, your subconscious mind will accept it as true and proceed to bring about results which must necessarily follow, because you consciously assumed it to be true.

EXPERIMENTS BY PSYCHOLOGISTS

Innumerable experiments by psychologists and others on persons in the hypnotic state have shown that the subconscious mind is incapable of making selections and comparisons which are necessary for a reasoning process. They have shown repeatedly that your subconscious mind will accept any suggestions, however false. Having once accepted any suggestion, it responds according to the nature of the suggestion given.

To illustrate the amenability of your subconscious mind to suggestion, if a practiced hypnotist suggests to one of his subjects that he is Napoleon Bonaparte, or even a cat or a dog, he will act out the part with inimitable accuracy. His personality becomes changed for the time being. He believes himself to be whatever the operator tells him he is.

A skilled hypnotist may suggest to one of his students in the hypnotic state that his back itches, to another that his nose is bleeding, to another that he is a marble statue, to another that he is freezing and the temperature is below zero. Each one will follow out the line of his particular suggestion, totally oblivious to all his surroundings which do not pertain to his idea.

These simple illustrations portray clearly the difference between your conscious reasoning mind and your subconscious mind which is impersonal, non-selective, and accepts as true whatever your conscious mind believes to be true. Hence, the importance of selecting thoughts, ideas, and premises which bless, heal, inspire, and fill your soul with joy.

THE TERMS OBJECTIVE AND SUBJECTIVE MIND CLARIFIED

Your conscious mind is sometimes referred to as your objective mind because it deals with outward objects. The objective mind takes cognizance of the objective world. Its media of observation are your five physical senses. Your objective mind is your guide and director in your contact with your environment. You gain knowledge through your five senses. Your objective mind learns through observation, experience, and education. As previously pointed out, the greatest function of the objective mind is that of reasoning.

Suppose you are one of the thousands of tourists who come to Los Angeles annually. You would come to the conclusion that it is a beautiful city based upon your observation of the parks, pretty gardens, majestic buildings, and lovely homes. This is the working of your objective mind.

Your subconscious mind is oftentimes referred to as your subjective mind. Your subjective mind takes cognizance of its environment by means independent of the five senses. Your subjective mind perceives by intuition. It is the seat of your emotion and the storehouse of memory. Your subjective mind performs its highest functions when your objective senses are in abeyance. In a word, it is that intelligence which makes itself manifest when the objective mind is suspended or in a sleepy, drowsy state.

Your subjective mind sees without the use of the natural organs of vision. It has the capacity of clairvoyance and clairaudience. Your subjective mind can leave your body, travel to distant lands, and bring back information oftentimes of the most exact and truthful character. Through your subjective mind you can read the thoughts of others, read the contents of sealed envelopes and closed safes. Your subjective mind has the ability to apprehend the thoughts of others without the use of the ordinary objective means of communication. It is of the greatest importance that we understand the interaction of the objective and subjective mind in order to learn the true art of prayer.

THE SUBCONSCIOUS CANNOT REASON LIKE YOUR CONSCIOUS MIND

Your subconscious mind cannot argue controversially. Hence, if you give it wrong suggestions, it will accept them as true and will proceed to bring them to pass as conditions, experiences, and events. All things that have happened to you are based on thoughts impressed on your subconscious mind through belief. If you have conveyed erroneous concepts to your subconscious mind, the sure method of overcoming them is by the repetition of constructive, harmonious thoughts frequently repeated which your subconscious mind accepts, thus forming new and healthy habits of thought and life, for your subconscious mind is the seat of habit.

The habitual thinking of your conscious mind establishes deep grooves in your subconscious mind. This is very favorable for you if your habitual thoughts are harmonious, peaceful, and constructive.

If you have indulged in fear, worry, and other obstructive forms of thinking, the remedy is to recognize the omnipotence of your subconscious mind and decree freedom, happiness, and perfect health. Your subconscious mind, being creative and one with your divine source, will proceed to create the freedom and happiness which you have earnestly decreed.

THE TREMENDOUS POWER OF SUGGESTION

You must realize by now that your conscious mind is the "watchman at the gate," and its chief function is to protect your subconscious mind from false impressions. You are now aware of one of the basic laws of mind: Your subconscious mind is amenable to suggestion. As you know, your subconscious mind does not make comparisons, or contrasts, neither does it reason and think things out for itself. This latter function belongs to your conscious mind. It simply reacts to the impressions given to it by your conscious mind. It does not show a preference for one course of action over another.

The following is a classic example of the tremendous power of suggestion. Suppose you approach a timid-looking passenger on board ship and say to him something like this: "You look very ill. How pale you are! I feel certain you are going to be seasick. Let me help you to your cabin." The passenger turns pale. Your suggestion of seasickness associates itself with his own fears and forebodings. He accepts your aid down to the berth, and there your negative suggestion, which was accepted by him, is realized.

DIFFERENT REACTIONS TO THE SAME SUGGESTION

It is true that different people will react in different ways to the same suggestion because of their subconscious conditioning or belief. For example, if you go to a sailor on the ship and say to him sympathetically, "My dear fellow, you're looking very ill. Aren't you feeling sick? You look to me as if you were going to be seasick."

According to his temperament he either laughs at your "joke," or expresses a mild irritation. Your suggestion fell on deaf ears in this instance because your suggestion of seasickness was associated in his mind with his own immunity from it. Therefore, it called up not fear or worry, but self-confidence.

The dictionary says that a suggestion is the act or instance of putting something into one's mind, the mental process by which the thought or idea suggested is entertained, accepted, or put into effect. You must remember that a suggestion cannot impose something on the subconscious mind against the will of the conscious mind. In other words, your conscious mind has the power to reject the suggestion given. In the case of the sailor, he had no fear of seasickness. He had convinced himself of his immunity, and the negative suggestion had absolutely no power to evoke fear.

The suggestion of seasickness to the other passenger called forth his indwelling fear of seasickness. Each of us has his own inner fears, beliefs, opinions, and these inner assumptions rule and govern our lives. A suggestion has no power in and of itself except it is accepted mentally by you. This causes your subconscious powers to flow in a limited and restricted way according to the nature of the suggestion.

HOW HE LOST HIS ARM

Every two or three years I give a series of lectures at the London Truth Forum in Caxton Hall. This is a Forum I founded a number of years ago. Dr. Evelyn Fleet, the director, told me about an article which appeared in the English newspapers dealing with the power of suggestion. This is the suggestion a man gave to his subconscious mind over a period of about two years: "I would give my right arm to see my daughter cured." It appeared that his daughter had a crippling form of arthritis together with a so-called incurable form of skin disease. Medical treatment had failed to alleviate the condition, and the father had an intense longing for his daughter's healing, and expressed his desire in the words just quoted.

Dr. Evelyn Fleet said that the newspaper article pointed out that one day the family was out riding when their car collided with another. The father's right arm was torn off at the shoulder, and immediately the daughter's arthritis and skin condition vanished.

You must make certain to give your subconscious only suggestions which heal, bless, elevate, and inspire you in all your ways. Remember that your subconscious mind cannot take a joke. It takes you at your word.

HOW AUTOSUGGESTION BANISHES FEAR

Illustrations of autosuggestion: Autosuggestion means suggesting something definite and specific to oneself. Herbert Parkyn, in his excellent manual of autosuggestion,* records the following incident. It has its amusing side, so that one remembers it. "A New York visitor in Chicago looks at his watch, which is set an hour ahead of Chicago time, and tells a Chicago friend that it is twelve o'clock. The Chicago friend, not considering the difference in time between Chicago and New York, tells the New Yorker that he is hungry and that he must go to lunch."

Autosuggestion may be used to banish various fears and other negative conditions. A young singer was invited to give an audition. She had been looking forward to the interview, but on three previous occasions she had failed miserably due to fear of failure. This young lady had a very good voice, but she had been saying to herself, "When the time comes for me to sing, maybe they won't like me. I will try, but I'm full of fear and anxiety."

Her subconscious mind accepted these negative autosuggestions as a request and proceeded to manifest them and bring them into her experience. The cause was an involuntary autosuggestion, i.e., silent fear thoughts emotionalized and subjectified.

She overcame it by the following technique: Three times a day she isolated herself in a room. She sat down comfortably in an armchair, relaxed her body, and closed her eyes. She stilled her mind and body as best she could. Physical inertia favors mental passivity

* Herbert Parkyn, *Autosuggestion* (London: Fowler, 1916).

and renders the mind more receptive to suggestion. She counteracted the fear suggestion by saying to herself, "I sing beautifully. I am poised, serene, confident, and calm." She repeated this statement slowly, quietly, and with feeling from five to ten times at each sitting. She had three such "sittings" every day and one immediately prior to sleep. At the end of a week she was completely poised and confident. When the invitation to audition came, she gave a remarkable, wonderful audition.

HOW SHE RESTORED HER MEMORY

A woman, aged seventy-five, was in the habit of saying to herself, "I am losing my memory." She reversed the procedure and practiced induced autosuggestion several times a day as follows: "My memory from today on is improving in every department. I shall always remember whatever I need to know at every moment of time and point of space. The impressions received will be clearer and more definite. I shall retain them automatically and with ease. Whatever I wish to recall will immediately present itself in the correct form in my mind. I am improving rapidly every day, and very soon my memory will be better than it has ever been before." At the end of three weeks, her memory was back to normal, and she was delighted.

HOW HE OVERCAME A NASTY TEMPER

Many men who complained of irritability and bad temper proved to be very susceptible to autosuggestion and obtained marvelous results by using the following statements three or four times a day—morning, noon, and at night prior to sleep for about a month. "Henceforth, I shall grow more good-humored. Joy, happiness, and cheerfulness are now becoming my normal states of mind. Every day I am becoming more and more lovable and understanding. I am now becoming the center of cheer and good will to all those about me, infecting them with good humor. This happy, joyous, and cheerful mood is now becoming my normal, natural state of mind. I am grateful."

THE CONSTRUCTIVE AND DESTRUCTIVE POWER OF SUGGESTION

Some illustrations and comments on heterosuggestion: Heterosuggestion means suggestions from another person. In all ages the power of suggestion has played a part in the life and thought of man in every period of time and in each country of the earth. In many parts of the world it is the controlling power in religion.

Suggestion may be used to discipline and control ourselves, but it can also be used to take control and command over others who do not know the laws of mind. In its constructive form it is wonderful and magnificent. In its negative aspects it is one of the most destructive of all the response patterns of the mind, resulting in patterns of misery, failure, suffering, sickness, and disaster.

HAVE YOU ACCEPTED ANY OF THESE?

From infancy on the majority of us have been given many negative suggestions. Not knowing how to thwart them, we unconsciously accepted them. Here are some of the negative suggestions: "You can't." "You'll never amount to anything." "You mustn't." "You'll fail." "You haven't got a chance." "You're all wrong." "It's no use." "It's not what you know, but who you know." "The world is going to the dogs." "What's the use, nobody cares." "It's no use trying so hard." "You're too old now." "Things are getting worse and worse." "Life is an endless grind." "Love is for the birds." "You just can't win." "Pretty soon you'll be bankrupt." "Watch out, you'll get the virus." "You can't trust a soul," etc.

Unless, as an adult, you use constructive autosuggestion, which is a reconditioning therapy, the impressions made on you in the past can cause behavior patterns that cause failure in your personal and social life. Autosuggestion is a means releasing you from the mass of negative verbal conditioning that might otherwise distort your life pattern, making the development of good habits difficult.

YOU CAN COUNTERACT NEGATIVE SUGGESTIONS

Pick up the paper any day, and you can read dozens of items that could sow the seeds of futility, fear, worry, anxiety, and impending doom. If accepted by you, these thoughts of fear could cause you to lose the will for life. Knowing that you can reject all these negative suggestions by giving your subconscious mind constructive autosuggestions, you counteract all these destructive ideas.

Check regularly on the negative suggestions that people make to you. You do not have to be influenced by destructive heterosuggestion. All of us have suffered from it in our childhood and in our teens. If you look back, you can easily recall how parents, friends, relatives, teachers, and associates contributed in a campaign of negative suggestions. Study the things said to you, and you will discover much of it was in the form of propaganda. The purpose of much of what was said was to control you or instill fear into you.

This heterosuggestion process goes on in every home, office, factory, and club. You will find that many of these suggestions are for the purpose of making you think, feel, and act as others want you to and in ways that are to their advantage.

HOW SUGGESTION KILLED A MAN

Here is an illustration of heterosuggestion: A relative of mine went to a crystal gazer in India who told him that he had a bad heart and predicted that he would die at the next new moon. He began to tell all members of his family about this prediction, and he arranged his will.

This powerful suggestion entered into his subconscious mind because he accepted it completely. My relative also told me that this crystal gazer was believed to have some strange occult powers, and he could do harm or good to a person. He died as predicted not knowing that he was the cause of his own death. I suppose many of us have heard similar stupid, ridiculous, superstitious stories.

Let us look at what happened in the light of our knowledge of the way the subconscious mind works. Whatever the conscious, reasoning mind of man believes, the subconscious mind will accept and act upon. My relative was happy, healthy, vigorous, and robust when he went to see the fortune-teller. She gave him a very negative suggestion which he accepted. He became terrified, and constantly dwelt upon the fact that he was going to die at the next new moon. He proceeded to tell everyone about it, and he prepared for the end. The activity took place in his own mind, and his own thought was the cause. He brought about his own so-called death, or rather destruction of the physical body, by his fear and expectation of the end.

The woman who predicted his death had no more power than the stones and sticks in the field. Her suggestion had no power to create or bring about the end she suggested. If he had known the laws of his mind, he would have completely rejected the negative suggestion and refused to give her words any attention, knowing in his heart that he was governed and controlled by his own thought and feeling. Like tin arrows aimed at a battleship, her prophecy could have been completely neutralized and dissipated without hurting him.

The suggestions of others in themselves have absolutely no power whatever over you except the power that you give them through your own thoughts. You have to give your mental consent; you have to entertain the thought. Then, it becomes your thought, and you do the thinking. Remember, you have the capacity to choose. Choose life! Choose love! Choose health!

THE POWER OF AN ASSUMED MAJOR PREMISE

Your mind works like a syllogism. This means that whatever major premise your conscious mind assumes to be true determines the conclusion your subconscious mind comes to in regard to any particular question or problem in your mind. If your premise is true, the conclusion must be true as in the following example:

Every virtue is laudable;
Kindness is a virtue;
Therefore, kindness is laudable.

Another example is as follows:

All formed things change and pass away;
The Pyramids of Egypt are formed things;
Therefore, some day the Pyramids will pass away.

The first statement is referred to as the major premise, and the right conclusion must necessarily follow the right premise.

A college professor, who attended some of my science of mind lectures in May 1962, at Town Hall, New York, said to me, "Everything in my life is topsy-turvy, and I have lost health, wealth, and friends. Everything I touch turns out wrong."

I explained to him that he should establish a major premise in his thinking, that the infinite intelligence of his subconscious mind was guiding, directing, and prospering him spiritually, mentally, and materially. Then, his subconscious mind would automatically direct him wisely in his investments, decisions, and also heal his body and restore his mind to peace and tranquillity.

This professor formulated an overall picture of the way he wanted his life to be, and this was his major premise:

"Infinite intelligence leads and guides me in all my ways. Perfect health is mine, and the Law of Harmony operates in my mind and body. Beauty, love, peace, and abundance are mine. The principle of right action and divine order govern my entire life. I know my major premise is based on the eternal truths of life, and I know, feel, and believe that my subconscious mind responds according to the nature of my conscious mind thinking."

He wrote me as follows: "I repeated the above statements slowly, quietly, and lovingly several times a day knowing that they were sinking deep down into my subconscious mind, and that results must follow. I am deeply grateful for the interview you gave me, and I would like to add that all departments of my life are changing for the better. It works!"

THE SUBCONSCIOUS DOES NOT ARGUE CONTROVERSIALLY

Your subconscious mind is all-wise and knows the answers to all questions. It does not argue with you or talk back to you. It does not say, "You must not impress me with that." For example, when you say, "I can't do this," "I am too old now," "I can't meet this obligation," "I was born on the wrong side of the tracks," "I don't know the right politician," you are impregnating your subconscious with these negative thoughts, and it responds accordingly. You are actually blocking your own good, thereby bringing lack, limitation, and frustration into your life.

When you set up obstacles, impediments, and delays in your conscious mind, you are denying the wisdom and intelligence resident in your subconscious mind. You are actually saying in effect that your subconscious mind cannot solve your problem. This leads to mental and emotional congestion, followed by sickness and neurotic tendencies.

To realize your desire and overcome your frustration, affirm boldly several times a day: "The infinite intelligence which gave me this desire leads, guides, and reveals to me the perfect plan for the unfolding of my desire. I know the deeper wisdom of my subconscious is now responding, and what I feel and claim within is expressed in the without. There is a balance, equilibrium, and equanimity."

If you say, "There is no way out; I am lost; there is no way out of this dilemma; I am stymied and blocked," you will get no answer or response from your subconscious mind. If you want the subconscious to work for you, give it the right request, and attain its co-operation. It is always working for you. It is controlling your heartbeat this minute and also your breathing. It heals a cut on your finger, and its tendency is lifeward, forever seeking to take care of you and preserve you. Your subconscious has a mind of its own, but it accepts your patterns of thought and imagery.

When you are seeking an answer to a problem, your subconscious will respond, but it expects you to come to a decision and to a true judgment in your conscious mind. You must acknowledge the answer is in your subconscious mind. However, if you say, "I don't think there is any way out; I am all mixed up and confused; why don't I get an answer?" you are neutralizing your prayer. Like the soldier marking time, you do not get anywhere.

Still the wheels of your mind, relax, let go, and quietly affirm: "My subconscious knows the answer. It is responding to me now. I give thanks because I know the infinite intelligence of my subconscious knows all things and is revealing the perfect answer to me now. My real conviction is now setting free the majesty and glory of my subconscious mind. I rejoice that it is so."

REVIEW OF HIGHLIGHTS

1. Think good, and good follows. Think evil, and evil follows. You are what you think all day long.
2. Your subconscious mind does not argue with you. It accepts what your conscious mind decrees. If you say, "I can't afford it," it may be true, but do not say it. Select a better thought, decree, *"I'll buy it. I accept it in my mind."*
3. You have the power to choose. Choose health and happiness. You can choose to be friendly, or you can choose to be unfriendly. Choose to be co-operative, joyous, friendly, lovable, and the whole world will respond. This is the best way to develop a wonderful personality.
4. Your conscious mind is the "watchman at the gate." Its chief function is to protect your subconscious mind from false impressions. Choose to believe that something good can happen and is happening now. Your greatest power is your capacity to choose. *Choose happiness and abundance.*
5. The suggestions and statements of others have no power to hurt you. The only power is the movement of your own thought. You can choose to reject the thoughts or statements of others and affirm the good. You have the power to choose how you will react.
6. Watch what you say. You have to account for every idle word. Never say, "I will fail; I will lose my job; I can't pay the rent." *Your subconscious cannot take a joke.* It brings all these things to pass.

7. Your mind is not evil. No force of nature is evil. It depends how you use the powers of nature. Use your mind to bless, heal, and inspire all people everywhere.
8. Never say, "I can't." Overcome that fear by substituting the following: "I can do all things through the power of my own subconscious mind."
9. Begin to think from the standpoint of the eternal truths and principles of life and not from the standpoint of fear, ignorance, and superstition. *Do not let others do your thinking for you.* Choose your own thoughts and make your own decisions.
10. You are the captain of your soul (subconscious mind) and the master of your fate. Remember, you have the capacity to choose. Choose life! Choose love! Choose health! Choose happiness!
11. Whatever your conscious mind assumes and believes to be true, your subconscious mind will accept and bring to pass. Believe in good fortune, divine guidance, right action, and all the *blessings* of life.

CHAPTER THREE

THE MIRACLE-WORKING POWER OF YOUR SUBCONSCIOUS

The power of your subconscious is enormous. It inspires you, it guides you, and it reveals to you names, facts, and scenes from the storehouse of memory. Your subconscious started your heartbeat, controls the circulation of your blood, regulates your digestion, assimilation, and elimination. When you eat a piece of bread, your subconscious mind transmutes it into tissue, muscle, bone, and blood. This process is beyond the ken of the wisest man who walks the earth. Your subconscious mind controls all the vital processes and functions of your body and knows the answer to all problems.

Your subconscious mind never sleeps, never rests. It is always on the job. You can discover the miracle-working power of your subconscious by plainly stating to your subconscious prior to sleep that you wish a certain specific thing accomplished. You will be delighted to discover that forces within you will be released, leading to the desired result. Here, then, is a source of power and wisdom which places you in touch with omnipotence or the power that moves the world, guides the planets in their course, and causes the sun to shine.

Your subconscious mind is the source of your ideals, aspirations, and altruistic urges.

It was through the subconscious mind that Shakespeare perceived great truths hidden from the average man of his day. Undoubtedly, it was the response of his subconscious mind that caused the Greek sculptor, Phidias, to portray beauty, order, symmetry, and proportion in marble and bronze. It enabled the Italian artist, Raphael, to paint Madonnas, and Ludwig van Beethoven to compose symphonies.

In 1955 I lectured at the Yoga Forest University, Rishikesh, India, and there I chatted with a visiting surgeon from Bombay. He told me about Dr. James Esdaille, a Scotch surgeon, who worked in Bengal before ether or other modern methods of anesthesia were discovered. Between 1843 and 1846, Dr. Esdaille performed about four hundred major operations of all kinds, such as amputations, removal of tumors and cancerous growths, as well as operations on the eye, ear, and throat. All operations were conducted under mental anesthesia only. This Indian doctor at Rishikesh informed me that the postoperative mortality rate of patients operated on by Dr. Esdaille was extremely low, probably two or three percent. Patients felt no pain, and there were no deaths during the operations.

Dr. Esdaille suggested to the subconscious minds of all his patients, who were in a hypnotic state, that no infection or septic condition would develop. You must remember that this was before Louis Pasteur, Joseph Lister, and others who pointed out the bacterial origin of disease and causes of infection due to unsterilized instruments and virulent organisms.

This Indian surgeon said that the reason for the low mortality rate and the general absence of infection, which was reduced to a minimum, was undoubtedly due to the suggestions of Dr. Esdaille to the subconscious minds of his patients. They responded according to the nature of his suggestion.

It is simply wonderful, when you conceive how a surgeon, over one hundred twenty years ago, discovered the miraculous wonder-working powers of the subconscious mind. Doesn't it cause you to be seized with a sort of mystic awe when you stop and think of the transcendental powers of your subconscious mind? Consider its extrasensory perceptions, such as its capacity for clairvoyance and clairaudience, its independence of time and space, its capacity to render you free from all pain and suffering, and its capacity to get the answer to all problems, be they what they may. All these and many more reveal to you that there is a power and an intelligence within you that far transcends your intellect, causing you to marvel at the wonders of it all. All these experiences cause you to rejoice and believe in the miracle-working powers of your own subconscious mind.

YOUR SUBCONSCIOUS IS YOUR BOOK OF LIFE

Whatever thoughts, beliefs, opinions, theories, or dogmas you write, engrave, or impress on your subconscious mind, you shall experience them as the objective manifestation of circumstances, conditions, and events. What you write on the inside, you will experience on the outside. You have two sides to your life, objective and subjective, visible and invisible, thought and its manifestation.

Your thought is received by your brain, which is the organ of your conscious reasoning mind. When your conscious or objective mind accepts the thought completely, it is sent to the solar plexus, called the brain of your abdomen, where it becomes flesh and is made manifest in your experience.

As previously outlined, your subconscious cannot argue. It acts only from what you write on it. It accepts your verdict or the conclusions of your conscious mind as final. This is why you are always writing on the book of life, because your thoughts become your experiences. The American essayist Ralph Waldo Emerson said, "Man is what he thinks all day long."

WHAT IS IMPRESSED IN THE SUBCONSCIOUS IS EXPRESSED

William James, the father of American psychology, said that the power to move the world is in your subconscious mind. Your subconscious mind is one with infinite intelligence and boundless wisdom. It is fed by hidden springs, and is called the law of life. Whatever you impress upon your subconscious mind, the latter will move heaven and earth to bring it to pass. You must, therefore, impress it with right ideas and constructive thoughts.

The reason there is so much chaos and misery in the world is because people do not understand the interaction of their conscious and subconscious minds. When these two principles work in accord, in concord, in peace, and synchronously together, you will have health, happiness, peace and joy. There is no sickness or discord when the conscious and subconscious work together harmoniously and peacefully.

The tomb of Hermes was opened with great expectancy and a sense of wonder because people believed that the greatest secret of the ages was contained therein. The secret was *as within, so without; as above, so below.*

In other words, whatever is impressed in your subconscious mind is expressed on the screen of space. This same truth was proclaimed by Moses, Isaiah, Jesus, Buddha, Zoroaster, Laotze, and the illumined seers of the ages. Whatever you feel as true subjectively is expressed as conditions, experiences, and events. Motion and emotion must balance. *As in heaven* [your own mind], *so on earth* [in your body and environment]. This is the great law of life.

You will find throughout all nature the law of action and reaction, of rest and motion. These two must balance, then there will be harmony and equilibrium. You are here to let the life principle flow through you rhythmically and harmoniously. The intake and the outgo must be equal. The impression and the expression must be equal. All your frustration is due to unfulfilled desire.

If you think negatively, destructively, and viciously, these thoughts generate destructive emotions which must be expressed and find an outlet. These emotions, being of a negative nature, are frequently expressed as ulcers, heart trouble, tension, and anxieties.

What is your idea or feeling about yourself now? Every part of your being expresses that idea. Your vitality, body, financial status, friends, and social status represent a perfect reflection of the idea you have of yourself. This is the real meaning of what is impressed in your subconscious mind, and which is expressed in all phases of your life.

We injure ourselves by the negative ideas which we entertain. How often have you wounded yourself by getting angry, fearful, jealous, or vengeful? These are the poisons that enter your subconscious mind. You were not born with these negative attitudes. Feed your subconscious mind life-giving thoughts, and you will wipe out all the negative patterns lodged therein. As you continue to do this, all the past will be wiped out and remembered no more.

THE SUBCONSCIOUS HEALS A MALIGNANCY OF THE SKIN

A personal healing will ever be the most convincing evidence of the healing power of the subconscious mind. Over forty years ago I resolved a malignancy of the skin through prayer. Medical therapy had failed to check the growth, and it was getting progressively worse.

A clergyman, with a deep psychological knowledge, explained to me the inner meaning of the 139th Psalm wherein it says, *In thy book all my members were written, which in continuance were fashioned, when as yet there was none of them.* He explained that the term *book* meant my subconscious mind which fashioned and molded all my organs from an invisible cell. He also pointed out that inasmuch as my subconscious mind made my body, it could also re-create it and heal it according to the perfect pattern within it.

This clergyman showed me his watch and said, "This had a maker, and the watchmaker had to have the idea first in mind before the watch became an objective reality, and if the watch was out of order, the watchmaker could fix it." My friend reminded me that the subconscious intelligence which created my body was like a watchmaker, and it also knew exactly how to heal, restore, and direct all the vital functions and processes of my body, but that I had to give it the perfect idea of health. This would act as cause, and the effect would be a healing.

I prayed in a very simple way as follows: "My body and all its organs were created by the infinite intelligence in my subconscious mind. It knows how to heal me. Its wisdom fashioned all my organs, tissues, muscles, and bones. This infinite healing presence within me is now transforming every atom of my being making me whole and perfect now. I give thanks for the healing I know is taking place now. Wonderful are the works of the creative intelligence within me."

I prayed aloud for about five minutes two or three times a day repeating the above simple prayer. In about three months my skin was whole and perfect.

As you can see, all I did was give life-giving patterns of wholeness, beauty, and perfection to my subconscious mind, thereby obliterating the negative images and patterns of thought lodged in my subconscious mind which were the cause of all my trouble. Nothing appears on your body except when the mental equivalent is first in your mind, and as you change your mind by drenching it with incessant affirmatives, you change your body. This is the basis of all healing. . . . *Marvellous are thy works; and that my soul* [subconscious mind] *knoweth right well.* PSALMS 139:14.

HOW THE SUBCONSCIOUS CONTROLS ALL FUNCTIONS OF THE BODY

While you are awake or sound asleep upon your bed, the ceaseless, tireless action of your subconscious mind controls all the vital functions of your body without the help of your conscious mind. For example, while you are asleep your heart continues to beat rhythmically, your lungs do not rest, and the process of inhalation and exhalation, whereby your blood absorbs fresh air, goes on just the same as when you are awake. Your subconscious controls your digestive processes and glandular secretions, as well as all the other mysterious operations of your body. The hair on your face continues to grow whether you are asleep or awake. Scientists tell us that the skin secretes much more perspiration during sleep than during the waking hours. Your eyes, ears, and other senses are active during sleep. For instance, many of our great scientists have received answers to perplexing problems while they were asleep. They saw the answers in a dream.

Oftentimes your conscious mind interferes with the normal rhythm of the heart, lungs, and functioning of the stomach and intestines by worry, anxiety, fear, and depression. These patterns of thought interfere with the harmonious functioning of your subconscious mind. When mentally disturbed, the best procedure is to let go, relax, and still the wheels of your thought processes. Speak to your subconscious mind, telling it to take over in peace, harmony, and divine order. You will find that all the functions of your body will become normal again. Be sure to speak to your subconscious mind with authority and conviction, and it will conform to your command.

Your subconscious seeks to preserve your life and restore you to health at all costs. It causes you to love your children which also illustrates an instinctive desire to preserve all life. Let us suppose you accidentally ate some bad food. Your subconscious mind would cause you to regurgitate it. If you inadvertently took some poison, your subconscious powers would proceed to neutralize it. If you completely entrusted yourself to its wonder-working power, you would be entirely restored to health.

HOW TO GET THE SUBCONSCIOUS TO WORK FOR YOU

The first thing to realize is that your subconscious mind is always working. It is active night and day, whether you act upon it or not. Your subconscious is the builder of your body, but you cannot consciously perceive or hear that inner silent process. Your business is with your conscious mind and not your subconscious mind. Just keep your conscious mind busy with the expectation of the best, and make sure the thoughts you habitually think are based on whatsoever things are lovely, true, just, and of good report. Begin now to take care of your conscious mind, knowing in your heart and soul that your subconscious mind is always expressing, reproducing, and manifesting according to your habitual thinking.

Remember, just as water takes the shape of the pipe it flows through, the life principle in you flows through you according to the nature of your thoughts. Claim that the healing presence in your subconscious is flowing through you as harmony, health, peace, joy, and abundance. Think of it as a living intelligence, a lovely companion on the way. Firmly believe it is continually flowing through you vivifying, inspiring, and prospering you. It will respond exactly this way. It is done unto you as you believe.

HEALING PRINCIPLE OF THE SUBCONSCIOUS RESTORES ATROPHIED OPTIC NERVES

There is the well-known, duly authenticated case of Madame Bire of France, recorded in the archives of the medical department of Lourdes, France. She was blind, the optic nerves were atrophied and useless. She visited Lourdes and had what she termed a miraculous healing. Ruth Cranston, a Protestant young lady who investigated and wrote about healings at Lourdes in *McCall's* magazine, November, 1955, writes about Madame Bire as follows: "At Lourdes she regained her sight incredibly, with the optic nerves still lifeless and useless, as several doctors could testify after repeated examinations. A month later, upon re-examination, it was found that the seeing mechanism had been restored to normal. But at first, so far as medical examination could tell, she was seeing with 'dead eyes.'"

I have visited Lourdes several times where I, too, witnessed some healings, and of course, as we shall explain in the next chapter, there is no doubt that healings take place at many shrines throughout the world, Christian and non-Christian.

Madame Bire, to whom we just referred, was not healed by the waters of the shrine, but by her own subconscious mind which responded to her belief. The healing principle within her subconscious mind responded to the nature of her thought. Belief is a thought in the subconscious mind. It means to accept something as true. The thought accepted executes itself automatically. Undoubtedly, Madame Bire went to the shrine with expectancy and great faith, knowing in her heart she would receive a healing. Her subconscious mind responded accordingly, releasing the ever present healing forces. The subconscious mind which created the eye can certainly bring a dead nerve back to life. What the creative principle created, it can re-create. *According to your belief is it done unto you.*

HOW TO CONVEY THE IDEA OF PERFECT HEALTH TO YOUR SUBCONSCIOUS MIND

A Protestant minister I knew in Johannesburg, South Africa, told me the method he used to convey the idea of perfect health to his subconscious mind. He had cancer of the lung.

His technique, as given to me in his own handwriting, is exactly as follows: "Several times a day I would make certain that I was completely relaxed mentally and physically. I relaxed my body by speaking to it as follows, 'My feet are relaxed, my ankles are relaxed, my legs are relaxed, my abdominal muscles are relaxed, my heart and lungs are relaxed, my head is relaxed, my whole being is completely relaxed.' After about five minutes I would be in a sleepy drowsy state, and then I affirmed the following truth: 'The perfection of God is now being expressed through me. The idea of perfect health is now filling my subconscious mind. The image God has of me is a perfect image, and my subconscious mind re-creates my body in perfect accordance with the perfect image held in the mind of God.'" This minister had a remarkable healing. This is a simple easy way of conveying the idea of perfect health to your subconscious mind.

Another wonderful way to convey the idea of health to your subconscious is through disciplined or scientific imagination. I told a man who was suffering from functional paralysis to make a vivid picture of himself walking around in his office, touching the desk, answering the telephone, and doing all the things he ordinarily would do if he were healed. I explained to him that this idea and mental picture of perfect health would be accepted by his subconscious mind.

He lived the role and actually felt himself back in the office. He knew that he was giving his subconscious mind something definite to work upon. His subconscious mind was the film upon which the picture was impressed. One day, after several weeks of frequent conditioning of the mind with this mental picture, the telephone rang by prearrangement and kept ringing while his wife and nurse were out. The telephone was about twelve feet away, but nevertheless he managed to answer it. He was healed at that hour. The healing power of his subconscious mind responded to his mental imagery, and a healing followed.

This man had a mental block which prevented impulses from the brain reaching his legs, therefore, he said he could not walk. When he shifted his attention to the healing power within him, the power flowed through his focused attention, enabling him to walk.

Whatsoever ye shall ask in prayer, believing, ye shall receive. MATTHEW 21:22.

IDEAS WORTH REMEMBERING

1. Your subconscious mind controls all the vital processes of your body and knows the answer to all problems.
2. Prior to sleep, turn over a specific request to your subconscious mind and prove its miracle-working power to yourself.
3. Whatever you impress on your subconscious mind is expressed on the screen of space as conditions, experiences, and events. Therefore, you should carefully watch all ideas and thoughts entertained in your conscious mind.
4. The law of action and reaction is universal. Your thought is action, and the reaction is the automatic response of your subconscious mind to your thought. Watch your thoughts!
5. All frustration is due to unfulfilled desires. If you dwell on obstacles, delays, and difficulties, your subconscious mind responds accordingly, and you are blocking your own good.
6. The Life Principle will flow through you rhythmically and harmoniously if you consciously affirm: "I believe that the subconscious power which gave me this desire is now fulfilling it through me." This dissolves all conflicts.
7. You can interfere with the normal rhythm of your heart, lungs, and other organs by worry, anxiety, and fear. Feed your subconscious with thoughts of harmony, health, and peace, and all the functions of your body will become normal again.

8. Keep your conscious mind busy with the expectation of the best, and your subconscious will faithfully reproduce your habitual thinking.
9. Imagine the happy ending or solution to your problem, feel the thrill of accomplishment, and what you imagine and feel will be accepted by your subconscious mind and bring it to pass.

CHAPTER FOUR

MENTAL HEALINGS IN ANCIENT TIMES

Down through the ages men of all nations have somehow instinctively believed that somewhere there resided a healing power which could restore to normal the functions and sensations of man's body. They believed that this strange power could be invoked under certain conditions, and that the alleviation of human suffering would follow. The history of all nations presents testimony in support of this belief.

In the early history of the world the power of secretly influencing men for good or evil, including the healing of the sick, was said to be possessed by the priests and holy men of all nations. Healing of the sick was supposed to be a power derived directly by them from God, and the procedures and processes of healing varied throughout the world. The healing processes took the form of supplications to God attended by various ceremonies, such as the laying on of hands, incantations, and the application of amulets, talismans, rings, relics, and images.

For example, in the religions of antiquity priests in the ancient temples gave drugs to the patient and practiced hypnotic suggestions prior to the patient's sleep, telling him that the gods would visit him in his sleep and heal him. Many healings followed. Obviously, all this was the work of potent suggestions to the subconscious mind.

After the performance of certain mysterious rites, the devotees of Hecate would see the goddess during sleep, provided that before going to sleep they had prayed to her according to weird and fantastic instructions. They were told to mix lizards with resin, frankincense, and myrrh, and pound all this together in the open air under the crescent moon. Healings were reported in many cases following this grotesque procedure.

It is obvious that these strange procedures, as mentioned in the illustrations given, favored suggestion and acceptance by the subconscious mind of these people by making a powerful appeal to their imagination. Actually, in all these healings, the subconscious mind of the subject was the healer.

In all ages unofficial healers have obtained remarkable results in cases where authorized medical skill has failed. This gives cause for thought. How do these healers in all parts of the world effect their cures? The answer to all these healings is due to the blind belief of the sick person which released the healing power resident in his subconscious mind. Many of the remedies and methods employed were rather strange and fantastic which fired the imagination of the patients, causing an aroused emotional state. This state of mind facilitated the suggestion of health, and was accepted both by the conscious and subconscious mind of the sick. This will be elaborated on further in the next chapter.

BIBLICAL ACCOUNTS ON THE USE OF THE SUBCONSCIOUS POWERS

What things soever ye desire, when ye pray, believe that ye receive them, and ye shall have them. MARK 11:24.

Note the difference in tenses. The inspired writer tells us to believe and accept as true the fact that our desire has already been accomplished and fulfilled, that it is already completed, and that its realization will follow as a thing in the future.

The success of this technique depends on the confident conviction that the thought, the idea, the picture is already a fact in mind. In order for anything to have substance in the realm of mind, it must be thought of as actually existing there.

Here in a few cryptic words is a concise and specific direction for making use of the creative power of thought by impressing upon the subconscious the particular thing which you desire. Your thought, idea, plan, or purpose is as real on its own plane as your hand or your heart. In following the Biblical technique, you completely eliminate from your mind all consideration of conditions, circumstances, or anything which might imply adverse contingencies. You are planting a seed (concept) in the mind which, if you leave it undisturbed, will infallibly germinate into external fruition.

The prime condition which Jesus insisted upon was faith. Over and over again you read in the Bible, *According to your faith is it done unto you.* If you plant certain types of seeds in the ground, you have faith they will grow after their kind. This is the way of seeds, and trusting the laws of growth and agriculture, you know that the seeds will come forth after their kind. Faith as mentioned in the Bible is a way of thinking, an attitude of mind, an inner certitude, knowing that the idea you fully accept in your conscious mind will be embodied in your subconscious mind and made manifest. Faith is, in a sense, accepting as true what your reason and senses deny, i.e., a shutting out of the little, rational, analytical, conscious mind and embracing an attitude of complete reliance on the inner power of your subconscious mind.

A classical instance of Bible technique is recorded in MATTHEW 9:28–30. *And when he was come into the house, the blind men came to him: and Jesus saith unto them, Believe ye that I am able to do this? They said unto him, Yea, Lord. Then touched he their eyes, saying, according to your faith be it unto you. And their eyes were opened; and Jesus straitly charged them, saying, See that no man know it.*

In the words *according to your faith be it unto you,* you can see that Jesus was actually appealing to the co-operation of the subconscious mind of the blind men. Their faith was their great expectancy, their inner feeling, their inner conviction that something miraculous would happen, and that their prayer would be answered, and it was. This is the time-honored technique of healing, utilized alike by all healing groups throughout the world regardless of religious affiliation.

In the words *see that no man know it,* Jesus enjoins the newly healed patients not to discuss their healing because they might be subjected to the skeptical and derogatory criticisms of the unbelieving. This might tend to undo the benefits they had received at the hand of Jesus by depositing thoughts of fear, doubt, and anxiety in the subconscious mind.

. . . *for with authority and power he commandeth the unclean spirits, and they come out.* LUKE 4:36.

When the sick came to Jesus to be healed, they were healed by their faith together with his faith and understanding of the healing power of the subconscious mind. Whatever he decreed, he felt inwardly to be true. He and the people needing help were in the one universal subjective mind, and his silent inner knowing and conviction of the healing power changed the negative destructive patterns in the patients' subconscious. The resultant healings were the automatic response to the internal mental change. His command was his appeal to the subconscious mind of the patients plus his awareness, feeling, and absolute trust in the response of the subconscious mind to the words which he spoke with authority.

MIRACLES AT VARIOUS SHRINES THROUGHOUT THE WORLD

It is an established fact that cures have taken place at various shrines throughout the world, such as in Japan, India, Europe, and America. I have visited several of the famous shrines in Japan. At the world famous shrine called Diabutsu is a gigantic divinity of bronze where Buddha is seated with folded hands, and the head is inclined in an attitude of profound contemplative ecstasy. It is 42 feet in height and is called the great Buddha. Here I saw young and old making offerings at its feet. Money, fruit, rice, and oranges were offered. Candles were lit, incense was burned, and prayers of petition recited.

The guide explained the chant of a young girl as she murmured a prayer, bowed low, and placed two oranges as an offering. She also lit a candle. He said she had lost her voice, and it was restored at the shrine. She was thanking Buddha for restoring her voice. She had the simple faith that Buddha would give her back her singing voice if she followed a certain ritual, fasted, and made certain offerings. All this helped to kindle faith and expectancy, resulting in a conditioning of her mind to the point of belief. Her subconscious mind responded to her belief.

To illustrate further the power of imagination and blind belief I will relate the case of a relative of mine who had tuberculosis. His lungs were badly diseased. His son decided to heal his father. He came home to Perth, Western Australia, where his father lived, and said to him that he had met a monk who had returned from one of the healing shrines in Europe. This monk sold him a piece of the true cross. He said that he gave the monk the equivalent of $500 for it.

This young man had actually picked up a splinter of wood from the sidewalk, went to the jeweler's, and had it set in a ring so that it looked real. He told his father that many were healed just by touching the ring or the cross. He inflamed and fired his father's imagination to the point that the old gentleman snatched the ring from him, placed it over his chest, prayed silently, and went to sleep. In the morning he was healed. All the clinic's tests proved negative.

You know, of course, it was not the splinter of wood from the sidewalk that healed him. It was his imagination aroused to an intense degree, plus the confident expectancy of a perfect healing. Imagination was joined to faith or subjective feeling, and the union of the two brought about a healing. The father never learned of the trick that had been played upon him. If he had, he probably would have had a relapse. He remained completely cured and passed away fifteen years later at the age of 89.

ONE UNIVERSAL HEALING PRINCIPLE

It is a well-known fact that all of the various schools of healing effect cures of the most wonderful character. The most obvious conclusion, which strikes your mind is that there must be some underlying principle which is common to them all, namely, the subconscious mind, and the one process of healing is faith.

It will now be in order to recall to your mind once more the following fundamental truths:

First that you possess mental functions which have been distinguished by designating one the conscious mind and the other the subconscious mind.

Secondly, your subconscious mind is constantly amenable to the power of suggestion. Furthermore, your subconscious mind has complete control of the functions, conditions, and sensations of your body.

I venture to believe that all the readers of this book are familiar with the fact that symptoms of almost any disease can be induced in hypnotic subjects by suggestion. For example, a subject in the hypnotic state can develop a high temperature, flushed face, or chills according to the nature of the suggestion given. By experiment, you can suggest to the person that he is paralyzed and cannot walk: it will be so. By illustration, you can hold a cup of cold water under the nose of the hypnotic subject and tell him, "This is full of pepper; smell it!" He will proceed to sneeze. What do you think caused him to sneeze, the water or the suggestion?

If a man says he is allergic to Timothy grass, you can place a synthetic flower or an empty glass in front of his nose, when he is in a hypnotic state, and tell him it is Timothy grass. He will portray the usual allergic symptoms. This indicates that the cause of the disease is in the mind. The healing of the disease can also take place mentally.

You realize that remarkable healings take place through osteopathy, chiropractic medicine, and naturopathy, as well as through all the various religious bodies throughout the world, but it is obvious that all of these healings are brought about through the subconscious mind—the only healer there is.

Notice how it heals a cut on your face caused by shaving. It knows exactly how to do it. The doctor dresses the wound and says, "Nature heals it!" Nature refers to natural law, the law of the subconscious mind, or self-preservation which is the function of the subconscious mind. The instinct of self-preservation is the first law of nature. Your strongest instinct is the most potent of all autosuggestions.

WIDELY DIFFERENT THEORIES

It would be tedious and unprofitable to discuss to any great extent the numerous theories advanced by different religious sects and prayer therapy groups. There are a great number who claim that because their theory produces results it is, therefore, the correct one. This, as explained in this chapter, cannot be true.

You are aware that there are all types of healing. Franz Anton Mesmer, a German physician (1734–1815) who practiced in Paris, discovered that by applying magnets to the diseased body, he could cure that disease miraculously. He also performed cures with various other pieces of glass and metals. He discontinued this form of healing and claimed that his cures were due to "animal magnetism," theorizing that this substance was projected from the healer to the patient.

His method of treating disease from then on was by hypnotism which was called mesmerism in his day. Other physicians said that all his healings were due to suggestion and nothing else.

All of these groups, such as psychiatrists, psychologists, osteopaths, chiropractors, physicians, and all the churches are using the one universal power resident in the subconscious mind. Each may proclaim the healings are due to their theory. The process of all healing is a definite, positive, mental attitude, an inner attitude, or a way of thinking, called faith. Healing is due to a confident expectancy which acts as a powerful suggestion to the subconscious mind releasing its healing potency.

One man does not heal by a different power than another. It is true he may have his own theory or method. There is only one process of healing and that is faith. There is only one healing power, namely, your subconscious mind. Select the theory and method you prefer. You can rest assured, if you have faith, you shall get results.

VIEWS OF PARACELSUS

Philippus Paracelsus, a famous Swiss alchemist and physician, who lived from 1493 to 1541, was a great healer in his day. He stated what is now an obvious scientific fact when he uttered these words, "Whether the object of your faith be real or false, you will nevertheless obtain the same effects. Thus, if I believed in Saint Peter's statue as I should have believed in Saint Peter himself, I shall obtain the same effects that I should have obtained from Saint Peter. But that is superstition. Faith, however, produces miracles; and whether it is true or false faith, it will always produce the same wonders."

The views of Paracelsus were also entertained in the sixteenth century by Pietro Pomponazzi, an Italian philosopher and contemporary of Paracelsus, who said, "We can easily conceive the marvelous effects which confidence and imagination can produce, particularly when both qualities are reciprocated between the subjects and the person who influences them. The cures attributed to the influence of certain relics are the effect of their imagination and confidence. Quacks and philosophers know that if the bones of any skeleton were put in place of the saint's bones, the sick would nonetheless experience beneficial effects, if they believed that they were veritable relics."

Then, if you believe in the bones of saints to heal, or if you believe in the healing power of certain waters, you will get results because of the powerful suggestion given to your subconscious mind. It is the latter that does the healing.

BERNHEIM'S EXPERIMENTS

Hippolyte Bernheim, professor of medicine at Nancy, France, 1910–1919, was the expounder of the fact that the suggestion of the physician to the patient was exerted through the subconscious mind.

Bernheim, in his *Suggestive Therapeutics,* page 197, tells a story of a man with paralysis of the tongue which had yielded to no form of treatment. His doctor told the patient that he had a new instrument with which he promised to heal him. He introduced a pocket thermometer into the patient's mouth. The patient imagined it to be the instrument which was to save him. In a few moments he cried out joyfully that he could once more move his tongue freely.

"Among our cases," continues Bernheim, "facts of the same sort will be found. A young girl came into my office, having suffered from complete loss of speech for nearly four weeks. After making sure of the diagnosis, I told my students that loss of speech sometimes yielded instantly to electricity, which might act simply by its suggestive influence. I sent for the induction apparatus. I applied my hand over the larynx and moved a little, and said, 'Now you can speak aloud.' In an instant I made her say 'a,' then 'b,' then 'Maria.' She continued to speak distinctly; the loss of voice had disappeared."

Here Bernheim is showing the power of faith and expectancy on the part of the patient which acts as a powerful suggestion to the subconscious mind.

PRODUCING A BLISTER BY SUGGESTION

Bernheim states that he produced a blister on the back of a patient's neck by applying a postage stamp and suggesting to the patient that it was a fly-plaster. This has been confirmed by the experiments and experiences of many doctors in many parts of the world, which leave no doubt that structural changes are a possible result of oral suggestion to patients.

THE CAUSE OF BLOODY STIGMATA

In Hudson's *Law of Psychic Phenomena,* page 153, he states, "Hemorrhages and bloody stigmata may be induced in certain subjects by means of suggestion.

"Dr. M. Bourru put a subject into the somnambulistic condition, and gave him the following suggestion: 'At four o'clock this afternoon, after the hypnosis, you will come into my office, sit down in the armchair, cross your arms upon your breast, and your nose will begin to bleed.' At the hour appointed the young man did as directed. Several drops of blood came from the left nostril.

"On another occasion the same investigator traced the patient's name on both his forearms with the dull point of an instrument. Then when the patient was in the somnambulistic condition, he said, 'At four o'clock this afternoon you will go to sleep, and your arms will bleed along the lines which I have traced, and your name will appear written on your arms in letters of blood.' He was watched at four o'clock and seen to fall asleep. On the left arm the letters stood out in bright relief, and in several places there were drops of blood. The letters were still visible three months afterward, although they had gradually grown faint."

These facts demonstrate at once the correctness of the two fundamental propositions previously stated, namely, the constant amenability of the subconscious mind to the power of suggestion and the perfect control which the subconscious mind exercises over the functions, sensations, and conditions of the body.

All the foregoing phenomena dramatize vividly abnormal conditions induced by suggestion, and are conclusive proof that *as a man thinketh in his heart* [subconscious mind] *so is he.*

HEALING POINTS IN REVIEW

1. Remind yourself frequently that the healing power is in your own subconscious mind.
2. Know that faith is like a seed planted in the ground; it grows after its kind. Plant the idea (seed) in your mind, water and fertilize it with expectancy, and it will manifest.
3. The idea you have for a book, new invention, or play is real in your mind. This is why you can believe you have it now. Believe in the reality of your idea, plan, or invention, and as you do, it will become manifest.

4. In praying for another, know that your silent inner knowing of wholeness, beauty, and perfection can change the negative patterns of the other's subconscious mind and bring about wonderful results.
5. The miraculous healings you hear about at various shrines are due to imagination and blind faith which act on the subconscious mind, releasing the healing power.
6. All disease originates in the mind. Nothing appears on the body unless there is a mental pattern corresponding to it.
7. The symptoms of almost any disease can be induced in you by hypnotic suggestion. This shows you the power of your thought.
8. There is only one process of healing and that is faith. There is only one healing power, namely, your subconscious mind.
9. Whether the object of your faith is real or false, you will get results. Your subconscious mind responds to the thought in your mind. Look upon faith as a thought in your mind, and that will suffice.

CHAPTER FIVE

MENTAL HEALINGS IN MODERN TIMES

Everyone is definitely concerned with the healing of bodily conditions and human affairs. What is it that heals? Where is this healing power? These are questions asked by everyone. The answer is that this healing power is in the subconscious mind of each person, and a changed mental attitude on the part of the sick person releases this healing power.

No mental or religious science practitioner, psychologist, psychiatrist, or medical doctor ever healed a patient. There is an old saying, "The doctor dresses the wound, but God heals it." The psychologist or psychiatrist proceeds to remove the mental blocks in the patient so that the healing principle may be released, restoring the patient to health. Likewise, the surgeon removes the physical block enabling the healing currents to function normally. No physician, surgeon, or mental science practitioner claims that "he healed the patient." The one healing power is called by many names—Nature, Life, God, Creative Intelligence, and Subconscious Power.

As previously outlined, there are many different methods used to remove the mental, emotional, and physical blocks which inhibit the flow of the healing life principle animating all of us. The healing principle resident in your subconscious mind can and will, if properly directed by you or some other person, heal your mind and body of all disease. This healing principle is operative in all men regardless of creed, color, or race. You do not have to belong to some particular church in order to use and participate in this healing process. Your subconscious will heal the burn or cut on your hand even though you profess to be an atheist or agnostic.

The modern mental therapeutic procedure is based on the truth that the infinite intelligence and power of your subconscious mind responds according to your faith. The mental science practitioner or minister follows the injunction of the Bible, i.e., he goes into his closet and shuts the door, which means he stills his mind, relaxes, lets go, and thinks of the infinite healing presence within him. He closes the door of his mind to all outside distractions as well as appearances, and then he quietly and knowingly turns over his request or desire to his subconscious mind, realizing that the intelligence of his mind will answer him according to his specific needs.

The most wonderful thing to know is this: Imagine the end desired and feel its reality; then the infinite life principle will respond to your conscious choice and your conscious request. This is the meaning of *believe you have received, and you shall receive.* This is what the modern mental scientist does when he practices prayer therapy.

ONE PROCESS OF HEALING

There is only one universal healing principle operating through everything—the cat, the dog, the tree, the grass, the wind, the earth—for everything is alive. This life principle operates through the animal, vegetable, and mineral kingdoms as instinct and the law of growth. Man is consciously aware of this life principle, and he can consciously direct it to bless himself in countless ways.

There are many different approaches, techniques, and methods in using the universal power, but there is only one process of healing, which is faith, for *according to your faith is it done unto you.*

THE LAW OF BELIEF

All religions of the world represent forms of belief, and these beliefs are explained in many ways. The law of life is belief. What do you believe about yourself, life, and the universe? *It is done unto you as you believe.*

Belief is a thought in your mind which causes the power of your subconscious to be distributed into all phases of your life according to your thinking habits. You must realize the Bible is not talking about your belief in some ritual, ceremony, form, institution, man, or formula. It is talking about belief itself. The belief of your mind is simply the thought of your mind. *If thou canst believe, all things are possible to him that believeth.* MARK 9:23.

It is foolish to believe in something to hurt or harm you. Remember, it is not the thing believed in that hurts or harms you, but the belief or thought in your mind which creates the result. All your experiences, all your actions, and all the events and circumstances of your life are but the reflections and reactions to your own thought.

PRAYER THERAPY IS THE COMBINED FUNCTION OF THE CONSCIOUS AND SUBCONSCIOUS MIND SCIENTIFICALLY DIRECTED

Prayer therapy is the synchronized, harmonious, and intelligent function of the conscious and subconscious levels of mind specifically directed for a definite purpose. In scientific prayer or prayer therapy, you must know what you are doing and why you are doing it. You trust the law of healing. Prayer therapy is sometimes referred to as mental treatment, and another term is scientific prayer.

In prayer therapy you consciously choose a certain idea, mental picture, or plan which you desire to experience. You realize your capacity to convey this idea or mental image to your subconscious by feeling the reality of the state assumed. As you remain faithful in your mental attitude, your prayer will be answered. Prayer therapy is a definite mental action for a definite specific purpose.

Let us suppose that you decide to heal a certain difficulty by prayer therapy. You are aware that your problem or sickness, whatever it may be, must be caused by negative thoughts charged with fear and lodged in your subconscious mind, and that if you can succeed in cleansing your mind of these thoughts, you will get a healing.

You, therefore, turn to the healing power within your own subconscious mind and remind yourself of its infinite power and intelligence and its capacity to heal all conditions. As you dwell on these truths, your fear will begin to dissolve, and the recollection of these truths also corrects the erroneous beliefs.

You give thanks for the healing that you know will come, and then you keep your mind off the difficulty until you feel guided, after an interval, to pray again. While you are praying, you absolutely refuse to give any power to the negative conditions or to admit for a second that the healing will not come. This attitude of mind brings about the harmonious union of the conscious and subconscious mind, which releases the healing power.

FAITH HEALING, WHAT IT MEANS, AND HOW BLIND FAITH WORKS

What is popularly termed faith healing is not the faith mentioned in the Bible, which means a knowledge of the interaction of the conscious and subconscious mind. A faith healer is one who heals without any real scientific understanding of the powers and forces involved. He may claim that he has a special gift of healing, and the sick person's blind belief in him or his powers may bring results.

The voodoo doctor in South Africa and other parts of the world may heal by incantations, or a person may be healed by touching the so-called bones of saints, or anything else which cause the patients to honestly believe in the method or process.

Any method which causes you to move from fear and worry to faith and expectancy will heal. There are many persons, each of whom claims that because his personal theory produces results, it is, therefore, the correct one. This, as already explained in this chapter, cannot be true.

To illustrate how blind faith works: You will recall our discussion of the German physician Franz Anton Mesmer. In 1776 he claimed many cures when he stroked diseased bodies with artificial magnets. Later on he threw away his magnets and evolved the theory of animal magnetism. This he held to be a fluid which pervades the universe, but is most active in the human organism.

He claimed that this magnetic fluid which was going forth from him to his patients healed them. People flocked to him, and many wonderful cures were effected.

Mesmer moved to Paris, and while there the Government appointed a commission composed of physicians and members of the Academy of Science, of which Benjamin Franklin was a member, to investigate his cures. The report admitted the leading facts claimed by Mesmer, but held that there was no evidence to prove the correctness of his magnetic fluid theory, and said the effects were due to the imagination of the patients.

Soon after this, Mesmer was driven into exile, and died in 1815. Shortly afterwards, Dr. Braid of Manchester undertook to show that magnetic fluid had nothing to do with the production of the healings of Dr. Mesmer. Dr. Braid discovered that patients could be thrown into hypnotic sleep by suggestion, during which many of the well-known phenomena ascribed to magnetism by Mesmer could be produced.

You can readily see that all these cures were undoubtedly brought about by the active imagination of the patients together with a powerful suggestion of health to their subconscious minds. All this could be termed blind faith as there was no understanding in those days as to how the cures were brought about.

SUBJECTIVE FAITH AND WHAT IT MEANS

You will recall the proposition, which need not be repeated at length, that the subjective or subconscious mind of an individual is as amenable to the control of his own conscious objective mind as it is by the suggestions of another. It follows that whatever may be your objective belief, if you will assume to have faith actively or passively, your subconscious mind will be controlled by the suggestion, and your desire will be fulfilled.

The faith required in mental healings is a purely subjective faith, and it is attainable upon the cessation of active opposition on the part of the objective or conscious mind.

In the healing of the body it is, of course, desirable to secure the concurrent faith of both the conscious and subconscious mind. However, it is not always essential if you will enter into a state of passivity and receptivity by relaxing the mind and the body and getting into a sleepy state. In this drowsy state your passivity becomes receptive to subjective impression.

Recently, I was asked by a man, "How is it that I got a healing through a minister? I did not believe what he said when he told me that there is no such thing as disease and that matter does not exist."

This man at first thought his intelligence was being insulted, and he protested against such a palpable absurdity. The explanation is simple. He was quieted by soothing words and told to get into a perfectly passive condition, to say nothing, and think of nothing for the time being. His minister also became passive, and affirmed quietly, peacefully, and constantly for about one half hour that this man would have perfect health, peace, harmony, and wholeness. He felt immense relief and was restored to health.

It is easy to see that his subjective faith had been made manifest by his passivity under treatment, and the suggestions of perfect healthfulness by the minister were conveyed to his subconscious mind. The two subjective minds were men *en rapport.*

The minister was not handicapped by antagonistic autosuggestions of the patient arising from objective doubt of the power of the healer or the correctness of the theory. In this sleepy, drowsy state the conscious mind resistance is reduced to a minimum, and results followed. The subconscious mind of the patient being necessarily controlled by such suggestion exercised its functions in accordance therewith, and a healing followed.

THE MEANING OF ABSENT TREATMENT

Suppose you learned that your mother was sick in New York City and you lived in Los Angeles. Your mother would not be physically present where you are, but you could pray for her. *It is the Father within which doeth the work.*

The creative law of mind (subconscious mind) serves you and will do the work. Its response to you is automatic. Your treatment is for the purpose of inducing an inner realization of health and harmony in your mentality. This inner realization, acting through the subconscious mind, operates through your mother's subconscious mind as there is but one creative mind. Your thoughts of health, vitality, and perfection operate through the one universal subjective mind, and set a law in motion on the subjective side of life which manifests through her body as a healing.

In the mind principle there is no time or space. It is the same mind that operates through your mother no matter where she may be. In reality there is no absent treatment as opposed to present treatment for the universal mind is omnipresent. You do not try to send out thoughts or hold a thought. Your treatment is a conscious movement of thought, and as you become conscious of the qualities of health, well-being, and relaxation, these qualities will be resurrected in the experience of your mother, and results will follow.

The following is a perfect example of what is called absent treatment. Recently, a listener of our radio program in Los Angeles prayed as follows for her mother in New York who had a coronary thrombosis: "The healing presence is right where my mother is. Her bodily condition is but a reflection of her thought-life like shadows cast on the screen. I know that in order to change the images on the screen I must change the projection reel. My mind is the projection reel, and I now project in my own mind the image of wholeness, harmony, and perfect health for my mother. The infinite healing presence which created my mother's body and all her organs is now saturating every atom of her being, and a river of peace flows through every cell of her body. The doctors are divinely guided and directed, and whoever touches my mother is guided to do the right thing. I know that disease has no ultimate reality; if it had, no one could be healed. I now align myself with the infinite principle of love and life, and I know and decree that harmony, health, and peace are now being expressed in my mother's body."

She prayed in the above manner several times daily, and her mother had a most remarkable recovery after a few days, much to the amazement of her specialist. He complimented her on her great faith in the power of God.

The conclusion arrived at in the daughter's mind set the creative law of mind in motion on the subjective side of life, which manifested itself through her mother's body as perfect health and harmony. What the daughter felt as true about her mother was simultaneously resurrected in the experience of her mother.

RELEASING THE KINETIC ACTION OF THE SUBCONSCIOUS MIND

A psychologist friend of mine told me that one of his lungs was infected. X rays and analysis showed the presence of tuberculosis. At night before going to sleep he would quietly affirm, "Every cell, nerve, tissue, and muscle of my lungs is now being made whole, pure, and perfect. My whole body is being restored to health and harmony."

These are not his exact words, but they represent the essence of what he affirmed. A complete healing followed in about a month's time. Subsequent X rays showed a perfect healing.

I wanted to know his method, so I asked him why he repeated the words prior to sleep. Here is his reply: "The kinetic action of the subconscious mind continues throughout your sleep-time period. Hence, give the subconscious mind something good to work on as you drop off into slumber." This was a very wise answer. In thinking of harmony and perfect health, he never mentioned his trouble by name.

I strongly suggest that you cease talking about your ailments or giving them a name.

The only sap from which they draw life is your attention and fear of them. Like the above-mentioned psychologist, become a mental surgeon. Then your troubles will be cut off like dead branches are pruned from a tree.

If you are constantly naming your aches and symptoms, you inhibit the kinetic action, which means the release of the healing power and energy of your subconscious mind. Furthermore, by the law of your own mind, these imaginings tend to take shape, *As the thing I greatly feared.* Fill your mind with the great truths of life and walk forward in the light of love.

SUMMARY OF YOUR AIDS TO HEALTH

1. Find out what it is that heals you. Realize that correct directions given to your subconscious mind will heal your mind and body.
2. Develop a definite plan for turning over your requests or desires to your subconscious mind.
3. Imagine the end desired and feel its reality. Follow it through, and you will get definite results.
4. Decide what belief is. Know that belief is a thought in your mind, and what you think you create.
5. It is foolish to believe in sickness as something to hurt or to harm you. Believe in perfect health, prosperity, peace, wealth, and divine guidance.
6. Great and noble thoughts upon which you habitually dwell become great acts.
7. Apply the power of prayer therapy in your life. Choose a certain plan, idea, or mental picture. Mentally and emotionally unite with that idea, and as you remain faithful to your mental attitude, your prayer will be answered.
8. Always remember, if you really want the power to heal, you can have it through

faith, which means a knowledge of the working of your conscious and subconscious mind. Faith comes with understanding.

9. Blind faith means that a person may get results in healing without any scientific understanding of the powers and forces involved.
10. Learn to pray for your loved ones who may be ill. Quiet your mind, and your thoughts of health, vitality, and perfection operating through the one universal subjective mind will be felt and resurrected in the mind of your loved one.

CHAPTER SIX

PRACTICAL TECHNIQUES IN MENTAL HEALINGS

An engineer has a technique and a process for building a bridge or an engine. Like the engineer, your mind also has a technique for governing, controlling, and directing your life. You must realize that methods and techniques are primary.

In building the Golden Gate bridge, the chief engineer understood mathematical principles, stresses and strains. Secondly, he had a picture of the ideal bridge across the bay. The third step was his application of tried and proven methods by which the principles were implemented until the bridge took form and we drive on it. There also are techniques and methods by which your prayers are answered. If your prayer is answered, there is a way in which it is answered, and this is a scientific way. Nothing happens by chance. This is a world of law and order. In this chapter you will find practical techniques for the unfolding and nurture of your spiritual life. Your prayers must not remain up in the air like a balloon. They must go somewhere and accomplish something in your life.

When we come to analyze prayer we discover there are many different approaches and methods. We will not consider in this book the formal, ritual prayers used in religious services. These have an important place in group worship. We are immediately concerned with the methods of personal prayer as it is applied in your daily life and as it is used to help others.

Prayer is the formulation of an idea concerning something we wish to accomplish. Prayer is the soul's sincere desire. Your desire is your prayer. It comes out of your deepest needs and it reveals the things you want in life. *Blessed are they that hunger and thirst after righteousness: for they shall be filled.* That is really prayer, life's hunger and thirst for peace, harmony, health, joy, and all the other blessings of life.

THE PASSING-OVER TECHNIQUE FOR IMPREGNATING THE SUBCONSCIOUS

This consists essentially in inducing the subconscious mind to take over your request as handed it by the conscious mind. This passing-over is best accomplished in the reverie-like state. Know that in your deeper mind is Infinite Intelligence and Infinite Power. Just calmly think over what you want; see it coming into fuller fruition from this moment forward. Be like the little girl who had a very bad cough and a sore throat. She declared firmly and repeatedly, "It is passing away now. It is passing away now." It passed away in about an hour. Use this technique with complete simplicity and naïveté.

YOUR SUBCONSCIOUS WILL ACCEPT YOUR BLUEPRINT

If you were building a new home for yourself and family, you know that you would be intensely interested in regard to the blueprint for your home; you would see to it that the builders conformed to the blueprint. You would watch the material and select only the best wood, steel, in fact, the best of everything. What about your mental home and your mental blueprint for happiness and abundance? All your experiences and everything that enters into your life depend upon the nature of the mental building blocks which you use in the construction of your mental home.

If your blueprint is full of mental patterns of fear, worry, anxiety, or lack, and if you are despondent, doubtful, and cynical, then the texture of the mental material you are weaving into your mind will come forth as more toil, care, tension, anxiety, and limitation of all kinds.

The most fundamental and the most far-reaching activity in life is that which you build into your mentality every waking hour. Your word is silent and invisible; nevertheless, it is real.

You are building your mental home all the time, and your thought and mental imagery represent your blueprint. Hour by hour, moment by moment, you can build radiant health, success, and happiness by the thoughts you think, the ideas which you harbor, the beliefs that you accept, and the scenes that you rehearse in the hidden studio of your mind. This stately mansion, upon the construction of which you are perpetually engaged, is your personality, your identity in this plane, your whole life story on this earth.

Get a new blueprint; build silently by realizing peace, harmony, joy, and good will in the present moment. By dwelling upon these things and claiming them, your subconscious will accept your blueprint and bring all these things to pass. *By their fruits ye shall know them.*

THE SCIENCE AND ART OF TRUE PRAYER

The term "science" means knowledge which is co-ordinated, arranged, and systematized. Let us think of the science and art of true prayer as it deals with the fundamental principles of life and the techniques and processes by which they can be demonstrated in your life, as well as in the life of every human being when he applies them faithfully. The art is your technique or process, and the science behind it is the definite response of creative mind to your mental picture or thought.

Ask, and it shall be given you; seek, and ye shall find; knock, and it shall be opened unto you. MATTHEW 7:7.

Here you are told you shall receive that for which you ask. It shall be opened to you when you knock, and you shall find that for which you are searching. This teaching implies the definiteness of mental and spiritual laws. There is always a direct response from the Infinite Intelligence of your subconscious mind to your conscious thinking. If you ask for bread, you will not receive a stone. You must ask *believing,* if you are to receive. Your mind moves from the thought to the thing. Unless there is first an image in the mind, it cannot move, for there would be nothing for it to move toward. Your prayer, which is your mental act, must be accepted as an image in your mind before the power from your subconscious will play upon it and make it productive. You must reach a point of acceptance in your mind, an unqualified and undisputed state of agreement.

This contemplation should be accompanied by a feeling of joy and restfulness in foreseeing the certain accomplishment of your desire. The sound basis for the art and science of true prayer is your knowledge and complete confidence that the movement of your conscious mind will gain a definite response from your subconscious mind which is one with boundless wisdom and infinite power. By following this procedure, your prayers will be answered.

THE VISUALIZATION TECHNIQUE

The easiest and most obvious way to formulate an idea is to visualize it, to see it in your mind's eye as vividly as if it were alive. You can see with the naked eye only what already exists in the external world; in a similar way, that which you can visualize in your mind's eye already exists in the invisible realms of your mind. Any picture which you have in your mind is *the substance of things hoped for and the evidence of things not seen.* What you form in your imagination is as real as any part of your body. The idea and the thought are real and will one day appear in your objective world if you are faithful to your mental image.

This process of thinking forms impressions in your mind; these impressions in turn become manifested as facts and experiences in your life. The builder visualizes the type of building he wants; he sees it as he desires it to be completed. His imagery and thought processes become a plastic mold from which the building will emerge—a beautiful or an ugly one, a skyscraper or a very low one. His mental imagery is projected as it is drawn on paper. Eventually, the contractor and his workers gather the essential materials, and the building progresses until it stands finished, conforming perfectly to the mental patterns of the architect.

I use the visualization technique prior to speaking from the platform. I quiet the wheels of my mind in order that I may present to the subconscious mind my images of thought. Then, I picture the entire auditorium and the seats filled with men and women, and each one of them illumined and inspired by the infinite healing presence within each one. I see them as radiant, happy, and free.

Having first built up the idea in my imagination, I quietly sustain it there as a mental picture while I imagine I hear men and women saying, "I am healed," "I feel wonderful," "I've had an instantaneous healing," "I'm transformed." I keep this up for about ten minutes or more, knowing and feeling that each person's mind and body are saturated with love, wholeness, beauty, and perfection. My awareness grows to the point where in my mind I can actually hear the voices of the multitude proclaiming their health and happiness; then I release the whole picture and go onto the platform. Almost every Sunday some people stop and say that their prayers were answered.

MENTAL MOVIE METHOD

The Chinese say, "A picture is worth a thousand words." William James, the father of American psychology, stressed the fact that the subconscious mind will bring to pass any picture held in the mind and backed by faith. *Act as though I am, and I will be.*

A number of years ago I was in the Middle West lecturing in several states, and I desired to have a permanent location in the general area from which I could serve those who desired help. I traveled far, but the desire did not leave my mind. One evening, while in a hotel in Spokane, Washington, I relaxed completely on a couch, immobilized my attention, and in a quiet, passive manner imagined that I was talking to a large audience, saying in effect, "I am glad to be here; I have prayed for the ideal opportunity." I saw in my mind's eye the imaginary audience, and I felt the reality of it all. I played the role of the actor, dramatized this mental movie, and felt satisfied that this picture was being conveyed to my subconscious mind, which would bring it to pass in its own way. The next morning, on awakening, I felt a great sense of peace and satisfaction, and in a few days' time I received a telegram asking me to take over an organization in the Midwest, which I did, and I enjoyed it immensely for several years.

The method outlined here appeals to many who have described it as "the mental movie method." I have received numerous letters from people who listen to my radio talks and weekly public lectures, telling me of the wonderful results they get using this technique in the sale of their property. I suggest to those who have homes or property for sale that they satisfy themselves in their own mind that their price is right. Then, I claim that the Infinite Intelligence is attracting to them the buyer who really wants to have the property and who will love it and prosper in it. After having done this I suggest that they quiet their mind, relax, let go, and get into a drowsy, sleepy state which reduces all mental effort to a minimum. Then, they are to picture the check in their hands, rejoice in the check, give thanks for the check, and go off to sleep feeling the naturalness of the whole mental movie created in their own mind. They must act as though it were an objective reality, and the subconscious mind will take it as an impression, and through the deeper currents of the mind the buyer and the seller are brought together. A mental picture held in the mind, backed by faith, will come to pass.

THE BAUDOIN TECHNIQUE

Charles Baudoin was a professor at the Rousseau Institute in France. He was a brilliant psychotherapist and a research director of the New Nancy School of Healing, who in 1910 taught that the best way to impress the subconscious mind was to enter into a drowsy, sleepy state, or a state akin to sleep in which all effort was reduced to a minimum. Then in a quiet, passive, receptive way, by reflection, he would convey the idea to the subconscious. The following is his formula: "A very simple way of securing this (impregnation of the subconscious mind) is to condense the idea which is to be the object of suggestion, to sum it up in a brief phrase which can be readily graven on the memory, and to repeat it over and over again as a lullaby."

Some years ago, a young lady in Los Angeles was engaged in a prolonged bitter family lawsuit over a will. Her husband had bequeathed his entire estate to her, and his sons and daughters by a previous marriage were bitterly fighting to break the will. The Baudoin technique was outlined to her, and this is what she did: She relaxed her body in an armchair, entered into the sleepy state and, as suggested, condensed the idea of her need into a phrase consisting of six words easily graven on the memory. "It is finished in Divine Order." The significance to her of these words meant that Infinite Intelligence operating through the laws of her subconscious mind would bring about a harmonious adjustment through the principle of harmony. She continued this procedure every night for about ten nights. After she got into a sleepy state, she would affirm slowly, quietly, and feelingly the statement: "It is finished in Divine Order," over and over again, feeling a sense of inner peace and an all-pervading tranquility; then she went off into her deep, normal sleep.

On the morning of the eleventh day, following the use of the above technique, she awakened with a sense of well-being, a conviction that *it was finished*. Her attorney called her the same day, saying that the opposing attorney and his clients were willing to settle. A harmonious agreement was reached, and litigation was discontinued.

THE SLEEPING TECHNIQUE

By entering into a sleepy, drowsy state, effort is reduced to a minimum. The conscious mind is submerged to a great extent when in a sleepy state. The reason for this is that the highest degree of outcropping of the subconscious occurs prior to sleep and just after we awaken. In this state the negative thoughts, which tend to neutralize your desire and so prevent acceptance by your subconscious mind, are no longer present.

Suppose you want to get rid of a destructive habit. Assume a comfortable posture, relax your body, and be still. Get into a sleepy state, and in that sleepy state, say quietly, over and over again as a lullaby, "I am completely free from this habit; harmony and peace of mind reign supreme." Repeat the above slowly, quietly, and lovingly for five or ten minutes night and morning. Each time you repeat the words the emotional value becomes greater. When the urge comes to repeat the negative habit, repeat the above formula out loud by yourself. By this means you induce the subconscious to accept the idea, and a healing follows.

THE "THANK YOU" TECHNIQUE

In the Bible, Paul recommends that we make known our requests with praise and thanksgiving. Some extraordinary results follow this simple method of prayer. The thankful heart is always close to the creative forces of the universe, causing countless blessings to flow toward it by the law of reciprocal relationship, based on a cosmic law of action and reaction.

For instance, a father promises his son a car for graduation; the boy has not yet received the car, but he is very thankful and happy, and is as joyous as though he had actually received the car. He knows his father will fulfill his promise, and he is full of gratitude and joy even though he has not yet received the car, objectively speaking. He has, however, received it with joy and thankfulness in his mind.

I shall illustrate how Mr. Broke applied this technique with excellent results. He said, "Bills are piling up, I am out of work, I have three children and no money. What shall I do?" Regularly every night and morning, for a period of about three weeks, he repeated the words, "Thank you, Father, for my wealth," in a relaxed, peaceful manner until the feeling or mood of thankfulness dominated his mind. He imagined he was addressing the infinite power and intelligence within him knowing, of course, that he could not see the creative intelligence or infinite mind. He was seeing with the inner eye of spiritual perception, realizing that his thought-image of wealth was the *first cause,* relative to the money, position, and food he needed. His thought-feeling was the substance of wealth untrammeled by antecedent conditions of any kind. By repeating, "Thank you, Father," over and over again, his mind and heart were lifted up to the point of acceptance, and when fear, thoughts of lack, poverty, and distress came into his mind, he would say, "Thank you, Father," as often as necessary. He knew that as he kept up the thankful attitude he would recondition his mind to the idea of wealth, which is what happened.

The sequel to his prayer is very interesting. After praying in the above-mentioned manner, he met a former employer of his on the street whom he had not seen for twenty years. The man offered him a very lucrative position and advanced him $500 on a temporary loan. Today, Mr. Broke is vice president of the company for which he works. His recent remark to me was, "I shall never forget the wonders of 'Thank you, Father.' It has worked wonders for me."

THE AFFIRMATIVE METHOD

The effectiveness of an affirmation is determined largely by your understanding of the truth and the meaning back of the words, "*In praying use not vain repetition.*" Therefore, the power of your affirmation lies in the intelligent application of definite and specific positives. For example, a boy adds three and three and puts down seven on the blackboard. The teacher affirms with mathematical certainty that three and three are six; therefore, the boy changes his figures accordingly. The teacher's statement did not make three and three equal six because the latter was already a mathematical truth. The mathematical truth caused the boy to rearrange the figures on the blackboard. It is abnormal to be sick; it is normal to be healthy. Health is the truth of your being. When you affirm health, harmony, and peace for yourself or another, and when you realize these are universal principles of your own being, you will rearrange the negative patterns of your subconscious mind based on your faith and understanding of that which you affirm.

The result of the affirmative process of prayer depends on your conforming to the principles of life, regardless of appearances. Consider for a moment that there is a principle of mathematics and none of error; there is a principle of truth but none of dishonesty. There is a principle of intelligence but none of ignorance; there is a principle of harmony and none of discord. There is a principle of health but none of disease, and there is a principle of abundance but none of poverty.

The affirmative method was chosen by the author for use on his sister who was to be operated on for the removal of gallstones in a hospital in England. The condition described was based on the diagnosis of hospital tests and the usual X-ray procedures. She asked me to pray for her. We were separated geographically about 6,500 miles, but there is no time or space in the mind principle. Infinite mind or intelligence is present in its entirety at every point simultaneously. I withdrew all thought from the contemplation of symptoms and from the corporeal personality altogether. I affirmed as follows: "This prayer is for my sister Catherine. She is relaxed and at peace, poised, balanced, serene, and calm. The healing intelligence of her subconscious mind which created her body is now transforming every cell, nerve, tissue, muscle, and bone of her being according to the perfect pattern of all organs lodged in her subconscious mind. Silently, quietly, all distorted thought patterns in her subconscious mind are removed and dissolved, and the vitality, wholeness, and beauty of the life principle are made manifest in every atom of her being. She is now open and receptive to the healing currents which are flowing through her like a river, restoring her to perfect health, harmony, and peace. All distortions and ugly images are now washed away by the infinite ocean of love and peace flowing through her, and it is so."

I affirmed the above several times a day, and at the end of two weeks my sister had an examination which showed a remarkable healing, and the X ray proved negative.

To affirm is to state that it is so, and as you maintain this attitude of mind as true, regardless of all evidence to the contrary, you will receive an answer to your prayer. Your thought can only affirm, for even if you deny something, you are actually affirming the presence of what you deny. Repeating an affirmation, knowing what you are saying and why you are saying it, leads the mind to that state of consciousness where it accepts that which you state as true. Keep on affirming the truths of life until you get the subconscious reaction which satisfies.

THE ARGUMENTATIVE METHOD

This method is just what the word implies. It stems from the procedure of Dr. Phineas Parkhurst Quimby of Maine. Dr. Quimby, a pioneer in mental and spiritual healing, lived and practiced in Belfast, Maine, about one hundred years ago. A book called *The Quimby Manuscripts,* published in 1921 by Thomas Y. Crowell Company, New York City, and edited by Horatio Dresser, is available in your library. This book gives newspaper accounts of this man's remarkable results in prayer treatment of the sick. Quimby duplicated many of the healing miracles recorded in the Bible. In brief, the argumentative method employed according to Quimby consists of spiritual reasoning where you convince the patient and yourself that his sickness is due to his false belief, groundless fears, and negative patterns lodged in his subconscious mind. You reason it out clearly in your mind and convince your patient that the disease or ailment is due only to a distorted, twisted pattern of thought which has taken form in his body. This wrong belief in some external power and external causes has now externalized itself as sickness, and can be changed by changing the thought patterns.

You explain to the sick person that the basis of all healing is a change of belief. You also point out that the subconscious mind created the body and all its organs; therefore, it knows how to heal it, can heal it, and is doing so now as you speak. You argue in the courtroom of your mind that the disease is a shadow of the mind based on disease-soaked, morbid thought-imagery. You continue to build up all the evidence you can muster on behalf of the healing power within, which created all the organs in the first place, and which has a perfect pattern of every cell, nerve, and tissue within it. Then, you render a verdict in the courthouse of your mind in favor of yourself or your patient. You liberate the sick one by faith and spiritual understanding. Your mental and spiritual evidence is overwhelming; there being but one mind, what you feel as true will be resurrected in the experience of the patient. This procedure is essentially the argumentative method used by Dr. Quimby of Maine from 1849 to 1869.

THE ABSOLUTE METHOD IS LIKE MODERN SOUND WAVE THERAPY

Many people throughout the world practice this form of prayer treatment with wonderful results. The person using the absolute method mentions the name of the patient, such as John Jones, then quietly and silently thinks of God and His qualities and attributes, such as, God is all bliss, boundless love, infinite intelligence, all-powerful, boundless wisdom, absolute harmony, indescribable beauty, and perfection. As he quietly thinks along these lines he is lifted up in consciousness into a new spiritual wavelength, at which times he feels the infinite ocean of God's love is now dissolving everything unlike itself in the mind and body of John Jones for whom he is praying. He feels all the power and love of God are now focused on John Jones, and whatever is bothering or vexing him is now completely neutralized in the presence of the infinite ocean of life and love.

The absolute method of prayer might be likened to the sound wave or sonic therapy recently shown me by a distinguished physician in Los Angeles. He has an ultra sound wave machine which oscillates at a tremendous speed and sends sound waves to any area of the body to which it is directed. These sound waves can be controlled, and he told me of achieving remarkable results in dissolving arthritic calcareous deposits, as well as the healing and removal of other disturbing conditions.

To the degree that we rise in consciousness by contemplating qualities and attributes of God, do we generate spiritual electronic waves of harmony, health, and peace. Many remarkable healings follow this technique of prayer.

A CRIPPLE WALKS

Dr. Phineas Parkhurst Quimby, of whom we spoke previously in this chapter, used the absolute method in the latter years of his healing career. He was really the father of psychosomatic medicine and the first psychoanalyst. He had the capacity to diagnose clairvoyantly the cause of the patient's trouble, pains, and aches.

The following is a condensed account of the healing of a cripple as recorded in Quimby's Manuscripts:

Quimby was called on to visit a woman who was lame, aged, and bedridden. He states that her ailment was due to the fact that she was imprisoned by a creed so small and contracted that she could not stand upright and move about. She was living in the tomb of fear and ignorance; furthermore, she was taking the Bible literally, and it frightened her. "In this tomb," Quimby said, "was the presence and power of God trying to burst the bands, break through the bonds, and rise from the dead." When she would ask others for an explanation of some passage of the Bible, the answer would be a stone; then she would hunger for the bread of life. Dr. Quimby diagnosed her case as a mind cloudy and stagnated, due to excitation and fear, caused by the inability to see clearly the meaning of the passage of the Bible which she had been reading. This showed itself in the body by her heavy and sluggish feeling which would terminate as paralysis.

At this point Quimby asked her what was meant in the Bible verses: *Yet a little while am I with you, and then I go unto Him that sent me. Ye shall seek me, and shall not find me: and where I am, thither ye cannot come.* JOHN 7:33–34. She replied that it meant Jesus went to heaven. Quimby explained what it really meant by telling her that *being with her a little while* meant his explanation of her symptoms, feelings, and their causes; i.e., he had compassion and sympathy for her momentarily, but he could not remain in that mental state. The next step was *to go to Him that sent us,* which, as Quimby pointed out, was the creative power of God in all of us.

Quimby immediately traveled in his mind and contemplated the divine ideal; i.e., the vitality, intelligence, harmony, and power of God functioning in the sick person. This is why he said to the woman, "Therefore, where I go you cannot come, for you are in your narrow, restricted belief, and I am in health." This prayer and explanation produced an instantaneous sensation, and a change came over her mind. She walked without her crutches! Quimby said it was one of the most singular of all his healings. She was, as it were, dead to error, and to bring her to life or truth was to raise her from the dead. Quimby quoted the resurrection of Christ and applied it to her own Christ or health; this produced a powerful effect on her. He also explained to her that the truth which she accepted was the angel or idea which rolled away the stone of fear, ignorance, and superstition, thereby, releasing the healing power of God which made her whole.

THE DECREE METHOD

Power goes into our word according to the feeling and faith behind it. When we realize the power that moves the world is moving on our behalf and is backing up our word, our confidence and assurance grow. You do not try and add power to power; therefore, there must be no mental striving, coercion, force, or mental wrestling.

A young girl used the decree method on a young man who was constantly phoning her, pressing her for dates, and meeting her at her place of business; she found it very difficult to get rid of him. She decreed as follows: "I release . . . unto God. He is in his true place at all times. I am free, and he is free. I now decree that my words go forth into infinite mind and it brings it to pass. It is so." She said he vanished and she has never seen him since, adding, "It was as though the ground swallowed him up."

Thou shalt also decree a thing, and it shall be established unto thee: and the light shall shine upon thy ways. Job 22:28.

SERVE YOURSELF WITH SCIENTIFIC TRUTH

1. Be a mental engineer and use tried and proven techniques in building a grander and greater life.
2. Your desire is your prayer. Picture the fulfillment of your desire now and feel its reality, and you will experience the joy of the answered prayer.
3. Desire to accomplish things the easy way—with the sure aid of mental science.
4. You can build radiant health, success, and happiness by the thoughts you think in the hidden studio of your mind.
5. Experiment scientifically until you personally prove that there is always a direct response from the infinite intelligence of your subconscious mind to your conscious thinking.
6. Feel the joy and restfulness in foreseeing the certain accomplishment of your desire. Any mental picture which you have in your mind is the substance of things hoped for and the evidence of things not seen.
7. A mental picture is worth a thousand words. Your subconscious will bring to pass any picture held in the mind backed by faith.
8. Avoid all effort or mental coercion in prayer. Get into a sleepy, drowsy state and lull yourself to sleep feeling and knowing that your prayer is answered.

9. Remember that the thankful heart is always close to the riches of the universe.
10. To affirm is to state that it is so, and as you maintain this attitude of mind as true, regardless of all evidence to the contrary, you will receive an answer to your prayer.
11. Generate electronic waves of harmony, health, and peace by thinking of the love and the glory of God.
12. What you decree and feel as true will come to pass. Decree harmony, health, peace, and abundance.

CHAPTER SEVEN

THE TENDENCY OF THE SUBCONSCIOUS IS LIFEWARD

Over 90 percent of your mental life is subconscious, so men and women who fail to make use of this marvelous power live within very narrow limits.

Your subconscious processes are always lifeward and constructive. Your subconscious is the builder of your body and maintains all its vital functions. It is on the job 24 hours a day and never sleeps. It is always trying to help and preserve you from harm.

Your subconscious mind is in touch with infinite life and boundless wisdom, and its impulses and ideas are always lifeward. The great aspirations, inspirations, and visions for a grander and nobler life spring from the subconscious. Your profoundest convictions are those you cannot argue about rationally because they do not come from your conscious mind; they come from your subconscious mind. Your subconscious speaks to you in intuitions, impulses, hunches, intimations, urges, and ideas, and it is always telling you to rise, transcend, grow, advance, adventure, and move forward to greater heights. The urge to love, to save the lives of others comes from the depths of your subconscious. For example, during the great San Francisco earthquake and fire of April 18, 1906, invalids and cripples who had been confined to bed for long periods of time, rose up and performed some of the most amazing feats of bravery and endurance. The intense desire welled up within them to save others at all costs, and their subconscious responded accordingly.

Great artists, musicians, poets, speakers, and writers tune in with their subconscious powers and become animated and inspired. For example, Robert Louis Stevenson, before he went to sleep, used to charge his subconscious with the task of evolving stories for him while he slept. He was accustomed to ask his subconscious to give him a good, marketable thriller when his bank account was low. Stevenson said the intelligence of his deeper mind gave him the story piece by piece, like a serial. This shows how your subconscious will speak lofty and wise sayings through you which your conscious mind knows nothing about.

Mark Twain confided to the world on many occasions that he never worked in his life. All his humor and all his great writings were due to the fact that he tapped the inexhaustible reservoir of his subconscious mind.

HOW THE BODY PORTRAYS THE WORKINGS OF THE MIND

The interaction of your conscious and subconscious mind requires a similar interaction between the corresponding system of nerves. The cerebrospinal system is the organ of the conscious mind, and the sympathetic system is the organ of the subconscious mind. The cerebrospinal system is the channel through which you receive conscious perception by means of your five physical senses and exercise control over the movement of your body. This system has its nerves in the brain, and it is the channel of your volitional and conscious mental action.

The sympathetic system, sometimes referred to as the involuntary nervous system, has its center in a ganglionic mass at the back of the stomach known as the solar plexus, and is sometimes spoken of as the abdominal brain. It is the channel of that mental action which unconsciously supports the vital functions of the body.

The two systems may work separately or synchronously. Judge Thomas Troward* says, "The vagus nerve passes out of the cerebral region as a portion of the voluntary system, and through it we control the vocal organs; then it passes onward to the thorax sending out branches to the heart and lungs; finally, passing through the diaphragm, it loses the outer coating which distinguishes the nerves of the voluntary system and becomes identified with those of the sympathetic system, so forming a connecting link between the two and making the man physically a single entity.

"Similarly different areas of the brain indicate their connection with the objective and subjective activities of the mind respectively, and speaking in a general way we may assign the frontal portion of the brain to the former and the posterior portion to the latter, while the intermediate portion partakes of the character of both."

A rather simple way of looking at the mental and physical interaction is to realize that your conscious mind grasps an idea which induces a corresponding vibration in your voluntary system of nerves. This in turn causes a similar current to be generated in your involuntary system of nerves, thus handling the idea over to your subconscious mind which is the creative medium. This is how your thoughts become things.

Every thought entertained by your conscious mind and accepted as true is sent by your brain to your solar plexus, the brain of your subconscious mind, to be made into your flesh, and to be brought forth into your world as a reality.

* *The Edinburgh Lectures on Menial Science* (New York: Robert McBride & Co., 1909).

THERE IS AN INTELLIGENCE WHICH TAKES CARE OF THE BODY

When you study the cellular system and the structure of the organs, such as eyes, ears, heart, liver, bladder, etc., you learn they consist of groups of cells which form a group intelligence whereby they function together and are able to take orders and carry them out in deductive function at the suggestion of the master mind (conscious mind).

A careful study of the single-celled organism shows you what goes on in your complex body. Though the monocellular organism has no organs, it still gives evidence of mind action and reaction performing the basic functions of movement, alimentation, assimilation, and elimination.

Many say there is an intelligence which will take care of your body if you let it alone. That is true, but the difficulty is that the conscious mind always interferes with its five-sense evidence based on outer appearances, leading to the sway of false beliefs, fears, and mere opinion. When fear, false beliefs, and negative patterns are made to register in your subconscious mind through psychological, emotional conditioning, there is no other course open to the subconscious mind except to act on the blueprint specifications offered it.

THE SUBCONSCIOUS MIND WORKS CONTINUALLY FOR THE COMMON GOOD

The subjective self within you works continuously for the general good, reflecting an innate principle of harmony behind all things. Your subconscious mind has its own will, and it is a very real something in itself. It acts night and day whether you act upon it or not. It is the builder of your body, but you cannot see, hear, or feel it building, as all this is a silent process. Your subconscious has a life of its own which is always moving toward harmony, health, and peace. This is the divine norm within it seeking expression through you at all times.

HOW MAN INTERFERES WITH THE INNATE PRINCIPLE OF HARMONY

To think correctly, scientifically, we must know the "Truth." To know the truth is to be in harmony with the infinite intelligence and power of your subconscious mind which is always moving lifeward.

Every thought or action which is not harmonious, whether through ignorance or design, will result in discord and limitation of all kinds.

Scientists inform us that you build a new body every eleven months; so you are really only eleven months old from a physical standpoint. If you build defects back into your body by thoughts of fear, anger, jealousy, and ill will, you have no one to blame but yourself.

You are the sum total of your own thoughts. You can keep from entertaining negative thought and imagery. The way to get rid of darkness is with light; the way to overcome cold is with heat; the way to overcome the negative thought is to substitute the good thought. Affirm the good, and the bad will vanish.

WHY IT'S NORMAL TO BE HEALTHY, VITAL, AND STRONG—IT'S ABNORMAL TO BE SICK

The average child born into the world is perfectly healthy with all its organs functioning perfectly. This is the normal state, and we should remain healthy, vital, and strong. The instinct of self-preservation is the strongest instinct of your nature, and it constitutes a most potent, ever-present, and constantly operative truth, inherent in your nature. It is, therefore, obvious that all your thoughts, ideas, and beliefs must operate with greater potentiality when they are in harmony with the innate life-principle in you, which is forever seeking to preserve and protect you along all lines. It follows from this that normal conditions can be restored with greater ease and certainty than abnormal conditions can be induced.

It is abnormal to be sick; it simply means you are going against the stream of life and thinking negatively. The law of life is the law of growth; all nature testifies to the operation of this law by silently, constantly expressing itself in the law of growth. Where there is growth and expression, there must be life; where there is life there must be harmony, and where there is harmony, there is perfect health.

If your thought is in harmony with the creative principle of your subconscious mind, you are in tune with the innate principle of harmony. If you entertain thoughts which are not in accordance with the principle of harmony, these thoughts cling to you, harass you, worry you, and finally bring about disease, and if persisted in, possibly death.

In the healing of disease, you must increase the inflow and distribution of the vital forces of your subconscious mind throughout your system. This can be done by eliminating thoughts of fear, worry, anxiety, jealousy, hatred, and every other destructive thought which tends to tear down and destroy your nerves and glands—body tissue which controls the elimination of all waste material.

POTT'S DISEASE CURED

In the *Nautilus* magazine of March, 1917, there appears an article about a boy suffering from Pott's disease, or tuberculosis of the spine, who had a remarkable healing. His name was Frederick Elias Andrews of Indianapolis, now minister of Unity School of Christianity,

Kansas City, Missouri. His physician pronounced him incurable. He began to pray, and from a crooked, twisted cripple going about on hands and knees, he became a strong, straight, well-formed man. He created his own affirmation, mentally absorbing the qualities he needed.

He affirmed over and over again many times a day, "I am whole, perfect, strong, powerful, loving, harmonious, and happy." He persevered and said that this prayer was the last utterance on his lips at night and the first in the morning. He prayed for others also by sending out thoughts of love and health. This attitude of mind and way of prayer returned to him multiplied many times. His faith and perseverance paid off with big dividends. When thoughts of fear, anger, jealousy, or envy drew his attention, he would immediately start his counteracting force of affirmation going in his mind. His subconscious mind responded according to the nature of his habitual thinking. This is the meaning of the statement in the Bible, *Go thy way, thy faith hath made thee whole.* MARK 10:52.

HOW FAITH IN YOUR SUBCONSCIOUS POWERS MAKES YOU WHOLE

A young man, who came to my lectures on the healing power of the subconscious mind, had severe eye trouble which his doctor said necessitated an operation. He said to himself, "My subconscious made my eyes, and it can heal me."

Each night, as he went to sleep, he entered into a drowsy, meditative state, the condition akin to sleep. His attention was immobilized and focused on the eye doctor. He imagined the doctor was in front of him, and he plainly heard, or imagined he heard, the doctor saying to him, "A miracle has happened!" He heard this over and over again every night for perhaps five minutes or so before going to sleep. At the end of three weeks he again went to the ophthalmologist who had previously examined his eyes, and the physician said to this man, "This is a miracle!" What happened? This man impressed his subconscious mind using the doctor as an instrument or a means of convincing it or conveying the idea. Through repetition, faith, and expectancy he impregnated his subconscious mind. His subconscious mind made his eye; within it was the perfect pattern, and immediately it proceeded to heal the eye. This is another example of how faith in the healing power of your subconscious can make you whole.

POINTERS TO REVIEW

1. Your subconscious is the builder of your body and is on the job 24 hours a day. You interfere with its life-giving patterns by negative thinking.
2. Charge your subconscious with the task of evolving an answer to any problem, prior to sleep, and it will answer you.
3. Watch your thoughts. Every thought accepted as true is sent by your brain to your solar plexus—your abdominal brain—and is brought into your world as a reality.
4. Know that you can remake yourself by giving a new blueprint to your subconscious mind.
5. The tendency of your subconscious is always lifeward. Your job is with your conscious mind. Feed your subconscious mind with premises which are true. Your subconscious is always reproducing according to your habitual mental patterns.
6. You build a new body every eleven months. Change your body by changing your thoughts and keeping them changed.

7. It is normal to be healthy. It is abnormal to be ill. There is within the innate principle of harmony.
8. Thoughts of jealousy, fear, worry, and anxiety tear down and destroy your nerves and glands bringing about mental and physical diseases of all kinds.
9. What you affirm consciously and feel as true will be made manifest in your mind, body, and affairs. Affirm the good and enter into the joy of living.

CHAPTER EIGHT

HOW TO GET THE RESULTS YOU WANT

The principle reasons for failure are: lack of confidence and too much effort. Many people block answers to their prayers by failing to fully comprehend the workings of their subconscious mind. When you know how your mind functions, you gain a measure of confidence. You must remember whenever your subconscious mind accepts an idea, it immediately begins to execute it. It uses all its mighty resources to that end and mobilizes all the mental and spiritual laws of your deeper mind. This law is true for good or bad ideas. Consequently, if you use it negatively, it brings trouble, failure, and confusion. When you use it constructively, it brings guidance, freedom, and peace of mind.

The right answer is inevitable when your thoughts are positive, constructive, and loving. From this it is perfectly obvious that the only thing you have to do in order to overcome failure is to get your subconscious to accept your idea or request by feeling its reality now, and the law of your mind will do the rest. Turn over your request with faith and confidence, and your subconscious will take over and answer for you.

You will always fail to get results by trying to use mental coercion—your subconscious mind does not respond to coercion, it responds to your faith or conscious mind acceptance.

Your failure to get results may also arise from such statements as: "Things are getting worse." "I will never get an answer." "I see no way out." "It is hopeless." "I don't know what to do." "I'm all mixed up." When you use such statements, you get no response or co-operation from your subconscious mind. Like a soldier marking time, you neither go forward nor backward; in other words, you don't get anywhere.

If you get into a taxi and give a half dozen different directions to the driver in five minutes, he would become hopelessly confused and probably would refuse to take you anywhere. It is the same when working with your subconscious mind. There must be a clear-cut idea in your mind. You must arrive at the definite decision that there is a way out, a solution to the vexing problem in sickness. Only the infinite intelligence within your subconscious knows the answer. When you come to that clear-cut conclusion in your conscious mind, your mind is then made up, and according to your belief is it done unto you.

EASY DOES IT

A house owner once remonstrated with a furnace repairman for charging two hundred dollars for fixing the boiler. The mechanic said, "I charged five cents for the missing bolt and one hundred ninety-nine dollars and ninety-five cents for knowing what was wrong."

Similarly, your subconscious mind is the master mechanic, the all-wise one, who knows ways and means of healing any organ of your body, as well as your affairs. Decree health, and your subconscious will establish it, but relaxation is the key. "Easy does it." Do not be concerned with details and means, but know the end result. Get the *feel* of the happy solution to your problem whether it is health, finances, or employment. Remember how you felt after you had recovered from a severe state of illness. Bear in mind that your feeling is the touchstone of all subconscious demonstration. Your new idea must be felt subjectively in a finished state, not the future, but as coming about now.

INFER NO OPPONENT, USE IMAGINATION AND NOT WILLPOWER

In using your subconscious mind you infer no opponent, you use no willpower. You imagine the end and the freedom state. You will find your intellect trying to get in the way, but persist in maintaining a simple, childlike, miracle-making faith. Picture yourself without the ailment or problem. Imagine the emotional accompaniment of the freedom state you crave. Cut out all red tape from the process. The simple way is the best.

HOW DISCIPLINED IMAGINATION WORKS WONDERS

A wonderful way to get a response from your subconscious mind is through disciplined or scientific imagination. As previously pointed out, your subconscious mind is the builder of the body and controls all its vital functions.

The Bible says, *Whatsoever ye shall ask in prayer, believing, ye shall receive.* To believe is to accept something as true, or to live in the state of being it. As you sustain this mood, you shall experience the joy of the answered prayer!

THE THREE STEPS TO SUCCESS IN PRAYER

The usual procedure is as follows:

1. Take a look at the problem.
2. Turn to the solution or way out known only to the subconscious mind.
3. Rest in a sense of deep conviction that it is done.

Do not weaken your prayer by saying, "I wish I might be healed." "I hope so." Your feeling about the work to be done is "the boss." Harmony is yours. Know that health is yours. Become intelligent by becoming a vehicle for the infinite healing power of the subconscious mind. Pass on the idea of health to your subconscious mind to the point of conviction; then relax. Get yourself off your hands. Say to the condition and circumstance, "This, too, shall pass." Through relaxation you impress your subconscious mind enabling the kinetic energy behind the idea to take over and bring it into concrete realization.

THE LAW OF REVERSED EFFORT AND WHY YOU GET THE OPPOSITE OF WHAT YOU PRAY FOR

Coué, the famous psychologist from France who visited America about forty years ago, defined the law of reversed effort as follows: "When your desires and imagination are in conflict your imagination invariably gains the day."

If, for example, you were asked to walk a plank on the floor, you would do so without question. Now suppose the same plank were placed twenty feet up in the air between two walls, would you walk it? Your desire to walk it would be counteracted by your imagination or fear of falling. Your dominant idea which would be the picture of falling would conquer. Your desire, will, or effort to walk on the plank would be reversed, and the dominant idea of failure would be reinforced.

Mental effort is invariably self-defeated, eventuating always in the opposite of what is desired. The suggestions of powerlessness to overcome the condition dominate the mind; your subconscious is always controlled by the dominant idea. Your subconscious will accept the strongest of two contradictory propositions. The effortless way is the better.

If you say, "I want a healing, but I can't get it," "I try so hard," "I force myself to pray," "I use all the willpower I have," you must realize that your error lies in your effort. Never try to compel the subconscious mind to accept your idea by exercising willpower. Such attempts are doomed to failure, and you get the opposite of what you prayed for.

The following is a rather common experience. Students, when taking examinations and reading through their papers, find that all their knowledge has suddenly deserted them. Their minds become appalling blanks, and they are unable to recall one revelant thought. The more they grit their teeth and summon the powers of the will, the further the answers seem to flee. But, when they have left the examination room and the mental pressure relaxes, the answers they were seeking flow tantalizingly back into their minds. Trying to force themselves to remember was the cause of their failure. This is an example of the law of reversed effort whereby you get the opposite of what you asked or prayed for.

THE CONFLICT OF DESIRE AND IMAGINATION MUST BE RECONCILED

To use mental force is to presuppose that there is opposition. When your mind is concentrated on the means to overcome a problem, it is no longer concerned with the obstacle. MATTHEW 18:19 says, *If two of you shall agree on earth as touching anything that they shall ask, it shall be done for them of my Father which is in heaven.* Who are these two? It means the harmonious union or agreement between your conscious and subconscious on any idea, desire, or mental image. When there is no longer any quarrel in either part of your mind, your prayer will be answered. The two agreeing may also be represented as you and your desire, your thought and feeling, your idea and emotion, your desire and imagination.

You avoid all conflict between your desires and imagination by entering into a drowsy, sleepy state which brings all effort to a minimum. The conscious mind is submerged to a great extent when in a sleepy state. The best time to impregnate your subconscious is prior to sleep. The reason for this is that the highest degree of outcropping of the subconscious occurs prior to sleep and just after we awaken. In this state the negative thoughts and imagery which tend to neutralize your desire and so prevent acceptance by your subconscious mind no longer present themselves. When you imagine the reality of the fulfilled desire and feel the thrill of accomplishment, your subconscious brings about the realization of your desire.

A great many people solve all their dilemmas and problems by the play of their controlled, directed, and disciplined imagination, knowing that whatever they imagine and feel as true *will* and *must* come to pass.

The following will clearly illustrate how a young girl overcame the conflict between her desire and her imagination. She desired a harmonious solution to her legal problem, yet her mental imagery was constantly on failure, loss, bankruptcy, and poverty. It was a complicated lawsuit and there was one postponement after another with no solution in sight.

At my suggestion, she got into a sleepy, drowsy state each night prior to sleep, and she began to imagine the happy ending, feeling it to the best of her ability. She knew that the image in her mind had to agree with her heart's desire. Prior to sleep she began to dramatize as vividly as possible her lawyer having an animated discussion with her regarding the outcome. She would ask him questions, and he would answer her appropriately. He would say to her over and over again, "There has been a perfect, harmonious solution. The case has been settled out of court." During the day when fear thoughts came into her mind, she would run her mental movie with gestures, voice, and sound equipment. She could easily imagine the sound of his voice, smile, and mannerism. She ran this mental picture so often, it became a subjective pattern, a regular train track. At the end of a few weeks her attorney called her and confirmed objectively what she had been imagining and feeling as true subjectively.

This is really what the Psalmist meant when he wrote, *Let the words of my mouth* [your thoughts, mental images, good], *and the meditations of my heart* [your feeling, nature, emotion] *be acceptable in thy sight, O Lord* [the law of your subconscious mind], *my strength, and my redeemer* [the power and wisdom of your subconscious mind can redeem you from sickness, bondage, and misery]. PSALMS 19:14.

IDEAS WORTH RECALLING

1. Mental coercion or too much effort shows anxiety and fear which block your answer. Easy does it.
2. When your mind is relaxed and you accept an idea, your subconscious goes to work to execute the idea.
3. Think and plan independently of traditional methods. Know that there is always an answer and a solution to every problem.
4. Do not be overly concerned with the beating of your heart, with the breathing of your lungs, or the functions of any part of your anatomy. Lean heavily upon your subconscious and proclaim frequently that Divine right action is taking place.

5. The feeling of health produces health, the feeling of wealth produces wealth. How do you feel?
6. Imagination is your most powerful faculty. Imagine what is lovely and of good report. You are what you imagine yourself to be.
7. You avoid conflict between your conscious and subconscious in the sleepy state. Imagine the fulfillment of your desire over and over again prior to sleep. Sleep in peace and wake in joy.

CHAPTER NINE

HOW TO USE THE POWER OF YOUR SUBCONSCIOUS FOR WEALTH

If you are having financial difficulties, if you are trying to make ends meet, it means you have not convinced your subconscious mind that you will always have plenty and some to spare. You know men and women who work a few hours a week and make fabulous sums of money. They do not strive or slave hard. Do not believe the story that the only way you can become wealthy is by the sweat of your brow and hard labor. It is not so; the effortless way of life is the best. Do the thing you love to do, and do it for the joy and thrill of it.

I know an executive in Los Angeles who receives a salary of $75,000 yearly. Last year he went on a nine-month cruise seeing the world and its beauty spots. He said to me that he had succeeded in convincing his subconscious mind that he is worth that much money. He told me that many men in his organization getting about one hundred dollars a week knew more about the business than he did, and could manage it better, but they had no ambition, no creative ideas, and were not interested in the wonders of their subconscious mind.

WEALTH IS OF THE MIND

Wealth is simply a subconscious conviction on the part of the individual. You will not become a millionaire by saying, "I am a millionaire, I am a millionaire." You will grow into a wealth consciousness by building into your mentality the idea of wealth and abundance.

YOUR INVISIBLE MEANS OF SUPPORT

The trouble with most people is that they have no invisible means of support. When business falls away, the stock market drops, or they lose their investments, they seem helpless. The reason for such insecurity is that they do not know how to tap the subconscious mind. They are unacquainted with the inexhaustible storehouse within.

A man with a poverty-type mind finds himself in poverty-stricken conditions. Another man with a mind filled with ideas of wealth is surrounded with everything he needs. It was never intended that man should lead a life of indigence. You can have wealth, everything you need, and plenty to spare. Your words have power to cleanse your mind of wrong ideas and to instill right ideas in their place.

THE IDEAL METHOD FOR BUILDING A WEALTH CONSCIOUSNESS

Perhaps you are saying as you read this chapter, "I need wealth and success." This is what you do: Repeat for about five minutes to yourself three or four times a day, "Wealth—Success." These words have tremendous power. They represent the inner power of the subconscious mind. Anchor your mind on this substantial power within you; then conditions and circumstances corresponding to their nature and quality will be manifested in your life. You are not saying, "I am wealthy," you are dwelling on real powers within you. There is no conflict in the mind when you say, "Wealth." Furthermore, the feeling of wealth will well up within you as you dwell on the idea of wealth.

The feeling of wealth produces wealth; keep this in mind at all times. Your subconscious mind is like a bank, a sort of universal financial institution. It magnifies whatever you deposit or impress upon it whether it is the idea of wealth or of poverty. Choose wealth.

WHY YOUR AFFIRMATIONS FOR WEALTH FAIL

I have talked to many people during the past thirty-five years whose usual complaint is, "I have said for weeks and months, 'I am wealthy, I am prosperous,' and nothing has happened." I discovered that when they said, "I am prosperous, I am wealthy," they felt within that they were lying to themselves.

One man told me, "I have affirmed that I am prosperous until I am tired. Things are now worse. I knew when I made the statement that it was obviously not true." His statements were rejected by the conscious mind, and the very opposite of what he outwardly affirmed and claimed was made manifest.

Your affirmation succeeds best when it is specific and when it does not produce a mental conflict or argument; hence the statements made by this man made matters worse because they suggested his lack. Your subconscious accepts what you really feel to be true, not just idle words or statements. The dominant idea or belief is always accepted by the subconscious mind.

HOW TO AVOID MENTAL CONFLICT

The following is the ideal way to overcome this conflict for those who have this difficulty. Make this practical statement frequently, particularly prior to sleep: "By day and by night I am being prospered in all of my interests." This affirmation will not arouse any argument because it does not contradict your subconscious mind's impression of financial lack.

I suggested to one businessman whose sales and finances were very low and who was greatly worried, that he sit down in his office, become quiet, and repeat this statement over and over again: "My sales are improving every day." This statement engaged the co-operation of the conscious and subconscious mind; results followed.

DON'T SIGN BLANK CHECKS

You sign blank checks when you make such statements as, "There is not enough to go around." "There is a shortage." "I will lose the house because of the mortgage," etc. If you are full of fear about the future, you are also writing a blank check and attracting negative conditions to you. Your subconscious mind takes your fear and negative statement as your request and proceeds in its own way to bring obstacles, delays, lack, and limitation into your life.

YOUR SUBCONSCIOUS GIVES YOU COMPOUND INTEREST

To him that hath the feeling of wealth, more wealth shall be added; to him that hath the feeling of lack, more lack shall be added. Your subconscious multiplies and magnifies whatever you deposit in it. Every morning as you awaken deposit thoughts of prosperity, success, wealth, and peace. Dwell upon these concepts. Busy your mind with them as often as possible. These constructive thoughts will find their way as deposits in your subconscious mind, and bring forth abundance and prosperity.

WHY NOTHING HAPPENED

I can hear you saying, "Oh, I did that and nothing happened." You did not get results because you indulged in fear thoughts perhaps ten minutes later and neutralized the good you had affirmed. When you place a seed in the ground, you do not dig it up. You let it take root and grow.

Suppose, for example, you are going to say, "I shall not be able to make that payment." Before you get further than, "I shall—" stop the sentence and dwell on a constructive statement, such as, "By day and by night I am prospered in all my ways."

TRUE SOURCE OF WEALTH

Your subconscious mind is never short of ideas. There are within it an infinite number of ideas ready to flow into your conscious mind and appear as cash in your pocketbook in countless ways. This process will continue to go on in your mind regardless of whether the stock market goes up or down, or whether the pound sterling or dollar drops in value. Your wealth is never truly dependent on bonds, stocks, or money in the bank; these are really only symbols, necessary and useful, of course, but only symbols.

The point I wish to emphasize is that if you convince your subconscious mind that wealth is yours, and that it is always circulating in your life, you will always and inevitably have it, regardless of the form it takes.

TRYING TO MAKE ENDS MEET AND THE REAL CAUSE

There are people who claim that they are always trying to make ends meet. They seem to have a great struggle to meet their obligations. Have you listened to their conversation? In many instances their conversation runs along this vein: They are constantly condemning those who have succeeded in life and who have raised their heads above the crowd. Perhaps they are saying, "Oh, that fellow has a racket; he is ruthless; he is a crook." This is why they lack; they are condemning the thing they desire and want. The reason they speak critically of their more prosperous associates is because they are envious and covetous of the others' prosperity. The quickest way to cause wealth to take wings and fly away is to criticize and condemn others who have more wealth than you.

A COMMON STUMBLING BLOCK TO WEALTH

There is one emotion which is the cause of the lack of wealth in the lives of many. Most people learn this the hard way. It is envy. For example, if you see a competitor depositing large sums of money in the bank, and you have only a meager amount to deposit, does it make you envious? The way to overcome this emotion is to say to yourself, "Isn't it wonderful! I rejoice in that man's prosperity. I wish for him greater and greater wealth."

To entertain envious thoughts is devastating because it places you in a very negative position; therefore, wealth flows *from* you instead of *to* you. If you are ever annoyed or irritated by the prosperity or great wealth of another, claim immediately that you truly wish for him greater wealth in every possible way. This will neutralize the negative thoughts in your mind and cause an even greater measure of wealth to flow to you by the law of your own subconscious mind.

RUBBING OUT A GREAT MENTAL BLOCK TO WEALTH

If you are worried and critical about someone whom you claim is making money dishonestly, cease worrying about him. You know such a person is using the law of mind negatively; the law of mind takes care of him. Be careful not to criticize him for the reasons previously indicated. Remember: The block or obstacle to wealth is in your own mind. You can now destroy that mental block. This you may do by getting on mental good terms with everyone.

SLEEP AND GROW RICH

As you go to sleep at night, practice the following technique: Repeat the word "wealth" quietly, easily, and feelingly. Do this over and over again, just like a lullaby. Lull yourself to sleep with the one word, "wealth." You should be amazed at the result. Wealth should flow to you in avalanches of abundance. This is another example of the magic power of your subconscious mind.

SERVE YOURSELF WITH THE POWERS OF YOUR MIND

1. Decide to be wealthy the easy way, with the infallible aid of your subconscious mind.
2. Trying to accumulate wealth by the sweat of your brow and hard labor is one way to become the richest man in the graveyard. You do not have to strive or slave hard.
3. Wealth is a subconscious conviction. Build into your mentality the idea of wealth.
4. The trouble with most people is that they have no invisible means of support.

5. Repeat the word "wealth" to yourself slowly and quietly for about five minutes prior to sleep and your subconscious will bring wealth to pass in your experience.
6. The feeling of wealth produces wealth. Keep this in mind at all times.
7. Your conscious and subconscious mind must agree. Your subconscious accepts what you really feel to be true. The dominant idea is always accepted by your subconscious mind. The dominant idea should be *wealth*, not *poverty.*
8. You can overcome any mental conflict regarding wealth by affirming frequently, "By day and by night I am being prospered in all of my interests."
9. Increase your sales by repeating this statement over and over again, "My sales are improving every day; I am advancing, progressing, and getting wealthier every day."
10. Stop writing blank checks, such as, "There is not enough to go around," or "There is a shortage," etc. Such statements magnify and multiply your loss.
11. Deposit thoughts of prosperity, wealth, and success in your subconscious mind, and the latter will give you compound interest.
12. What you consciously affirm, you must not mentally deny a few moments later. This will neutralize the good you have affirmed.
13. Your true source of wealth consists of the ideas in your mind. You can have an idea worth millions of dollars. Your subconscious will give you the idea you seek.
14. Envy and jealousy are stumbling blocks to the flow of wealth. Rejoice in the prosperity of others.
15. The block to wealth is in your own mind. Destroy that block now by getting on good mental terms with everyone.

CHAPTER TEN

YOUR RIGHT TO BE RICH

It is your right to be rich. You are here to lead the abundant life and be happy, radiant, and free. You should, therefore, have all the money you need to lead a full, happy, and prosperous life.

You are here to grow, expand, and unfold spiritually, mentally, and materially. You have the inalienable right to fully develop and express yourself along all lines. You should surround yourself with beauty and luxury.

Why be satisfied with just enough to go around when you can enjoy the riches of your subconscious mind? In this chapter you can learn to make friends with money, and you should always have a surplus. Your desire to be rich is a desire for a fuller, happier, more wonderful life. It is a cosmic urge. It is not only good, but very good.

MONEY IS A SYMBOL

Money is a symbol of exchange. It means to you not only freedom from want, but beauty, luxury, abundance, and refinement. It is merely a symbol of the economic health of the nation. When your blood is circulating freely in your body, you are healthy. When money is circulating freely in your life, you are economically healthy. When people begin to hoard money, to put it away in tin boxes, and become charged with fear, there is economic illness. Money has taken many forms as a medium of exchange down through the centuries, such as salt, beads, and trinkets of various kinds. In early times a man's wealth was determined by the number of sheep and oxen he had. Now we use currency, and other negotiable instruments, as it is much more convenient to write a check than carry some sheep around with you to pay bills.

HOW TO WALK THE ROYAL ROAD TO RICHES

Knowledge of the powers of your subconscious mind is the means to the royal road to riches of all kinds—spiritual, mental, or financial. The student of the laws of mind believes and knows definitely that regardless of economic situations, stock market fluctuation, depression, strikes, war, or other conditions or circumstances, he will always be amply supplied, regardless of what form money takes. The reason for this is that he has conveyed the idea of wealth to his subconscious mind, and it keeps him supplied wherever he may be. He has convinced himself in his mind that money is forever flowing freely in his life and that there is always a wonderful surplus. Should there be a financial collapse of government tomorrow and all the man's present holdings become valueless, as the German marks did after the First World War, he would still attract wealth and be cared for, regardless of the form the new currency took.

WHY YOU DO NOT HAVE MORE MONEY

As you read this chapter, you are probably saying, "I am worthy of a higher salary than I am receiving." I believe most people are inadequately compensated. One of the causes many people do not have more money is that they are silently or openly condemning it. They refer to money as "filthy lucre" or "the love of money is the root of all evil." Another reason they do not prosper is that they have a sneaky subconscious feeling there is some virtue in poverty. This subconscious pattern may be due to early childhood training, superstition, or it could be based on a false interpretation of scriptures.

MONEY AND A BALANCED LIFE

One time a man said to me, "I am broke. I do not like money. It is the root of all evil." These statements represent a confused neurotic mind. Love of money to the exclusion of everything else will cause you to become lopsided and unbalanced. You are here to use your power or authority wisely. Some men crave power, others crave money. If you set your heart on money exclusively and say, "Money is all I want; I am going to give all my attention to amassing money; nothing else matters," you can get money and attain a fortune, but you have forgotten that you are here to lead a balanced life. You must also satisfy the hunger for peace of mind, harmony, love, joy, and perfect health.

By making money your sole aim, you simply made a wrong choice. You thought that was all you wanted, but you found after all your efforts that it was not only the money you needed. You also desired true expression of your hidden talents, true place in life, beauty, and the joy of contributing to the welfare and success of others. By learning the laws of your subconscious mind, you could have a million dollars or many millions, if you wanted them, and still have peace of mind, harmony, perfect health, and perfect expression.

POVERTY IS A MENTAL DISEASE

There is no virtue in poverty; it is a disease like any other mental disease. If you were physically ill, you would think there was something wrong with you. You would seek help and do something about the condition at once. Likewise, if you do not have money constantly circulating in your life, there is something radically wrong with you.

The urge of the life principle in you is toward growth, expansion, and the life more abundant. You are not here to live in a hovel, dress in rags, and go hungry. You should be happy, prosperous, and successful.

WHY YOU MUST NEVER CRITICIZE MONEY

Cleanse your mind of all weird and superstitious beliefs about money. Do not ever regard money as evil or filthy. If you do, you cause it to take wings and fly away from you. Remember that you lose what you condemn. You cannot attract what you criticize.

GETTING THE RIGHT ATTITUDE TOWARD MONEY

Here is a simple technique you may use to multiply money in your experience. Use the following statements several times a day, "I like money, I love it, I use it wisely, constructively, and judiciously. Money is constantly circulating in my life. I release it with joy, and it returns to me multiplied in a wonderful way. It is good and very good. Money flows to me in avalanches of abundance. I use it for good only, and I am grateful for my good and for the riches of my mind."

HOW THE SCIENTIFIC THINKER LOOKS AT MONEY

Suppose, for example, you found gold, silver, lead, copper, or iron in the ground. Would you pronounce these things evil? All evil comes from man's darkened understanding, from his ignorance, from his false interpretation of life, and from his misuse of his subconscious mind. Uranium, lead, or some other metal could have been used as a medium of exchange. We use paper bills, checks, nickel, and silver, surely, these are not evil. Physicists and chemists know today that the only difference between one metal and another is the number and rate of motion of electrons revolving around a central nucleus. They can now change one metal into another through a bombardment of the atoms in the powerful cyclotron. Gold under certain conditions becomes mercury. I believe that our modern scientists in the near future will be able to make gold, silver, and other metals synthetically in the chemical laboratory. The cost may be prohibitive now, but it can be done. I cannot imagine any intelligent person seeing anything evil in electrons, neutrons, protons, and isotopes.

The piece of paper in your pocket is composed of atoms and molecules with their electrons and protons arranged differently. Their number and rate of motion are different. That is the only way the paper differs from the silver in your pocket.

HOW TO ATTRACT THE MONEY YOU NEED

Many years ago I met a young boy in Australia who wanted to become a physician and surgeon, but he had no money. I explained to him how a seed deposited in the soil attracts to itself everything necessary for its unfolding, and that all he had to do was to take a lesson from the seed and deposit the required idea in his subconscious mind. For expenses this young, brilliant boy used to clean out doctors' offices, wash windows, and do odd repair jobs. He told me that every night, as he went to sleep, he used to picture in his mind's eye a medical diploma on a wall with his name on it in big, bold letters. He used to clean and shine the framed diplomas in the medical building where he worked. It was not hard for him to engrave the image of a diploma in his mind and develop it there. Definite results followed as he persisted with his mental picture every night for about four months.

The sequel of this story was very interesting. One of the doctors took a great liking to this young boy and after training him in the art of sterilizing instruments, giving hypodermic injections, and other miscellaneous first-aid work, he employed him as a technical assistant in his office. The doctor later sent him to medical school at his own expense. Today, this young man is a prominent medical doctor in Montreal, Canada. He discovered the law of attraction by using his subconscious mind the right way. He operated an age-old law which says, "Having seen the end, you have willed the means to the realization of the end." The *end* in this case was to become a medical doctor.

This young man was able to imagine, see, and feel the reality of being a doctor. He lived with that idea, sustained it, nourished it, and loved it until through his imagination it penetrated the layers of his subconscious mind and became a conviction, thereby attracting to him everything necessary for the fulfillment of his dream.

WHY SOME MEN DO NOT GET A RAISE IN PAY

If you are working in a large organization and you are silently thinking of and resenting the fact you are underpaid, that you are not appreciated, and that you deserve more money and greater recognition, you are subconsciously severing your ties with that organization. You are setting a law in motion, and the superintendent or manager will say to you, "We have to let you go." Actually, you dismissed yourself. The manager was simply the instrument through which your own negative mental state was confirmed. It was an example of the law of action and reaction. The action was your thought, and the reaction was the response of your subconscious mind.

OBSTACLES AND IMPEDIMENTS ON THE PATHWAY TO RICHES

I am sure you have heard men say, "That fellow has a racket." "He is a racketeer." "He is getting money dishonestly." "He is a faker." "I knew him when he had nothing." "He is a crook, a thief, and a swindler."

If you analyze the man who talks like that, you discover he is usually in want or suffering from some financial or physical illness. Perhaps his former college friends went up the ladder of success and excelled him. Now he is bitter and envious of their progress. In many instances this is the cause of his downfall. Thinking negatively of these classmates and condemning their wealth causes the wealth and prosperity he is praying for to vanish and flee away. He is condemning the thing he is praying for.

He is praying two ways. On the one hand he is saying, "Wealth is flowing to me now," and in the next breath, silently or audibly, he is saying, "I resent that fellow's wealth." Always make it a special point to rejoice in the wealth of the other person.

PROTECT YOUR INVESTMENTS

If you are seeking wisdom regarding investments, or if you are worried about your stocks or bonds, quietly claim, "Infinite intelligence governs and watches over all my financial transactions, and whatsoever I do shall prosper." Do this frequently and you will find that your investments will be wise; moreover, you will be protected from loss, as you will be prompted to sell your securities or holdings before any loss accrues to you.

YOU CANNOT GET SOMETHING FOR NOTHING

In large stores the management employs store detectives to prevent people from stealing. They catch a number of people every day trying to get something for nothing. All such people are living in the mental atmosphere of lack and limitation and are stealing from themselves peace, harmony, faith, honesty, integrity, good will, and confidence. Furthermore, they are attracting to themselves all manner of loss, such as loss of character, prestige, social status, and peace of mind. These people lack faith in the source of supply and the understanding of how their minds work. If they would mentally call on the powers of their subconscious mind and claim that they are guided to their true expression, they would find work and constant supply. Then by honesty, integrity, and perseverance, they would become a credit to themselves and to society at large.

YOUR CONSTANT SUPPLY OF MONEY

Recognizing the powers of your subconscious mind and the creative power of your thought or mental image is the way to opulence, freedom, and constant supply. Accept the abundant life in your own mind. Your mental acceptance and expectancy of wealth has its own mathematics and mechanics of expression. As you enter into the mood of opulence, all things necessary for the abundant life will come to pass.

Let this be your daily affirmation; write it in your heart: "I am one with the infinite riches of my subconscious mind. It is my right to be rich, happy, and successful. Money flows to me freely, copiously, and endlessly. I am forever conscious of my true worth. I give of my talents freely, and I am wonderfully blessed financially. It is wonderful!"

STEP UP THIS WAY TO RICHES

1. Be bold enough to claim that it is your right to be rich and your deeper mind will honor your claim.
2. You don't want just enough to go around. You want all the money you need to do all the things you want to do and when you want to do them. Get acquainted with the riches of your subconscious mind.
3. When money is circulating freely in your life, you are economically healthy. Look at money like the tide and you will always have plenty of it. The ebb and flow of the tide is constant. When the tide is out you are absolutely sure that it will return.
4. Knowing the laws of your subconscious mind, you will always be supplied regardless of what form money takes.
5. One reason many people simply make ends meet and never have enough money is that they condemn money. What you condemn takes wings and flies away.
6. Do not make a god of money. It is only a symbol. Remember that the real riches are in your mind. You are here to lead a balanced life—this includes acquiring all the money you need.
7. Don't make money your sole aim. Claim wealth, happiness, peace, true expression, and love, and personally radiate love and good will to all. Then your subconscious mind will give you compound interest in all these fields of expression.
8. There is no virtue in poverty. It is a disease of the mind, and you should heal yourself of this mental conflict or malady at once.
9. You are not here to live in a hovel, to dress in rags, or to go hungry. You are here to lead the life more abundant.

10. Never use the terms "filthy lucre" or "I despise money." You lose what you criticize. There is nothing good or bad, but thinking of it in either light makes it so.
11. Repeat frequently, "I like money. I use it wisely, constructively, and judiciously. I release it with joy, and it returns a thousandfold."
12. Money is not evil any more so than copper, lead, tin, or iron which you may find in the ground. All evil is due to ignorance and misuse of the mind's powers.
13. To picture the end result in your mind causes your subconscious to respond and fulfill your mental picture.
14. Stop trying to get something for nothing. There is no such thing as a free lunch. You must give to receive. You must give mental attention to your goals, ideals, and enterprises, and your deeper mind will back you up. The key to wealth is application of the laws of the subconscious mind by impregnating it with the idea of wealth.

CHAPTER ELEVEN

YOUR SUBCONSCIOUS MIND AS A PARTNER IN SUCCESS

Success means successful living. A long period of peace, joy, and happiness on this plane may be termed success. The eternal experience of these qualities is the everlasting life spoken of by Jesus. The real things of life, such as peace, harmony, integrity, security, and happiness are intangible. They come from the Deep Self of man. Meditating on these qualities builds these treasures of heaven in our subconscious. It is where *moth nor rust doth corrupt, and where thieves do not break through nor steal.* MATTHEW 6:20.

THE THREE STEPS TO SUCCESS

Let us discuss three steps to success: The first step to success is to find out the thing you love to do, then do it. Success is in loving your work. Although, if a man is a psychiatrist, it is not adequate for him to get a diploma and place it on the wall; he must keep up with the times, attend conventions, and continue studying the mind and its workings. The successful psychiatrist visits clinics and reads the latest scientific articles. In other words, he is informed in the most advanced methods of alleviating human suffering. The successful psychiatrist or doctor must have the interest of his patients at heart.

Someone may say, "How can I put the first step into operation? I do not know what I should do." In such a case, pray for guidance as follows: "The infinite intelligence of my subconscious mind reveals to me my true place in life." Repeat this prayer quietly, positively, and lovingly to your deeper mind. As you persist with faith and confidence, the answer will come to you as a feeling, a hunch, or a tendency in a certain direction. It will come to you clearly and in peace, and as an inner silent awareness.

The second step to success is to specialize in some particular branch of work and know more about it than anyone else. For example, if a young man chooses chemistry as his profession, he should concentrate on one of the many branches in this field. He should give all of his time and attention to his chosen specialty. He should become sufficiently enthusiastic to try to know all there is available about his field; if possible, he should know more than anyone else. The young man should become ardently interested in his work and should desire to serve the world.

He that is greatest among you, let him become your servant. There is a great contrast in this attitude of mind in comparison to that of the man who only wants to make a living or just "get by." "Getting by" is not true success. Man's motive must be greater, nobler, and more altruistic. He must serve others, thereby casting his bread upon the waters.

The third step is the most important one. You must be sure that the thing you want to do does not redound to your success only. Your desire must not be selfish; it must benefit humanity. The path of a complete circuit must be formed. In other words, your idea must go forth with the purpose of blessing or serving the world. It will then come back to you pressed down, shaken together, and running over. If it is to benefit yourself exclusively, the circle or complete circuit is not formed, and you may experience a short circuit in your life which may consist of limitation or sickness.

THE MEASURE OF TRUE SUCCESS

Some people may say, "But, Mr. James made a fortune in selling fraudulent oil stock." A man may seem to succeed for a while, but the money he obtained by fraud usually takes wings and flies away. When we rob from another, we rob from ourselves, because we are in a mood of lack and limitation which may manifest itself in our body, home life, and affairs. What we think and feel, we create. We create what we believe. Even though a man may have accumulated a fortune fraudulently, he is not successful. There is no success without peace of mind. What good is man's accumulated wealth if he cannot sleep nights, is sick, or has a guilt complex?

I knew a man in London who told me of his exploits. He had been a professional pickpocket and had amassed a large amount of money. He had a summer home in France and lived in a royal fashion in England. His story was that he was in constant dread of being arrested by Scotland Yard. He had many inner disorders which were undoubtedly caused by his constant fear and deep-seated guilt complex. He knew he had done wrong. This deep sense of guilt attracted all kinds of trouble to him. Subsequently, he voluntarily surrendered to the police and served a prison sentence. After his release from prison, he sought psychological and spiritual counsel and became transformed. He went to work and became an honest, law-abiding citizen. He found what he loved to do and was happy.

A successful person loves his work and expresses himself fully. Success is contingent upon a higher ideal than the more accumulation of riches. The man of success is the man who possesses great psychological and spiritual understanding. Many of the great industrialists today depend upon the correct use of their subconscious minds for their success.

There was an article published some years ago about Flagler, an oil magnate. He admitted that the secret of his success was his ability to see a project in its completion. For instance, in his case, he closed his eyes, imagined a big oil industry, saw trains running on tracks, heard whistles blowing, and saw smoke. Having seen and felt the fulfillment of his prayer, his subconscious mind brought about its realization. If you imagine an objective clearly, you will be provided with the necessities, in ways you know not of, through the wonder-working power of your subconscious mind.

In considering the three steps to success you must never forget the underlying power of the creative forces of your subconscious mind. This is the energy in back of all steps in any plan of success. Your thought is creative. Thought fused with feeling becomes a subjective faith or belief, and *according to your belief be it done unto you.* MATTHEW 9:29.

A knowledge of a mighty force in you which is capable of bringing to pass all your desires gives you confidence and a sense of peace. Whatever your field of action may be, you should learn the laws of your subconscious mind. When you know how to apply the powers of your mind, and when you are expressing yourself fully and giving of your talents to others, you are on the sure path to true success. If you are about God's business, or any part of it, God, by His very nature, is for you, so who can be against you? With this understanding there is no power in heaven or on earth to withhold success from you.

HOW HE MADE HIS DREAM COME TRUE

A movie actor told me that he had very little education, but he had a dream as a boy of becoming a successful movie actor. Out in the field mowing hay, driving the cows home, or even when milking them he said, "I would constantly imagine I saw my name in big lights at a large theater. I kept this up for years until finally I ran away from home. I got extra jobs in the motion-picture field, and the day finally came when I saw my name in great, big lights as I did when I was a boy!" Then he added, "I know the power of sustained imagination to bring success."

HIS DREAM PHARMACY BECAME A REALITY

Thirty years ago I knew a young pharmacist who was receiving forty dollars a week plus commission on sales. "After twenty-five years," he said to me, "I will get a pension and retire."

I said to this young man, "Why don't you own your own store? Get out of this place. Raise your sights! Have a dream for your children. Maybe your son wants to be a doctor; perhaps your daughter desires to be a great musician."

His answer was that he had no money! He began to awaken to the fact that whatever he could conceive as true, he could give conception.

The first step toward his goal was his awakening to the powers of his subconscious mind, which I briefly elaborated on for his benefit. His second step was his realization that if he could succeed in conveying an idea to his subconscious mind, the latter would somehow bring it to pass.

He began to imagine that he was in his own store. He mentally arranged the bottles, dispensed prescriptions, and imagined several clerks in the store waiting on customers. He also visualized a big bank balance. Mentally he worked in that imaginary store. Like a good actor he lived the role. *Act as though I am, and I will be.* This pharmacist put himself wholeheartedly into the act, living, moving, and acting on the assumption that he owned the store.

The sequel was interesting. He was discharged from his position. He found new employment with a large chain store, became manager, and later on, district manager. He saved enough money in four years to provide a down payment on a drugstore of his own. He called it his "Dream Pharmacy."

"It was," he said, "exactly the store I saw in my imagination." He became a recognized success in his chosen field, and was happy doing what he loved to do.

USING THE SUBCONSCIOUS MIND IN BUSINESS

Some years ago I gave a lecture to a group of businessmen on the powers of imagination and the subconscious mind. In this lecture I pointed out how Goethe used his imagination wisely when confronted with difficulties and predicaments.

His biographers point out that he was accustomed to fill many hours quietly holding imaginary conversations. It is well known that his custom was to imagine one of his friends before him in a chair answering him in the right way. In other words, if he were concerned over any problems, he imagined his friend giving him the right or appropriate answer, accompanied with the usual gestures and tonal qualities of the voice, and he made the entire imaginary scene as real and as vivid as possible.

One of the men present at this lecture was a young stockbroker. He proceeded to adopt the technique of Goethe. He began to have mental, imaginary conversations with a multimillionaire banker friend of his who used to congratulate him on his wise and sound judgment, and compliment him on his purchase of the right stocks. He used to dramatize this imaginary conversation until he had psychologically fixed it as a form of belief in his mind.

This broker's inner talking and controlled imagination certainly agreed with his aim which was to make sound investments for his clients. His main purpose in life was to make money for his clients and to see them prosper financially by his wise counsel. He is still using his subconscious mind in his business, and he is a brilliant success in his field of endeavor.

BOY OF SIXTEEN YEARS TURNS FAILURE INTO SUCCESS

A young boy who was attending high school said to me, "I am getting very poor grades. My memory is failing. I do not know what is the matter." I discovered that the only thing wrong with this boy was his attitude which was one of indifference and resentment toward some of his teachers and fellow students. I taught him how to use his subconscious mind, and how to succeed in his studies.

He began to affirm certain truths several times a day particularly at night prior to sleep, and also in the morning after awakening. These are the best times to impregnate the subconscious mind.

He affirmed as follows: "I realize that my subconscious mind is a storehouse of memory. It retains everything I read and hear from my teachers. I have a perfect memory, and the infinite intelligence in my subconscious mind constantly reveals to me everything I need to know at all my examinations, whether written or oral. I radiate love and good will to all my teachers and fellow students. I sincerely wish for them success and all good things."

This young man is now enjoying a greater freedom than he has ever known. He is now receiving all "A's." He constantly imagines the teachers and his mother congratulating him on his success in his studies.

HOW TO BECOME SUCCESSFUL IN BUYING AND SELLING

In buying and selling, remember that your conscious mind is the starter and your subconscious mind is the motor. You must start the motor to enable it to perform its work. Your conscious mind is the dynamo that awakens the power of your subconscious mind.

The first step in conveying your clarified desire, idea, or image to the deeper mind is to relax, immobilize the attention, get still, and be quiet. This quiet, relaxed, and peaceful attitude of mind prevents extraneous matter and false ideas from interfering with your mental absorption of your ideal. Furthermore, in the quiet, passive, and receptive attitude of mind, effort is reduced to a minimum.

The second step is to begin to imagine the reality of that which you desire. For example, you may wish to buy a home, and in your relaxed state of mind affirm as follows: "The infinite intelligence of my subconscious mind is all-wise. It reveals to me now the ideal home which is central, ideal, is in a lovely environment, meets with all my requirements, and is commensurate with my income. I am now turning this request over to my subconscious mind, and I know it responds according to the nature of my request. I release this request with absolute faith and confidence in the same way that a farmer deposits a seed in the ground, trusting implicitly in the laws of growth."

The answer to your prayer may come through an advertisement in the paper, through a friend, or you may be guided directly to a particular home which is exactly what you are seeking. There are many ways by which your prayer may be answered. The principal knowledge, in which you may place your confidence, is that the answer always comes, provided you trust the working of your deeper mind.

You may wish to sell a home, land, or any kind of property. In private consultation with real estate brokers I have told them of the way I sold my own home on Orlando Avenue in Los Angeles. Many of them have applied the technique I used with remarkable and speedy results. I placed a sign which read, "For sale by owner" in the garden in front of my home. The day after I said to myself as I was going to sleep, "Supposing you sold your house, what would you do?"

I answered my own question and I said, "I would take that sign down and throw it into the garage." In my imagination I took hold of the sign, pulled it up from the ground, placed it on my shoulder, went to the garage, threw it on the floor, and said jokingly to the sign, "I don't need you any more!" I felt the inner satisfaction of it all, realizing it was finished.

The next day a man gave me a deposit of $1,000 and said to me, "Take your sign down. We will go into escrow now."

Immediately I pulled the sign up and took it to the garage. The outer action conformed to the inner. There is nothing new about this. *As within, so without,* meaning according to the image impressed on your subconscious mind, so it is on the objective screen of your life. The outside mirrors the inside. External action follows internal action.

Here is another very popular method used in selling homes, land, or any kind of property. Affirm slowly, quietly, and feelingly as follows: "Infinite intelligence attracts to me the buyer for this home who wants it and who prospers in it. This buyer is being sent to me by the creative intelligence of my subconscious mind which makes no mistakes. This buyer may look at many other homes, but mine is the only one he wants and will buy, because he is guided by the infinite intelligence within him. I know the buyer is right, the time is right, and the price is right. Everything about it is right. The deeper currents of my subconscious mind are now in operation bringing both of us together in divine order. I know that it is so."

Remember always, that what you are seeking is also seeking you, and whenever you want to sell a home or property of any kind, there is always someone who wants what you have to offer. By using the powers of your subconscious mind correctly, you free your mind of all sense of competition and anxiety in buying and selling.

HOW SHE SUCCEEDED IN GETTING WHAT SHE WANTED

There is a young lady who regularly comes to my lectures and classes. She had to change buses three times; it took her one and a half hours each time to come to the lectures. In one lecture I explained how a young man who needed a car in his work received one.

She went home and experimented as outlined in my lecture. Here is her letter in part, narrating her application of my method, and published by her permission:

Dear Dr. Murphy:

This is how I received a Cadillac car—I wanted one to come to the lectures regularly. In my imagination I went through the identical process I would go through, if I were actually driving a car. I went to the showroom, and the salesman took me for a ride in one. I also drove it several blocks. I claimed the Cadillac car as my own over and over again.

I kept the mental picture of getting into the car, driving it, feeling the upholstery, etc., consistently for over two weeks. Last week I drove to your lectures in a Cadillac. My uncle in Inglewood passed away, and left me his Cadillac and his entire estate.

A SUCCESS TECHNIQUE EMPLOYED BY MANY OUTSTANDING EXECUTIVES AND BUSINESSMEN

There are many prominent businessmen who quietly use the abstract term, "success," over and over many times a day until they reach a conviction that *success* is theirs. They know that the *idea of success* contains all the essential elements of success. Likewise, you can begin now to repeat the word, "success," to yourself with faith and conviction. Your subconscious mind will accept it as true of you, and you will be under a subconscious compulsion to succeed.

You are compelled to express your subjective beliefs, impressions, and convictions. What does success imply to you? You want, undoubtedly, to be successful in your home life and in your relationships with others. You wish to be outstanding in your chosen work or profession. You wish to possess a beautiful home, and all the money you need to live comfortably and happily. You want to be successful in your prayer life and in your contact with the powers of your subconscious mind.

You are a businessman also because you are in the business of living. Become a successful businessman by imagining yourself doing what you long to do, and possessing the things you long to possess. Become imaginative; mentally participate in the reality of the successful state. Make a habit of it. Go to sleep feeling successful every night, and perfectly satisfied, and you will eventually succeed in implanting the idea of success in your subconscious mind. Believe you were born to succeed, and wonders will happen as you pray!

PROFITABLE POINTERS

1. Success means successful living. When you are peaceful, happy, joyous, and doing what you love to do, you are successful.
2. Find out what you love to do, then do it. If you don't know your true expression, ask for guidance, and the *lead* will come.
3. Specialize in your particular field and try to know more about it than anyone else.
4. A successful man is not selfish. His main desire in life is to serve humanity.
5. There is no true success without peace of mind.
6. A successful man possesses great psychological and spiritual understanding.
7. If you imagine an objective clearly, you will be provided with the necessities through the wonder-working power of your subconscious mind.

8. Your thought fused with feeling becomes a subjective belief, and *according to your belief is it done unto you.*
9. The power of sustained imagination draws forth the miracle-working powers of your subconscious mind.
10. If you are seeking promotion in your work, imagine your employer, supervisor, or loved one congratulating you on your promotion. Make the picture vivid and real. Hear the voice, see the gestures, and feel the reality of it all. Continue to do this frequently, and through frequent occupancy of your mind, you will experience the joy of the answered prayer.
11. Your subconscious mind is a storehouse of memory. For a perfect memory, affirm frequently: "The infinite intelligence of my subconscious mind reveals to me everything I need to know at all times, everywhere."
12. If you wish to sell a home or property of any kind, affirm slowly, quietly, and feelingly as follows: "Infinite intelligence attracts to me the buyer of this house or property, who wants it, and who prospers in it." Sustain this awareness, and the deeper currents of your subconscious mind will bring it to pass.
13. The idea of success contains all the elements of success. Repeat the word, "success," to yourself frequently with faith and conviction, and you will be under a subconscious compulsion to succeed.

CHAPTER TWELVE

SCIENTISTS USE THE SUBCONSCIOUS MIND

Many scientists realize the true importance of the subconscious mind. Edison, Marconi, Kettering, Poincaré, Einstein, and many others have used the subconscious mind. It has given them the insight and the "know-how" for all their great achievements in modern science and industry. Research has shown that the ability to bring into action the subconscious power has determined the success of all the great scientific and research workers.

An instance of how a famous chemist, Friedrich von Stradonitz, used his subconscious mind to solve his problem is as follows: He had been working laboriously for a long time trying to rearrange the six carbon and the six hydrogen atoms of the benzine formula, and he was constantly perplexed and unable to solve the matter. Tired and exhausted, he turned the request over completely to his subconscious mind. Shortly afterward, as he was about to board a London bus, his subconscious presented his conscious mind with a sudden flash of a snake biting its own tail and turning around like a pinwheel. This answer, from his subconscious mind, gave him the long-sought answer of the circular rearrangement of the atoms that is known as the benzine ring.

HOW A DISTINGUISHED SCIENTIST BROUGHT FORTH HIS INVENTIONS

Nikola Tesla was a brilliant electrical scientist who brought forth the most amazing innovations. When an idea for a new invention came into his mind, he would build it up in his imagination, knowing that his subconscious mind would reconstruct and reveal to his conscious mind all the parts needed for its manufacture in concrete form. Through quietly contemplating every possible improvement, he spent no time in correcting defects, and was able to give the technicians the perfect product of his mind.

He said, "Invariably, my device works as I imagined it should. In twenty years there has not been a single exception."

HOW A FAMOUS NATURALIST SOLVED HIS PROBLEM

Professor Agassiz, a distinguished American naturalist, discovered the indefatigable activities of his subconscious mind while he slept. The following has been reported by his widow in her biography of her famous husband.

"He had been for two weeks striving to decipher the somewhat obscure impression of a fossil fish on the stone slab in which it was preserved. Weary and perplexed, he put his work aside at last, and tried to dismiss it from his mind. Shortly after, he waked one night persuaded that while asleep he had seen his fish with all the missing features perfectly restored. But when he tried to hold and make fast the image it escaped him. Nevertheless, he went early to the Jardin des Plantes, thinking that on looking anew at the impression he should see something which would put him on the track of his vision. In vain—the blurred record was as black as ever. The next night he saw the fish again, but with no more satisfactory result. When he awoke it disappeared from his memory as before. Hoping that the same experience might be repeated, on the third night he placed a pencil and paper beside his bed before going to sleep.

"Accordingly, toward morning the fish reappeared in his dream, confusedly at first, but at last with such distinctness that he had no longer any doubt as to its zoological characters. Still half dreaming, in perfect darkness, he traced these characters on the sheet of paper at the bedside. In the morning he was surprised to see in his nocturnal sketch features which he thought it impossible the fossil itself should reveal. He hastened to the Jardin des Plantes, and, with his drawing as a guide, succeeded in chiselling away the surface of the stone under which portions of the fish proved to be hidden. When wholly exposed it corresponded with his dream and his drawing, and he succeeded in classifying it with ease."

AN OUTSTANDING PHYSICIAN SOLVED THE PROBLEM OF DIABETES

Some years ago I received a clipping from a magazine describing the origin of the discovery of insulin. This is the essence of the article as I recall it.

About forty years ago or more, Dr. Frederick Banting, a brilliant Canadian physician and surgeon, was concentrating his attention on the ravages of diabetes. At that time medical science offered no effective method of arresting the disease. Dr. Banting spent considerable time experimenting and studying the international literature on the subject. One night he was exhausted and fell asleep. While asleep, his subconscious mind instructed him to extract the residue from the degenerated pancreatic duct of dogs. This was the origin of insulin which has helped millions of people.

You will note that Dr. Banting had been consciously dwelling on the problem for some time seeking a solution, a way out, and his subconscious responded accordingly.

It does not follow that you will always get an answer overnight. The answer may not come for some time. Do not be discouraged. Keep on turning the problem over every night to the subconscious mind prior to sleep, as if you had never done it before.

One of the reasons for the delay may be that you look upon it as a major problem. You may believe it will take a long time to solve it.

Your subconscious mind is timeless and spaceless. Go to sleep believing you have the answer now. Do not postulate the answer in the future. Have an abiding faith in the outcome. Become convinced now as you read this book that there is an answer and a perfect solution for you.

HOW A FAMOUS SCIENTIST AND PHYSICIST ESCAPED FROM A RUSSIAN CONCENTRATION CAMP

Dr. Lothar von Blenk-Schmidt, a member of the Rocket Society and an outstanding research electronic engineer, gives the following condensed summary of how he used his subconscious mind to free himself from certain death at the hands of brutal guards in a Russian prison camp coal mine. He states as follows:

"I was a prisoner of war in a coal mine in Russia, and I saw men dying all around me in that prison compound. We were watched over by brutal guards, arrogant officers, and sharp, fast-thinking commissars. After a short medical checkup, a quota of coal was assigned to each person. My quota was three hundred pounds per day. In case any man did not fill his quota, his small food ration was cut down, and in a short time he was resting in the cemetery.

"I started concentrating on my escape. I knew that my subconscious mind would somehow find a way. My home in Germany was destroyed, my family wiped out; all my friends and former associates were either killed in the war or were in concentration camps.

"I said to my subconscious mind, 'I want to go to Los Angeles, and you will find the way.' I had seen pictures of Los Angeles and I remembered some of the boulevards very well as well as some of the buildings.

"Every day and night I would imagine I was walking down Wilshire Boulevard with an American girl whom I met in Berlin prior to the war (she is now my wife). In my imagination we would visit the stores, ride buses, and eat in the restaurants. Every night I made it a special point to drive my imaginary American automobile up and down the boulevards of Los Angeles. I made all this vivid and real. These pictures in my mind were as real and as natural to me as one of the trees outside the prison camp.

"Every morning the chief guard would count the prisoners as they were lined up. He would call out 'one, two, three' etc., and when seventeen was called out, which was my number in sequence, I stepped aside. In the meantime, the guard was called away for a minute or so, and on his return he started by mistake on the next man as number seventeen. When the crew returned in the evening, the number of men was the same, and I was not missed, and the discovery would take a long time.

"I walked out of the camp undetected and kept walking for twenty-four hours, resting in a deserted town the next day. I was able to live by fishing and killing some wildlife. I found coal trains going to Poland and traveled on them by night, until finally I reached Poland. With the help of friends, I made my way to Lucerne, Switzerland.

"One evening at the Palace Hotel, Lucerne, I had a talk with a man and his wife from the United States of America. This man asked me if I would care to be a guest at his home in Santa Monica, California. I accepted, and when I arrived in Los Angeles, I found that their chauffeur drove me along Wilshire Boulevard and many other boulevards which I had imagined so vividly in the long months in the Russian coal mines. I recognized the buildings which I had seen in my mind so often. It actually seemed as if I had been in Los Angeles before. I had reached my goal.

"I will never cease to marvel at the wonders of the subconscious mind. Truly, it has ways we know not of."

HOW ARCHAEOLOGISTS AND PALEONTOLOGISTS RECONSTRUCT ANCIENT SCENES

These scientists know that their subconscious mind has a memory of everything that has ever transpired. As they study the ancient ruins and fossils, through their imaginative perception, their subconscious mind aids them in reconstructing the ancient scenes. The dead past becomes alive and audible once more. Looking at these ancient temples and studying the pottery, statuary, tools, and household utensils of these ancient times, the scientist tells us of an age when there was no language. Communication was done by grunts, groans, and signs.

The keen concentration and disciplined imagination of the scientist awakens the latent powers of his subconscious mind enabling him to clothe the ancient temples with roofs, and surround them with gardens, pools, and fountains. The fossil remains are clothed with eyes, sinews, and muscles, and they again walk and talk. The past becomes the living present, and we find that in mind there is no time or space. Through disciplined, controlled, and directed imagination, you can be a companion of the most scientific and inspired thinkers of all time.

HOW TO RECEIVE GUIDANCE FROM YOUR SUBCONSCIOUS

When you have what you term "a difficult decision" to make, or when you fail to see the solution to your problem, begin at once to think constructively about it. If you are fearful and worried, you are not really thinking. True thinking is free from fear.

Here is a simple technique you can use to receive guidance on any subject: Quiet the mind and still the body. Tell the body to relax; it has to obey you. It has no volition, initiative, or self-conscious intelligence. Your body is an emotional disk which records your beliefs and impressions. Mobilize your attention; focus your thought on the solution to your problem. Try to solve it with your conscious mind. Think how happy you would be about the perfect solution. Sense the feeling you would have if the perfect answer were yours now. Let your mind play with this mood in a relaxed way; then drop off to sleep. When you awaken, and you do not have the answer, get busy about something else. Probably, when you are preoccupied with something else, the answer will come into your mind like toast pops out of a toaster.

In receiving guidance from the subconscious mind, the simple way is the best. This is an illustration: I once lost a valuable ring which was an heirloom. I looked everywhere for it and could not locate it. At night I talked to the subconscious in the same manner that I would talk to anyone. I said to it prior to dropping off to sleep, "You know all things; you know where that ring is, and you now reveal to me where it is."

In the morning I awoke suddenly with the words ringing in my ear, "Ask Robert!"

I thought it very strange that I should ask Robert, a young boy about nine years of age; however, I followed the inner voice of intuition.

Robert said, "Oh, yes, I picked it up in the yard while I was playing with the boys. I placed it on the desk in my room. I did not think it worth anything, so I did not say anything about it."

The subconscious mind will always answer you if you trust it.

HIS SUBCONSCIOUS REVEALED THE LOCATION OF HIS FATHER'S WILL

A young man who attends my lectures had this experience. His father died and apparently left no will. However, this man's sister told him that their father had confided to her that a will had been executed which was fair to all. Every attempt to locate the will failed.

Prior to sleep he talked to his deeper mind as follows: "I now turn this request over the the subconscious mind. It knows just where that will is, and reveals it to me." Then he condensed his request down to one word, "Answer," repeating it over and over again as a lullaby. He lulled himself to sleep with the word, "Answer."

The next morning this young man had an overpowering hunch to go to a certain bank in Los Angeles where he found a safe deposit vault registered in the name of his father, the contents of which solved all his problems.

Your thought, as you go to sleep, arouses the powerful latency which is within you. For example, let us suppose you are wondering whether to sell your home, buy a certain stock, sever partnership, move to New York or stay in Los Angeles, dissolve the present contract or take a new one. Do this: Sit quietly in your armchair or at the desk in your office. Remember that there is a universal law of action and reaction. The action is your thought. The reaction is the response from your subconscious mind. The subconscious mind is reactive and reflexive; this is its nature. It rebounds, rewards, and repays. It is the law of correspondence. It responds by corresponding. As you contemplate right action, you will automatically experience a reaction or response in yourself which represents the guidance or answer of your subconscious mind.

In seeking guidance, you simply think quietly about right action which means that you are using the infinite intelligence resident in the subconscious mind to the point where it begins to use you. From there on, your course of action is directed and controlled by the subjective wisdom within you which is all-wise and omnipotent. Your decision will be right. There will only be right action because you are under a subjective compulsion to do the right thing. I use the word *compulsion* because the law of the subconscious is compulsion.

THE SECRET OF GUIDANCE

The secret of guidance or right action is to mentally devote yourself to the right answer, until you find its response in you. The response is a feeling, an inner awareness, an overpowering hunch whereby you know that you know. You have used the power to the point where it begins to use you. You cannot possibly fail or make one false step while operating under the subjective wisdom within you. You will find that all your ways are pleasantness and all your paths are peace.

HIGHLIGHTS TO RECALL

1. Remember that the subconscious mind has determined the success and wonderful achievements of all great scientific workers.
2. By giving your conscious attention and devotion to the solution of a perplexing problem, your subconscious mind gathers all the necessary information and presents it full-blown to the conscious mind.
3. If you are wondering about the answer to a problem, try to solve it objectively. Get all the information you can from research and also from others. If no answer comes, turn it over to your subconscious mind prior to sleep, and the answer always comes. It never fails.

4. You do not always get the answer overnight. Keep on turning your request over to your subconscious until the day breaks and the shadows flee away.
5. You delay the answer by thinking it will take a long time or that it is a major problem. Your subconscious has no problem, it knows only the answer.
6. Believe that you have the answer now. Feel the joy of the answer and the way you would feel if you had the perfect answer. Your subconscious will respond to your feeling.
7. Any mental picture, backed by faith and perseverance, will come to pass through the miracle-working power of your subconscious. Trust it, believe in its power, and wonders will happen as you pray.
8. Your subconscious is the storehouse of memory, and within your subconscious are recorded all your experiences since childhood.
9. Scientists meditating on ancient scrolls, temples, fossils, etc., are able to reconstruct scenes of the past and make them alive today. Their subconscious mind comes to their aid.
10. Turn over your request for a solution to your subconscious prior to sleep. Trust it and believe in it, and the answer will come. It knows all and sees all, but you must not doubt or question its powers.
11. The action is your thought, and the reaction is the response of your subconscious mind. If your thoughts are wise, your actions and decisions will be wise.
12. Guidance comes as a feeling, an inner awareness, an overpowering hunch whereby you know that you know. It is an inner sense of touch. Follow it.

CHAPTER THIRTEEN

YOUR SUBCONSCIOUS AND THE WONDERS OF SLEEP

You spend about eight out of every twenty-four hours, or one-third of your entire life, in sleep. This is an inexorable law of life. This also applies to the animal and vegetable kingdoms. Sleep is a divine law, and many answers to our problems come to us when we are sound asleep upon the bed.

Many people have advocated the theory that you get tired during the day, that you go to sleep to rest the body, and that a reparative process takes place while you sleep. Nothing rests in sleep. Your heart, lungs, and all your vital organs function while you are asleep. If you eat prior to sleep, the food is digested and assimilated; also, your skin secretes perspiration, and your nails and hair continue to grow.

Your subconscious mind never rests or sleeps. It is always active, controlling all your vital forces. The healing process takes place more rapidly while you are asleep as there is no interference from your conscious mind. Remarkable answers are given to you while you are asleep.

WHY WE SLEEP

Dr. John Bigelow, a famous research authority on sleep,* demonstrated that at night while asleep you receive impressions showing that the nerves of the eyes, ears, nose, and taste buds are active during sleep, and also that the nerves of your brain are quite active. He says that the main reason we sleep is because "the nobler part of the soul is united by abstraction to our higher nature and becomes a participant in the wisdom and foreknowledge of the gods."

Dr. Bigelow states also, "The results of my studies have not only strengthened my convictions that the supposed exemption from customary toils and activities was not the final purpose of sleep, but have also made clearer to my mind the conviction that no part of a man's life deserves to be considered more indispensable to its symmetrical and perfect spiritual development than the while he is separated from the phenomenal world in sleep."

PRAYER, A FORM OF SLEEP

Your conscious mind gets involved with vexations, strife, and contentions of the day, and it is very necessary to withdraw periodically from sense evidence and the objective world, and commune silently with the inner wisdom of your subconscious mind. By claiming guidance, strength, and greater intelligence in all phases of your life, you will be enabled to overcome all difficulties and solve your daily problems.

This regular withdrawal from sense evidence and the noise and confusion of everyday living is also a form of sleep, i.e., you become asleep to the world of the senses and alive to the wisdom and power of your subconscious mind.

* Dr. John Bigelow, *The Mystery of Sleep* (New York and London: Harper Brothers, 1903).

STARTLING EFFECTS OF SLEEP DEPRIVATION

Lack of sleep can cause you to become irritable, moody, and depressed. Dr. George Stevenson of the National Association for Mental Health says, "I believe it can safely be said that all human beings need a minimum of six hours' sleep to be healthy. Most people need more. Those who think they can get along on less are fooling themselves."

Medical research scholars, investigating sleep processes and deprivation of sleep, point out that severe insomnia has preceded psychotic breakdown in some instances. Remember, you are spiritually recharged during sleep, and adequate sleep is essential to produce joy and vitality in life.

YOU NEED MORE SLEEP

Robert O'Brien, in an article, "Maybe You Need More Sleep," in an issue of *The Reader's Digest,* reports the following experiment on sleep:

"For the last three years experiments have been in progress at Walter Reed Army Institute of Research in Washington, D.C. Subjects—more than one hundred military and civilian volunteers—have been kept awake for as long as four days. Thousands of tests have measured the effects on their behavior and personality. Results of these tests have given scientists astonishingly new insights into the mysteries of sleep.

"They now know that the tired brain apparently craves sleep so hungrily that it will sacrifice anything to get it. After only a few hours of sleep loss, fleeting stolen naps called 'lapses,' or micro-sleep, occurred at the rate of three or four an hour. As in real sleep, eyelids drooped, heartbeat slowed. Each lapse lasted just a fraction of a second. Sometimes the lapses were periods of blankness; sometimes they were filled with images, wisps of dreams. As hours of sleep loss mounted, the lapses took place more often and lasted longer, perhaps two or three seconds. Even if the subjects had been piloting an airliner in a thunderstorm, they still couldn't have resisted micro-sleeps for those few priceless seconds. And it can happen to you, as many who have fallen asleep at the wheel of a car can testify.

"Another startling effect of sleep deprivation was its attack on human memory and perception. Many sleep-deprived subjects were unable to retain information long enough to relate it to the task they were supposed to perform. They were totally befuddled in situations requiring them to hold several factors in mind and act on them, as a pilot must when he skillfully integrates wind direction, air speed, altitude, and glide path to make a safe landing."

SLEEP BRINGS COUNSEL

A young lady in Los Angeles who listens to my morning radio talks told me that she had been offered a lucrative position in New York City at twice her present salary. She was wondering whether to accept or not and prayed prior to sleep as follows: "The creative intelligence of my subconscious mind knows what is best for me. Its tendency is always lifeward, and it reveals to me the right decision which blesses me and all concerned. I give thanks for the answer which I know will come to me."

She repeated this simple prayer over and over again as a lullaby prior to sleep, and in the morning she had a persistent feeling that she should not accept the offer. She rejected the offer and subsequent events verified her inward sense of knowing, because the company went bankrupt in a few months following their offer of employment to her.

The conscious mind may be correct on the facts objectively known, but the intuitive faculty of her subconscious mind saw the failure of the concern in question, and prompted her accordingly.

SAVED FROM CERTAIN DISASTER

I will illustrate how the wisdom of your subconscious mind can instruct you and protect you relative to your request for right action as you go to sleep.

Many years ago, before the Second World War, I was offered a very lucrative assignment in the Orient, and I prayed for guidance and the right decision as follows: "Infinite intelligence within me knows all things, and the right decision is revealed to me in divine order. I will recognize the answer when it comes."

I repeated this simple prayer over and over again as a lullaby prior to sleep, and in a dream came the vivid realization of things to come three years hence. An old friend appeared in the dream and said, "Read these headlines—do not go!" The headlines of the newspaper which appeared in the dream related to war and the attack on Pearl Harbor.

Occasionally, the writer dreams literally. The aforementioned dream was undoubtedly a dramatization of the subconscious mind which projected a person whom I trusted and respected. To some a warning may come in the form of a mother who appears in a dream. She tells the person not to go here or there, and the reason for the warning. Your subconscious mind is all-wise. It knows all things. Oftentimes it will speak to you only in a voice that your conscious mind will immediately accept as true. Sometimes your subconscious will warn you in a voice which sounds like that of your mother or some loved one which may cause you to stop on the street, and you find, if you had gone another foot, a falling object from a window might have struck you on the head.

My subconscious mind is one with the universal subconscious, and it knew the Japanese were planning a war, and it also knew when the war would start.

Dr. Rhine, director of the Department of Psychology at Duke University, has gathered together a vast amount of evidence showing that a great number of people all over the world see events before they happen, and in many instances are, therefore, able to avoid the tragic event which was foreseen vividly in a dream.

The dream which I had showed clearly the headlines in *The New York Times* about three years prior to the tragedy of Pearl Harbor. In consequence of this dream, I immediately cancelled the trip as I felt a subconscious compulsion to do so. Three years later the Second World War proved the truth of the inner voice of intuition.

YOUR FUTURE IS IN YOUR SUBCONSCIOUS MIND

Remember that the future, the result of your habitual thinking, is already in your mind except when you change it through prayer. The future of a country, likewise, is in the collective subconscious of the people of that nation. There is nothing strange in the dream I had wherein I saw the headlines of the New York newspapers long before the war began. The war had already taken place in mind, and all the plans of attack were already engraved on that great recording instrument, the subconscious mind or collective unconscious of the universal mind. Tomorrow's events are in your subconscious mind, so are next week's and next month's, and they may be seen by a highly psychic or clairvoyant person.

No disaster or tragedy can happen to you if you decide to pray. Nothing is predetermined or foreordained. Your mental attitude, i.e., the way you think, feel, and believe, determines your destiny. You can, through scientific prayer, which is explained in a previous chapter, mold, fashion, and create your own future. *Whatsoever a man soweth, that shall he also reap.*

A CATNAP NETS HIM $15,000

One of my students mailed me a newspaper clipping three or four years ago about a man called Ray Hammerstrom, a roller at the steel works in Pittsburgh operated by Jones and Laughlin Steel Corporation. He received $15,000 for his dream.

According to the article, the engineers could not fix a faulty switch in a newly installed bar mill which controlled the delivery of straight bars to the cooling beds. The engineers worked on the switch about eleven or twelve times to no avail.

Hammerstrom thought a lot about the problem and tried to figure out a new design which might work. Nothing worked. One afternoon he lay down for a nap, and prior to sleep he began to think about the answer to the switch problem. He had a dream in which a perfect design for the switch was portrayed. When he awoke, he sketched his new design according to the outline of his dream.

This visionary catnap won Hammerstrom a check for $15,000, the largest award the firm ever gave an employee for a new idea.

HOW A FAMOUS PROFESSOR SOLVED HIS PROBLEM IN SLEEP

Dr. H. V. Hilprecht, professor of Assyrian at the University of Pennsylvania, wrote as follows: "One Saturday evening . . . I had been wearying myself, in the vain attempt to decipher two small fragments of agate which were supposed to belong to the finger rings of some Babylonians.

"About midnight, weary and exhausted, I went to bed and dreamed the following remarkable dream: A tall, thin priest of Nippur, about forty years of age, led me to the treasure chamber of the temple . . . a small, low-ceilinged room without windows, while scraps of agate and lapis-lazuli lay scattered on the floor. Here he addressed me as follows:

'The two fragments which you have published separately on pages 22 and 26 belong together, are not finger rings. . . . The first two rings served as earrings for the statue of the god; the two fragments (you have) . . . are the portions of them. If you will put them together you will have confirmation of my words.' . . . I awoke at once . . . I examined the fragments . . . and to my astonishment found the dream verified. The problem was then at last solved."

This demonstrates clearly the creative manifestation of his subconscious mind which knew the answer to all his problems.

HOW THE SUBCONSCIOUS WORKED FOR A FAMOUS WRITER WHILE HE SLEPT

Robert Louis Stevenson in one of his books, *Across the Plains,* devotes a whole chapter to dreams. He was a vivid dreamer and had the persistent habit of giving specific instructions to his subconscious every night prior to sleep. He would request his subconscious to evolve stories for him while he slept. For example, if Stevenson's funds were at a low ebb, his command to his subconscious would be something like this: "Give me a good thrilling novel which will be marketable and profitable." His subconscious responded magnificently.

Stevenson says, "These little brownies [the intelligences and powers of his subconscious] can tell me a story piece by piece, like a serial, and keep me, its supposed creator, all the while in total ignorance of where they aim." And he added: "That part of my work which is done when I am up and about [while he is consciously aware and awake] is by no means necessarily mine, since all goes to show that the *brownies* have a hand in it even then."

SLEEP IN PEACE AND WAKE IN JOY

To those who suffer from insomnia, you will find the following prayer very effective. Repeat it slowly, quietly, and lovingly prior to sleep: "My toes are relaxed, my ankles are relaxed, my abdominal muscles are relaxed, my heart and lungs are relaxed, my hands and arms are relaxed, my neck is relaxed, my brain is relaxed, my face is relaxed, my eyes are relaxed, my whole mind and body are relaxed. I fully and freely forgive everyone, and I sincerely wish for them harmony, health, peace, and all the blessings of life. I am at peace, I am poised, serene, and calm. I rest in security and in peace. A great stillness steals over me, and a great calm quiets my whole being as I realize the Divine Presence within me. I know that the realization of life and love heals me. I wrap myself in the mantle of love and fall asleep filled with good will for all. Throughout the night peace remains with me, and in the morning I shall be filled with life and love. A circle of love is drawn around me. *I will fear no evil, for Thou art with me.* I sleep in peace, I wake in joy, and *in Him I live, move, and have my being.*"

SUMMARY OF YOUR AIDS TO THE WONDERS OF SLEEP

1. If you are worried that you will not wake up on time, suggest to your subconscious mind prior to sleep the exact time you wish to arise, and it will awaken you. It needs no clock. Do the same thing with all problems. There is nothing too hard for your subconscious.
2. Your subconscious never sleeps. It is always on the job. It controls all your vital functions. Forgive yourself and everyone else before you go to sleep, and healing will take place much more rapidly.

3. Guidance is given you while you are asleep, sometimes in a dream. The healing currents are also released, and in the morning you feel refreshed and rejuvenated.
4. When troubled by the vexations and strife of the day, still the wheels of your mind and think about the wisdom and intelligence lodged in your subconscious mind which is ready to respond to you. This will give you peace, strength, and confidence.
5. Sleep is essential for peace of mind and health of body. Lack of sleep can cause irritation, depression, and mental disorders. You need eight hours' sleep.
6. Medical research scholars point out that insomnia precedes psychotic breakdowns.
7. You are spiritually recharged during sleep. Adequate sleep is essential for joy and vitality in life.
8. Your tired brain craves sleep so hungrily that it will sacrifice anything to get it. Many who have fallen asleep at the wheel of an automobile can testify to this.
9. Many sleep-deprived people have poor memories and lack proper coordination. They become befuddled, confused, and disoriented.
10. Sleep brings counsel. Prior to sleep, claim that the infinite intelligence of your subconscious mind is guiding and directing you. Then, watch for the *lead* which comes, perhaps on awakening.
11. Trust your subconscious completely. Know that its tendency is always lifeward. Occasionally, your subconscious answers you in a very vivid dream and a vision in the night. You can be forewarned in a dream in the same way as the author of this book was warned.
12. Your future is in your mind now, based on your habitual thinking and beliefs. Claim infinite intelligence leads and guides you and that all good is yours,

and your future will be wonderful. Believe it and accept it. Expect the best, and invariably the best will come to you.

13. If you are writing a novel, play, or book, or are working on an invention, speak to your subconscious mind at night and claim boldly that its wisdom, intelligence, and power are guiding, directing, and revealing to you the ideal play, novel, book, or revealing the perfect solution whatever it may be. Wonders will happen as you pray this way.

CHAPTER FOURTEEN

YOUR SUBCONSCIOUS MIND AND MARITAL PROBLEMS

Ignorance of the functions and powers of the mind is the cause of all marital trouble. Friction between husband and wife can be solved by each using the law of mind correctly. By praying together they stay together. The contemplation of divine ideals, the study of the laws of life, the mutual agreement on a common purpose and plan, and the enjoyment of personal freedom bring about that harmonious marriage, that wedded bliss, that sense of oneness where the two become one.

The best time to prevent divorce is before marriage. It is not wrong to try to get out of a very bad situation. But why get into the bad situation in the first place? Would it not be better to give attention to the real cause of marital problems, in other words, to really get at the root of the matter involved?

As with all other problems of men and women, the problems of divorce, separation, annulment, and endless litigation are directly traceable to lack of knowledge of the working and interrelationship of the conscious and subconscious mind.

THE MEANING OF MARRIAGE

Marriage to be real must first be on a spiritual basis. It must be of the heart, and the heart is the chalice of love. Honesty, sincerity, kindness, and integrity are also forms of love. Each partner should be perfectly honest and sincere with the other. It is not a true marriage when a man marries a woman for her money, social position, or to lift his ego, because this indicates a lack of sincerity, honesty, and true love. Such a marriage is a farce, a sham, and a masquerade.

When a woman says, "I am tired working; I want to get married because I want security," her premise is false. She is not using the laws of mind correctly. Her security depends upon her knowledge of the interaction of the conscious and subconscious mind and its application.

For example, a woman will never lack for wealth or health if she applies the techniques outlined in the respective chapters of this book. Her wealth can come to her independent of her husband, father, or anyone else. A woman is not dependent on her husband for health, peace, joy, inspiration, guidance, love, wealth, security, happiness, or anything in the world. Her security and peace of mind come from her knowledge of the inner powers within her and from the constant use of the laws of her own mind in a constructive fashion.

HOW TO ATTRACT THE IDEAL HUSBAND

You are now acquainted with the way your subconscious mind works. You know that whatever you impress upon it will be experienced in your world. Begin now to impress your subconscious mind with the qualities and characteristics you desire in a man.

The following is an excellent technique: Sit down at night in your armchair, close your eyes, let go, relax the body, become very quiet, passive, and receptive. Talk to your subconscious mind and say to it, "I am now attracting a man into my experience who is honest, sincere, loyal, faithful, peaceful, happy, and prosperous. These qualities which I admire are sinking down into my subconscious mind now. As I dwell upon these characteristics, they become a part of me and are embodied subconsciously.

"I know there is an irresistible law of attraction and that I attract to me a man according to my subconscious belief. I attract that which I feel to be true in my subconscious mind.

"I know I can contribute to his peace and happiness. He loves my ideals, and I love his ideals. He does not want to make me over; neither do I want to make him over. There is mutual love, freedom, and respect."

Practice this process of impregnating your subconscious mind. Then, you will have the joy of attracting to you a man possessing the qualities and characteristics you mentally dwelt upon. Your subconscious intelligence will open up a pathway, whereby both of you will meet, according to the irresistible and changeless flow of your own subconscious mind. Have a keen desire to give the best that is in you of love, devotion, and cooperation. Be receptive to this gift of love which you have given to your subconscious mind.

HOW TO ATTRACT THE IDEAL WIFE

Affirm as follows: "I now attract the right woman who is in complete accord with me. This is a spiritual union because it is divine love functioning through the personality of someone with whom I blend perfectly. I know I can give to this woman love, light, peace, and joy. I feel and believe I can make this woman's life full, complete, and wonderful.

"I now decree that she possesses the following qualities and attributes: She is spiritual, loyal, faithful, and true. She is harmonious, peaceful, and happy. We are irresistibly attracted to each other. Only that which belongs to love, truth, and beauty can enter my experience. I accept my ideal companion now."

As you think quietly and with interest on the qualities and attributes which you admire in the companion you seek, you will build the mental equivalent into your mentality. Then, the deeper currents of your subconscious mind will bring both of you together in divine order.

NO NEED FOR THIRD MISTAKE

Recently a teacher said to me, "I have had three husbands and all three have been passive, submissive, and dependent on me to make all decisions and govern everything. Why do I attract such type men?"

I asked her whether she had known that her second husband was the effeminate type, and she replied, "Of course not. Had I known, I would not have married him." Apparently she had not learned anything from the first mistake. The trouble was with her own personality makeup. She was very masculine, domineering, and unconsciously wanted someone who would be submissive and passive so that she could play the dominant role. All this was unconscious motivation, and her subconscious picture attracted to her what she subjectively wanted. She had to learn to *break the pattern by adopting the right prayer process.*

HOW SHE BROKE THE NEGATIVE PATTERN

The above-mentioned woman learned a simple truth. When you believe you can have the type of man you idealize, it is done unto you as you believe. The following is the specific prayer she used to break the old subconscious pattern and attract to her the ideal mate: "I am building into my mentality the type of man I deeply desire. The man I attract for a husband is strong, powerful, loving, very masculine, successful, honest, loyal, and faithful. He finds love and happiness with me. I love to follow where he leads.

"I know he wants me, and I want him. I am honest, sincere, loving, and kind. I have wonderful gifts to offer him. They are good will, a joyous heart, and a healthy body. He offers me the same. It is mutual. I give and I receive. Divine intelligence knows where this man is, and the deeper wisdom of my subconscious mind is now bringing both of us together in its own way, and we recognize each other immediately. I release this request to my subconscious mind which knows how to bring my request to pass. I give thanks for the perfect answer."

She prayed in the above manner night and morning, affirming these truths and knowing that through frequent occupation of the mind she would reach the mental equivalent of that which she sought.

THE ANSWER TO HER PRAYER

Several months went by. She had a great number of dates and social engagements, none of which was agreeable to her. When she was about to question, waiver, doubt, and vacillate, she reminded herself that the infinite intelligence was bringing it to pass in its own way and that there was nothing to be concerned about. Her final decree in her divorce proceedings was granted which brought her a great sense of release and mental freedom.

Shortly afterward she went to work as a receptionist in a doctor's office. She told me that the minute she saw the physician she knew he was the man she was praying about. Apparently he knew it, too, because he proposed to her the first week she was in the office, and their subsequent marriage was ideally happy. This physician was not the passive or submissive type, but was a real man, a former football player, an outstanding athlete, and was a deeply spiritual man though he was completely devoid of any sectarian or denominational affiliation.

She got what she prayed for because she claimed it mentally until she reached the point of saturation. In other words, she mentally and emotionally united with her idea, and it became a part of her in the same way that an apple becomes a part of her bloodstream.

SHOULD I GET A DIVORCE?

Divorce is an individual problem. It cannot be generalized. In some cases, of course, there never should have been a marriage. In some cases, divorce is not the solution, no more so than marriage is the solution for a lonely man. Divorce may be right for one person and wrong for another. A divorced woman may be far more sincere and noble than many of her married sisters who perhaps are living a lie.

For example, I once talked with a woman whose husband was a dope fiend, an ex-convict, a wife-beater, and a non-provider. She had been told it was wrong to get a divorce. I explained to her that marriage is of the heart. If two hearts blend harmoniously, lovingly, and sincerely, that is the ideal marriage. The pure action of the heart is love.

Following this explanation she knew what to do. She knew in her heart that there is no divine law which compelled her to be browbeaten, intimidated, and beaten because someone said, "I pronounce you man and wife."

If you are in doubt as to what to do, ask for guidance, knowing that there is always an answer and you will receive it. Follow the *lead* that comes to you in the silence of your soul. It speaks to you in peace.

DRIFTING INTO DIVORCE

Recently a young couple, married for only a few months, were seeking a divorce. I discovered that the young man had a constant fear that his wife would leave him. He expected rejection, and he believed that she would be unfaithful. These thoughts haunted his mind, and became an obsession with him. His mental attitude was one of separation and suspicion. She felt unresponsive to him; it was his own feeling or atmosphere of loss and separation operating through them. This brought about a condition or action in accordance with the mental pattern behind it. There is a law of action and reaction, or cause and effect. The thought is the action, and the response of the subconscious mind is the reaction.

His wife left home and asked for a divorce which is what he feared and believed she would do.

DIVORCE BEGINS IN THE MIND

Divorce takes place first in the mind; the legal proceedings follow after. These two young people were full of resentment, fear, suspicion, and anger. These attitudes weaken, exhaust, and debilitate the whole being. They learned that hate divides and that love unites. They began to realize what they had been doing with their minds. Neither one of them knew the law of mental action, and they were misusing their minds and bringing on chaos and misery. These two people went back together at my suggestion and experimented with prayer therapy.

They began to radiate love, peace, and good will to each other. Each one practiced radiating harmony, health, peace, and love to the other, and they alternated in the reading of the Psalms every night. Their marriage is growing more beautiful everyday.

THE NAGGING WIFE

Many times the reason the wife nags is because she gets no attention. Oftentimes, it is a craving for love and affection. Give your wife attention, and show your appreciation. Praise and exalt all her many good points. There is also the nagging type of woman who wants to make the man conform to her particular pattern. This is about the quickest way in the world to get rid of a man.

The wife and the husband must cease being scavengers—always looking at the petty faults or errors in each other. Let each give attention and praise for the constructive and wonderful qualities in the other.

THE BROODING HUSBAND

If a man begins to brood, grows morbid against his wife because of the things she said or did, he is, psychologically speaking, committing adultery. One of the meanings of adultery is idolatry, i.e., giving attention to or uniting mentally with that which is negative and destructive. When a man is silently resenting his wife and is full of hostility toward her, he is unfaithful. He is not faithful to his marriage vows, which are to love, cherish, and honor her all the days of his life.

The man who is brooding, bitter, and resentful can swallow his sharp remarks, abate his anger, and he can go to great lengths to be considerate, kind, and courteous. He can deftly skirt the differences. Through praise and mental effort, he can get out of the habit of antagonism. Then, he will be able to get along better, not only with his wife, but with business associates also. Assume the harmonious state, and eventually you will find peace and harmony.

THE GREAT MISTAKE

A great mistake is to discuss your marital problems or difficulties with neighbors and relatives. Suppose, for example, a wife says to the neighbor, "John never gives me any money. He treats my mother abominably, drinks to excess, and is constantly abusive and insulting."

Now, this wife is degrading and belittling her husband in the eyes of all the neighbors and relatives. He no longer appears as the ideal husband to them. Never discuss your marital problems with anyone except a trained counselor. Why cause numerous people to think negatively of your marriage? Moreover, as you discuss and dwell upon these shortcomings of your husband, you are actually creating these states within yourself. Who is thinking and feeling it? You are! As you think and feel, so are you.

Relatives will usually give you the wrong advice. It is usually biased and prejudiced because it is not given in an impersonal way. Any advice you receive which violates the golden rule, which is a cosmic law, is not good or sound.

It is well to remember that no two human beings ever lived beneath the same roof without clashes of temperament, periods of hurts and strain. Never display the unhappy side of your marriage to your friends. Keep your quarrels to yourself. Refrain from criticism and condemnation of your partner.

DON'T TRY TO MAKE YOUR WIFE OVER

A husband must not try to make his wife over into a second edition of himself. The tactless attempt to change her in many ways is foreign to her nature. These attempts are always foolish, and many times result in a dissolution of the marriage. These attempts to alter her destroy her pride and self-esteem, and arouse a spirit of contrariness and resentment that proves fatal to the marriage bond.

Adjustments are needed, of course, but if you have a good look inside your own mind, and study your character and behavior, you will find so many shortcomings, they will keep you busy the rest of your life. If you say, "I will make him over into what I want," you are looking for trouble and the divorce court. You are asking for misery. You will have to learn the hard way that there is no one to change but yourself.

PRAY TOGETHER AND STAY TOGETHER THROUGH STEPS IN PRAYER

The first step: Never carry over from one day to another accumulated irritations arising from little disappointments. Be sure to forgive each other for any sharpness before you retire at night. The moment you awaken in the morning, claim infinite intelligence is guiding you in all your ways. Send out loving thoughts of peace, harmony, and love to your marriage partner, to all members of the family, and to the whole world.

The second step: Say grace at breakfast. Give thanks for the wonderful food, for your abundance, and for all your blessings. Make sure that no problems, worries, or arguments shall enter into the table conversation; the same applies at dinner time. Say to your wife or husband, "I appreciate all you are doing, and I radiate love and good will to you all day long."

The third step: The husband and wife should alternate in praying each night. Do not take your marriage partner for granted. Show your appreciation and love. Think appreciation and good will, rather than condemnation, criticism, and nagging. The way to build a peaceful home and a happy marriage is to use a foundation of love, beauty, harmony, mutual respect, faith in God, and all things good. Read the 23rd, 27th, and 91st Psalms, the 11th chapter of Hebrews, the 13th chapter of I Corinthians, and other great texts of the Bible before going to sleep. As you practice these truths, your marriage will grow more and more blessed through the years.

REVIEW YOUR ACTIONS

1. Ignorance of mental and spiritual laws is the cause of all marital unhappiness. By praying scientifically together, you stay together.
2. The best time to prevent divorce is before marriage. If you learn how to pray in the right way, you will attract the right mate for you.
3. Marriage is the union of a man and woman who are bound together by love. Their hearts beat as one, and they move onward, upward, and Godward.
4. Marriage does not bequeath happiness. People find happiness by dwelling on the eternal truths of God and the spiritual values of life. Then, the man and woman can contribute to each other's happiness and joy.
5. You attract the right mate by dwelling on the qualities and characteristics you admire in a woman or a man, and then your subconscious mind will bring you together in divine order.
6. You must build into your mentality the mental equivalent of what you want in a marriage partner. If you want to attract an honest, sincere, and loving partner in life, you must be honest, sincere, and loving yourself.
7. You do not have to repeat mistakes in marriage. When you really believe you can have the type man or woman you idealize, it is done unto you as you believe. To believe is to accept something as true. Accept your ideal companion now mentally.
8. Do not wonder how, why, or where you will meet the mate you are praying for. Trust implicitly the wisdom of your subconscious mind. It has the "know-how," and you don't have to assist it.
9. You are mentally divorced when you indulge in peeves, grudges, ill will, and hostility toward your marriage partner. You are mentally dwelling with error

in the bed of your mind. Adhere to your marriage vows, "I promise to cherish, love, and honor him (or her) all the days of my life."

10. Cease projecting fear patterns to your marriage partner. Project love, peace, harmony, and good will, and your marriage will grow more beautiful and more wonderful through the years.
11. Radiate love, peace, and good will to each other. These vibrations are picked up by the subconscious mind resulting in mutual trust, affection, and respect.
12. A nagging wife is usually seeking attention and appreciation. She is craving for love and affection. Praise and exalt her many good points. Show her that you love her and appreciate her.
13. A man who loves his wife does not do anything unloving or unkind in word, manner, or action. Love is what love does.
14. In marital problems, always seek expert advice. You would not go to a carpenter to pull a tooth; neither should you discuss your marriage problems with relatives or friends. You should go to a trained person for counsel.
15. Never try to make your wife or husband over. These attempts are always foolish and tend to destroy the pride and self-esteem of the other. Moreover, it arouses a spirit of resentment that proves fatal to the marriage bond. Cease trying to make the other a second edition of yourself.
16. Pray together and you will stay together. Scientific prayer solves all problems. Mentally picture your wife as she ought to be, joyous, happy, healthy, and beautiful. See your husband as he ought to be, strong, powerful, loving, harmonious, and kind. Maintain this mental picture, and you will experience the marriage made in heaven which is harmony and peace.

CHAPTER FIFTEEN

YOUR SUBCONSCIOUS MIND AND YOUR HAPPINESS

William James, father of American psychology, said that the greatest discovery of the nineteenth century was not in the realm of physical science. The greatest discovery was the power of the subconscious touched by faith. In every human being is that limitless reservoir of power which can overcome any problem in the world.

True and lasting happiness will come into your life the day you get the clear realization that you can overcome any weakness—the day you realize that your subconscious can solve your problems, heal your body, and prosper you beyond your fondest dream.

You might have felt very happy when your child was born, when you got married, when you graduated from college, or when you won a great victory or a prize. You might have been very happy when you became engaged to the loveliest girl or the most handsome man. You could go on and list innumerable experiences which have made you happy. However, no matter how marvelous these experiences are, they do not give real lasting happiness—they are transitory.

The Book of Proverbs gives the answer: *Whosoever trusteth in the Lord, happy is he.*

When you trust in the Lord (the power and wisdom of your subconscious mind) to lead, guide, govern, and direct all your ways, you will become poised, serene, and relaxed. As you radiate love, peace, and good will to all, you are really building a superstructure of happiness for all the days of your life.

YOU MUST CHOOSE HAPPINESS

Happiness is a state of mind. There is a phrase in the Bible which says, *Choose ye this day whom ye will serve.* You have the freedom to choose happiness. This may seem extraordinarily simple, and it is. Perhaps this is why people stumble over the way to happiness; they do not see the simplicity of the key to happiness. The great things of life are simple, dynamic, and creative. They produce well-being and happiness.

St. Paul reveals to you how you can think your way into a life of dynamic power and happiness in these words: *Finally, brethren, whatsoever things are true, whatsoever things are honest, whatsoever things are just, whatsoever things are pure, whatsoever things are lovely, whatsoever things are of good report; if there be any virtue, and if there be any praise, think on these things.* PHIL. 4:8.

HOW TO CHOOSE HAPPINESS

Begin now to choose happiness. This is how you do it: When you open your eyes in the morning, say to yourself, "Divine order takes charge of my life today and every day. All things work together for good for me today. This is a new and wonderful day for me. There will never be another day like this one. I am divinely guided all day long, and whatever I do will prosper. Divine love surrounds me, enfolds me, and enwraps me, and I go forth in peace. Whenever my attention wanders away from that which is good and constructive, I will immediately bring it back to the contemplation of that which is lovely and of good report. I am a spiritual and mental magnet attracting to myself all things which bless and prosper me. I am going to be a wonderful success in all my undertakings today. I am definitely going to be happy all day long."

Start each day in this manner; then you will be choosing happiness, and you will be a radiant joyous person.

HE MADE IT A HABIT TO BE HAPPY

A number of years ago, I stayed for about a week in a farmer's house in Connemarra on the west coast of Ireland. He seemed to be always singing and whistling and was full of humor. I asked him the secret of his happiness, and his reply was: "It is a habit of mine to be happy. Every morning when I awaken and every night before I go to sleep, I bless my family, the crops, the cattle, and I thank God for the wonderful harvest."

This farmer had made a practice of this for over forty years. As you know, thoughts repeated regularly and systematically sink into the subconscious mind and become habitual. He discovered that happiness is a habit.

YOU MUST DESIRE TO BE HAPPY

There is one very important point about being happy. You must sincerely *desire* to be happy. There are people who have been depressed, dejected, and unhappy so long that were they suddenly made happy by some wonderful, good, joyous news, they would actually be like the woman who said to me, "It is wrong to be so happy!" They have been so accustomed to the old mental patterns that they do not feel at home being happy! They long for the former, depressed, unhappy state.

I knew a woman in England who had rheumatism for many years. She would pat herself on the knee and say, "My rheumatism is bad today. I cannot go out. My rheumatism keeps me miserable."

This dear elderly lady got a lot of attention from her son, daughter, and the neighbors. She really wanted her rheumatism. She enjoyed her "misery" as she called it. This woman did not really want to be happy.

I suggested a curative procedure to her. I wrote down some biblical verses and told her that if she gave attention to these truths, her mental attitude would undoubtedly change and would result in her faith and confidence in being restored to health. She was not interested. There seems to be a peculiar, mental, morbid streak in many people, whereby they seem to enjoy being miserable and sad.

WHY CHOOSE UNHAPPINESS?

Many people choose unhappiness by entertaining these ideas: "Today is a black day; everything is going to go wrong." "I am not going to succeed." "Everyone is against me." "Business is bad, and it is going to get worse." "I'm always late." "I never get the breaks." "He can, but I can't." If you have this attitude of mind the first thing in the morning, you will attract all these experiences to you, and you will be very unhappy.

Begin to realize that the world you live in is determined largely by what goes on in your mind. Marcus Aurelius, the great Roman philosopher and sage, said, "A man's life is what his thoughts make of it." Emerson, America's foremost philosopher, said, "A man is what he thinks all day long." The thoughts you habitually entertain in your mind have the tendency to actualize themselves in physical conditions.

Make certain you do not indulge in negative thoughts, defeatist thoughts, or unkind, depressing thoughts. Recall frequently to your mind that you can experience nothing outside your own mentality.

IF I HAD A MILLION DOLLARS, I WOULD BE HAPPY

I have visited many men in mental institutions who were millionaires, but they insisted they were penniless and destitute. They were incarcerated because of psychotic, paranoic, and manic-depressive tendencies. Wealth in and of itself will not make you happy. On the other hand, it is not a deterrent to happiness. Today, there are many people trying to buy happiness through the purchase of radios, television sets, automobiles, a home in the country, a private yacht, and a swimming pool, but happiness cannot be purchased or procured in that way.

The kingdom of happiness is in your thought and feeling. Too many people have the idea that it takes something artificial to produce happiness. Some say, "If I were elected mayor, made president of the organization, promoted to general manager of the corporation, I would be happy."

The truth is that happiness is a mental and spiritual state. None of these positions mentioned will necessarily bequeath happiness. Your strength, joy, and happiness consist in finding out the law of divine order and right action lodged in your subconscious mind and by applying these principles in all phases of your life.

HE FOUND HAPPINESS TO BE THE HARVEST OF A QUIET MIND

Lecturing in San Francisco some years ago, I interviewed a man who was very unhappy and dejected over the way his business was going. He was the general manager. His heart was filled with resentment toward the vice president and the president of the organization. He claimed that they opposed him. Because of this internal strife, business was declining; he was receiving no dividends or stock bonuses.

This is how he solved his business problem: The first thing in the morning he affirmed quietly as follows, "All those working in our corporation are honest, sincere, co-operative, faithful, and full of good will to all. They are mental and spiritual links in the chain of this corporation's growth, welfare, and prosperity. I radiate love, peace, and good will in my thoughts, words, and deeds to my two associates and to all those in the company. The president and the vice president of our company are divinely guided in all their undertakings. The infinite intelligence of my subconscious mind makes all decisions through me. There is only right action in all our business transactions and in our relationship with each other. I send the messengers of peace, love, and good will before me to the office. Peace and harmony reign supreme in the minds and hearts of all those in the company including myself. I now go forth into a new day, full of faith, confidence, and trust."

This business executive repeated the above meditation slowly three times in the morning, feeling the truth of what he affirmed. When fearful or angry thoughts came into his mind during the day, he would say to himself, "Peace, harmony, and poise govern my mind at all times."

As he continued disciplining his mind in this manner, all the harmful thoughts ceased to come, and peace came into his mind. He reaped the harvest.

Subsequently, he wrote me to the effect that at the end of about two weeks of reordering his mind, the president and the vice president called him into the office, praised his operations and his new constructive ideas, and remarked how fortunate they were in having him as general manager. He was very happy in discovering that man finds happiness within himself.

THE BLOCK OR STUMP IS NOT REALLY THERE

I read a newspaper article some years ago which told about a horse who had shied when he came to a stump on the road. Subsequently, every time the horse came to that same stump, he shied. The farmer dug the stump out, burned it, and leveled the old road. Yet, for twenty-five years, every time the horse passed the place where the former stump was, he shied. The horse was shying at the memory of a stump.

There is no block to your happiness save in your own thought life and mental imagery. Are fear or worry holding you back? Fear is a thought in your mind. You can dig it up this very moment by supplanting it with faith in success, achievement, and victory over all problems.

I knew a man who failed in business. He said to me, "I made mistakes. I've learned a lot. I am going back into business, and I will be a tremendous success." He faced up to that stump in his mind. He did not whine or complain, but he tore up the stump of failure, and through believing in his inner powers to back him up, he banished all fear thoughts and old depressions. Believe in yourself, and you will succeed and be happy.

THE HAPPIEST PEOPLE

The happiest man is he who constantly brings forth and practices what is best in him. Happiness and virtue complement each other. The best are not only the happiest, but the happiest are usually the best in the art of living life successfully. God is the highest and best in you. Express more of God's love, light, truth, and beauty, and you will become one of the happiest persons in the world today.

Epictetus, the Greek Stoic philosopher, said, "There is but one way to tranquillity of mind and happiness; let this, therefore, be always ready at hand with thee, both when thou wakest early in the morning, and all the day long, and when thou goest late to sleep, to account no external things thine own, but commit all these to God."

SUMMARY OF STEPS TO HAPPINESS

1. William James said that the greatest discovery of the 19th century was the power of the subconscious mind touched by faith.
2. There is tremendous power within you. Happiness will come to you when you acquire a sublime confidence in this power. Then, you will make your dreams come true.
3. You can rise victorious over any defeat and realize the cherished desires of your heart through the marvelous power of your subconscious mind. This is the meaning of *Whosoever trusteth in the Lord* [spiritual laws of the subconscious mind], *happy is he.*
4. You must choose happiness. Happiness is a habit. It is a good habit to ponder often on *Whatsoever things are true, whatsoever things are honest, whatsoever things are just, whatsoever things are pure, whatsoever things are lovely, whatsoever things are of good report; if there be any virtue, and if there be any praise, think on these things.* PHILIPPIANS 4:8.
5. When you open your eyes in the morning, say to yourself, I choose happiness today. I choose success today. I choose right action today. I choose love and good will for all today. I choose peace today. Pour life, love, and interest into this affirmation, and you have chosen happiness.
6. Give thanks for all your blessings several times a day. Furthermore, pray for the peace, happiness, and prosperity of all members of your family, your associates, and all people everywhere.
7. You must sincerely desire to be happy. Nothing is accomplished without desire. Desire is a wish with wings of imagination and faith. Imagine the fulfill-

ment of your desire, and feel its reality, and it will come to pass. Happiness comes in answered prayer.

8. By constantly dwelling on thoughts of fear, worry, anger, hate, and failure, you will become very depressed and unhappy. Remember, your life is what your thoughts make of it.
9. You cannot buy happiness with all the money in the world. Some millionaires are very happy, some are very unhappy. Many people with very little worldly goods are very happy, and some are very unhappy. Some married people are happy, and some very unhappy. Some single people are happy, and some are very unhappy. The kingdom of happiness is in your thought and feeling.
10. Happiness is the harvest of a quiet mind. Anchor your thoughts on peace, poise, security, and divine guidance, and your mind will be productive of happiness.
11. There is no block to your happiness. External things are not causative, these are effects, not cause. Take your cue from the only creative principle within you. Your thought is cause, and a new cause produces a new effect. Choose happiness.
12. The happiest man is he who brings forth the highest and the best in him. God is the highest and the best in him, for the kingdom of God is within.

CHAPTER SIXTEEN

YOUR SUBCONSCIOUS MIND AND HARMONIOUS HUMAN RELATIONS

In studying this book, you learn that your subconscious mind is a recording machine which faithfully reproduces whatever you impress upon it. This is one of the reasons for the application of the Golden Rule in human relations.

MATTHEW 7:12 says, *All things whatsoever ye would that men should do unto you, do ye even so to them.* This quotation has outer and inner meanings. You are interested in its inner meaning from the standpoint of your subconscious mind which is: As you would that men should *think* about you, think you about them in like manner. As you would that men should *feel* about you, feel you also about them in like manner. As you would want men to *act* toward you, act you toward them in like manner.

For example, you may be polite and courteous to someone in your office, but when his back is turned, you are very critical and resentful toward him in your mind. Such negative thoughts are highly destructive to you. It is like taking poison. You are actually taking mental poisons which rob you of vitality, enthusiasm, strength, guidance, and good will. These negative thoughts and emotions sink down into your subconscious, and cause all kinds of difficulties and maladies in your life.

THE MASTER KEY TO HAPPY RELATIONSHIPS WITH OTHERS

Judge not, that ye be not judged. For with what judgment ye judge, ye shall be judged: and with what measure ye mete, it shall be measured to you again. MATTHEW 7:1-2.

A study of these verses and the application of the inner truths therein contained represent the real key to harmonious relations. To judge is to think, to arrive at a mental verdict or conclusion in your mind. The thought you have about the other person is your thought, because you are thinking it. Your thoughts are creative, therefore, you actually create in your own experience what you think and feel about the other person. It is also true that the suggestion you give to another, you give to yourself because your mind is the creative medium.

This is why it is said, *For with what judgment ye judge, ye shall be judged.* When you know this law and the way your subconscious mind works, you are careful to think, feel, and act right toward the other. These verses teach you about the emancipation of man and reveal to you the solution to your individual problems.

AND WITH WHAT MEASURE YE METE, IT SHALL BE MEASURED TO YOU AGAIN

The good you do for others comes back to you in like measure; and the evil you do returns to you by the law of your own mind. If a man cheats and deceives another, he is actually cheating and deceiving himself. His sense of guilt and mood of loss inevitably will attract loss to him in some way, at some time. His subconscious records his mental act and reacts according to the mental intention or motivation.

Your subconscious mind is impersonal and unchanging, neither considering persons nor respecting religious affiliations or institutions of any kind. It is neither compassionate nor vindictive. The way you think, feel, and act toward others returns at last upon yourself.

THE DAILY HEADLINES MADE HIM SICK

Begin now to observe yourself. Observe your reactions to people, conditions, and circumstances. How do you respond to the events and news of the day? It makes no difference if all the other people were wrong and you alone were right. If the news disturbs you, it is your evil because your negative emotions robbed you of peace and harmony.

A woman wrote me about her husband, saying that he goes into a rage when he reads what certain newspaper columnists write in the newspaper. She added that this constant reaction of anger and suppressed rage on his part brought on bleeding ulcers, and his physician recommended an emotional reconditioning.

I invited this man to see me and I explained to him the way his mind functions indicating how emotionally immature it was to get angry when others write articles with which he disapproves or disagrees.

He began to realize that he should give the newspaperman freedom to express himself even though the latter disagreed with him politically, religiously, or in any other way. In the same manner, the newspaperman would give him freedom to write a letter to the newspaper disagreeing with his published statements. He learned that he could disagree without being disagreeable. He awakened to the simple truth that it is never what a person says or does that affects him, it is his reaction to what is said or done that matters.

This explanation was the cure for this man, and he realized that with a little practice he could master his morning tantrums. His wife told me, subsequently, that he laughed at himself and also at what the columnists say. They no longer have power to disturb, annoy, and irritate him. His ulcers have disappeared due to his emotional poise and serenity.

I HATE WOMEN, BUT I LIKE MEN

A private secretary was very bitter toward some of the girls in her office because they were gossiping about her, and as she said, spreading vicious lies about her. She admitted that she did not like women. She said, "I hate women, but I like men." I discovered also that she spoke to the girls who were under her in the office in a very haughty, imperious, and irritable tone of voice. She pointed out that they took a delight in making things difficult for her. There was a certain pomposity in her way of speaking, and I could see where her tone of voice would affect some people unpleasantly.

If all the people in the office or factory annoy you, isn't it a possibility that the vibration, annoyance, and turmoil may be due to some subconscious pattern or mental projection from you? We know that a dog will react ferociously if you hate or fear dogs. Animals pick up your subconscious vibrations and react accordingly. Many undisciplined human beings are just as sensitive as dogs, cats, and other animals.

I suggested a process of prayer to this private secretary who hated women, explaining to her that when she began to identify herself with spiritual values and commenced to affirm the truths of life, her voice, mannerisms, and hatred of women would completely disappear. She was surprised to know that the emotion of hatred shows up in a person's speech, actions, in his writings, and in all phases of his life. She ceased reacting in the typical resentful and angry way. She established a pattern of prayer which she practiced regularly, systematically, and conscientiously in the office.

The prayer was as follows: "I think, speak, and act lovingly, quietly, and peacefully. I now radiate love, peace, tolerance, and kindliness to all the girls who criticized me and gossiped about me. I anchor my thoughts on peace, harmony, and good will to all. Whenever I am about to react negatively, I say firmly to myself, 'I am going to think, speak, and act from the standpoint of the principle of harmony, health, and peace within myself.' Creative intelligence leads, rules, and guides me in all my ways."

The practice of this prayer transformed her life, and she found that all criticism and annoyance ceased. The girls became co-workers and friends along life's journey. She discovered that *there is no one to change but myself.*

HIS INNER SPEECH HELD BACK HIS PROMOTION

One day a salesman came to see me and described his difficulties in working with the sales manager of his organization. He had been with the company ten years and had received no promotion or recognition of any kind. He showed me his sales figures which were greater proportionately than the other men in the territory. He said that the sales manager did not like him, that he was unjustly treated, and that at conferences the manager was rude to him, and at times ridiculed his suggestions.

I explained that undoubtedly the cause was to a great degree within himself, and that his concept and belief about his superior bore witness to the reaction of this man. *The measure we mete, shall be measured to us again.* His mental measure or concept of the sales manager was that he was mean and cantankerous. He was filled with bitterness and hostility toward the executive. On his way to work he conducted a vigorous conversation with himself filled with criticism, mental arguments, recriminations, and denunciations of his sales manager.

What he gave out mentally, he was inevitably bound to get back. This salesman realized that his inner speech was highly destructive because the intensity and force of his silent thoughts and emotions, and personally conducted mental condemnation and vilification of the sales manager, entered into his own subconscious mind. This brought about the negative response from his boss as well as creating many other personal, physical, and emotional disorders.

He began to pray frequently as follows: "I am the only thinker in my universe. I am responsible for what I think about my boss. My sales manager is not responsible for the way I think about him. I refuse to give power to any person, place, or thing to annoy me or disturb me. I wish health, success, peace of mind, and happiness for my boss. I sincerely wish him well, and I know he is divinely guided in all his ways."

He repeated this prayer out loud slowly, quietly, and feelingly, knowing that his mind is like a garden, and that whatever he plants in the garden will come forth like seeds after their kind.

I also taught him to practice mental imagery prior to sleep in this way: He imagined that his sales manager was congratulating him on his fine work, on his zeal and enthusiasm, and on his wonderful response from customers. He felt the reality of all this, felt his handshake, heard the tone of his voice, and saw him smile. He made a real mental movie, dramatizing it to the best of his ability. Night after night he conducted this mental movie, knowing that his subconscious mind was the receptive plate on which his conscious imagery would be impressed.

Gradually by a process of what may be termed mental and spiritual osmosis, the impression was made on his subconscious mind, and the expression automatically came forth. The sales manager subsequently called him up to San Francisco, congratulated him, and gave him a new assignment as Division Sales Manager over one hundred men with a big increase in salary. He changed his concept and estimate of his boss, and the latter responded accordingly.

BECOMING EMOTIONALLY MATURE

What the other person says or does cannot really annoy or irritate you except you permit him to disturb you. The only way he can annoy you is through your own thought. For example, if you get angry, you have to go through four stages in your mind: You begin to think about what he said. You decide to get angry and generate an emotion of rage. Then, you decide to act. Perhaps, you talk back and react in kind. You see that the thought, emotion, reaction, and action all take place in your mind.

When you become emotionally mature, you do not respond negatively to the criticism and resentment of others. To do so would mean that you had descended to that state of low mental vibration and become one with the negative atmosphere of the other. Identify yourself with your aim in life, and do not permit any person, place, or thing to deflect you from your inner sense of peace, tranquillity, and radiant health.

THE MEANING OF LOVE IN HARMONIOUS HUMAN RELATIONS

Sigmund Freud, the Austrian founder of psychoanalysis, said that unless the personality has love, it sickens and dies. Love includes understanding, good will, and respect for the divinity in the other person. The more love and good will you emanate and exude, the more comes back to you.

If you puncture the other fellow's ego and wound his estimate of himself, you cannot gain his good will. Recognize that every man wants to be loved and appreciated, and made to feel important in the world. Realize that the other man is conscious of his true worth, and that, like yourself, he feels the dignity of being an expression of the One Life-Principle animating all men. As you do this consciously and knowingly, you build the other person up, and he returns your love and good will.

HE HATED AUDIENCES

An actor told me that the audience booed and hissed him on his first appearance on the stage. He added that the play was badly written and that undoubtedly he did not play a good role. He admitted openly to me that for months afterward he hated audiences. He called them dopes, dummies, stupid, ignorant, gullible, etc. He quit the stage in disgust and went to work in a drugstore for a year.

One day a friend invited him to hear a lecture in Town Hall, New York City, on "How to Get Along With Ourselves." This lecture changed his life. He went back to the stage and began to pray sincerely for the audience and himself. He poured out love and good will every night before appearing on the stage. He made it a habit to claim that the peace of God filled the hearts of all present, and that all present were lifted up and inspired. During each performance he sent out love vibrations to the audience. Today, he is a great actor, and he loves and respects people. His good will and esteem are transmitted to others and are felt by them.

HANDLING DIFFICULT PEOPLE

There are difficult people in the world who are twisted and distorted mentally. They are malconditioned. Many are mental delinquents, argumentative, uncooperative, cantankerous, cynical, and sour on life. They are sick psychologically. Many people have deformed and distorted minds, probably warped during childhood. Many have congenital deformities. You would not condemn a person who had tuberculosis, nor should you condemn a person who is mentally ill. No one, for example, hates or resents a hunchback; there are many mental hunchbacks. You should have compassion and understanding. *To understand all is to forgive all.*

MISERY LOVES COMPANY

The hateful, frustrated, distorted, and twisted personality is out of tune with the Infinite. He resents those who are peaceful, happy, and joyous. Usually he criticizes, condemns, and vilifies those who have been very good and kind to him. His attitude is this: Why should they be so happy when he is so miserable? He wants to drag them down to his own level. Misery loves company. When you understand this you remain unmoved, calm, and dispassionate.

THE PRACTICE OF EMPATHY IN HUMAN RELATIONS

A girl visited me recently stating that she hated another girl in her office. She gave as her reason that the other girl was prettier, happier, and wealthier than she, and, in addition, was engaged to the boss of the company where they worked. One day after the marriage had taken place, the crippled daughter (by a former marriage) of the woman whom she hated came into the office. The child put her arms around her mother and said, "Mommy, Mommy, I love my new daddy! Look what he gave me!" She showed her mother a wonderful new toy.

She said to me, "My heart went out to that little girl, and I knew how happy she must feel. I got a vision of how happy this woman was. All of a sudden I felt love for her, and I went into the office and wished her all the happiness in the world, and I meant it."

In psychological circles today, this is called empathy, which simply means the imaginative projection of your mental attitude into that of another. She projected her mental mood or the feeling of her heart into that of the other woman, and began to think and look out through the other woman's brain. She was actually thinking and feeling as the other woman, and also as the child, because she likewise had projected herself into the mind of the child. She was looking out from that vantage point on the child's mother.

If tempted to injure or think ill of another, project yourself mentally into the mind of Moses and think from the standpoint of the Ten Commandments. If you are prone to be envious, jealous, or angry, project yourself into the mind of Jesus and think from that standpoint, and you will feel the truth of the words *Love ye one another.*

APPEASEMENT NEVER WINS

Do not permit people to take advantage of you and gain their point by temper tantrums, crying jags, or so-called heart attacks. These people are dictators who try to enslave you and make you do their bidding. Be firm but kind, and refuse to yield. Appeasement never wins. Refuse to contribute to their delinquency, selfishness, and possessiveness. Remember, do that which is right. You are here to fulfill your ideal and remain true to the eternal verities and spiritual values of life which are eternal.

Give no one in all the world the power to deflect you from your goal, your aim in life, which is to express your hidden talents to the world, to serve humanity, and to reveal more and more of God's wisdom, truth, and beauty to all people in the world. Remain true to your ideal. Know definitely and absolutely that whatever contributes to your peace, happiness, and fulfillment must of necessity bless all men who walk the earth. The harmony of the part is the harmony of the whole, for the whole is in the part, and the part is in the whole. All you owe the other, as Paul says, is love, and love is the fulfilling of the law of health, happiness, and peace of mind.

PROFITABLE POINTERS IN HUMAN RELATIONS

1. Your subconscious mind is a recording machine which reproduces your habitual thinking. Think good of the other, and you are actually thinking good about yourself.
2. A hateful or resentful thought is a mental poison. Do not think ill of another for to do so is to think ill of yourself. You are the only thinker in your universe, and your thoughts are creative.
3. Your mind is a creative medium; therefore, what you think and feel about the other, you are bringing to pass in your own experience. This is the psychological meaning of the Golden Rule. As you would that man should think about you, think you about them in the same manner.
4. To cheat, rob, or defraud another brings lack, loss, and limitation to yourself. Your subconscious mind records your inner motivations, thoughts, and feelings. These being of a negative nature, loss, limitation, and trouble come to you in countless ways. Actually, what you do to the other, you are doing to yourself.
5. The good you do, the kindness proffered, the love and good will you send forth, will all come back to you multiplied in many ways.
6. You are the only thinker in your world. You are responsible for the way you think about the other. Remember, the other person is not responsible for the way you think about him. Your thoughts are reproduced. What are you thinking now about the other fellow?
7. Become emotionally mature and permit other people to differ from you. They have a perfect right to disagree with you, and you have the same freedom to disagree with them. You can disagree without being disagreeable.

8. Animals pick up your fear vibrations and snap at you. If you love animals, they will never attack you. Many undisciplined human beings are just as sensitive as dogs, cats, and other animals.
9. Your inner speech, representing your silent thoughts and feelings, is experienced in the reactions of others toward you.
10. Wish for the other what you wish for yourself. This is the key to harmonious human relations.
11. Change your concept and estimate of your employer. Feel and know he is practicing the Golden Rule and the Law of Love, and he will respond accordingly.
12. The other person cannot annoy you or irritate you except you permit him. Your thought is creative; you can bless him. If someone calls you a skunk, you have the freedom to say to the other, "God's peace fills your soul."
13. Love is the answer to getting along with others. Love is understanding, good will, and respecting the divinity of the other.
14. You would not hate a hunchback or cripple. You would have compassion. Have compassion and understanding for mental hunchbacks who have been conditioned negatively. To understand all is to forgive all.
15. Rejoice in the success, promotion, and good fortune of the other. In doing so, you attract good fortune to yourself.
16. Never yield to emotional scenes and tantrums of others. Appeasement never wins. Do not be a doormat. Adhere to that which is right. Stick to your ideal, knowing that the mental outlook which gives you peace, happiness, and joy is right, good, and true. What blesses you, blesses all.
18. All you owe any person in the world is love, and love is wishing for everyone what you wish for yourself—health, happiness, and all the blessings of life.

CHAPTER SEVENTEEN

HOW TO USE YOUR SUBCONSCIOUS MIND FOR FORGIVENESS

Life plays no favorites. God is Life, and this Life-Principle is flowing through you this moment. God loves to express Himself as harmony, peace, beauty, joy, and abundance through you. This is called the will of God or the tendency of Life.

If you set up resistance in your mind to the flow of Life through you, this emotional congestion will get snarled up in your subconscious mind and cause all kinds of negative conditions. God has nothing to do with unhappy or chaotic conditions in the world. All these conditions are brought about by man's negative and destructive thinking. Therefore, it is silly to blame God for your trouble or sickness.

Many persons habitually set up mental resistance to the flow of Life by accusing and reproaching God for the sin, sickness, and suffering of mankind. Others cast the blame on God for their pains, aches, loss of loved ones, personal tragedies, and accidents. They are angry at God, and they believe He is responsible for their misery.

As long as people entertain such negative concepts about God, they will experience the automatic negative reactions from their subconscious minds. Actually, such people do not know that they are punishing themselves. They must see the truth, find release, and give up all condemnation, resentment, and anger against anyone or any power outside themselves. Otherwise, they cannot go forward into a healthy, happy, or creative activity. The minute these people entertain a God of love in their minds and hearts, and when they believe that God is their Loving Father who watches over them, cares for them, guides them, sustains and strengthens them, this concept and belief about God or the Life-Principle will be accepted by their subconscious mind, and they will find themselves blessed in countless ways.

LIFE ALWAYS FORGIVES YOU

Life forgives you when you cut your finger. The subconscious intelligence within you sets about immediately to repair it. New cells build bridges over the cut. Should you take some tainted food by error, Life forgives you and causes you to regurgitate it in order to preserve you. If you burn your hand, the Life-Principle reduces the edema and congestion, and gives you new skin, tissue, and cells. Life holds no grudges against you, and it is always forgiving you. Life brings you back to health, vitality, harmony, and peace, if you co-operate by thinking in harmony with nature. Negative, hurtful memories, bitterness, and ill will clutter up and impede the free flow of the Life-Principle in you.

HOW HE BANISHED THAT FEELING OF GUILT

I knew a man who worked every night until about one o'clock in the morning. He paid no attention to his two boys or his wife. He was always too busy working hard. He thought people should pat him on the back because he was working so arduously and persistently past midnight every night. He had a blood pressure of over two hundred and was full of guilt. Unconsciously, he proceeded to punish himself by hard work and he completely ignored his children. A normal man does not do that. He is interested in his boys and in their development. He does not shut his wife out of his world.

I explained to him why he was working so arduously, "There is something eating you inside, otherwise, you would not act this way. You are punishing yourself, and you have to learn to forgive yourself." He did have a deep sense of guilt. It was toward a brother.

I explained to him that God was not punishing him, but that he was punishing himself. For example, if you misuse the laws of life, you will suffer accordingly. If you put your hand on a naked charged wire, you will get burned. The forces of nature are not evil; it is your use of them that determines whether they have a good or evil effect. Electricity is not evil; it depends on how you use it, whether to burn down a structure or light up a home. The only sin is ignorance of the law, and the only punishment is the automatic reaction of man's misuse of the law.

If you misuse the principle of chemistry, you may blow up the office or the factory. If you strike your hand on a board, you may cause your hand to bleed. The board is not for that purpose. Its purpose may be to lean upon or to support your feet.

This man realized that God does not condemn or punish anyone, and that all his suffering was due to the reaction of his subconscious mind to his own negative and destructive thinking. He had cheated his brother at one time, and the brother had now passed on. Still, he was full of remorse and guilt.

I asked him, "Would you cheat your brother now?"

He said, "No."

"Did you feel you were justified at the time?"

His reply was, "Yes."

"But, you would not do it now?"

He added, "No, I am helping others to know how to live."

I added the following comment, "You have a greater reason and understanding now.

Forgiveness is to forgive yourself. Forgiveness is getting your thoughts in line with the divine law of harmony. Self-condemnation is called hell (bondage and restriction); forgiveness is called heaven (harmony and peace)."

The burden of guilt and self-condemnation was lifted from his mind, and he had a complete healing. The doctor tested his blood pressure, and it had become normal. The explanation was the cure.

A MURDERER LEARNED TO FORGIVE HIMSELF

A man who murdered his brother in Europe visited me many years ago. He was suffering from great mental anguish and torture believing that God must punish him. He explained that his brother had been having an affair with his wife, and that he had shot him on the spur of the moment. This had happened about fifteen years previous to his interview with me. In the meantime, this man had married an American girl and had been blessed with three lovely children. He was in a position where he helped many people, and he was a transformed man.

My explanation to him was that physically and psychologically he was not the same man who shot his brother, since scientists inform us that every cell of our bodies changes every eleven months. Moreover, mentally and spiritually he was a new man. He was now full of love and good will for humanity. The "old" man who committed the crime fifteen years before was mentally and spiritually dead. Actually, he was condemning an innocent man!

This explanation had a profound effect upon him, and he said it was as if a great weight had been lifted from his mind. He realized the significance of the following truth in the Bible: *Come now, let us reason together, saith the Lord: though your sins be as scarlet, they shall be as white as snow; though they be red like crimson, they shall be as wool.* ISAIAH 1:18.

CRITICISM CANNOT HURT YOU WITHOUT YOUR CONSENT

A schoolteacher told me that one of her associates criticized a speech she had given, saying to her that she spoke too fast, she swallowed some of her words, she couldn't be heard, her diction was poor, and her speech ineffective. This teacher was furious and full of resentment toward her critic.

She admitted to me that the criticisms were just. Her first reaction was really childish, and she agreed that the letter was really a blessing and a marvelous corrective. She proceeded immediately to supplement her deficiencies in her speech by enrolling in a course in public speaking at City College. She wrote and thanked the writer of the note for her interest, expressing appreciation for her conclusions and findings which enabled the teacher to correct the matter at once.

HOW TO BE COMPASSIONATE

Suppose none of the things mentioned in the letter had been true of the teacher. The latter would have realized that her class material had upset the prejudices, superstitions, or narrow sectarian beliefs of the writer of the note, and that a psychologically ill person was simply pouring forth her resentment because a psychological boil had been hurt.

To understand this fact is to be compassionate. The next logical step would be to pray for the other person's peace, harmony, and understanding. You cannot be hurt when you know that you are master of your thoughts, reactions, and emotions. Emotions follow thoughts, and you have the power to reject all thoughts which may disturb or upset you.

LEFT AT THE ALTAR

Some years ago I visited a church to perform a marriage ceremony. The young man did not appear, and at the end of two hours, the bride-to-be shed a few tears, and then said to me, "I prayed for divine guidance. This might be the answer for He never faileth."

That was her reaction—faith in God and all things good. She had no bitterness in her heart because as she said, "It must not have been right action because my prayer was for right action for both of us." Someone else having a similar experience would have gone into a tantrum, have had an emotional fit, required sedation, and perhaps needed hospitalization.

Tune in with the infinite intelligence within your subconscious depths, trusting the answer in the same way that you trusted your mother when she held you in her arms. This is how you can acquire poise and mental and emotional health.

IT IS WRONG TO MARRY. SEX IS EVIL AND I AM EVIL

Some time ago I talked to a young lady aged twenty-two. She was taught that it was a sin to dance, to play cards, to swim, and to go out with men. She was threatened by her mother who told her she would burn eternally in hell-fire if she disobeyed her will and her religious teachings. This girl wore a black dress and black stockings. She wore no rouge, lipstick, or any form of make-up because her mother said that these things were sinful. Her mother told her that all men were evil, and that sex was of the devil and simply diabolic debauchery.

This girl had to learn how to forgive herself as she was full of guilt. To forgive means to give for. She had to give up all these false beliefs for the truths of life and a new estimate of herself. When she went out with young men in the office where she worked, she had a deep sense of guilt and thought that God would punish her. Several eligible young men proposed to her, but she said to me, "It is wrong to marry. Sex is evil and I am evil." This was her conscience or early conditioning speaking.

She came to me once weekly for about ten weeks, and I taught her the workings of the conscious and subconscious mind as set forth in this book. This young girl gradually came to see that she had been completely brainwashed, mesmerized, and conditioned by an ignorant, superstitious, bigoted, and frustrated mother. She broke away completely from her family and started to live a wonderful life.

At my suggestion she dressed up and had her hair attended to. She took lessons in dancing from a *man*, and she also took driving lessons. She learned to swim, play cards, and had a number of dates. She began to love life. She prayed for a divine companion by claiming that Infinite Spirit would attract to her a man who harmonized with her thoroughly. Eventually this came to pass. As she left my office one evening, there was a man waiting to see me and I casually introduced them. They are now married and harmonize with each other perfectly.

FORGIVENESS IS NECESSARY FOR HEALING

And when ye stand praying, forgive, if ye have ought against any . . . MARK 11:25.

Forgiveness of others is essential to mental peace and radiant health. You must forgive everyone who has ever hurt you if you want perfect health and happiness. Forgive yourself by getting your thoughts in harmony with divine law and order. You cannot really forgive yourself completely until you have forgiven others first. To refuse to forgive yourself is nothing more or less than spiritual pride or ignorance.

In the psychosomatic field of medicine today, it is being constantly stressed that resentment, condemnation of others, remorse, and hostility are behind a host of maladies ranging from arthritis to cardiac disease. They point out that these sick people, who were hurt, mistreated, deceived, or injured, were full of resentment and hatred for those who hurt them. This caused inflamed and festering wounds in their subconscious minds. There is only one remedy. They have to cut out and discard their hurts, and the one and only sure way is by forgiveness.

FORGIVENESS IS LOVE IN ACTION

The essential ingredient in the art of forgiveness is the willingness to forgive. If you sincerely desire to forgive the other, you are fifty-one percent over the hurdle. I feel sure you know that to forgive the other does not necessarily mean that you like him or want to associate with him. You cannot be compelled to like someone, neither can a government legislate good will, love, peace, or tolerance. It is quite impossible to like people because someone in Washington issues an edict to that effect. We can, however, love people without liking them.

The Bible says, *Love ye one another.* This, anyone can do who really wants to do it. Love means that you wish for the other health, happiness, peace, joy, and all the blessings of life. There is only one prerequisite, and that is sincerity. You are not being magnanimous when you forgive, you are really being selfish, because what you wish for the other, you are actually wishing for yourself. The reason is that you are thinking it and you are feeling it. As you think and feel, so are you. Could anything be simpler than that?

TECHNIQUE OF FORGIVENESS

The following is a simple method which works wonders in your life as you practice it: Quiet your mind, relax, and let go. Think of God and His love for you, and then affirm, "I fully and freely forgive (mention the name of the offender); I release him mentally and spiritually. I completely forgive everything connected with the matter in question. I am free, and he/she is free. It is a marvelous feeling. It is my day of general amnesty. I release anybody and everybody who has ever hurt me, and I wish for each and everyone health, happiness, peace, and all the blessings of life. I do this freely, joyously, and lovingly, and whenever I think of the person or persons who hurt me, I say, 'I have released you, and all the blessings of life are yours.' I am free and you are free. It is wonderful!"

The great secret of true forgiveness is that once you have forgiven the person, it is unnecessary to repeat the prayer. Whenever the person comes to your mind, or the particular hurt happens to enter your mind, wish the delinquent well, and say, "Peace be to you." Do this as often as the thought enters your mind. You will find that after a few days the thought of the person or experience will return less and less often, until it fades into nothingness.

THE ACID TEST FOR FORGIVENESS

There is an acid test for gold. There is also an acid test for forgiveness. If I should tell you something wonderful about someone who has wronged you, cheated you, or defrauded you, and you sizzled at hearing the good news about this person, the roots of hatred would still be in your subconscious mind, playing havoc with you.

Let us suppose you had a painful abscess on your jaw a year ago, and you told me about it. I would casually ask you if you had any pain now. You would automatically say, "Of course not, I have a memory of it but no pain." That is the whole story. You may have a memory of the incident but no sting or hurt anymore. This is the acid test, and you must meet it psychologically and spiritually, otherwise, you are simply deceiving yourself and not practicing the true art of forgiveness.

TO UNDERSTAND ALL IS TO FORGIVE ALL

When man understands the creative law of his own mind, he ceases to blame other people and conditions for making or marring his life. He knows that his own thoughts and feelings create his destiny. Furthermore, he is aware that externals are not the causes and conditioners of his life and his experiences. To think that others can mar your happiness, that you are the football of a cruel fate, that you must oppose and fight others for a living—all these and others like them are untenable when you understand that thoughts are things. The Bible says the same thing. *For as a man thinketh in his heart, so is he.* PROVERBS 23:7.

SUMMARY OF YOUR AIDS TO FORGIVENESS

1. God, or Life, is no respecter of persons. Life plays no favorites. Life, or God, seems to favor you when you align yourself with the principle of harmony, health, joy, and peace.
2. God, or Life, never sends disease, sickness, accident, or suffering. We bring these things on ourselves by our own negative destructive thinking based upon the law *as we sow, so shall we reap.*
3. Your concept of God is the most important thing in your life. If you really believe in a God of love, your subconscious mind will respond in countless blessings to you. Believe in a God of love.
4. Life, or God, holds no grudge against you. Life never condemns you. Life heals a severe cut on your hand. Life forgives you if you burn your finger. It reduces the edema and restores the part to wholeness and perfection.
5. Your guilt complex is a false concept of God and Life. God, or Life, does not

punish or judge you. You do this to yourself by your false beliefs, negative thinking, and self-condemnation.

6. God, or Life, does not condemn or punish you. The forces of nature are not evil. The effect of their use depends on how you use the power within you. You can use electricity to kill someone or to light the house. You can use water to drown a child, or quench his thirst. Good and evil come right back to the thought and purpose in man's own mind.
7. God, or life, never punishes. Man punishes himself by his false concepts of God, Life, and the Universe. His thoughts are creative, and he creates his own misery.
8. If another criticizes you, and these faults are within you, rejoice, give thanks, and appreciate the comments. This gives you the opportunity to correct the particular fault.
9. You cannot be hurt by criticism when you know that you are master of your thoughts, reactions, and emotions. This gives you the opportunity to pray and bless the other, thereby blessing yourself.
10. When you pray for guidance and right action, take what comes. Realize it is good and very good. Then there is no cause for self-pity, criticism, or hatred.
11. There is nothing good or bad, but thinking makes it so. There is no evil in sex, the desire for food, wealth, or true expression. It depends on how you use these urges, desires, or aspirations. Your desire for food can be met without killing someone for a loaf of bread.
12. Resentment, hatred, ill will, and hostility are behind a host of maladies. Forgive yourself and everybody else by pouring out love, life, joy, and good will to all those who have hurt you. Continue until such time as you meet them in your mind and you are at peace with them.

13. To forgive is to *give something for.* Give love, peace, joy, wisdom, and all the blessings of life to the other, until there is no sting left in your mind. This is really the acid test of forgiveness.
14. Let us suppose you had an abscess in your jaw about a year ago. It was very painful. Ask yourself if it is painful now. The answer is in the negative. Likewise, if someone has hurt you, lied about and vilified you, and said all manner of evil about you, is your thought of that person negative? Do you sizzle when he or she comes into your mind? If so, the roots of hatred are still there, playing havoc with you and your good. The only way is to wither them with love by wishing for the person all the blessings of life, until you can meet the person in your mind, and you can sincerely react with a benediction of peace and good will. This is the meaning of *forgive until seventy times seven.*

CHAPTER EIGHTEEN

HOW YOUR SUBCONSCIOUS REMOVES MENTAL BLOCKS

The solution lies within the problem. The answer is in every question. If you are presented with a difficult situation and you cannot see your way clear, the best procedure is to assume that infinite intelligence within your subconscious mind knows all and sees all, has the answer, and is revealing it to you now. Your new mental attitude that the creative intelligence is bringing about a happy solution will enable you to find the answer. Rest assured that such an attitude of mind will bring order, peace, and meaning to all your undertakings.

HOW TO BREAK OR BUILD A HABIT

You are a creature of habit. Habit is the function of your subconscious mind. You learned to swim, ride a bicycle, dance, and drive a car by consciously doing these things over and over again until they established tracks in your subconscious mind. Then, the automatic habit action of your subconscious mind took over. This is sometimes called second nature, which is a reaction of your subconscious mind to your thinking and acting.

You are free to choose a good habit or a bad habit. If you repeat a negative thought or act over a period of time, you will be under the compulsion of a habit. The law of your subconscious is compulsion.

HOW HE BROKE A BAD HABIT

Mr. Jones said to me, "An uncontrollable urge to drink seizes me, and I remain drunk for two weeks at a time. I can't give up this terrible habit."

Time and time again these experiences had occurred to this unfortunate man. He had grown into the habit of drinking to excess. Although he had started drinking of his own initiative, he also began to realize that he could change the habit and establish a new one. He said that while through his willpower he was able to suppress his desires temporarily, his continued efforts to suppress the many urges only made matters worse. His repeated failures convinced him that he was hopeless and powerless to control his urge or obsession. This idea of being powerless operated as a powerful suggestion to his subconscious mind and aggravated his weakness, making his life a succession of failures.

I taught him to harmonize the functions of the conscious and subconscious mind. When these two co-operate, the idea or desire implanted in the subconscious mind is realized. His reasoning mind agreed that if the old habit path or track had carried him into trouble, he could consciously form a new path to freedom, sobriety, and peace of mind. He knew that his destructive habit was automatic, but since it was acquired through his conscious choice, he realized that if he had been conditioned negatively, he also could be conditioned positively. As a result, he ceased thinking of the fact that he was powerless to overcome the habit. Moreover, he understood clearly that there was no obstacle to his healing other than his own thought. Therefore, there was no occasion for great mental effort or mental coercion.

THE POWER OF HIS MENTAL PICTURE

This man acquired a practice of relaxing his body and getting into a relaxed, drowsy, meditative state. Then he filled his mind with the picture of the desired end, knowing his subconscious mind could bring it about the easiest way. He imagined his daughter congratulating him on his freedom, and saying to him, "Daddy, it's wonderful to have you home!" He had lost his family through drink. He was not allowed to visit them, and his wife would not speak to him.

Regularly, systematically, he used to sit down and meditate in the way outlined. When his attention wandered, he made it a habit to immediately recall the mental picture of his daughter with her smile and the scene of his home enlivened by her cheerful voice. All this brought about a reconditioning of his mind. It was a gradual process. He kept it up. He persevered knowing that sooner or later he would establish a new habit pattern in his subconscious mind.

I told him that he could liken his conscious mind to a camera, that his subconscious mind was the sensitive plate on which he registered and impressed the picture. This made a profound impression on him, and his whole aim was to firmly impress the picture on his mind and develop it there. Films are developed in the dark; likewise, mental pictures are developed in the darkroom of the subconscious mind.

FOCUSED ATTENTION

Realizing that his conscious mind was simply a camera, he used no effort. There was no mental struggle. He quietly adjusted his thoughts and focused his attention on the scene before him until he gradually became identified with the picture. He became absorbed in the mental atmosphere, repeating the mental movie frequently. There was no room for doubt that a healing would follow. When there was any temptation to drink, he would switch his imagination from any reveries of drinking bouts to the feeling of being at home with his family. He was successful because he confidently expected to experience the picture he was developing in his mind. Today he is president of a multimillion-dollar concern and is radiantly happy.

HE SAID A JINX WAS FOLLOWING HIM

Mr. Block said that he had been making an annual income of $20,000, but for the past three months all doors seemed to jam tightly. He brought clients up to the point where they were about to sign on the dotted line, and then at the eleventh hour the door closed. He added that perhaps a jinx was following him.

In discussing the matter with Mr. Block, I discovered that three months previously he had become very irritated, annoyed, and resentful toward a dentist who, after he had promised to sign a contract, had withdrawn at the last moment. He began to live in the unconscious fear that other clients would do the same, thereby setting up a history of frustration, hostility, and obstacles. He gradually built up in his mind a belief in obstruction and last minute cancellations until a vicious circle had been established. *What I fear most has come upon me.* Mr. Block realized that the trouble was in his own mind, and that it was essential to change his mental attitude.

His run of so-called misfortune was broken in the following way: "I realize I am one with the infinite intelligence of my subconscious mind which knows no obstacle, difficulty, or delay. I live in the joyous expectancy of the best. My deeper mind responds to my thoughts. I know that the work of the infinite power of my subconscious cannot be hindered. Infinite intelligence always finishes successfully whatever it begins. Creative wisdom works through me bringing all my plans and purposes to completion. Whatever

I start, I bring to a successful conclusion. My aim in life is to give wonderful service, and all those whom I contact are blessed by what I have to offer. All my work comes to full fruition in divine order."

He repeated this prayer every morning before going to call on his customers, and he also prayed each night prior to sleep. In a short time he had established a new habit pattern in his subconscious mind, and he was back in his old accustomed stride as a successful salesman.

HOW MUCH DO YOU WANT WHAT YOU WANT?

A young man asked Socrates how he could get wisdom. Socrates replied, "Come with me." He took the lad to a river, pushed the boy's head under the water, held it there until the boy was gasping for air, then relaxed and released his head. When the boy regained his composure, he asked him, "What did you desire most when you were under water?"

"I wanted air," said the boy.

Socrates said to him, "When you want wisdom as much as you wanted air when you were immersed in the water, you will receive it."

Likewise, when you really have an intense desire to overcome any block in your life, and you come to a clear-cut decision that there is a way out, and that is the course you wish to follow, then victory and triumph are assured.

If you really want peace of mind and inner calm, you will get it. Regardless of how unjustly you have been treated, or how unfair the boss has been, or what a mean scoundrel someone has proved to be, all this makes no difference to you when you awaken to your mental and spiritual powers. You know what you want, and you will definitely refuse to let the thieves (thoughts) of hatred, anger, hostility, and ill will rob you of peace, harmony, health, and happiness. You cease to become upset by people, conditions, news, and events by identifying your thoughts immediately with your aim in life. Your aim is peace, health, inspiration, harmony, and abundance. Feel a river of peace flowing through you now. Your thought is the immaterial and invisible power, and you choose to let it bless, inspire, and give you peace.

WHY HE COULD NOT BE HEALED

This is a case history of a married man with four children who was supporting and secretly living with another woman during his business trips. He was ill, nervous, irritable, and cantankerous, and he could not sleep without drugs. The doctor's medicine failed to bring down his high blood pressure of over two hundred. He had pains in numerous organs of his body which doctors could not diagnose or relieve. To make matters worse, he was drinking heavily.

The cause of all this was a deep unconscious sense of guilt. He had violated the marriage vows, and this troubled him. The religious creed he was brought up on was deeply lodged in his subconscious mind, and he drank excessively to heal the wound of guilt. Some invalids take morphine and codeine for severe pains; he was taking alcohol for the pain or wound in his mind. It was the old story of adding fuel to the fire.

THE EXPLANATION AND THE CURE

He listened to the explanation of how his mind worked. He faced his problem, looked at it, and gave up his dual role. He knew that his drinking was an unconscious attempt to escape. The hidden cause lodged in his subconscious mind had to be eradicated; then the healing would follow.

He began to impress his subconscious mind three or four times a day by using the following prayer: "My mind is full of peace, poise, balance, and equilibrium. The infinite lies stretched in smiling repose within me. I am not afraid of anything in the past, the present, or the future. The infinite intelligence of my subconscious mind leads, guides, and directs me in all ways. I now meet every situation with faith, poise, calmness, and confidence. I am now completely free from the habit. My mind is full of inner peace, freedom, and joy. I forgive myself; then I am forgiven. Peace, sobriety, and confidence reign supreme in my mind."

He repeated this prayer frequently as outlined, being fully aware of what he was doing and why he was doing it. Knowing what he was doing gave him the necessary faith and confidence. I explained to him that as he spoke these statements out loud, slowly, lovingly, and meaningfully, they would gradually sink down into his subconscious mind. Like seeds, they would grow after their kind. These truths, on which he concentrated, went in through his eyes, his ears heard the sound, and the healing vibrations of these words reached his subconscious mind and obliterated all the negative mental patterns which caused all the trouble. Light dispels darkness. The constructive thought destroys the negative thought. He became a transformed man within a month.

REFUSING TO ADMIT IT

If you are an alcoholic or drug addict; admit it. Do not dodge the issue. Many people remain alcoholics because they refuse to admit it.

Your disease is an instability, an inner fear. You are refusing to face life, and so you try to escape your responsibilities through the bottle. As an alcoholic you have no free will, although you think you have, and you may even boast about your willpower. If you are a habitual drunkard and say bravely, "I will not touch it anymore," you have no power to make this assertion come true, because you do not know where to locate the power.

You are living in a psychological prison of your own making, and you are bound by your beliefs, opinions, training, and environmental influences. Like most people, you are a creature of habit. You are conditioned to react the way you do.

BUILDING IN THE IDEA OF FREEDOM

You can build the idea of freedom and peace of mind into your mentality so that it reaches your subconscious depths. The latter, being all-powerful, will free you from all desire for alcohol. Then, you will have the new understanding of how your mind works, and you can truly back up your statement and prove the truth to yourself.

FIFTY-ONE PERCENT HEALED

If you have a keen desire to free yourself from any destructive habit, you are fifty-one percent healed already. When you have a greater desire to give up the bad habit than to continue it, you will not experience too much difficulty in gaining complete freedom.

Whatever thought you anchor the mind upon, the latter magnifies. If you engage the mind on the concept of freedom (freedom from the habit) and peace of mind, and if you keep it focused on this new direction of attention, you generate feelings and emotions which gradually emotionalize the concept of freedom and peace. Whatever idea you emotionalize is accepted by your subconscious and brought to pass.

THE LAW OF SUBSTITUTION

Realize that something good can come out of your suffering. You have not suffered in vain. However, it is foolish to continue to suffer.

If you continue as an alcoholic, it will bring about mental and physical deterioration and decay. Realize that the power in your subconscious is backing you up. Even though you may be seized with melancholia, you should begin to imagine the joy of freedom that is in store for you. This is the law of substitution. Your imagination took you to the bottle; let it take you now to freedom and peace of mind. You will suffer a little bit, but it is for a constructive purpose. You will bear it like a mother in the pangs of childbirth, and you will, likewise, bring forth a child of the mind. Your subconscious will give birth to sobriety.

CAUSE OF ALCOHOLISM

The real cause of alcoholism is negative and destructive thinking; for as a man thinketh, so is he. The alcoholic has a deep sense of inferiority, inadequacy, defeat, and frustration, usually accompanied by a deep inner hostility. He has countless alibis as to his reason for drinking, but the sole reason is in his *thought life.*

THREE MAGIC STEPS

The first step: Get still; quiet the wheels of the mind. Enter into a sleepy, drowsy state. In this relaxed, peaceful, receptive state, you are preparing for the second step.

The second step: Take a brief phrase, which can readily be graven on the memory, and repeat it over and over as a lullaby. Use the phrase, "Sobriety and peace of mind are mine now, and I give thanks." To prevent the mind from wandering, repeat it aloud or sketch its pronunciation with the lips and tongue as you say it mentally. This helps its entry into the subconscious mind. Do this for five minutes or more. You will find a deep emotional response.

The third step: Just before going to sleep, practice what Johann von Goethe, German author, used to do. Imagine a friend, a loved one in front of you. Your eyes are closed, you are relaxed and at peace. The loved one or friend is subjectively present, and is saying to you, "Congratulations!" You see the smile; you hear the voice. You mentally touch the hand; it is all real and vivid. The word *congratulations* implies complete freedom. Hear it over and over again until you get the subconscious reaction which satisfies.

KEEP ON KEEPING ON

When fear knocks at the door of your mind, or when worry, anxiety, and doubt cross your mind, behold your vision, your goal. Think of the infinite power within your subconscious mind, which you can generate by your thinking and imagining, and this will give you confidence, power, and courage. Keep on, persevere, *until the day breaks, and the shadows flee away.*

REVIEW YOUR THOUGHT POWER

1. The solution lies within the problem. The answer is in every question. Infinite intelligence responds to you as you call upon it with faith and confidence.
2. Habit is the function of your subconscious mind. There is no greater evidence of the marvelous power of your subconscious than the force and sway habit holds in your life. You are a creature of habit.
3. You form habit patterns in your subconscious mind by repeating a thought and act over and over again until it establishes tracks in the subconscious mind

and becomes automatic, such as swimming, dancing, typing, walking, driving your car, etc.

4. You have freedom to choose. You can choose a good habit or a bad habit. Prayer is a good habit.
5. Whatever mental picture, backed by faith, you behold in your conscious mind, your subconscious mind will bring to pass.
6. The only obstacle to your success and achievement is your own thought or mental image.
7. When your attention wanders, bring it back to the contemplation of your good or goal. Make a habit of this. This is called disciplining the mind.
8. Your conscious mind is the camera, and your subconscious mind is the sensitive plate on which you register or impress the picture.
9. The only jinx that follows anyone is a fear thought repeated over and over in the mind. Break the jinx by knowing that whatever you start you will bring to a conclusion in divine order. Picture the happy ending and sustain it with confidence.
10. To form a new habit, you must be convinced that it is desirable. When your desire to give up the bad habit is greater than your desire to continue, you are fifty-one percent healed already.
11. The statements of others cannot hurt you except through your own thoughts and mental participation. Identify yourself with your aim which is peace, harmony, and joy. You are the only thinker in your universe.
12. Excessive drinking is an unconscious desire to escape. The cause of alcoholism is negative and destructive thinking. The cure is to think of freedom, sobriety, and perfection, and to feel the thrill of accomplishment.
13. Many people remain alcoholics because they refuse to admit it.

14. The law of your subconscious mind, which held you in bondage and inhibited your freedom of action, will give you freedom and happiness. It depends on how you use it.
15. Your imagination took you to the bottle; let it take you to freedom by imagining you are free.
16. The real cause of alcoholism is negative and destructive thinking. *As a man thinketh in his heart* [subconscious mind], *so is he.*
17. When fear knocks at the door of your mind, let faith in God and all things good open the door.

CHAPTER NINETEEN

HOW TO USE YOUR SUBCONSCIOUS MIND TO REMOVE FEAR

One of our students told me that he was invited to speak at a banquet. He said he was panic-stricken at the thought of speaking before a thousand people. He overcame his fear this way: For several nights he sat down in an armchair for about five minutes and said to himself slowly, quietly, and positively, "I am going to master this fear. I am overcoming it now. I speak with poise and confidence. I am relaxed and at ease." He operated a definite law of mind and overcame his fear.

The subconscious mind is amenable to suggestion and is controlled by suggestion. When you still your mind and relax, the thoughts of your conscious mind sink down into the subconscious through a process similar to osmosis, whereby fluids separated by a porous membrane intermingle. As these positive seeds, or thoughts, sink into the subconscious area, they grow after their kind, and you become poised, serene, and calm.

MAN'S GREATEST ENEMY

It is said that fear is man's greatest enemy. Fear is behind failure, sickness, and poor human relations. Millions of people are afraid of the past, the future, old age, insanity, and death. Fear is a thought in your mind, and you are afraid of your own thoughts.

A little boy can be paralyzed with fear when he is told there is a boogie man under his bed who is going to take him away. When his father turns on the light and shows him there is no boogie man, he is freed from fear. The fear in the mind of the boy was as real as if there really was a boogie man there. He was healed of a false thought in his mind. The thing he feared did not exist. Likewise, most of your fears have no reality. They are merely a conglomeration of sinister shadows, and shadows have no reality.

DO THE THING YOU FEAR

Ralph Waldo Emerson, philosopher and poet, said, "Do the thing you are afraid to do, and the death of fear is certain."

There was a time when the writer of this chapter was filled with unutterable fear when standing before an audience. The way I overcame it was to stand before the audience, do the thing I was afraid to do, and the death of fear was certain.

When you affirm positively that you are going to master your fears, and you come to a definite decision in your conscious mind, you release the power of the subconscious, which flows in response to the nature of your thought.

BANISHING STAGE FRIGHT

A young lady was invited to an audition. She had been looking forward to the interview. However, on three previous occasions, she had failed miserably due to stage fright.

She possessed a very good voice, but she was certain that when the time came for her to sing, she would be seized with stage fright. The subconscious mind takes your fears as a request, proceeds to manifest them, and brings them into your experience. On three previous auditions she sang wrong notes, and she finally broke down and cried. The cause, as previously outlined, was an involuntary autosuggestion, i.e., a silent fear thought emotionalized and subjectified.

She overcame it by the following technique: Three times a day she isolated herself in a room. She sat down comfortably in an armchair, relaxed her body, and closed her eyes. She stilled her mind and body to the best of her ability. Physical inertia favors passivity and renders the mind more receptive to suggestion. She counteracted the fear suggestion by its converse, saying to herself, "I sing beautifully. I am poised, serene, confident, and calm."

She repeated the words slowly, quietly, and with feeling from five to ten times at each sitting. She had three such "sittings" every day and one immediately prior to sleep at night. At the end of a week she was completely poised and confident, and gave a definitely outstanding audition. Carry out the above procedure, and the death of fear is certain.

FEAR OF FAILURE

Occasionally young men from the local university come to see me, as well as schoolteachers, who often seem to suffer from suggestive amnesia at examinations. The complaint is always the same: "I know the answers after the examination is over, but I can't remember the answers during the examination."

The idea, which realizes itself, is the one to which we invariably give concentrated attention. I find that each one is obsessed with the idea of failure. Fear is behind the temporary amnesia, and it is the cause of the whole experience.

One young medical student was the most brilliant person in his class, yet he found himself failing to answer simple questions at the time of written or oral examinations. I explained to him that the reason was he had been worrying and was fearful for several days previous to the examination. These negative thoughts became charged with fear.

Thoughts enveloped in the powerful emotion of fear are realized in the subconscious mind. In other words, this young man was requesting his subconscious mind to see to it that he failed, and that is exactly what it did. On the day of the examination he found himself stricken with what is called, in psychological circles, suggestive amnesia.

HOW HE OVERCAME THE FEAR

He learned that his subconscious mind was the storehouse of memory, and that it had a perfect record of all he had heard and read during his medical training. Moreover, he learned that the subconscious mind was responsive and reciprocal. The way to be *en rapport* with it was to be relaxed, peaceful, and confident.

Every night and morning he began to imagine his mother congratulating him on his wonderful record. He would hold an imaginary letter from her in his hand. As he began to contemplate the happy result, he called forth a corresponding or reciprocal response or reaction in himself. The all-wise and omnipotent power of the subconscious took over, dictated, and directed his conscious mind accordingly. He imagined the end, thereby willing the means to the realization of the end. Following this procedure, he had no trouble passing subsequent examinations. In other words, the subjective wisdom took over, compelling him to give an excellent account of himself.

FEAR OF WATER, MOUNTAINS, CLOSED PLACES, ETC.

There are many people who are afraid to go into an elevator, climb mountains, or even swim in the water. It may well be that the individual had unpleasant experiences in the water in his youth, such as having been thrown forcibly into the water without being able to swim. He might have been forcibly detained in an elevator, which failed to function properly, causing resultant fear of closed places.

I had an experience when I was about ten years of age. I accidentally fell into a pool and went down three times. I can still remember the dark water engulfing my head, and my gasping for air until another boy pulled me out at the last moment. This experience sank into my subconscious mind, and for years I feared the water.

An elderly psychologist said to me, "Go down to the swimming pool, look at the water, and say out loud in strong tones, 'I am going to master you. I can dominate you.' Then go into the water, take lessons, and overcome it." This I did, and I mastered the water. Do not permit water to master you. Remember, you are the master of the water.

When I assumed a new attitude of mind, the omnipotent power of the subconscious responded, giving me strength, faith, and confidence, and enabling me to overcome my fear.

MASTER TECHNIQUE FOR OVERCOMING ANY PARTICULAR FEAR

The following is a process and technique for overcoming fear which I teach from the patform. It works like a charm. Try it!

Suppose you are afraid of the water, a mountain, an interview, an audition, or you fear closed places. If you are afraid of swimming, begin now to sit still for five or ten minutes three or four times a day, and imagine you are swimming. Actually, you are swimming in your mind. It is a subjective experience. Mentally you have projected yourself into the water. You feel the chill of the water and the movement of your arms and legs. It is all real, vivid, and a joyous activity of the mind. It is not idle daydreaming, for you know that what you are experiencing in your imagination will be developed in your subconscious mind. Then you will be compelled to express the image and likeness of the picture you impressed on your deeper mind. This is the law of the subconscious.

You could apply the same technique if you are afraid of mountains or high places. Imagine you are climbing the mountain, feel the reality of it all, enjoy the scenery, knowing that as you continue to do this mentally, you will do it physically with ease and comfort.

HE BLESSED THE ELEVATOR

I knew an executive of a large corporation who was terrified to ride in an elevator. He would walk up five flights of stairs to his office every morning. He said that he began to bless the elevator every night and several times a day. He finally overcame his fear. This was how he blessed the elevator: "The elevator in our building is a wonderful idea. It came out of the universal mind. It is a boon and a blessing to all our employees. It gives wonderful service. It operates in divine order. I ride in it in peace and joy. I remain silent now while the currents of life, love, and understanding flow through the patterns of my thought. In my imagination I am now in the elevator, and I step out into my office. The elevator is full of our employees. I talk to them, and they are friendly, joyous, and free. It is a wonderful experience of freedom, faith, and confidence. I give thanks."

He continued this prayer for about ten days, and on the eleventh day, he walked into the elevator with other members of the organization and felt completely free.

NORMAL AND ABNORMAL FEAR

Man is born only with two fears, the fear of falling and the fear of noise. These are a sort of alarm system given you by nature as a means of self-preservation. Normal fear is good. You hear an automobile coming down the road, and you step aside to survive. The momentary fear of being run over is overcome by your action. All other fears were given to you by parents, relatives, teachers, and all those who influenced your early years.

ABNORMAL FEAR

Abnormal fear takes place when man lets his imagination run riot. I knew a woman who was invited to go on a trip around the world by plane. She began to cut out of the newspapers all reports of airplane catastrophes. She pictured herself going down in the ocean, being drowned, etc. This is abnormal fear. Had she persisted in this, she would undoubtedly have attracted what she feared most.

Another example of abnormal fear is that of a businessman in New York, who was very prosperous and successful. He had his own private mental motion picture of which he was the director. He would run this mental movie of failure, bankruptcy, empty shelves, and no bank balance until he sank into a deep depression. He refused to stop this morbid imagery and kept reminding his wife that "this can't last," "there will be a recession," "I feel sure we will go bankrupt," etc.

His wife told me that he finally did go into bankruptcy, and all the things he imagined and feared came to pass. The things he feared did not exist, but he brought them to pass by constantly fearing, believing, and expecting financial disaster. *Job said, the thing I feared has come upon me.*

There are people who are afraid that something terrible will happen to their children, and that some dread catastrophe will befall them. When they read about an epidemic or rare disease, they live in fear that they will catch it, and some imagine they have the disease already. All this is abnormal fear.

THE ANSWER TO ABNORMAL FEAR

Move mentally to the opposite. To stay at the extreme of fear is stagnation plus mental and physical deterioration. When fear arises, there immediately comes with it a desire for something opposite to the thing feared. Place your attention on the thing immediately desired. Get absorbed and engrossed in your desire, knowing that the subjective always overturns the objective. This attitude will give you confidence and lift your spirits. The infinite power of your subconscious mind is moving on your behalf, and it cannot fail. Therefore, peace and assurance are yours.

EXAMINE YOUR FEARS

The president of a large organization told me that when he was a salesman he used to walk around the block five or six times before he called on a customer. The sales manager came along one day and said to him, "Don't be afraid of the boogie man behind the door. There is no boogie man. It is a false belief."

The manager told him that whenever he looked at his own fears he stared them in the face and stood up to them, looking them straight in the eye. Then they faded and shrank into insignificance.

HE LANDED IN THE JUNGLE

A chaplain told me of his experiences in the Second World War. He had to parachute from a damaged plane and land in the jungle. He said he was frightened, but he knew there were two kinds of fear, normal and abnormal, which we have previously pointed out.

He decided to do something about the fear immediately, and began to talk to himself saying, "John, you can't surrender to your fear. Your fear is a desire for safety and security, and a way out."

He began to claim, "Infinite intelligence which guides the planets in their courses is now leading and guiding me out of this jungle."

He kept saying this out loud to himself for ten minutes or more. "Then," he added, "something began to stir inside me. A mood of confidence began to seize me, and I began to walk. After a few days, I miraculously came out of the jungle, and was picked up by a rescue plane."

His changed mental attitude saved him. His confidence and trust in the subjective wisdom and power within him was the solution to his problem.

He said, "Had I begun to bemoan my fate and indulge my fears, I would have succumbed to the monster fear, and probably would have died of fear and starvation."

HE DISMISSED HIMSELF

The general manager of an organization told me that for three years he feared he would lose his position. He was always imagining failure. The thing he feared did not exist, save as a morbid anxious thought in his own mind. His vivid imagination dramatized the loss of his job until he became nervous and neurotic. Finally he was asked to resign.

Actually, he dismissed himself. His constant negative imagery and fear suggestions to his subconscious mind caused the latter to respond and react accordingly. It caused him to make mistakes and foolish decisions, which resulted in his failure as a general manager. His dismissal would never have happened, if he had immediately moved to the opposite in his mind.

THEY PLOTTED AGAINST HIM

During a recent world lecture tour, I had a two-hour conversation with a prominent government official. He had a deep sense of inner peace and serenity. He said that all the abuse he receives politically from newspapers and the opposition party never disturb him. His practice is to sit still for fifteen minutes in the morning and realize that in the center of himself is a deep still ocean of peace. Meditating in this way, he generates tremendous power which overcomes all manner of difficulties and fears.

Some time previously, a colleague called him at midnight and told him a group of people were plotting against him. This is what he said to his colleague: "I am going to sleep now in perfect peace. You can discuss it with me at 10:00 A.M. tomorrow."

He said to me, "I know that no negative thought can ever manifest except I emotionalize the thought and accept it mentally. I refuse to entertain their suggestion of fear. Therefore, no harm can come to me."

Notice how calm he was, how cool, how peaceful! He did not start getting excited, tearing his hair, or wringing his hands. At his center he found the still water, an inner peace, and there was a great calm.

DELIVER YOURSELF FROM ALL YOUR FEARS

Use this perfect formula for casting out fear. *I sought the Lord, and he heard me, and delivered me from all my fears.* PSALMS 34:4. The *Lord* is an ancient word meaning *law*—the power of your subconscious mind.

Learn the wonders of your subconscious, and how it works and functions. Master the techniques given to you in this chapter. Put them into practice now, today! Your subconscious will respond, and you will be free of all fears. *I sought the Lord, and he heard me, and delivered me from all my fears.*

STEP THIS WAY TO FREEDOM FROM FEAR

1. Do the thing you are afraid to do, and the death of fear is certain. Say to yourself and mean it, "I am going to master this fear," and you will.
2. Fear is a negative thought in your mind. Supplant it with a constructive thought. Fear has killed millions. Confidence is greater than fear. Nothing is more powerful than faith in God and the good.
3. Fear is man's greatest enemy. It is behind failure, sickness, and bad human relations. Love casts out fear. Love is an emotional attachment to the good things of life. Fall in love with honesty, integrity, justice, good will, and success. Live in the joyous expectancy of the best, and invariably the best will come to you.
4. Counteract the fear suggestions with the opposite, such as "I sing beautifully; I am poised, serene, and calm." It will pay fabulous dividends.
5. Fear is behind amnesia at oral and written examination time. You can overcome this by affirming frequently, "I have a perfect memory for everything I

need to know," or you can imagine a friend congratulating you on your brilliant success on the examination. Persevere and you will win.

6. If you are afraid to cross water, swim. In your imagination swim freely, joyously. Project yourself into the water mentally. Feel the chill and thrill of swimming across the pool. Make it vivid. As you do this subjectively, you will be compelled to go into the water and conquer it. This is the law of your mind.
7. If you are afraid of closed places, such as elevators, lecture halls, etc., mentally ride in an elevator blessing all its parts and functions. You will be amazed how quickly the fear will be dissipated.
8. You were born with only two fears, the fear of falling and the fear of noise. All your other fears were acquired. Get rid of them.
9. Normal fear is good. Abnormal fear is very bad and destructive. To constantly indulge in fear thoughts results in abnormal fear, obsessions, and complexes. To fear something persistently causes a sense of panic and terror.
10. You can overcome abnormal fear when you know the power of your subconscious mind can change conditions and bring to pass the cherished desires of your heart. Give your immediate attention and devotion to your desire which is the opposite of your fear. This is the love that casts out fear.
11. If you are afraid of failure, give attention to success. If you are afraid of sickness, dwell on your perfect health. If you are afraid of an accident, dwell on the guidance and protection of God. If you are afraid of death, dwell on Eternal Life. God is Life, and that is your life now.
12. The great law of substitution is the answer to fear. Whatever you fear has its solution in the form of your desire. If you are sick, you desire health. If you are in the prison of fear, you desire freedom. Expect the good. Mentally con-

centrate on the good, and know that your subconscious mind answers you always. It never fails.

13. The things you fear do not really exist except as thoughts in your mind. Thoughts are creative. This is why Job said, *The thing I feared has come upon me.* Think good and good follows.
14. Look at your fears; hold them up to the light of reason. Learn to laugh at your fears. That is the best medicine.
15. Nothing can disturb you but your own thought. The suggestions, statements, or threats of other persons have no power. The power is within you, and when your thoughts are focused on that which is good, then God's power is with your thoughts of good. There is only one Creative Power, and It moves as harmony. There are no divisions of quarrels in it. Its source is Love. This is why God's power is with your thoughts of good.

CHAPTER TWENTY

HOW TO STAY YOUNG IN SPIRIT FOREVER

Your subconscious mind never grows old. It is timeless, ageless, and endless. It is a part of the universal mind of God which was never born, and it will never die.

Fatigue or old age cannot be predicated on any spiritual quality or power. Patience, kindness, veracity, humility, good will, peace, harmony, and brotherly love are attributes and qualities which never grow old. If you continue to generate these qualities here on this plane of life, you will always remain young in spirit.

I remember reading an article in one of our magazines some years ago which stated that a group of eminent medical men at the De Courcy Clinic, in Cincinnati, Ohio, reported that years alone are not responsible for bringing about degenerative disorders. These same physicians stated that it is the fear of time, not time itself, that has a harmful aging effect on our minds and bodies, and that the neurotic fear of the effects of time may well be the cause of premature aging.

During the many years of my public life, I have had occasion to study the biographies of the famous men and women who have continued their productive activities into the years well beyond the normal span of life. Some of them achieve their greatness in old age.

At the same time, it has been my privilege to meet and to know countless individuals of no prominence who, in their lesser sphere, belonged to those hardy mortals who have proved that old age of itself does not destroy the creative powers of the mind and body.

HE HAD GROWN OLD IN HIS THOUGHT LIFE

A few years ago I called on an old friend in London, England. He was over 80 years of age, very ill, and obviously was yielding to his advancing years. Our conversation revealed his physical weakness, his sense of frustration, and a general deterioration almost approaching lifelessness. His cry was that he was useless and that no one wanted him. With an expression of hopelessness he betrayed his false philosophy, "We are born, grow up, become old, good for nothing, and that's the end."

This mental attitude of futility and worthlessness was the chief reason for his sickness. He was looking forward only to senescence, and after that—nothing. Indeed, he had grown old in his thought life, and his subconscious mind brought about all the evidence of his habitual thinking.

AGE IS THE DAWN OF WISDOM

Unfortunately, many people have the same attitude as this unhappy man. They are afraid of what they term "old age," the end, and extinction, which really means that they are afraid of life. Yet, life is endless. Age is not the flight of years, but the dawn of wisdom.

Wisdom is an awareness of the tremendous spiritual powers in your subconscious mind and the knowledge of how to apply these powers to lead a full and happy life. Get it out of your head once and for all that 65, 75, or 85 years of age is synonymous with the end for you or anybody else. It can be the beginning of a glorious, fruitful, active, and most productive life pattern, better than you have ever experienced. Believe this, expect it, and your subconscious will bring it to pass.

WELCOME THE CHANGE

Old age is not a tragic occurrence. What we call the aging process is really change. It is to be welcomed joyfully and gladly as each phase of human life is a step forward on the path which has no end. Man has powers which transcend his bodily powers. He has senses which transcend his five physical senses.

Scientists today are finding positive indisputable evidence that something conscious in man can leave his present body and travel thousands of miles to see, hear, touch, and speak to people even though his physical body never leaves the couch on which it reclines.

Man's life is spiritual and eternal. He need never grow old for Life, or God, cannot grow old. The Bible says that God is Life. Life is self-renewing, eternal, indestructible, and is the reality of all men.

EVIDENCE FOR SURVIVAL

The evidence gathered by the psychical research societies both in Great Britain and America is overwhelming. You may go into any large metropolitan library and get volumes on *The Proceedings of the Psychical Research Society* based on findings of distinguished scientists on survival following so-called death. You will find a startling report on scientific experiments establishing the reality of life after death in *The Case for Psychic Survival* by Hereward Carrington, Director of the American Psychical Institute.

LIFE IS

A woman asked Thomas Edison, the electrical wizard, "Mr. Edison, what is electricity?"

He replied, "Madame, electricity is. Use it."

Electricity is a name we give an invisible power which we do not fully comprehend, but we learn all we can about the principle of electricity and its uses. We use it in countless ways.

The scientist cannot see an electron with his eyes, yet he accepts it as a scientific fact, because it is the only valid conclusion which coincides with his other experimental evidence. We cannot see life. However, we know we are alive. Life is, and we are here to express it in all its beauty and glory.

MIND AND SPIRIT DO NOT GROW OLD

The Bible says, *And this is life eternal, that they might know thee the only true God.* JOHN 17:3.

The man who thinks or believes that the earthly cycle of birth, adolescence, youth, maturity, and old age is all there is to life, is indeed to be pitied. Such a man has no anchor, no hope, no vision, and to him life has no meaning.

This type of belief brings frustration, stagnation, cynicism, and a sense of hopelessness resulting in neurosis and mental aberrations of all kinds. If you cannot play a fast game of tennis, or swim as fast as your son, or if your body has slowed down, or you walk with a slow step, remember life is always clothing itself anew. What men call death is but a journey to a new city in another dimension of Life.

I say to men and women in my lectures that they should accept what we call old age gracefully. Age has its own glory, beauty, and wisdom which belong to it. Peace, love, joy, beauty, happiness, wisdom, good will, and understanding are qualities which never grow old or die.

Ralph Waldo Emerson, poet and philosopher, said, "We do not count a man's years until he has nothing else to count."

Your character, the quality of your mind, your faith, and your convictions are not subject to decay.

YOU ARE AS YOUNG AS YOU THINK YOU ARE

I give public lectures in Caxton Hall, London, England, every few years, and following one of these lectures, a surgeon said to me, "I am 84 years of age. I operate every morning, visit patients in the afternoons, and I write for medical and other scientific journals in the evening."

His attitude was that he was as useful as he believed himself to be, and that he was as young as his thoughts. He said to me, "It's true what you said, 'Man is as strong as he thinks he is, and as valuable as he thinks he is.'"

This surgeon has not surrendered to advancing years. He knows that he is immortal. His final comment to me was, "If I should pass on tomorrow, I would be operating on people in the next dimension, not with a surgeon's scalpel, but with mental and spiritual surgery."

YOUR GRAY HAIRS ARE AN ASSET

Don't ever quit a job and say, "I am retired; I am old; I am finished." That would be stagnation, death, and you would be finished. Some men are old at 30, while others are young at 80. The mind is the master weaver, the architect, the designer, and the sculptor. George

Bernard Shaw was active at 90, and the artistic quality of his mind had not relaxed from active duty.

I meet men and women who tell me that some employers almost slam the door in their faces when they say they are over 40. This attitude on the part of the employers is to be considered cold, callous, evil, and completely void of compassion and understanding. The total emphasis seems to be on youth, i.e., you must be under 35 years of age to receive consideration. The reasoning behind this is certainly very shallow. If the employer would stop and think, he would realize that the man or woman was not selling his age or gray hair, rather, he was willing to give of his talents, his experience, and his wisdom gathered through years of experience in the marketplace of life.

AGE IS AN ASSET

Your age should be a distinct asset to any organization, because of your practice and application through the years of the principles of the Golden Rule and the law of love and good will. Your gray hair, if you have any, should stand for greater wisdom, skill, and understanding. Your emotional and spiritual maturity should be a tremendous blessing to any organization.

A man should not be asked to resign when he is 65 years of age. That is the time of life when he could be most useful in handling personnel problems, making plans for the future, making decisions, and guiding others in the realm of creative ideas based on his experience and insight into the nature of the business.

BE YOUR AGE

A motion-picture writer in Hollywood told me that he had to write scripts which would cater to the twelve-year-old mind. This is a tragic state of affairs if the great masses of people are expected to become emotionally and spiritually mature. It means that the emphasis is placed on youth in spite of the fact that youth stands for inexperience, lack of discernment, and hasty judgment.

I CAN KEEP UP WITH THE BEST OF THEM

I am now thinking of a man 65 years of age who is trying frantically to keep young. He swims with young men every Sunday, goes on long hikes, plays tennis, and boasts of his prowess and physical powers, saying, "Look, I can keep up with the best of them!"

He should remember the great truth: *As a man thinketh in his heart, so is he.* PROV. 23:7.

Diets, exercises, and games of all kinds will not keep this man young. It is necessary for him to observe that he grows old or remains young in accordance with his processes of thinking. Your subconscious mind is conditioned by your thoughts. If your thoughts are constantly on the beautiful, the noble, and the good, you will remain young regardless of the chronological years.

FEAR OF OLD AGE

Job said, *The thing which I greatly feared is come upon me.* There are many people who fear old age and are uncertain about the future, because they anticipate mental and physical deterioration as the years advance. What they think and feel comes to pass.

You grow old when you lose interest in life, when you cease to dream, to hunger after new truths, and to search for new worlds to conquer. When your mind is open to new ideas, new interests, and when you raise the curtain and let in the sunshine and inspiration of new truths of life and the universe, you will be young and vital.

YOU HAVE MUCH TO GIVE

If you are 65 or 95 years of age, realize you have much to give. You can help stabilize, advise, and direct the younger generation. You can give the benefit of your knowledge, your experience, and your wisdom. You can always look ahead for at all times you are gazing into infinite life. You will find that you can never cease to unveil the glories and wonders of life. Try to learn something new every moment of the day, and you will find your mind will always be young.

ONE HUNDRED AND TEN YEARS OLD

Some years ago while lecturing in Bombay, India, I was introduced to a man who said he was 110 years old. He had the most beautiful face I have ever seen. He seemed transfigured by the radiance of an inner light. There was a rare beauty in his eyes indicating he had grown old in years with gladness and with no indication that his mind had dimmed its lights.

RETIREMENT—A NEW VENTURE

Be sure that your mind never retires. It must be like a parachute which is no good unless it opens up. Be open and receptive to new ideas. I have seen men of 65 and 70 retire. They seemed to rot away, and in a few months passed on. They obviously felt that life was at an end.

Retirement can be a new venture, a new challenge, a new path, the beginning of the fulfillment of a long dream. It is inexpressibly depressing to hear a man say, "What shall I do now that I am retired?" He is saying in effect, "I am mentally and physically dead. My mind is bankrupt of ideas."

All this is a false picture. The real truth is that you can accomplish more at 90 than you did at 60, because each day you are growing in wisdom and understanding of life and the universe through your new studies and interest.

HE GRADUATED TO A BETTER JOB

An executive, who lives near me, was forced to retire a few months ago because he had reached the age of 65. He said to me, "I look upon my retirement as promotion from kindergarten to the first grade." He philosophized in this manner: He said that when he left high school, he went up the ladder by going to college. He realized this was a step forward in his education and understanding of life in general. Likewise, he added, now he could do the things he had always wanted to do, and therefore, his retirement was still another step forward on the ladder of life and wisdom.

He came to the wise conclusion that he was no longer going to concentrate on making a living. Now he was going to give all his attention to living life. He is an amateur photographer, and he took additional courses on the subject. He took a trip around the world and took movies of famous places. He now lectures before various groups, lodges, and clubs, and is in popular demand.

There are countless ways of taking an interest in something worthwhile outside yourself. Become enthusiastic over new creative ideas, make spiritual progress, and continue to learn and to grow. In this manner you remain young in heart, because you are hungering and thirsting after new truths, and your body will reflect your thinking at all times.

YOU MUST BE A PRODUCER AND NOT A PRISONER OF SOCIETY

The newspapers are taking cognizance of the fact that the voting population of the elderly in California elections is increasing by leaps and bounds. This means that their voices will be heard in the legislature of the state and also in the halls of Congress. I believe there will be enacted a federal law prohibiting employers from discrimination against men and women because of age.

A man of 65 years may be younger mentally, physically, and physiologically than many men at 30. It is stupid and ridiculous to tell a man he cannot be hired because he is over 40. It is like saying to him that he is ready for the scrap heap or the junk pile.

What is a man of 40 or over to do? Must he bury his talents and hide his light under a bushel? Men who are deprived and prevented from working because of age must be sustained by government treasuries at county, state, and federal levels. The many organizations who refuse to hire them and benefit from their wisdom and experience will be taxed to support them. This is a form of financial suicide.

Man is here to enjoy the fruit of his labor, and he is here to be a producer and not a prisoner of society which compels him to idleness.

Man's body slows down gradually as he advances through the years, but his conscious mind can be made much more active, alert, alive, and quickened by the inspiration from his subconscious mind. His mind, in reality, never grows old. Job said, *Oh that I were as in months past, as in the days when God preserved me; When his candle shined upon my head, and when by his light I walked through darkness; As I was in the days of my youth, when the secret of God was upon my tabernacle.* Job 29:2-4.

SECRET OF YOUTH

To recapture the days of your youth, feel the miraculous, healing, self-renewing power of your subconscious mind moving through your whole being. Know and feel that you are inspired, lifted up, rejuvenated, revitalized, and recharged spiritually. You can bubble over with enthusiasm and joy, as in the days of your youth, for the simple reason that you can always mentally and emotionally recapture the joyous state.

The candle which shines upon your head is divine intelligence, and reveals to you everything you need to know; it enables you to affirm the presence of your good, regardless of appearances. You walk by the guidance of your subconscious mind, because you know that the dawn appears and the shadows flee away.

GET A VISION

Instead of saying, "I am old," say, "I am wise in the way of the Divine Life." Don't let the corporation, newspapers, or statistics hold a picture before you of old age, declining years, decrepitude, senility, and uselessness. Reject it, for it is a lie. Refuse to be hypnotized by such propaganda. Affirm life—not death. Get a vision of yourself as happy, radiant, successful, serene, and powerful.

YOUR MIND DOES NOT GROW OLD

Former President Herbert Hoover, now 88 years old, is very active and is performing monumental work. I interviewed him a few years ago in his suite at the Waldorf-Astoria, New York City. I found him healthy, happy, vigorous, and full of life and enthusiasm. He was keeping several secretaries busy handling his correspondence and was himself writing books of a political and historical nature. Like all great men, I found him affable, genial, amiable, loving, and most understanding.

His mental acumen and sagacity gave me the thrill of a lifetime. He is a deeply religious man, and is full of faith in God and in the triumph of the eternal truth of life. He was subjected to a barrage of criticism and condemnation in the years of the Great Depression, but he weathered the storm and did not grow old in hatred, resentment, ill will, and bitterness. On the contrary, he went into the silence of his soul, and communing with the Divine Presence within him, he found the peace which is the power at the heart of God.

HIS MIND ACTIVE AT NINETY-NINE

My father learned the French language at 65 years of age, and became an authority on it at 70. He made a study of Gaelic when he was over 60, and became an acknowledged and famous teacher of the subject. He assisted my sister in a school of higher learning and continued to do so until he passed away at 99. His mind was as clear at 99 as it was when he was 20. Moreover, his handwriting and his reasoning powers had improved with age. Truly, you are as old as you think and feel.

WE NEED OUR SENIOR CITIZENS

Marcus Porcius Cato, the Roman patriot, learned Greek at 80. Madame Ernestine Schumann-Heink, the great German-American contralto, reached the pinnacle of her musical success after she became a grandmother. It is wonderful to behold the accomplishments of the oldsters. General Douglas MacArthur, Harry S Truman, General Dwight David Eisenhower, and American financier Bernard Baruch are interesting, active, and contributing their talents and wisdom to the world.

The Greek philosopher Socrates learned to play musical instruments when he was 80 years old. Michelangelo was painting his greatest canvases at 80. At 80, Cios Simonides won the prize for poetry, Johann von Goethe finished *Faust*, and Leopold von Ranke commenced his *History of the World*, which he finished at 92.

Alfred Tennyson wrote a magnificent poem, "Crossing the Bar," at 83. Isaac Newton was hard at work close to 85. At 88 John Wesley was directing, preaching, and guiding Methodism. We have several men of 95 years who come to my lectures, and they tell me they are in better health now than they were at 20.

Let us place our senior citizens in high places and give them every opportunity to bring forth the flowers of Paradise.

If you are retired, get interested in the laws of life and the wonders of your subconscious mind. Do something you have always wanted to do. Study new subjects, and investigate new ideas.

Pray as follows: *As the hart panteth after the water brooks, so panteth my soul after thee, O God.* PSALMS 42:1.

THE FRUITS OF OLD AGE

His flesh shall be fresher than a child's: he shall return to the days of his youth. JOB 33:25.

Old age really means the contemplation of the truths of God from the highest standpoint. Realize that you are on an endless journey, a series of important steps in the ceaseless, tireless, endless ocean of life. Then, with the Psalmist you will say, *They shall still bring forth fruit in old age; they shall be fat and flourishing.* PSALMS 92:14.

But the fruit of the Spirit is love, joy, peace, longsuffering, gentleness, goodness, faith, meekness, temperance; against such there is no law. GALATIANS 5:22–23.

You are a son of Infinite Life which knows no end, and you are a child of Eternity.

PROFITABLE POINTERS

1. Patience, kindness, love, good will, joy, happiness, wisdom, and understanding are qualities which never grow old. Cultivate them and express them, and remain young in mind and body.
2. Some research physicians say that the neurotic fear of the effects of time may well be the cause of premature aging.
3. Age is not the flight of years; it is the dawn of wisdom in the mind of man.
4. The most productive years of your life can be from 65 to 95.
5. Welcome the advancing years. It means you are moving higher on the path of life which has no end.
6. God is Life, and that is your life now. Life is self-renewing, eternal, and indestructible, and is the reality of all men. You live forever, because your life is God's life.
7. Evidence of survival after death is overwhelming. Study *Proceedings of Psychical Research Society of Great Britain and America* in your library. The work is based on the scientific research by outstanding scientists for over 75 years.
8. You cannot see your mind, but you know you have a mind. You cannot see spirit, but you know that the spirit of the game, the spirit of the artist, the spirit of the musician, and the spirit of the speaker is real. Likewise, the spirit of goodness, truth, and beauty moving in your mind and heart are real. You cannot see life, but you know you are alive.

9. Old age may be called the contemplation of the truths of God from the highest standpoint. The joys of old age are greater than those of youth. Your mind is engaged in spiritual and mental athletics. Nature slows down your body so that you may have the opportunity to meditate on things divine.
10. We do not count a man's years until he has nothing else to count. Your faith and convictions are not subject to decay.
11. You are as young as you think you are. You are as strong as you think you are. You are as useful as you think you are. You are as young as your thoughts.
12. Your gray hairs are an asset. You are not selling your gray hairs. You are selling your talent, abilities, and wisdom which you have garnered through the years.
13. Diets and exercises won't keep you young. *As a man thinketh, so is he.*
14. Fear of old age can bring about physical and mental deterioration. *The thing I greatly feared has come upon me.*
15. You grow old when you cease to dream, and when you lose interest in life. You grow old if you are irritable, crotchety, petulant, and cantankerous. Fill your mind with the truths of God and radiate the sunshine of His love—this is youth.
16. Look ahead, for at all times you are gazing into infinite life.
17. Your retirement is a new venture. Take up new studies and new interests. You can now do the things you always wanted to do when you were so busy making a living. Give your attention to living life.
18. Become a producer and not a prisoner of society. Don't hide your light under a bushel.
19. The secret of youth is love, joy, inner peace, and laughter. *In Him there is fullness of joy. In Him there is no darkness at all.*

20. You are needed. Some of the great philosophers, artists, scientists, writers, and others accomplished their greatest work after they were 80 years old.
21. The fruits of old age are love, joy, peace, patience, gentleness, goodness, faith, meekness, and temperance.
22. You are a son of Infinite Life which knows no end. You are a child of Eternity. You are wonderful!

ABOUT THE AUTHORS

NAPOLEON HILL was born in 1883 in Wise County, Virginia. He worked as a secretary, a "mountain reporter" for a local newspaper, and the manager of a coal mine and a lumber yard, and attended law school, before he began working as a journalist for *Bob Taylor's Magazine*—a job that led to his meeting steel magnate Andrew Carnegie, which changed the course of his life. Carnegie urged Hill to interview the greatest industrialists, inventors, and statesmen of the era in order to discover the principles that led them to success. Hill took on the challenge, which lasted twenty years, and formed the building block first for *The Law of Success* (1928), and later for *Think and Grow Rich* (1937)—the wealth-building classic and all-time bestseller of its kind. After a long and varied career as an author, magazine publisher, lecturer, and consultant to business leaders, the motivational pioneer died in 1970 in South Carolina.

JAMES ALLEN was born in Leicester, England, in 1864. He took his first job at fifteen to support his family, after his father was murdered while looking for work in America in 1879. Allen worked as a factory knitter and later as a private secretary with various manufacturing companies. In 1901, he published his first book, *From Poverty to Power.* The following year, he left secretarial work to devote himself full time to writing and in 1903 completed his third, and best-known, work: *As a Man Thinketh.* Allen soon moved with his wife, Lily, and daughter, Nora, to Ilfracombe, England, where he continued to write books and articles, and, with Lily, to publish his spiritual journal *The Light of Reason*, later retitled *The Epoch.* He died at age 47 in 1912, most likely of consumption. Allen completed nineteen books during his career, several of which were published posthumously by his wife. Allen came to be seen as a pioneering voice of contemporary inspirational literature, his work touching many of the twentieth century's leading writers of motivational thought, including Norman Vincent Peale, Napoleon Hill, Robert Collier, and Dale Carnegie.

A native of Ireland who resettled in America, **Joseph Murphy**, Ph.D., D.D., (1898–1981), was a prolific and widely admired New Thought minister and writer, best known for his metaphysical classic, *The Power of Your Subconscious Mind*—an international bestseller since it first appeared on the self-help scene in 1963. A popular speaker, Murphy lectured on both American coasts and in Europe, Asia, and South Africa. His many books and pamphlets on the autosuggestive and metaphysical faculties of the human mind have entered multiple editions. Murphy is considered one of the pioneering voices of affirmative-thinking philosophy.